# The Reception of Blake in the Orient

Continuum Reception Studies Series

*Forthcoming volumes include:*

*The International Reception of T. S. Eliot*
Edited by Shyamal Bagchee and Elisabeth Daümer

*Writers Reading Shakespeare*
By William Baker

# The Reception of Blake in the Orient

Edited by Steve Clark and Masashi Suzuki

continuum

Continuum
The Tower Building      80 Maiden Lane
11 York Road      Suite 704
London SE1 7NX      New York, NY 10038

www.continuumbooks.com

First published 2006
Paperback edition 2008

**British Library Cataloguing-in-Publication Data**
A catalogue record for this book is available from the British Library.

ISBN: PB: 978–0–8264–3805–8

**Library of Congress Cataloging-in-Publication Data**
A catalog record for this book is available from the Library of Congress.

Typeset by RefineCatch Limited, Bungay, Suffolk
Printed and bound by Lightning Source

# Contents

# List of Illustrations

# Notes on Contributors

**Ching-erh Chang** is Professor at the National Taiwan University. His major areas of research include, in addition to Chinese–Western comparative literature, the Chinese novel, Chinese literary theory and English drama. His most recent publication is the *Research Bibliography of Western Literature in Taiwan 1946–2000* (2 vols).

**Steve Clark** is currently Visiting Professor at the University of Tokyo. Other publications include *Historicising Blake* (1994), *Blake in the 90s* (1999) and *Blake, Nation and Empire* (2006), all co-edited with David Worrall.

**Tristanne Connolly** is Assistant Professor in the English Department of St Jerome's University, Waterloo, Canada. She is the author of *William Blake and the Body* (2002).

**Keri Davies** is Secretary of the Blake Society. He is currently research fellow on the Arts and Humanities Research Council-funded project at Nottingham Trent University, 'East Midlands Moravian Belief Communities with Special Reference to William Blake'.

**Sibylle Erle** completed her PhD on Blake's 1790s creation myth in 2004. She is now teaching at Warwick and the Open University and is completing a book on Blake and European concepts of physiognomy with special emphasis on Johann Caspar Lavater.

**Yumiko Goto** is Assistant Curator at Kyoto Municipal Museum of Art. Her publications include 'Blake's Illuminated Books and the Reproductive Prints of the 18th Century' (2001) and 'A New View to the Past: Delacroix and Walter Scott' (Exh. cat.)(2005).

**Yoko Ima-Izumi** is Professor of English and Film Studies at the University of Tsukuba. Her publications include *English Literature on Screen* (1999), *Blake's Re-vision of the Female in His Composite Art* (2001) and *Film Syntax: Shot Analysis of Japanese Film* (2004).

**Susan Matthews** is Senior Lecturer at the University of Roehampton and currently completing a study of Blake and the public sphere of sentiment.

**Ashton Nichols** is the John and Ann Conser Curley Professor of Language and Literature at Dickinson College in Carlisle, Pennsylvania, USA. He is the author of *The Poetics of Epiphany* (1987), *The Revolutionary 'I'* (1998), and most recently the editor of *Romantic Natural Histories: William Wordsworth, Charles Darwin, and*

*Others* (2004). He is at work on a study of the relationship between poetry and natural science from 1750 to 1859.

**Hatsuko Nimii** is Professor of English at Japan Women's University. Her publications include 'The Proverbial Language of Blake's *Marriage of Heaven and Hell*'(1982) and '*The Book of Ahania*: A Metatext' (2000).

**Kazuyoshi Oishi** is Associate Professor of English at the University of the Air. His publications include 'Philanthropy and Literature of the 1790s: The Division, Revision and Reconstruction of Early Romantic Discourses on Poverty'(PhD, 2002) and 'Coleridge's Philanthropy: Poverty, Dissenting Radicalism, and the Language of Benevolence' (2000).

**Kazuya Okada** is Associate Professor of English at Okayama University. His publications include 'Romantic Radicalism: Discourses of Liberty in Blake' (1999) and 'Orc under a Veil Revealed: Family Relationships and their Symbols in *Europe* and *The Book of Urizen*' (2000).

**Peter Otto** holds a chair in English Literature at the University of Melbourne. His most recent publications include *Blake's Critique of Transcendence* (2000) and *Gothic Fictions* (2002–3), a large microfilm collection of gothic novels and chapbooks published between 1764 and 1830. He is currently completing a monograph mapping the pre-history of virtual reality, while assembling a new microfilm collection of primary texts, entitled *Entertaining the Supernatural: Mesmerism, Spiritualism, Conjuring and Psychical Science*.

**John Phillips** is Associate Professor in the Department of English Language and Literature at The National University of Singapore. He is the author of *Contested Knowledge: A Guide To Critical Theory* (2000) and editor, with Lyndsey Stonebridge, of *Reading Melanie Klein* (1998). He is also co-editor of two books on cities, *Postcolonial Urbanism: Southeast Asian Cities and Global Processes* (2003) and *Beyond Description: Space Historicity Singapore* (2004).

**Hikari Sato** is Associate Professor of English at Kobe University. His publications include 'Creative Contradiction in Proverbs of Hell: On the Media and Contents of *The Marriage of Heaven and Hell*' (2000) and 'The Devil's Progress: Blake, Bunyan and *The Marriage of Heaven and Hell*' (2001).

**Elinor Shaffer** is Senior Research Fellow at the Institute of Germanic and Romance Studies, University of London, and Project Director of *The Reception of British and Irish Authors in Europe*. She is a Fellow of the British Academy, editor of *Comparative Criticism* (1979–2002) and Comparative Critical Studies (Edinburgh University Press).

**Masashi Suzuki** is Professor of English at Kyoto University. His publications include *Visionary Poetics: A Study of William Blake* (1994) and ' "Signal of Solemn Mourning": Los/Blake's Sandals and Ancient Israelite Custom' (2001), and he is co-author of *Gnosticism* (2001) and *William Blake: Trans-Boundary Artist* (2002).

**Jeremy Tambling** is Professor of Comparative Literature at the University of Hong Kong, and author of *Blake's Night Thoughts* (2004) and of other books on nineteenth-century literature and on critical theory. He has also written on Dante. He is about to take up a chair at Manchester University.

**Minne Tanaka** is currently completing her PhD on 'William Blake's Large Colour Prints 1985/1804' at Nottingham Trent University.

**Shunsuke Tsurumi** is one of the most famous philosophers in Japan. His many publications include *Takano Choei* (1975), *Yanagi Muneyoshi* (1976; 1994) and *Collected Works of Tsurumi Shunsuke* (12 vols, 1992).

**Barnard Turner** is Associate Professor in the Department of English and Academic Convenor for European Studies at the National University of Singapore. He has published widely on British, American and European literature, from Friedrich Hölderlin to Edwin Morgan and Richard Brautigan's Japanese books. His book *Cultural Tropes of the Contemporary American West* appeared in early 2005, and he is currently working on a book on D. H. Lawrence's poetry.

**Mei-Ying Sung** finished her PhD on the *Technical and Material Studies of William Blake's Engraved Illustrations of the Book of Job (1826)* at Nottingham Trent University, 2005.

**Ayako Wada** is Associate Professor of English at Tottori University. Her publications include 'Blake's *Vala/The Four Zoas*: the Genesis of Night I as a Preludium' (1996) and 'Encountering One's Own Spectre: Tharmas as Urthona/ Blake's Alter Ego in *Vala/The Four Zoas*' (1999).

**Jason Whittaker** is a lecturer in English with Media Studies at University College Falmouth. He is the author of *William Blake and the Myths of Britain* (1999) and (with Shirley Dent) of *Radical Blake: Influence and Afterlife since 1827* (2002), and his interests include the reception of Blake's work in the twentieth century.

**David Worrall** is Professor of English at Nottingham Trent University. He is editor of *The Urizen Books* (1995) and co-editor (with Steve Clark) of *Historicizing Blake* (1994), *Blake in the Nineties* (1999) and *Blake, Nation and Empire* (2006). He is also the author of *Theatric Revolution: Drama, Censorship and Romantic Period Subcultures, 1774–1832* (2006). He is currently Vice-President of the British Association for Romantic Studies.

# 1 Introduction

## Steve Clark and Masashi Suzuki

### 1 Blake in the Orient

The Orient might seem an unlikely location for William Blake, a notorious non-traveller, whose visionary flights 'from Ireland to Japan' in *Jerusalem* (67.8; E 177)[1] contrast with the more mundane fact of never having physically journeyed more than 60 miles to Felpham in Sussex. In simple biographical terms, therefore, Blake would seem an implausible candidate to attract the attentions of post-colonial criticism. Yet the emphasis on political imaginaries, imbalances of cultural power and various constructions of otherness over the last decade has had the effect of making much of what had seemed most wayward and idiosyncratic in his work both comprehensible and mainstream.[2] In so doing, it has rectified what had been a conspicuous anomaly in Blake criticism: the absence of extended treatments of nation and empire. Certain texts had previously received detailed commentary from such a perspective ('The Little Black Boy'; slavery in *Visions of the Daughters of Albion*; the illustrations to Stedman) but there had been no sustained overview until a recent flurry of publications: Saree Makdisi's *William Blake and the Impossible History of the 1790s* (2003), Julia Wright's *Blake, Nationalism and the Politics of Alienation* (2004), and the collection of essays edited by Steve Clark and David Worrall, *Blake Nation Empire* (2006).[3]

For Makdisi, Blake's achievement lies in remaining outside the ideologies shared even by his radical contemporaries: his work is startlingly devoid of the orientalist props that supersaturate the period – turbans, janissaries, harems, genies and so on – even in texts far removed from direct treatment of the East. In many ways, this remains a highly traditional reading of Blake as an oppositional and utopian figure either indifferent to or fervently antagonistic to the processes of nation-building and empire-formation that occurred during his lifetime, relying upon a highly selective account restricted to less than a single decade. Wright's study divides between chapters (1,3,4) on formal subversion of a linear temporality identified with classicism; and others (2,5,6) on how the antiquarian mythology which suffuses *Poetical Sketches*, crucial to the mid-eighteenth-century formation of British nationalism, re-emerges in Blake's work after 1800 to prefigure an imperial imaginary that would dominate the following century. The majority of contributors to *Blake Nation Empire* share the basic premise that prophecy against empire necessarily includes within itself a prophecy of empire (Wright 2004: xxxii–iii): attempts to imagine a future outside and beyond its domain must necessarily oscillate between complicity and critique. All three works, however, are united in their determination to challenge the still powerful orthodoxy of a retreat from radical engagement into visionary other-worldliness, and to re-examine the interactions between apparently private inspiration and the emergent discourses of nation and empire.

This volume hopes to approach these issues by addressing a different set of questions:

1. The majority of current post-colonial studies have tended to regard Enlightenment rationality and Romanticist exoticism as equally manifestations of a will-to-power, with its corollary of the inevitable passivity of an Orient formed according to European projections of Otherness. Can support be found in Blake's own time for a less bleakly dystopian model, one closer to a world-systems theory model of the continual circulation of images, ideas and commodities? Can the model of violent incursion followed by ideological imposition be jettisoned in favour of the postulate of an already-global eighteenth century, engaged in vigorous two-way interchange?

2. Blake criticism has tended to be fascinated if not obsessed by origins. In an earlier generation, both Kathleen Raine and E.P. Thompson sought to uncover occluded intellectual traditions of Platonist perennial philosophy and non-conformist dissent; an emphasis mirrored more recently by Jon Mee's dangerous enthusiasm and Saree Makdisi's Asiatic pantheism.[4] This mode of explanation through genealogy is accompanied by its own constraints: reactivation and trans-mission of pre-existent imagery and belief take precedence over the possibility of the generation of new meaning in altered and contingent circumstances. The focus of reception history had circled somewhat myopically around the problematic of Blake's contemporary audience (or lack thereof), until Shirley Dent and Jason Whittaker's ground-breaking *Radical Blake: Influence and Afterlife from 1827* (2002).[5] *Blake in the Orient* instead adopts the central postulate that the text means what it will become: in Blake's own words, 'And tho I call them Mine I know they are not Mine' (to Dr Trusler 16 August 1799; E701). Interaction with the interpretative horizons of future audiences matters at least as much as the original context of enunciation.

3. More specifically, what happens to the study of Blake when his work is assimilated in not merely a non-British but also a non-European context? Our focus is specifically on the long and distinguished Japanese tradition of reception, but in principle the same issue could be raised with regard to the classic products of European Romanticism in other Asian and Pacific Rim contexts. What questions are posed by (and to) Blake's texts when viewed from such a perspec-tive? To what degree can the assumption of an intense and parochial insularity (the flipside of any celebration of Blake as quintessentially English) be overcome? The contributors to this volume do not argue for a universal or archetypal Blake, but instead respond to the power of his work to produce novel and unpredictable configurations in radically different cultural and historical contexts from his own.

## 2  The Orient in Blake

In our opening section, the chapters explore a variety of perspectives that reveal an international Blake rather than the more familiar icon of embattled visionary solipsist. These may be based not only on specific empirical connections within an extended biographical milieu, but also within the larger perspectives of trading networks already permitting an unexpected degree of global integration.

In 'Thel in Africa', David Worrall draws on recent critical studies of romantic sociability, in order to reconstruct the personal networks constituting the Swedenborgian communities of the early 1790s. The role of alternative spiritualities has long been a focus of attention in Blake criticism, but usually in terms of the recovery of the lost voices of exotic minority sects. The chapter in contrast emphasizes their impressive cosmopolitanism, the very this-worldly agenda in their proposed colonization of Sierra Leone, and, on a methodological level, the principle of historical alterity; these individuals/subcultures were different from us and we can only begin to understand them by accepting that difference.[6]

In 'Typhon, the lower nature: Blake and Egypt as the Orient', Kazukya Okada, like Worrall, emphasizes Blake's internationalism, here in the context of Masonic allusions that underpin his presentation of Egypt. The complex iconographies that Blake adapts from eighteenth-century antiquarianism have usually been assimilated to archetypalist readings. In contrast, this chapter demonstrates the immediate political resonances of the figure of Typhon which simultaneously conforms to and resists the subordination of the Orient to the imperial centre represented by the body of Albion. Myth is not the antithesis of history, but engaged in a continuous two-way process of mutual redefinition.

The automatic identification of Blake with a radical artisan (and highly masculinist) culture is also questioned by Keri Davies in 'Rebekah Bliss: Collector of William Blake and Oriental Books'. He expands his previous bibliographical work on the importance of the collection of the first female British book-collector, as a significant intellectual in her own right, as a proponent of independent female homosocial relations, and, in the context of her relation with Blake, as a source of patronage and repository of both Chinese and, more unexpectedly, Japanese books. Blake's access to Hindi mythology has been comparatively thoroughly documented, but the potential influence of East Asian culture has been less fully considered.[7] The availability to him of such exquisite oriental manuscripts raises the intriguing possibility of actual cross-fertilization between these apparently incommensurate traditions.

Similar routes of interconnection can be detailed in mercantile terms. In 'Blake and the Chinamen', Mei-Ying Sung explores the commercial networks that developed around the importation of Chinese porcelain in the eighteenth century. Technological developments in English ceramics allowed what were previously elite aesthetic artefacts to be reproduced as part of a general diffusion of commodity culture during the period. Though Blake's direct involvement in this sphere was limited to a single engraving for a Wedgwood catalogue in 1816, his very failure poses intriguing questions: most notably, what prevented him from capitalizing on his skills in this buoyant market, and, more generally, why were his attempts at entrepreneurial participation in the emergent capitalist economy so fallible?

Adopting a larger-scale comparative perspective, Minne Tanaka, in 'Colour Printing in the West and the East', examines Blake's famous 1795 large prints in the context of the parallel developments of European colour printing and the techniques employed by Japanese Ukiyo-e. These traditions may seem entirely separate, particularly with the self-imposed isolation of Edo Japan (*sakoku*), yet at precisely the same historical conjuncture, they both offer comparable solutions to the technical problems of the medium, and dramatize the complexly interim status of engraving as a form of mass culture rather than artefacts of fine art.

Moving away from commodity production to cognitive models, Sibylle Erle explores the importance of physiognomy for concepts of a fixed anatomical hierarchy in 'Representing Race: The Meaning of Colour and Line in William Blake's 1790s Bodies'. Blake's annotations to Lavater's aphorism have received extensive critical attention: her chapter assesses the degree to which his pseudo-scientific taxonomies may have influenced (or contaminated) Blake's use of skin colouring, depiction of soul–body relations, and premise that the differing geographical–eugenic conditions produce unique and essential identities.

Concentrating on a specific continent, in 'Africa and Utopia: Refusing a "Local Habitation"', Susan Matthews explores various inter-texts for Blake's presentation of Africa, notably George Cumberland's gothic novel, *The Captive of the Castle of Senaar* (1798) and James Bruce's *Travels to discover the source of the Nile* (1790). It is argued that spatial demarcations are underpinned by an eroticized racial imaginary; that blackness cannot be dissociated from identification with a fallen state, and that apparently emancipatory exhortations are inevitably conditioned by a residual colonial topography.

Not only definition of human species but also more general discourses of natural history permeate Blake's 1790s lyrics. As Ashton Nichols' 'An Empire of Exotic Nature' demonstrates, apparently symbolist lyrics such as 'The Tyger' and 'A Poison Tree' are rooted in geographical specificities. Despite such famous proclamations as 'Natural Objects always did & do now Weaken deaden & obliterate Imagination in Me' (Annotations to Wordsworth's *Poems*, E 665), Blake is shown as both willing to incorporate recent scientific data and to dramatize and contest its latent structures of colonial power.

The degree of access to imperial knowledge is explored by Hikari Sato in 'Blake, Hayley and India: On *Designs to a Series of Ballads* (1802)', which argues against the customary critical neglect, even vilification, of Blake's most munificent patron. It is argued that Hayley's elegiac ballads employ Indian iconography as part of their rites of mourning for his deceased son, Thomas Alphonso, and that the *Designs* provided a primary conduit for Blake's increasing familiarity with the East. The expansion and accentuation of natural history motifs in his illustrations, made possible by access to Hayley's extensive library, may be seen as a crucial point of transition to the enlarged geographical panoramas of his late prophecies.

Blake's relation to India is also examined by Tristanne Connolly, 'The Authority of the Ancients', in 'Blake and Wilkins' translation of the *Bhagvat-Geeta*', which focuses on the complex triangulation of the influence of Sir Charles Wilkins's version of the classic Indian scripture, its context of production within East India Company patronage as embodied by Warren Hastings, and its British reception. Through detailed reconstruction of the now lost painting *The Brahmins*, part of his abortive 1809 exhibition, Blake's own stance is found to be already anachronistic, belonging to a pre-utilitarian phase of respect for, even veneration of, cultural difference. It is argued that the late-eighteenth-century Orientalist recovery of a distant Indian history, and Blake's speculations on comparative mythology, both involve similar paradoxes of pursuit of a lost origin, which, once located, must inevitably compromise and displace the priority of both Christian revelation and visionary imagination.

No clear-cut opposition can be drawn between a material and an idealist Blake, practising artist and speculative mythologist. His work is worldly both in the sense of its intellectual ambition and geographical inclusiveness, and in its receptivity to the continuous interchange of images, ideas and commodities between East and West already in place during his lifetime. Hence the subtitle to this section: the Orient in Blake. In this, his career may be seen as culturally representative rather than irredeemably peripheral: Europe, far from unilaterally imposing its technological, cultural and racial superiority on the rest of the world, has already been formed by complex processes of reciprocal interchange.

The second section of this volume offers a detailed case study of the material specifics of one particular genealogy of cross-cultural assimilation: that of Japan. It will therefore be appropriate at this point to consider the general context of the early reception history and offer some more detail on figures not covered in the chapters themselves.

## 3  Blake in the Orient: the early-twentieth-century Japanese reception

The exhibition, 'The Glad Days in the Reception of Blake in Japan', was held from 27 November to 27 December 2003 at Kyoto University Museum, concurrent with the conference on which this volume is based. It demonstrated Japan's encounter with Blake in the *Meiji*, *Taisho* and early *Showa* periods (roughly from 1893 to 1938) through documents of literature, philosophy and arts. The exhibition catalogue with notes on the items on display was the most detailed account ever published on the history of the reception of Blake in Japan.[8] What follows is a supplementary outline based on that catalogue, and a brief comment on Blake studies in the academic fields which the present volume does not cover directly.

Blake's influence was enormous and extensive on philosophers like Tetsuro Watsuji (1889–1960), Professor of the Kyoto Imperial University, and Soetsu Yanagi (1889–1961), the founder of the Japan Folk Crafts Museum in Tokyo, who devoted a lot of energy to writing a book of more than 750 pages on Blake at the age of 25, on young painters in the *Taisho* period like Ryusei Kishida (1891–1929) and Kagaku Murakami (1888–1939) who claimed himself as a 'Blakean', and on writers like Kenzaburo Oe (1935–), the winner of the Nobel Prize for Literature in 1994, who has had a lifelong creative relationship with Blake's texts.

The first appearance of William Blake in Japan dates from 1893, when Bimyo Yamada (1868–1910) published *Bankoku Jimmei Jisho* (A Dictionary of Famous Names in the World). In 1894, *Obei Meika Shishu, Jokan* (An Anthology of Western and American Poetry, Part I) by Takeki Owada was published in which a translation of 'The Ecchoing Green' was collected. Around the turn of the century, in the 1890s, Lafcadio Hearn (Yakumo Koizumi; 1850–1904)[9] gave a few lectures on Blake, referring to him as 'The First Mystic' at the Tokyo Imperial University.[10] The most important introductions of Blake were made through the translations by leading literary figures such as Ariake Kanbara (1876–1952) and Choko Ikuta (1882–1936). Ikuta's translation of 'The Sick Rose' had a strong impact on Rofu Miki (1889–1964), a poet, who was so much inspired by the poem as to write the striking counterpart, 'Yameru Bara', which means 'the sick rose'. It is thus mostly as a poet that Blake was first introduced and accepted in

Japan. It seems, however, Harold Bloom's 'anxiety of influence' was not much of an issue in Japanese literary history. Several collections of the Japanese translations of Blake's poems have appeared since then, but a complete translation of his whole poems and prose works had to wait until 1989 when Narumi Umetsu (1917–96) published *Bureiku Zen Chosaku* (The Complete Translation of William Blake's Works) in two volumes.[11]

The reception in the second and third decades of the twentieth century was characterized by the interest in both Blake's poems and artworks, and the magazine *Shirakaba* (White Birch) was very much instrumental in initiating the Japanese people into Blake's world. *Shirakaba* was a humanistic magazine, founded in 1910 by a group of young literati; Saneatsu Mushanokoji (1885–1976), Naoya Shiga (1883–1971), Soetsu Yanagi and others. It not only stimulated new ideas in the Japanese literary world but also functioned as an art magazine to introduce new movements of western art into Japan. Blake was one of those artists *Shirakaba* promoted with great enthusiasm in the cultural milieu of the times. Yanagi's long essay, 'William Blake' (*Shirakaba*, April 1914), was the first to introduce Blake's visual artworks to Japanese readers and spectators. After this, Blake's designs and pictures appeared again and again in *Shirakaba* and numerous other related magazines such as *Seimei no Kawa* (River of Life, 1917) and *Junbungei Zasshi: Geijutsu* (Belle Lettres Magazine: Arts, 1921). Western-style painter Kishida was greatly influenced by the Blake circle of *Shirakaba*, and his *Ningen no Ishi* (Will of Humanity, *c.* 1914) even reminds us of the composition of Blake's *Last Judgment*.

The year 1919 saw 'The Exhibition of Reproductions from the Works of William Blake: For the Establishment of Shirakaba Art Museum' which exerted a large influence on young Japanese-style painters in Kyoto; they formed a private art group in opposition to a government-sponsored exhibition, *Kokuga Sosaku Kyokai* (Association for the Creation of National Painting) in 1918. The members included Bakusen Tsuchida (1887–1936), Kagaku Murakami and Hako Irie (1887–1984).

In 1914, another literary journal, *Dai-Sanji Shinshicho* (New Currents of Thought, the third series) was published by the students of the Department of Literature of the Tokyo Imperial University. Among them were Makoto Sangu (1892–1967), who would later become a distinguished scholar of English literature, and Ryunosuke Akutagawa (1892–1927), who would later become one of the greatest writers in Japan. For the title-page design of the first issue of the journal, Blake's 'The Ancient of Days' was selected by Sangu who had become familiar with his work through his study of William Butler Yeats, and in 1919 he published the first collection of Japanese translations of Blake's poems.

Along with the exhibition commemorating the 100th anniversary of the death of Blake held in Kyoto in 1927, a number of issues of *Eigoseinen* (The Rising Generation) featuring Blake were released, from Nos. 8 to 12 of Vol. 57. The contributors were Takeshi Saito, Rintaro Fukuhara, Soufu Taketomo and others; they were all professors of prestigious universities and specialists on subjects other than Blake. Two in particular were not given enough attention in the exhibition catalogue and are not directly treated in the present volume: Kochi Doi (1886–1979), Professor of English at the Tohoku Imperial University, and Bunsho Jugaku (1900–92), Professor of English at Kansai Gakuin University, Bibliographer and Researcher on *washi* (Japanese paper). They might be considered precursors of the present 'Blakeology' in Japan.[12]

Doi's fields of interest covered a wide spectrum of humanities, including literature, comparative culture, comparative mythology, folklore, philosophy, ethnology and linguistics; in short, his fields of research included anything concerning human beings. His first book *Bungaku Josetsu* (An Introduction to Literature) (1922) dealt primarily with the evolution of literary genres of Japanese literature. The book, written by a scholar of English literature, was warmly received and highly evaluated by scholars of Japanese literature who were particularly inspired by Doi's interest in cultural exchanges between East and West.

One of Doi's Blake essays 'On William Blake's Symbolism' appeared in 1927, in which he discussed artistic symbols in Blake in relation to the unconscious. His essay on Blake's illustrations to *Job* excellently deciphered the text and images. In 'On Blake's Long Poem *Milton*' (1943), Doi traced the influences on Blake of the glories and miseries of the French Revolution in early-nineteenth-century England, with reference to history and myths, and succeeded in offering a version of Blake comparable to, and arguably far in advance of anything available in Europe at that time.

Doi is often compared to Northrop Frye, although they never met (Frye was born in 1912, Doi in 1886) nor could any influences on each other be seen among their works;[13] but both were greatly influenced by the dynamic concept of general vs. particular, and their creative academic activities were often considered to be based upon this dynamism. Nicholas Halmi notes in the introduction to Vol. 14 of *Collected Works of Northrop Frye* that Frye draws the critical inference 'from the interpenetrating dynamic Blake posits between the particular (and even the "peculiar") visions of individual creator and the "Divine Vision" of a universal Creator'.[14] Doi is said to have learned the concept from Walter Pater, and he founded his dynamic aestheticism and his concept of global world literature upon it.[15] His essays on Blake still have intellectual impact on us because of their close and rigorous analysis of the unconscious out of which Blakean symbols, he thought, were formed.

Bunsho Jugaku, a close friend of Yanagi, was one of the great precursors of Blake studies in Japan. When Jugaku and Yanagi were living in Kyoto nearby, they worked together to publish a journal, *Blake and Whitman* (1931–2), and to hold the exhibition commemorating the 100th anniversary of the death of Blake (1927). One of his most important contributions to Blake Studies in Japan as well as in the world was *William Blake: A Bibliography* (1929), the first to be compiled in Japan. It collected 1470 items, including not only all the books and articles on Blake cited in Geoffrey Keynes's *Bibliography* (1921), but also other works published after that date. Two types of binding were used for Jugaku's *Bibliography*. It showed how meticulous Jugaku was about book design, and we are inevitably reminded of the private press *Kojitsu-an* (the Sunward Press), reminiscent of the Kelmscott Press, which he and his wife Shizu established in 1932; Jugaku, as a connoisseur and expert on *washi*, prepared hand-made papers for printing and did the binding himself. Indeed, the first book published from the *Kojitsu-an* was a translation of *The Book of Urizen*.

Jugaku's understanding of Blake was particularly impressive for the way in which it sought to grasp Blake as a whole, not as a poet alone but both as a poet and an engraver; his essays, 'The Outline of Blake's Myth' and 'Blake's Theory of Paintings', still have a lot to offer to us.[16]

Blake's reception in Japan has late-nineteenth-century roots, but its major efflorescence comes slightly later with Yanagi Soetsu and the Shirakaba group.[17] In 'Blake's Oriental Heterodoxy: Yanagi's Perception of Blake', Ayako Wada explores the intellectual antecedents of Yanagi's critical biography, which is shown to be both fully informed by and in some ways superior to British precursors such as Gilchrist and Swinburne. The chapter will examine how, through Blake, Yanagi 'loved the East in the West', as his friend the potter Bernard Leach commented) and attempt to detail the factors that made such a generous and uninhibited assessment possible: for instance, in the way it bypasses the recoil from the imputation of religious heterodoxy or the problematic of madness and sanity that dominates and restricts reception in Blake's native culture throughout the nineteenth century.

Similarly, the Japanese reception shows no inclination to contrast a simplistic version of an accessible politically-engaged early Blake against the mystical obscurity of the later work. In 'Self-Annihilation in *Milton*', Hatsuko Nimii's essay demonstrates how in Yanagi's exposition, Buddhist thought becomes eminently compatible with the broadly Christian mysticism dramatized in Blake's late epic. The ethic of 'Self-Annihilation', shown to have both source and analogue in Boehme's doctrine of signatures and Hartley's associationist psychology, becomes the redemptive ideal that is the culmination of a mock-epic pilgrimage, whose mythological coinages and conceptual neologisms (often cited as evidence of obscurity if not derangement) become immediate and accessible points of cross-cultural engagement.

A more sceptical contextualization of the political ambiguities of the Taisho intellectual milieu is offered by Kazuyoshi Oishi in 'An Ideological Map of (Mis)reading: William Blake and Yanagi Muneyoshi in early-twentieth-century Japan'. Though Blake undoubtedly helped Yanagi formulate his own aesthetic and theological ideals, and also his later resistance to Japanese militarization, there are also subtle but significant misreadings: most notably the idealization of labour as art (excluding the possibility of oppressive toil) and the excision of the more turbulently insurrectionary aspects of Blake. The apparent symmetry between their politico-religious positions belies the ideological gap between an English 'radical enthusiast' and a 'polite' Japanese philosopher.

The commentary of Yanagi is assessed within the context of gender developments in early-twentieth-century Japan by Yoko Ima-Izumi in 'The Female Voice in Blake Studies in Japan, 1910s–1930s', focusing specifically on the formation of a parallel intellectual community to *Shirakaba* in the journal *Seito* (or 'Bluestocking'). Yanagi was particularly responsive to a femme fatale exuberance expressed by Blake's emanations, and may be seen as simultaneously venerating and oppressive in his domestic relations with his wife, the singer Kaneko Nakajima. Jugaku was much more responsive to the changing role of women, and indeed his collaboration with his wife Shizu in the physical production of books and journals offers an intriguing and poignant parallel to Blake's relation to Catherine. Shizu's remains the only female voice within early Japanese Blake studies, whose ideological constraints may be illustrated through contemporary Hollywood cinema, with the specific example of Lubitsch's *The Man I Killed* (1932).

In his biographical memoir, 'Yanagi and Jukagu in the Fifteen Years War', Shunsuke Tsurumi indicates how difficult it was for Japanese intellectuals to preserve their independence during the 1930s and the period of the Great Pacific War. Outright opposition was too dangerous an option to be contemplated; however, Yanagi and his collaborator Jukagu sought to sustain a domestic republic against pressure exerted by the wartime state, and to resist the preoccupation with national status that has characterized Japan's post-war economic resurgence.

The collective role of Yanagi's generation of intellectuals is explored by Yumiko Goto, in 'Individuality and Expression: The *Shirakaba* Group's Reception of Blake's Visual Art in Japan'. Their importance lies firstly in their promotion of Blake in their journal and through their 1915 and 1919 exhibitions, and secondly through presenting his image as the embodiment of a new and distinctive aesthetic of individuality and expression. Particular emphasis is paid to the paradox that it was new technologies of reproduction that allowed the circulation of images supposedly produced by autonomous vision; and to the simultaneous assimilation of Blake with later generations of Western art such as impressionism and post-impressionism, up to and including Dada and Surrealism. As more specific influences on Japanase painting, exposure to Blake's work facilitated transition from genre themes and landscapes, to celestial or supernatural scenes based on Buddhism, but also strongly indebted to the weightlessness and corporeal contortions of his spiritual forms. Their visual grammar is able to bypass the mediation of verbal translation and become an immediate resource for the practising artist.[18]

This section of the book focuses on Yanagi and his contemporaries as an impressive modernist avant-garde (what might facetiously but not altogether inaccurately be termed 'Bloomsbury in kimonos'). What is perhaps most striking is the absence of certain preconceptions and dichotomies that structure and restrict the early-twentieth-century reception in Blake's own culture: madness–sanity, poetry–philosophy, accessibility–obscurity, orthodoxy–heresy. Reading through the Japanese context offers a version of Blake taken very much whole and on his own terms, in a way perhaps not matched in the West until Northrop Frye's *Fearful Symmetry* (1947), and one refreshingly devoid of the parochial nationalism and jejeune politicization of much British criticism, however celebratory in intent.

## 4 Blake in the Orient: later responses

The final chapters supplement this account of Blake's reputation at its peak with a range of contemporary responses to his work from Japan and the Pacific Rim.

In 'Blake's Night', Jeremy Tambling compares a European tradition of the sublime involving night, darkness and secrecy exemplified by Edward Young's graveyard-school meditation with the aesthetics of Tanizaki's *In Praise of Shadows* (1933). The former develops via dream, nightmare and the gothic into surrealism and contemporary theorizations of the writing of pure absence; the latter defends, even in relinquishing it, a realm with a preference for the fleetingness of shadows over the stark ideal of illumination promoted by Western Enlightenment. It is argued that Blake's work, though overtly committed to a redemptive aesthetic of daybreak, cannot escape from the realm of darkness, and remains formed by that which it denies in ways that render it compatible with the traditions invoked by Tanizaki.

The changes undergone by speculative, even metaphysical, introspection in the process of transcultural reception are analysed by Barnard Turner in 'Ōe Kenzaburo's Reading of Blake'. His mythopoeia interacts with representational practices characteristic of a tradition that is radically other to European romanticism, in such a way as to offer the possibility of a retranslation back into the native culture of a text so transformed. Ōe in particular offers a densely allusive tessellation in *Rouse up O ye Young Men of the New Age* (1983), which is specifically concerned with the difficulties and responsibilities of his relationship with his handicapped son, who both personifies innocence within the realm of adult experience, and suffers the agonies of entrapment within a fallen body. Here the polysemous fragments of Blake's mythology are reworked in a deftly anecdotal prose that seeks to contain and redefine them within an apparently naturalistic and autobiographical narrative.[19]

An antipodean context is offered by Peter Otto in 'Nebuchadnezzar's Sublime Torment: William Blake, Arthur Boyd and the East', which examines their revisions of the iconography of the Biblical patriarch. For both Blake and the Australian painter Arthur Boyd (1920–99), the extremity of Nebuchadnezzar's sufferings marks the collapse of the division between body and soul, vice and virtue, that in imperialist discourse often underpins binary oppositions between East and West. Thus while acknowledging different inflections and contexts, for both of them this becomes the occasion for a potential undoing of the division between Europe and what it sets up as 'other', and therefore, for all its bestial grotesquerie, a redemptive moment.

A Taiwanese perspective is offered by Ching-erh Chang in 'William Blake in Taiwan', which examines the degree to which Blake's work both solicits and resists processes of cultural appropriation. Translation may be seen not only as cultural homage but also as a means of commentary and critical analysis. Particular attention will be paid to Blake as an embodiment of the European romantic sublime, and ways in which specific critiques seek to utilize or contain the force of his texts.

The ambiguous status of the urban sublime is examined by Jason Whittaker in ' "Walking thro' Eternity": Blake's Psychogeography and other Pedestrian Practices'. By moving away from centre-periphery models of empire that characterize London as imperial capital, the possibilities raised by contemporary practices of psychogeography become apparent. In a European context, the movement derives from French situationism (see Debord 1967, 2002) though comparable debates occur in a Japanese context with the avant-garde group Fluxus. It seeks to restore a degree of autonomy to the experience of the individual in contemporary urban life by symbolic (de)territorialization, for which parallels may be found in Blake in Los's metropolitan streetwalking and Milton's descent through the mundane universe. Coordinates based on the personal body allow a phenomenological remapping that undercuts the symbolic cartographies through which Albion has tried to 'overspread the Nations of the whole Earth' (E100).

A more general assessment of interrogative taxonomies is proposed by John Phillips in 'Blake's Question (from the Orient)': questions answered, questions without answers, questions unstated but with answers latent within his texts. The final category would be situated in the future of the address which is in principle illimitable. Blake's work can be seen as a question posed for Asia from within the tradition of European Romanticism: individualism, imagination, transcendence.

Conversely, in terms of ideological significance, economic and geographical boundaries and the complexity of global culture, the reverse may be the case. Where Tambling sees Blake unable to emerge from the darkness of the sublime tradition, Phillips argues that his aubades, exhortations to a new dawn, seek to proclaim an end to a history of imperial domination; they posit a possible outside exemplified in the development of Asia itself, which may be regarded as an implicit response to the question of the future of Europe.

Makdisi posits a Blake considered *a priori* ethically outside of a dominant Orientalist discourse; although what is perhaps more striking, in view of his overall thesis, is the absence of state-sponsored imperialism in the early 1790s, specifically with regard to territorial acquisition; it is the ostensibly oppositional manifestos proliferating out of the intellectual ferment of the decade which prefigure later ideologies of empire. This volume presents Blake as a more compromised but also more engaged figure, linked to a wide variety of geographical locations and cultural traditions. Support for this enlarged referent for the term Orient can be found in contemporary eighteenth-century usage, where it would include not only Asia but also any realm poised tantalizingly on the boundaries of a Eurocentric cartography.[20] There is no automatic subordination but instead a wide variety of mechanisms of cultural exchange, in which the ascendancy of European culture and technology cannot simply be taken for granted.

In conclusion, one might compare the Japanese and Pacific Rim reception history with that of Blake's own culture or the somewhat later psychedelically-inflected North American tradition of Beat Zen, from Huxley to Ginsberg and Leary (see Dent and Whittaker, 2002, 104–12). 'Blake in the Orient' has certainly been assimilated somewhat anachronistically alongside earlier and later traditions of European art, and removed from certain formative political and economic contexts. This must be weighed against the strengths of this tradition, compared to, say, Yanagi's almost exact contemporary, T.S. Eliot. There is no problematic of madness and sanity; no break discerned between accessible early lyrics and obscure later mythology; no sense of inherent contradiction between thought and artwork. Indeed the commemorative silence precisely on the very moment of the 100 year anniversary of Blake's death on Japanese state broadcaster NHK in 1927 preceded by 30 years canonization ceremonies in his own culture, symbolized by reburial in Westminster Abbey in 1957. Perhaps this is a version of Blake, partially remade but still recognizable and powerfully resonant, that can more than hold its own against the current Anglo-American orthodoxies.

## Notes

1  All quotations from David V. Erdman (ed.) (1988), *The Complete Poetry and Prose of William Blake*. Newly Revised Edition. New York: Doubleday. Henceforth referred to as E.

2  The Anglo-Hebraism, the mingling of British with Biblical place names, which initially looks among the most idiosyncratic of Blake's techniques, prompting Southey's appalled 'Oxford Street is in Jerusalem', (Bentley 2004a: 310) is seen by Linda Colley in *Britons* (Colley 1992: 42–3) as central to the national ideal of a chosen people predestined to triumph over a catholic and tyrannical France.

3  For Makdisi, see especially *Impossible History* (Makdisi 2003a: 204–59). In some ways the chapter on Blake in the earlier *Romantic Imperialism: Universal Empire and the Culture*

*of Modernity* (Makdisi 1998: 154–72) is both considerably more nuanced and more compatible with the perspective of the other two volumes: 'a vision of an anti-imperial imperialism . . . it is only at the very height of empire that the possibility of destroying it can be imagined' (172). For Wright, see especially ' "Whence came they"; contesting National Narrative' (27–56); ' "A State about to be Created": Modelling the Nation in *Milton*' (111–34); and ' "Artfully Propagated": Hybridity, Disease, and the Transformation of the Body Politick' (135–68).

4  Kathleen Raine, *Blake and Tradition* (1969); E. P. Thompson, *The Making of the English Working Class* (1963); Jon Mee, *Dangerous Enthusiasm: William Blake and the Culture of Radicalism in the 1790s* (1992); Makdisi, *Impossible History* (2003).

5  Until Dent and Whittaker opened up the issue of broader dissemination within popular culture, the only comparable studies were Deborah Dorfman's somewhat narrow genealogy in *Blake in the Nineteenth Century* (1969), and the collection edited by Robert J. Berfhoff and Annette S. Levitt, *Blake and the Moderns* (1982), dealing with intra-poetic influences.

6  The Sierra Leone project is also analysed at length (though without Blakean inflections) by Deidre Coleman, in *Romantic Colonization and British Anti-Slavery* (2005).

7  See especially Weir 2003.

8  More than 100 items were on display for the concurrent exhibition. The exhibition catalogue (ii+93pp.) consists of 'Master Writers of the *Meiji* Period and Blake', 'The Introduction of Blake's Art by Soetsu Yanagi and the *Shirakaba* Group', 'Blake Exhibition Organized by *Shirakaba*', 'The Development of Blake Reception and the 100th Anniversary of the Death of Blake', 'Ryusei Kishida and the Artists of the *Shirakaba* Group', 'Kagaku Murakami and *Kokuga Sosaku Kyokai*', and 'Blake Collector: Taro Nagasaki'.

9  See Vol. 14 of *Koizumi Yakumo Zenshu* (The Complete Works of Yakumo Koizumi) (1927).

10  At the original conference, David Taylor discussed ' "The First English Mystic": Lafcadio Hearn, Blake, and late romantic perception of Japan', in a paper unfortunately not available for this collection.

11  *Bureiku Zen Chosaku* (The Complete Translation of Blake's Works), 2 vols, trans. Narumi Umetsu (1989).

12  Jugaku contributed an essay, 'Blake and Japan' to *Gakuto* (a pamphlet published and distributed by the *Maruzen* book company; Vol.70, 3 March 1973) in which Jugaku, after briefly surveying the current Blake studies, referred to the difficulty of studying Blake, and especially of establishing 'Blakeology' (a coinage after Foster Damon's 'Blake cult') in Japan. Jugaku confessed that perhaps Yanagi and he himself were at first attracted only to Blakean ideas and expressions which they found very similar to those of the mysticism of Buddhism, but that the older he got the less confident he became in his Blake studies; he wondered if it was really possible for the Japanese to reach the core of Blake.

13  See Zenzo Suzuki, 'Kochi Doi and Northrop Frye', *Eigoseinen* (The Rising Generation) (1999): 14–16.

14  Nicholas Halmi, 'Introduction', Vol. 14 of *Collected Works of Northrop Frye* (2004), xxv.

15  'Walter Pater's Literary Criticism', Vol. 5 of *Selected Works of Kochi Doi* (1977), 344–82. See also Kenzaburo Ohashi, 'Doi Kochi', *Eigoseinen* (1984): 8–9 and 'Kochi Doi on Literary Criticism', *Eigoseinen* (November 1986): 18–19.

16  Bunsho Jugaku, *Essays on Blake* (1931; 1992)

17  However, the earliest recorded response from the Pacific Rim is probably Anon, 'Mr Swinburne on Mr Blake', *Argus* (Melbourne) 2 June 1868, 5–6.

18  At the original conference, Kozo Shioe discussed 'Blake and the Young Painters of the Kyoto School', specifically Bakusen Tsuchida, Kagaku Murakami and Hako Irie, in a paper unfortunately unavailable for this collection. For further discussion, see Shioe (1995).

19 At the original conference, the father–son motif in 'Blake and Oe Kenzaburo' was examined by Keiko Kobayashi, whose paper was unfortunately not available for this collection.

20 For example, the French deistical philosopher, Nicolas A. Boulanger, quite happily situates the 'orient' variously in the 'Mogul-territory' of India, Japan, Israel, Mexico and Ethiopia, all within the space of a few pages: *Origins and Progress of Despotism in the Oriental, and Other Empires, of Africa, Europe, and America* (1764), translated in an Amsterdam imprint by the radical Member of Parliament, John Wilkes (185–91). For further discussion, see Larrissy 2005.

# PART I

## The Orient in Blake:
## The Global Eighteenth
## Century

# 2 Thel in Africa: William Blake and the Post-colonial, Post-Swedenborgian Female Subject

David Worrall

This chapter will argue that Thel's refusal, confirmed 'with a shriek' (6: 21; E 6), to join the mode of life offered to her by Clay, Lilly and Cloud is a specific refusal of Swedenborg's doctrine of conjugal love, a subject topical to contemporary Swedenborgians who were proposing to establish an African colony based on its principles.[1] In other words, *The Book of Thel*'s structure, which is organized around a narrative of her modes of refusal, can be contextualized with reference to Swedenborgian principles of conjugal love and their proposed west African colony. Thel's refusals are a rejection of her co-option into such a community and, implicitly, a rejection of the entire colonization project. Although *The Book of Thel* (etched with a title page date of 1789) never refers to Africa, this essay will argue that the figure of Thel embodies Blake's misgivings about the role of women in the Swedenborgian project.[2] To contemporary historians of Africa and slavery, the Sierra Leone colony, as founded by the Sierra Leone Company with the support of Granville Sharp, was highly regarded ideologically and recognized as equivalent to the seventeenth-century 'free states' of Brazil, a type of 'republic . . . which might have revolutionized the new world.'[3] The Swedenborgian version was never actually established – that was done by the Sierra Leone Company – but its principal enthusiast, Carl Bernhard Wadström, struggled with the project over several years from 1788 onwards, coinciding with the time when Blake's connections with the London Swedenborgian community were at their height. The theological foundation for such a project arose from Swedenborg's frequent assertion that Africans have retained the clearest intuition of God.[4] Blake's most definitive allusion to this aspect of his teaching occurs in *America: A Prophecy* (1793) where he writes of Orc, 'Thou art the image of God who dwells in darkness of Africa' (2: 8; E 52).[5] In other words, not only is *The Book of Thel* an intervention into a topical debate figured within this specific but recoverable London belief community, it is also resonant with the wider contemporary politics of colonization, slavery and the role of women in the era immediately before Mary Wollstonecraft.

At the start of the poem, Blake establishes Thel's antipathy to the role model of women exemplified by her unadventurous shepherdess sisters: while 'All' the other 'daughters of Mne Seraphim' are content to lead 'round their sunny flocks', Thel 'the youngest . . . in paleness sought the secret air' (1: 1–2; E 3). *Thel*'s recent critical reception has indicated that such a largely decontextualized feminist mode of interpretation continues to be intelligible and has attracted a fair amount of critical interest, notably as a cause célèbre in Helen Bruder's challenging survey of *Thel* scholarship in 1994. Her analysis, together with a pivotal essay by Kelvin Everest in 1987, allowed us to rethink Thel as a young woman on the verge of entering a particularly unprepossessing society, one which was both patriarchal and hierarchical in nature. That Blake was inclined towards doctrinal engagement with contemporary Swedenborgians is manifest both from his attendance at the 1789 Eastcheap conference and his trenchant sparring with the church's founder in *The Marriage of Heaven and Hell* (1789–90). It may also be the case that Catherine Blake's presence at the Eastcheap conference was more potentially influential at a domestic level than has hitherto been realized. Otherwise, a possible controversial doctrinal schism over concubinage apart, the issue which in 1789 most engaged the attention of the church's activists was Wadström's Sierra Leone project (see Rubinstein and Townsend).

Swedenborgian influences or allusions in *The Book of Thel* have long been noted, particularly in connection with Blake's repeated reference to the doctrine of 'use' which Thel appears to echo (e.g. 'And all shall say, without a use this shining woman liv'd' (3: 22; E 5)).[6] In three essays published in 1997, 1998 and 1999, Joseph Viscomi has argued that the near-contemporary *Marriage of Heaven and Hell* originated as a specifically anti-Swedenborgian pamphlet gathered around a four-plate core. The present author (2000) has also contributed towards figuring something of the spiritual complexity of Blake's anti-Swedenborgian peers in the contemporary London engraving trade. The establishment of the Great Eastcheap New Jerusalem Church had been heralded by the distribution of a circular letter and set of propositions on 7 December 1788, to which Wadström was a signatory. In April 1789 they held a four day conference of establishment.[7] As first conjectured by Mark Schorer in *William Blake: The Politics of Vision* (1946) and discussed in greater detail by Marsha Keith Schuchard, there were probably also doctrinal schisms within the London Swedenborgians over the issue of polygamy and the notion of 'Conjugial Love'.[8] In the contemporary capital, the copper-plate printer William Bryan's visionary carpenter friend, John Wright, had attended worship with the Eastcheap Swedenborgians in 1788 but by early 1789 both men had journeyed to Avignon, France, to meet up with European illuminists who styled themselves the Society of Avignon, staying there until around September 1789 when they both returned to London. Their dissidence was probably more symptomatic than influential during this fairly turbulent period but Wright and Bryan help materialize the context of a New Church peopled by a congregation fired by idealism but also committed to internationalism rather than missionary endeavour. Meanwhile in Europe, certainly more momentously, the Bastille was stormed in July 1789 and the French Revolution began.

Amidst the reverberations of the Revolution, the fractured spiritualities of London Swedenborgians must have been quickly outpaced by the imperatives of the political and social cataclysms across the English Channel. For Blake's part, he also quickly followed a more politicized impetus in his writings. His finely laid out typeset quarto proof poem *The French Revolution* (1791) was produced about the same time as the *Song of Liberty* suffix to *The Marriage*, and they were both followed by the Paineite tendencies of *America* (1793). In other words, *The Book of Thel*, along with many of the poems which went into *Songs of Innocence* (some of whose moments of inception can be dated back to the late 1780s composition of 'an Island in the Moon'), occurred at a particularly transitional moment. Not only was the national situation changing, Blake's increasing skill with stereotype relief-etching was allowing him to master the fluid and vivid combinations of uncluttered text and design which are much more a characteristic of *The Book of Thel* than the *Songs of Innocence* or of the so-called 1788 tractates, *All Religions are One* and *There is No Natural Religion*.

Wadström laid out his plans for the Sierra Leone colony in the Richard Hindmarsh printed *A Plan For A Free Community Upon The Coast Of Africa, Under The Protection Of Great Britain; But Intirely [sic] Independent Of All European Laws And Governments* published in June 1789.[9] Startlingly, the political economy of the colony was to be run entirely on the principles of conjugal love as outlined by Swedenborg. This analysis is not an overstatement. The latest point by which Blake would have encountered news of the Sierra Leone project and its underlying doctrine would have been in 1790 when Wadström's *New Jerusalem Magazine* appended to its first volume an English translation of Swedenborg's *The Delights of Wisdom Respecting Conjugal Love. After which follow the Pleasures of Insanity Respecting Scortatory Love* (1790). Significantly, Wadström ensured that the *New Jerusalem Magazine* carried disproportionately frequent references to the project.[10] However, the earliest date by which time Blake is likely to have read Swedenborg on conjugal love, and to have encountered the idea of the colony project, was in the abridgement of *The Delights of Wisdom Respecting Conjugal Love* published as *A Sketch of the Chaste Delights of Conjugal Love, and the Impure Pleasures of Adulterous Love. Translated from the Apocalypsis Explicata, a manuscript of the posthumous works of the Hon. Emanuel Swedenborg* (1789). This can be dated to the spring of that year when it carried an advertisement declaring that 'Soon Will be Published, A Plan for Establishing a Free Community on the Western Coast of Africa.'[11] Wadström's *Plan For A Free Community* was dated 29 June 1789, only a couple of months after the Eastcheap conference, so *A Sketch of the Chaste Delights* must have been printed a few weeks earlier. It is possible the African project was also discussed at the conference where Wadström played such a forward role. To glance at the publication background of *A Sketch* is to briefly re-enter that community of late 1780s London spiritualities within which Blake moved and in which Catherine and William had conclusively confirmed their presence by registering at the Eastcheap conference.

*A Sketch*'s printer was John Denew, an engraver, letterpress and copper-plate printer who worked from premises in Wardour Street, Soho, moving from No. 91 to No. 109 at some time between 1788 and 1790.[12] It was perhaps his engraving and copper-plate printing skills which led him to become Anthony Pasquin's printer for his closet drama, *The Royal Academicians. A Farce. As it was Performed To the Astonishment of Mankind, by His Majesty's Servants, at the Stone House, in Utopia, in the Summer of 1786* (1786). Pasquin's gentle satire (in the idiom of *An Island in the Moon*) featured the painters 'Monsieur Lethimhumbug' (Phillipe de Loutherbourg) and 'Tiny Cosmetic' (Richard Cosway) who both had well-known mystical leanings – although it notably shielded Blake's friend Henry Fuseli from lampoon. *The Royal Academicians*'s half-title page vignette, captioned 'Oh Dear! / Diploma' and presumably executed by Denew, was a delightful parody of incompetent copper-plate printing. The etched vignette was manufactured from one plate but done as if to show two plates, one misregistered with the image inverted – the spoof over-inked plate marks included. This device was probably intended to satirize the Royal Academy's dependence on its poorer cousins in engraving. As well as Denew's acquaintanceship with these spiky edges of London's fine art trades, his interest in socially progressive liberal causes is typified in his printing of (by 'A Young Lady') *The Deserter. A Poem, in Four Cantos: Describing the Premature Death of a Youth of Eighteen, Who perished through ill-timed Severity in Dover-Castle on the 5th of March, 1788* (1788) which promoted the anti-flogging cause by focusing on the case of a soldier killed by a court martial's imposition of a thousand lashes. The printer must also have been known to the lodge of Lambeth Freemasons established in September 1783 who called themselves The Royal Grand Modern (or Constitutional) Jerusalem Sols because he later printed one of their sermons and an anniversary ode.[13] In other words, Denew's printing of *A Sketch of the Chaste Delights of Conjugal Love* fits into an identifiable context of late 1780s metropolitan mentalities linked through common connections with liberal politics, fine art, alternative religions and, not least, the engraving and print trade.

This belief community, into which Blake can be firmly dated from April 1789, was probably sociable enough to discuss Wadström's ideas and it seems likely Blake would have been aware of the discussions concerning conjugal love which created the London schism. He could have read Swedenborg directly in Denew's edition. If Blake knew of Wadström's *Plan For A Free Community* in 1789, at a time when he was contemplating some of the ideas presented in *The Marriage of Heaven and Hell* nominally dated to the same year, he would have also understood the startling philosophical basis of the colony's proposed articles of governance: 'This Government must exactly resemble a Marriage, which consists of two distinct Powers, the Active on the part of the Husband, and the Re-active on the part of the Wife.'[14] This specific gendering of government, with its legion of social and sexual implications, is the context of *The Book of Thel*'s intervention into a debate championed by Wadström. In its political instruments, the proposed colony was to be articulated as a series of contrary institutions: 'This Government must consequently consist of two distinct Powers, one *Active* and the other *Re-active*. The former proposes and executes, the latter deliberates and determines.'[15] In other words, Wadström's proposed colony was to be the political embodiment of Swedenborgian doctrines of contraries with its government divided into an executive body and a house of representatives. The executive, 'The Active Power of a Free Community,' was to be headed by 'Four Chief Magistrates' while the 'Reactive Power of a Free Community' consisted of 'Twenty-Four Representatives of the People in the Supreme Council.'[16] Beneath these executives, the prevailing social compact was to be constructed around the supposition of conjugal love.

However, the *Plan For A Free Community* became less and less involved with the anti-slavery issues which had probably initially impelled its moral direction. Instead, it became increasingly concerned with setting up a viable colony. Remarkably, although he was yet to encounter John Gabriel Stedman, whose *Narrative, of a Five Years' Expedition, against the Revolted Negroes of Surinam . . . 1772 to 1777* (1796) itself formed a critique of colonialism and slavery, Blake realized that the idea of a utopian African community was fundamentally flawed, particularly in the roles it envisaged for women as well as for slaves. Some of the rather credulous contemporary descriptions of the Sierra Leone landscape may be partially satirized in the rich pastoral depicted in *The Book of Thel*'s designs.

Christopher Fyfe, the modern historian of Sierra Leone, points out that the attempt to establish a colony was first prompted by the entrepreneurial amateur botanist, Henry Smeathman, who received £4 per head from the British government to persuade destitute American blacks in London to migrate to Africa in order to free the capital's authorities of the necessity of providing for them.[17] Smeathman had proposed his project in February 1786 to the Committee for the Black Poor, an organization aimed at relieving the distress of the London black population and headed by Jonas Hanway, the chimney sweep philanthropist.[18] It is also possible that Blake knew something of Smeathman through his acquaintance with George Cumberland, Blake's patron, with whom he had directly discussed an embryonic Sierra Leone project as early as 1783.[19] The role of Smeathman as instigator of the initial African project, and Blake's possible awareness of his well-established connection to Cumberland, is another facet of London's complex networks of social, racial, political and religious allegiance. Beneath the Swedenborgian utopias and Smeathman's entrepreneurial machinations, lay the poverty-stricken American blacks, ex-slave migrants who had been freed after fighting for the British only to find themselves relocated to the inhospitable climate of Nova Scotia.[20] Smeathman's promotion of Sierra Leone's viability as a colonial site proved hopelessly over-optimistic (and amounted to a betrayal of London blacks) but he was not alone in his plausible claims.

Many of the problems of health and climate that the early colonists in the area encountered had been outlined in the philanthropist Granville Sharp's *Short Sketch of Temporary Regulations (Until Better Shall Be Proposed) For the Intended Settlement on the Grain Coast of Africa, Near Sierra Leona* (1786) but the warnings seem to have been ignored. Two important sources for Wadström's knowledge about Sierra Leone were accounts written by Royal Navy Lieutenant John Matthews and Wadström's personal correspondence in 1788 with one Henry Gandy who had not only made two voyages there but was himself a Swedenborgian. Curiously, Wadström's own *Observations on the Slave Trade, and a Description of some part of the Coast of Guinea, During a Voyage Made in 1787, and 1788* (1789) was as optimistic about the natural fertility of Sierra Leone as Matthew's and Gandy's accounts. Gandy's counsel that Sierra Leone would be the ideal environment in which to preach 'the rudiments of the everlasting Gospel . . . and cause the blessing to extend, beyond the limits of our narrow perceptions' must have been a crucial endorsement. Gandy, who claimed that he had spent 'a considerable time' in the country, wrote that it was 'rich, healthy and exceeding fertile', and he appeared to verify much of Matthews' *A Voyage to the River Sierra-Leone* (1788) in extolling its natural productivity.[21] For example, Matthews wrote that 'Sugar canes are a native plant, and grow wild to a size beyond any I ever saw in the West Indies.'[22] Gandy similarly claimed there were above '192,000 acres of exceeding rich and fertile land' and compared it favourably to Barbados while Wadström claimed that 'Millet, rice, potatoes . . . and many other excellent vegetables, are cultivated . . . with very little trouble, and in a profusion perfectly astonishing to an European.'[23] It is perhaps this notion of Sierra Leone's botanical fertility which Blake alludes to in what one commentator has called *The Book of Thel*'s 'fable of flowers' and which is illustrated in recognizable depictions of amaryllis formosissima, monotropa, anenome pulsatilla, lily of the valley, fuschia coccinea and, in Copy I, a middle distance of extra-illustrated cypresses (Erdman 1974: 33, 9; Baine 1986: 3, 168). Later Sierra Leone Company reports also alluded to how the colonists had 'in some measure trusted' Matthews' account which was 'far more favourable than further observation of that . . . country would have justified.'[24] While Gandy certainly kept in mind some general objective of using the African colony 'to stab in measure, the vitals of the slave-trade', and they later managed to gather the support of William Wilberforce, the anti-slavery issue was secondary to their intentions.[25] Instead, subscribers and correspondents to *The New Jerusalem Magazine* continued to express their 'pleasing astonishment' when they received Wadström's plan, 'believing it to be a system of legislation, the most likely if adopted, to root out vice, and introduce virtue among mankind.' Wadström's proposition was thought to be ideally suited to coastal Africa 'where the people's manners are not corrupted with vice, nor their principles contaminated with false and inconsistent ideas of the Supreme Being.'[26] The sexual politics of this uneasy combination of utopian idealism and Swedenborgian missionary zeal are debated in *The Book of Thel*.

Thel's decisive response to her attempted seduction into the material world by Clay makes clear her total unsuitability for the version of the world described in the voice from 'the hollow pit' (6: 10; E 6). Her reaction is decisive, 'The Virgin started from her seat, & with a shriek. / Fled back unhindered till she came into the vales of Har' (6: 21–2; E 6). As has often been noted, part of the psychic structure of Thel's flight appears to be her repulsion at the physical discomforts of human sexuality: 'Why a tender curb upon the youthful burning boy! / Why a little curtain of flesh on the bed of our desire?' (6: 19–20; E 6). If Thel had known what Wadström had in mind for women in his ideal Swedenborgian community, she might have run faster. The sexual act was to be incorporated into the Sierra Leone colony's very notion of citizenship. This stressed that 'The true exercise of civil duties is founded in an unboundedly active Industry, in what is useful; and true Religion, in an unlimited exercise of regular Conjugal Life.'[27] Wadström reiterated that every husband was pledged to 'keep sacred Union with his Wife, by a diligent observance of *the ultimate endearment*' (my italics).[28] Thel's position would have been untenable within the kind of Swedenborgian utopian colony Wadström envisaged yet its ideologies would have coerced her inclusion. Perhaps some of this comes across in the Cloud, Thel's haughtiest interlocutor, with his declaration, 'Then if thou art the food of worms. O virgin of the skies, / How great thy use, how great thy blessing; every thing that lives, / Lives not alone. Nor for itself' (3: 25–6; E 5). The Cloud's doctrine is a distillation of the Swedenborgian principles articulated by Wadström:

'Society is no other than a Conjunction, a Combination of Uses; or, in other words, of Men formed into a vast variety of useful Occupations. It's [*sic*] Life consists of Uses, and the perfection of that Life is according to the excellency of those Uses, and at the same time according to their multiplicity. The Strength of Society consists in the order and connection of those Uses, in one Form or body . . .'[29]

For a 'virgin of the skies' (3: 25, E 5) like Thel (her virginity is emphasized at 3: 1, 14, 5: 17, 6: 21; E 4, 5, 6), the Sierra Leone colony was dauntingly intended to have been founded on 'the Love of the Sex, and the constant exercise thereof, which is the Virile Potency, is the very basis to the accession of all other kinds of permanent Powers'.[30] Wadström believed that these 'permanent Powers', whether of vision or generation, lay exclusively through the 'true Conjugal Life, agreeable to the order of Creation'.[31] As *Thel's* most recent editors Morris Eaves, Robert N. Essick and Joseph Viscomi note, 'The Cloud claims for his very impermanence an eternal purpose that he characterizes as spiritual or sexual "raptures holy" ' (Blake 1993: 75).[32] Wadström explicitly presented the conjugal relationship as based upon different gendered roles. He wrote that 'The Conjugal Alliance of the Community, which is between the Sexes' is constituted 'between the Understanding in the Man and the Will in the Woman; or, Man's Wisdom and Woman's Love.'[33] Peter F. Fisher first pointed out that 'Thel' may derive from the Greek θέλω, meaning 'will' or 'desire', while *Thel's* most recent editors have noted that the title of *The Wisdom of Angels, Concerning Divine Love and Divine Wisdom* (annotated *c.*1789), 'contains two key words in "Thel's Motto" and hints at deeper [Swedenborgian] influences' (Fisher 1961: 205–35; Blake 1993: 78). The extent to which Blake's own beliefs intersect with Wadström's principles of citizenship (founded upon the exercise of 'the ultimate endearment' within marriage) is both striking and complex.

For Wadström, upon 'the Conjugal Unions' of marriages 'depends intirely the improvement of the very elements in all Communities'. That is, conjugally exercised marriage was the basis of civil society, active matrimony being the foundational 'Conjugal Alliance of the Community'.[34] *The Book of Thel* is Blake's working out of the civil situation of women prompted by what appears to be his own view that the path to eternity or vision would 'come to pass', as he similarly expressed it in *The Marriage of Heaven and Hell*, 'by an improvement of sensual enjoyment', a rather more extreme version of Wadström's citizenry of conjugal union (*MHH* 14; E 39) and yet one freed from the fixed gender stations envisaged by Wadström. The patriarchal implications of such doctrines are debated in *The Book of Thel* where everything about Thel suggests that she is 'Anti-conjugal'. *Thel's* recent editors note that 'the Cloud extols the pleasures of sex', or what Wadström or Swedenborg might call the 'Conjugal Life', but Thel's rejection is adamant: 'I fear I am not like thee' (3: 17, E 5) (Blake 1993: 78). The Swedenborgian Sierra Leone colony was partially motivated by an attempt to escape 'the state of Marriages, poisoned by an Anti-conjugal Life, in all the Communities of Europe'. For Wadström, marriage's civil and civic bases 'constitute the very elements of Society, and every Marriage is representative, in miniature, of the Civil society in it's [*sic*] principles or beginnings'.[35] The issue of concubinage was one Wadström carefully avoided, making it clear that 'By Anti-conjugal Life, I do not here mean the attachment of one unmarried Man to one free Woman, and simply Concubinage, which under certain regulations never ought to be forbidden in a Free State.'[36] However, Wadström didn't entirely rule it out for his 'Free State'. Consulted or not, the future for European women in Sierra Leone was frequent participation in the sexual consummation of marriage. Wadström even daydreamed of a global conjugal empire, contemplating that such 'a Community might, without the least disorder or confusion, by a multiplication of itself, extend over the face of the whole Earth'.[37]

Women do not seem to have been consulted about this conjugal union. The colony's house of representatives, for example, was to be comprised of a 'Corps of Free-men'.[38] Wadström assumed the complicit integration of women into the community without encompassing them within its electoral franchise. If Blake kept up with news about the Sierra Leone expedition of 1786–7, he might have learned that white women, presumed to be prostitutes, travelled with the original black settlers. Both the 1791 *Substance of the Report of the Court of Directors of the Sierra Leone Company* and Anna Maria Falconbridge's first-hand account of 1794 attested to this occurrence of miscegenation.[39] Blake's satire on the social role of women may also be embedded in *The Book of Thel*'s allusion to Martin Madan's *Thelyphthora; Or, A Treatise on Female Ruin, in its Causes, Effects, Consequences, Prevention, and Remedy* (1780). Madan was an ardent advocate of polygamy ('we find it *allowed, owned*, and even *blessed* of God') which he contrasted to '*Popish* schemes of celibacy, which have been set up against the command of God'.[40] Madan discussed the scriptural evidence for polygamy but ignored women (while considering polyandry 'too aborrent [*sic*] from *nature, reason*, and *scripture*, to admit of a single argument in its favour, or even to deserve a moment's consideration').[41] Blake's allusion to *Thelyphthora* in his title may be aimed at creating a specific critique of the Wadström project.

If the passive conformities implicit in the discourse of conjugal love were discussed at the Eastcheap conference, it seems inconceivable Catherine Blake would not have intervened, possibly in public, certainly in the domestic context of her relationship with her husband. It is a complex and probably irrecoverable issue, but that ideas or views about polygamy surfaced in Blake's mind seems confirmed by his large colour print of 'Lamech and his Two Wives' (1795/1805). Lamech had a coveted place in Madan's book with the patriarch's twin marriages triumphantly noted as 'The first instance of *polygamy* which is recorded.'[42] Keri Davies and Keith Schuchard have also recently discovered that Blake's mother, Catherine Wright, was brought up in a Moravian household, a spiritual community which, although not advocating polygamy, had advanced ideas of pastoral sex education and specific customs of marriage including the choosing of marriage partners by the elders of the congregation.[43] Discussions of the conduct and sexuality of marriage in public forums was a practice with which Blake would have been familiar.

While some aspects of conjugal love doctrine may have been attractive, Blake recognized they lacked the voluntary incorporation of women. The fully constituted Swedenborgian church, founded in 1789, would have materialized Blake's doubts. However, the inception of the Sierra Leone colony was predicated by its followers on the possibility of its functioning as a credible independent state with its own polity. That Wadström himself was heavily personally committed to establishing such a west African colony is evidenced by his later promotion of another joint stock 'Sierra Leone Company' which issued a subscription for shares and published in two volumes *An Essay on Colonization Particularly Applied to the Western Coast of Africa with some Free Thoughts on Cultivation and Commerce* (1794), written by Wadström and illustrated with fine copper-engraved illustrations. By the time of the *Essay*, Wadström had dropped any reference to establishing the colony upon principles of conjugal love. Instead, by June 1792, he had gathered hundreds of subscriptions at the considerable price of £50 per share. Wadström reprinted the shareholder list in full together with a further list of those who subscribed to the quarto volume. The shareholders constitute a definitive list of the British great and good of the early 1790s. Among them is a 'wrong' William Blake (of Aldersgate Street, who bought three shares for £150 in total) but also several who are of much more interest and whose presence is indicative of the circulation of Wadström's proposal amongst the country's affluent and liberally inclined intelligentsia.[44] The subscribers include Erasmus Darwin (one share), author of *The Botanic Garden* (1791) and Ann Whitaker (two shares) of Enfield, Middlesex. Whitaker was the live-in partner of Rebekah Bliss who was the first collector of Blake's illuminated books (see Chapter 4). The shareholder list is not noticeably Swedenborgian in leaning but John Augustus Tulk, the father of the later Swedenborgian Blake collector, Charles Augustus Tulk, and himself an organizer of the 1789 Eastcheap conference, bought two shares (£100) and subscribed for a copy of Wadström's *Essay*.[45] Assuming Ann Whitaker sympathized with her partner Rebekah Bliss's life-long allegiance to the Independent Chapel, Carey Street, then something of the contemporary appeal of the project to the broad range of English nonconformism becomes apparent (Davies 1999).

Alongside Blake's response to the sexual politics of the Sierra Leone conjugal love colony lies the broader hinterland of British progressive politics on the eve of the French Revolution. As Wadström put it, 'To what purpose is Spiritual Liberty without Civil Liberty? All our Spiritual Light . . . will but serve to agitate our Political Hell.'[46] According to Wadström's original subtitle, the colony was to be *Intirely* [sic] *Independent Of All European Laws And Governments*. It was probably this utopian idealism, founded on aspects of political disenchantment, which motivated Wadström and his followers. Despite his assertions, however, Wadström's anti-slavery views quickly dissipated. One of his opening statements, 'Every one feels a sort of Political and Oeconomical Slavery', quickly became an apology for an amelioration rather than abolition.[47] On the second to last page of the book he merely proposed that in the colony 'instead of Slavery, a gentle Servitude is to be instantly adopted, and every Native redeemed from Slavery shall be free after a Service or Apprenticeship of a few Years'.[48] 'A gentle Servitude . . . of a few Years' was not clarified.

The cruel paradox of the colonizing project was that the challenge of founding a viable, economic and philosophically coherent colony rapidly diminished self-reflection on the problems of slavery and the acquisition of African land by Europeans. Like Granville Sharp's *Short Sketch of Temporary Regulations* (1786), which conferred a version of Saxon constitutionalism on his Sierra Leone colony, Wadström's plan envisaged a quasi-republican 'Corps of Free-men' intended to be self-reliant and self-governing. As with Wadström, the intricacies of its elaboration only serve to highlight its blindness to the effects of colonization on the indigenous people. Sharp's *Sketch* set out a polity based upon the 'Frank-pledge', a division of the land and the people into representative units based upon twelfths but retaining the traditional names of 'tithing' and 'decenary'. Like the Swedenborgian colony, with some important exceptions as to land ownership, Sharp's plan was based upon a male franchise awarded to the 'masters of families or householders', 'good men and true' headed by a '*Hundreder*, or centurion'.[49] This excepted, Sharp's proposals set out democratic principles by stating that those who 'equally contribute to support all the burthens of the state . . . must be entitled to an *equal* voice in the "common council", or parliament . . . in a due and *equal* proportion to their numbers'.[50] The extent to which these mechanisms have been worked out is as striking as their failure to envisage the impact on native Africans.

These constitutional issues provide the larger context for Blake's interest in contemplating the viability of Wadström's colony. *The Book of Thel* may even fall into a recognizable tradition of early modern utopias fictionalized in Africa (such as in Simon Berington's *The Adventures of Sig. Gaudentio di Lucca*).[51] However, *The Book of Thel* doesn't just simply posit a utopia but critiques the practical implications of what *Tiriel* terms as the 'Vales of Har' (pl. 2; 4 E 277), the place the poem seems to imply as the region of Swedenborgian sexual union and conjugal polity – and from which Thel flees. In this respect, Blake's critique of colonization was probably more thoroughly conceptualized than Coleridge's or Southey's contemporary plans for a 'Pantisocratic' community on the Susquehanna River, Pennsylvania.[52] Blake's imaginative engagement with the specific gender problems of the conjugal colony, probably prompted by Catherine, also denotes a surprising degree of realism and predictive engagement with the consequences of colonization on the colonizers (if not on the colonized).

The Swedenborgian Sierra Leone colony as an aspect of contemporary utopian temperament helps locate it firmly within the context of London's politics and alternative spiritualities. *The Book of Thel* manifests a more materialized ideology than one might have expected. It is certainly rather different from the notion of the utopian writing and the place of *Visions of the Daughters of Albion* envisaged by Nicholas Williams in *Ideology and Utopia in the Poetry of William Blake*: 'Whatever its status, utopian discourse in *Visions* remains, even in the representational world of the poem, precisely at the level of discourse, not yet as a part of any actual reconfiguration of social constructions' (Williams 1998: 96). This essay has suggested that the recovery of the Sierra Leone context means that *The Book of Thel* has gone further than to merely suggest 'the utopian valency of its method of unpresentability' (Williams 1998: 219). Indeed, Thel's predicament in 1789 appears to have been precisely the apparent imminence of her presentability and even, quite conceivably, Catherine Blake's co-option into its ideological support. Women could, and did, become colonists. Anna Maria Falconbridge, the wife of the first manager of the Sierra Leone colony, wrote an account of her experiences in *Narrative of Two Voyages to the River Sierra Leone, During the Years 1791–2–3* (1794).[53] She survived her drunken husband's death and challenged the Sierra Leone Company's inconsiderate treatment of them.[54] Her case is a striking parallel for how the gender politics of African colonization were concurrently considered by European women.

The Wadström project was floated on the vast template of eighteenth-century nonconformism, proto-republicanism and anti-slavery idealism. To its supporters, the colony must have looked real and practicable. At its basis, however, lay not only the assumed passivity of native Africans but the co-option of women within the conjugal state of marriage. Driven by a heady mix of Anglo-Scandinavian alternative spiritualities, and blind to the implications of empire, Wadström intended the colony to be an idealized social and political compact figured around the distinctive concept of Swedenborgian conjugal love. In this sense at least, Thel's refusal to be co-opted into the terms of its foundation makes her Blake's first post-Swedenborgian, post-colonial female.

### Notes

1  Robert Carr (1987: 78) points out that, properly, Swedenborg differentiated between 'conjugal' and 'conjugial' love: 'Conjugial love is defined as "the conjunction of love and wisdom" . . . Conjugal love is defined as "the connubial principle of evil and the false".' The two early translations referred to in this essay do not appear to observe such a

distinction. The idea for this essay was suggested by reading Robert W. Rix, 'Bibles of Hell': PhD thesis (University of Copenhagen, 2001).

2  The most authoritative history is Braidwood 1994.

3  Grégoire 1810: 144–51.

4  See Ogude 1976; Paley 1979.

5  As far as the continent itself is concerned, Blake went on to denote 'Africa' as part of *The Song of Los*'s (1795) continental theme in continuation of *America: A Prophecy* (1793) and *Europe: A Prophecy* (1794).

6  See Davies 1948; Heppner 1977; Carr 1987.

7  The texts of the circular, propositions and proceedings, as recorded by Robert Hindmarsh, have been conveniently reprinted (Bellin and Ruhl 1985: 121–31). The originals are in Hindmarsh 1861: 79–84, 97, 101–8. Hindmarsh refers to Wadström's abolitionist activism but not to the Sierra Leone colony.

8  Schorer 1946: 105; Schuchard 2000.

9  Rix (2003) notes that Wadström's friend, August Nordenskold, is sometimes credited with the authorship of *A Plan for a Free Community* but both the BL and ESTC attribute the work to Wadström.

10  *New Jerusalem Magazine* (1790): 70–3, 125–32, 157–74, 181–6, 217–19, 278–94.

11  Swedenborg 1789: 91.

12  See entries, Maxted 2001; Berch and Maxted 2001.

13  Barry 1788; anon. 1790.

14  The etched date on *The Marriage*'s title page is '1789' but Blake penned '1790' into Copy F (Blake 1993: 113–16); Wadström 1789: 20. Paley notes that a different, more elaborated, constitution for the colony was drafted in Nordenskjöld 1790.

15  Wadström 1789: 19–20.

16  Wadström 1789: 11, 17.

17  Fyfe 1962: 14–16.

18  See the handbill distributed to the 'Black Poor', Smeathman 1786: 23–4.

19  BL Add. MS 3694, Smeathman to Cumberland, 31 August 1783, 10 October 1783, cited in Braidwood 1994a: 11.

20  Fyfe 1962: 31–7.

21  Gandy adopted typical Swedenborgian practices of dating his letter, i.e. '17$^{th}$ of 9$^{th}$ Mo. 1788' (17$^{th}$ September), *New Jerusalem Magazine* (1790): 166.

22  Matthews 1788: 53.

23  Wadström 1789: 42.

24  *An Account of the Colony of Sierra Leone, From Its First Establishment in 1793* (1795), p. 19.

25  *New Jerusalem Magazine* (1790) '3$^{d}$ of 12$^{th}$ Mo. 1788' (3 December): 168–9.

26  *New Jerusalem Magazine* (1790) '7$^{th}$ of 7$^{th}$ Mo. 1789' (7 July): 171, 173.

27  Wadström 1789: xi.

28  Wadström 1789: 28.

29  Wadström 1789: 4.

30  Wadström 1789: 35.

31  Wadström 1789: 31.

32  Carr notes that 'The Cloud is . . . urging a selfless "conjugial" love that is certainly not sexless' (Carr 1987: 81).

33  Wadström 1789: 29–30.

34  Wadström 1789: 29–30.

35  Wadström 1789: v.

36  Wadström 1789: 32.

37  Wadström 1789: xii.

38  Wadström 1789: 19.

39  Braidwood 1994: Appendix 2, 280–8.

40  Madan 1780: 1, 75; 2, 299.

41  Madan 1780: I. 75.

42  Madan 1780: I. 147.
43  Davies 2003. On the 'love-feast' and sex education in Moravian communities, see Podmore 1998: 31–2, 130–1.
44  It is presumably this 'William Blake, Esq' who is a member of the African Institution in 1815 (Thorpe 1815: xxi).
45  Hindmarsh 1861: 70, 78, 83, 104, 106.
46  Wadström 1789: xi–xii.
47  Wadström 1789: iv.
48  Wadström 1789: 50.
49  Sharp 1786: 5.
50  Sharp 1786: 6.
51  There were a number of editions, including Berington (1763).
52  McKusick 1998.
53  Alexander Falconbridge had written a memorable account in *An Account of the Slave Trade on the Coast of Africa* (1788).
54  The traumas of life in the colony destroyed their relationship. She wrote at the time of his death, 'I will not be guilty of such meanness as to tell a falsehood on this occasion, by saying I regret his death, no! I really do not, his life had become burthensome to himself and all around him, and his conduct to me, for more than two years past, was so unkind (not to give a harsher term), as long since to wean every spark of affection or regard I had for him.' (Falconbridge 1792: 169–70)

# 3 'Typhon, the lower nature'[1]: Blake and Egypt as the Orient

Kazuya Okada

John Flaxman wrote in a letter to William Hartley:

> The best modern books on this subject [of Egyptian monuments] are Pococke's Voyages, Savary's Travels in Egypt, Norden's Egypt, Denon's Egypt; to which may be added, the most magnificent work of ancient and modern Egypt, now publishing [sic] in Paris.[2]

Here, as we can see, are included several important works on Egypt – the last one quite definitely referring to the *Description de l'Egypte* of Jomard – all of which are familiar to students keen on the topic of the Orientalism of romantic travel narratives.[3] Flaxman and Hartley had both been friends of Blake for many years (Blake was entrusted with illustrating some works by them). Accordingly, the passage above may strengthen our assumption that Blake had access, either directly or indirectly, to important information on Egypt and Egyptology. In terms of Blake's symbolism, 'Egypt is an analogue of the fallen world', as John Beer notes, summarizing from Roe's pioneering and extensive exploration, which illustrates that '[t]he concept of Egypt thus came to serve Blake as a perfect symbol of the Fallen World' (Roe 1969: 174). Moreover, it can also be pointed out that, to use Beer's own definition, 'Egypt [is] opposed to Eden' (Beer 1969: 256).[4] In the developed mythology Egypt is given the important function of paying 'homage to Urizen, the God of the Fallen World' (Roe 1969: 174), which is reconfirmed by the descriptions, for example, in the final section of *The Book of Urizen* (1794):

> So Fuzon call'd all together
> The remaining children of Urizen:
> And they left the pendulous earth:
> They called it Egypt, & left it.
> (Pl. 28, ll. 19–22; E 83)[5]

In addition to these descriptions, as Morton Paley suggests, the typical Egyptian imagery of the pyramids 'emblematise[s] the not-human in Blake's texts' (Paley 1983: 189). As Paley further notes, the 'pyramids of pride' (*Jerusalem* 91: 43 E 252) form a representative image through his particular descriptions of them, as, for example; 'pyramids loom[ing] ominously over the human figures'; or 'pyramids that represent the now eclipsed negation of the divine human form' (Paley 1983: 188–9). As for the issue of Egyptian fertility in a plate from *The Book of Ahania* (1795), we can note that Blake describes the image of eggs in typical association with the obnoxious:

> . . . [Urizen's] dire Contemplations
> Rush'd down like floods from his mountains
> In torrents of mud settling thick
> With Eggs of unnatural production
> Forthwith hatching;
>
> (Pl. 3, ll. 7–11; E 85)

Here Blake expresses Urizen's 'dire Contemplations' in the metaphor of a flood rushing like 'torrents of mud . . . With Eggs'. We recognize here that Blake has transformed the traditional 'egg-in-mud' image in the description of *Antony and Cleopatra* (i.e. an image of eggs spawning from the Nile-mud: 'the seedsman scatters / Upon the slime and ooze scatters his grain, / And shortly comes to harvest', II. iv. 21–3).

Seen in this light, Blake's Egypt seems to invite a number of rather straight-forward interpretations in terms of his cosmology. Hence it is not surprising that recent critics have not been keener to reinvestigate the deeper significance of Blake's relationship with Egypt to his work. I have previously referred to the Egyptian Cupid/Eros figure as a possible archetypal image of Blake's Orc (Okada 2000) and here I will further reinvestigate the deeper significance of the relationship between Blake and Egypt. I will argue that Blake's knowledge of Egyptian iconography among other Egyptian backgrounds can be inferred to fundamentally motivate him in the formulation of his own mythology. To illustrate this I will elucidate, in particular, the symbolic meaning of the Typhon figure and also highlight the issue of Egypt–Freemasonry associations in order to re-evaluate the role of Egypt in his works. I believe that the discussion here will contribute to Blake studies a view in which it is possible to recognize the profundity of Blake's distinctive understanding of Egypt as the Orient.

Blake places the image of a pyramid behind the Orc figure in a plate from *The Marriage of Heaven and Hell*.[6] Blake's reader might be encouraged to connect it with his well-known Newton picture (1795) and might be eager to discuss the image in the context of the discourse of science in romanticism. Yet, in spite of such a critical climate an illustration of Isis, from Lenoir's *La Franche-Maconnerie*, should encourage further investigation of this topic.[7] For this illustration of Isis contains a depiction – familiar in Egyptian mythologies – of symbolic stars, which are used to describe the Isis figure who laments for the slain sun god, Osiris, and his lost power. This particular description should encourage careful students of Blake's iconographical symbolism to recognize a symbolical identification – that is, that 'all stars are Urizen's' (Damon 1965: 116–7), remembering then that Blake uses stars in a similar style for the illustrations of Thomas Gray's 'The Bard' and 'The Triumphs of Owen'.[8] This relation is strengthened by the bard figure holding a compass-formed harp, which can be connected with Urizen's repressive force exemplifying a compass-holder. Furthermore, it should be noted that Blake endows the same bard with thick and highly misshapen harp-cords,[9] which can be considered as an alternative representation of Blake's symbolic imagery of 'The Net of Urizen' in a plate from *The Book of Urizen*, pl. 128: 11.13, E 83, although the icon of stars disappears from the depiction. With the likeness of the description of stars, we can assume that Blake might well have been acquainted with a similar image of Isis's garment with stars, and used it with the intention of embodying such a depiction of his own cosmology, with the bard figure representing his vehement dislike of repression (i.e. his dislike of Egypt as the fallen world which is founded upon power only, based on abundance of 'meer [*sic*] Nature' (Keynes [1949] 1971: 93). Thus the rendering of stars of Isis stimulates us to reinvestigate Blake's relationship with Egypt. Blake was, I believe, endeavouring to define his ironic view of Egypt as the Orient. His knowledge and understanding – and more importantly, his reworking of Egyptian mythologies – need to be carefully re-examined.

Erasmus Darwin's *Botanic Garden* (1791) contains an Egyptian illustration, entitled *Fertilization of Egypt*,[10] which Blake engraved after Fuseli's design. This engraving illustrates the passage of Darwin, namely section IV, entitled 'Overflowing of the Nile from African Monsoons'. In the additional note accompanying the passage, Darwin draws on a comment by Volney, who observed that:

> the time of the rising of the Nile commences about the 19th of June, and that Abyssinia and the adjacent parts of Africa are deluged with rain in May, June, and July, and produce a mass of water which is three months in draining off. The Abbé La Pluche observes that Sirius, or the dog-star, rose at the time of the commencement of the flood[,] its rising was watched by the astronomers, and notice given of the approach of inundation by hanging the figure of Anubis, which was that of a man with a dog's head, upon all their temples. (Darwin 1791: I. 145–6)

Volney's observation evidently influenced the descriptions of the engraving by Fuseli/Blake, in particular the standing figure with a dog's head, i.e. Anubis, praying that lands may be deluged with rain. In the engraving, Anubis is represented in a giant body which differs from Volney's description, yet one of the most important differences is that in the engraving the bringer of the deluge is given an ominous quality. As for this hovering figure over the Nile, many critics agree that it represents 'the Urizenic River God' (Roe 1969: 167). Damon more precisely judges that 'it is Urizen who answers the prayer with lightnings and storm-floods of water' (Damon 1965: 117).[11] In the Blakean cosmology, as I have suggested, Egypt and Egyptian things connote a destructive power, as the poet himself articulated: 'Egypt . . . Whose Gods are the Powers of this World, Goddess Nature, Who spoil & then destroy Imaginative Art' (Laocoön E 274; Keynes [1949] 1971: 777; cf. Roe 1969: 162). Blake's emphasis upon the 'spoiling'/ 'destroying' phase of the Egyptian world highlights the platonic tendencies of his philosophy, that is, his habit of contrasting everyday reality or 'this-world-ness' with an imaginative power within the human mind. Blake's position is that material thriving ultimately results in internal destruction; hence, I would argue, we should interpret the hovering figure in question as a 'mistaken Demon of heaven'.[12] Consequently, the Urizenic hovering figure in question appears to represent a false or illegitimate god, that is to say, the denounced figure of a seducer into the world of material abundance.

Another plate of a storm-god, which is entitled *Tornado*, was added to the third edition of *The Botanic Garden* (1795).[13] In an analysis of this figure with wings and a snakelike form, some critics, such as Mary Jackson, identify 'symbolic features of the Mithraic god' in it (Jackson 1977: 74). It is true that the Mithraic tradition can explain some features of the figure, yet I tend rather to agree with Beer's suggestion that the serpentine form with the wings 'follow[s] Darwin's detail fairly closely but may also be based on Egyptian mythology' (Beer 1993: 41).[14]

Darwin himself mentioned the phenomena in Abyssinia in the following section where he makes use of Bruce's exploration:

> This circumstance of the eddies produced by the monsoon-winds was seen by Mr. Bruce in Abyssinia; he relates that for many successive mornings, at the commencement of the rainy monsoon, he observed a cloud of apparently small dimension whirling round with great rapidity, and in a few minutes the heavens became covered with dark clouds with consequent great rains. (Darwin 1791: I.392)

Relating these two hovering figures in the two engravings – though we cannot tell what details, if any, Blake added or altered from the information he had obtained – we can infer that, as John Beer points out, '[i]t is conceivable that . . . Blake had in mind the destructive Egyptian deity Typhon, who is linked etymologically to the phenomenon of the Typhoon' (Beer 1993: 260).[15] As for the Typhon figure, Jacob Bryant's *A New System, an Analysis of Ancient Mythologies* (1774–6) – probably one of the most accessible and practical sources for Blake's understanding of Egyptian mythologies – includes extensive descriptions of the Egyptian god. For example, Bryant writes: 'Typhon signified a Deluge. The over-flowing of the Nile was called by the Egyptians Typhon'; and '*By Typhon is meant a violent wind*. The history of Typhon was taken from hieroglyphical descriptions' (Bryant [1774] 1979: II.319, 321). Bryant further illustrates the Egyptian god, particularly emphasizing his role as bringer of the Deluge:

> In respect to Typhon, it must be confessed that the history given of him is attended with some obscurity. The Grecians have comprehended several characters under one term, which the Egyptians undoubtedly distinguished. The term was used for a title, as well as name: several of those personages, who had a relation to the Deluge, were styled Typhonian, or Diluvian. All these the Grecians have included under one and the same name, Typhon. The real Deity, by whom the Deluge was brought upon the earth, had the appellation of Typhonian; by which was meant Diluvii Deus. (Bryant [1774] 1979: II.323)

Bryant also mentions two different personages of the Egyptian god, who are described as follows:

> This has arisen from two different personages being included under one name; who undoubtedly were distinguished in the language of Egypt. Typhon was a compound of Tuph, or Tupha-On; and signified a high altar of the Deity. There were several such in Egypt; upon which they offered human sacrifices; and those cities, which had these altars, were styled Typhonian. But there was another Typhon, who was very different from the former, however by mistake blended with that character. By this was signified a mighty whirlwind, and inundation . . . (Bryant [1774] 1979: II.320)

With these analyses in mind, it will be recognized that Blake's figuration of the Urizenic hovering figure in *Fertilization of Egypt* is clearly influenced by the Typhonic figure of Egyptian mythology. Concerning the aspect of Typhon's being a mistaken god, or a fake one, the relationships between Osiris, Isis and Typhon seem particularly important. In his study Bryant explores these relationships, emphasizing the following story from Egyptian mythology:

... it is said, that Typhon made an Ark of curious workmanship, that he might dispose of the body of Osiris. Into this Osiris entered, and was shut up by Typhon. (Bryant [1774] 1979: II.323)[16]

John Beer has speculated on the deeper implication of the dynamism of these relationships in order to connect the mythology with the hovering figure in question.[17] Though Beer has not explored the fuller implications of the Typhonic–Urizen figure over the Nile in relation to the hovering figure, his identification lends support to my interpretation: namely that Blake might have attempted to embody the temptation of Egyptian fertility, i.e. Egypt as the Orient, by means of his reworking of Typhonic features. I believe it may well be further investigated how Blake stylized the hovering form in such a way as to express his rejection of the domination of materialism, representing it in images of Egypt. Such an exploration will show how the hovering figures – a complex image recurring frequently in Blake's designs, and sometimes given snake-like markings – were expanded, and also developed, within his pictorial corpus. In order to do this, however, we need to analyse the hitherto scarcely discussed Egyptian god, Typhon, more deeply.

Curiously, the hovering figure of Tornado(/Typhon) in *The Botanic Garden* (1795) resembles Satan alighting in Fuseli's illustration entitled *Eve's Dream*.[18] This resemblance appears so consistently in Blake illustrations as to suggest that we can infer that Blake might have intended to imply, within the form of the seducer figure of Typhon, the idea of a false god deriving from the mythology – an idea which might have been developed through Blake's own concept of Egypt as the fallen world.[19]

Beer demonstrates that Swedenborgian knowledge serves as the evocative, and crucial, structure of Blake's idiosyncratic reworking of Egyptian mythologies. Accordingly, we are encouraged to adopt the view that Blake might have intended to amplify distinctive, yet so far little recognized, implications in his refiguration of the Egyptian god, Typhon. Beer comments that:

> Interest in Egyptian mythology, coupled with knowledge of Swedenborg's presupposition that the true sun is in this world divided into heat and light, would lead Blake naturally enough to bring the two traditions together and fit them to his ideas. The story of Isis and Osiris, with its figures of Osiris, the lost true sun, Isis the moon-goddess who is constantly seeking to re-create him and Typhon the fallen sun, a sun of heat alone, would fall quite naturally into the Swedenborgian pattern. (Beer 1969: 28–9)[20]

Furthermore, Beer also mentions an 'essay on the Mythology and Worship of the Serpent' by Hugh Downman whom Coleridge knew as a member of the Society of Gentlemen at Exeter. The essay contains the description of an ambiguous

> serpent in Egyptian mythology, pointing out that under the name of 'Cneph' it signified the 'good principle', but under the name of 'Typhon' the 'destructive principle' . . . (Beer 1970: 128)

With this view in mind, it will be noted that Blake depicted a female figure in a plate from *Jerusalem* (*WBIB* 1: Pl. 63) which curiously resembles 'a charming eighteenth-century ceramic figurine called Cleopatra',[21] where the snake seems destructive and seductive.

More significantly, this vicious snake of the 'destructive principle' can be connected with a remarkable snake image of Freemasonry, though no critics have so far noted this connection. The particular image appears in the illustration of Athanasius Kircher's *Oedipus Aegyptiacus*,[22] which Manly P. Hall uses in his commentary, *Freemasonry of the Ancient Egyptians*, mentioning 'Typhon, the lower nature'. Hall rightly describes the image of Typhon thus embodied; 'Typhon is the inferior or lower self, the Human Will of Boehme',[23] or 'he is the same as Mephistopheles in Goethe's *Faust*' (Hall 1937: 122–3). This image corresponds with what we have emphasized as a 'mistaken Demon of heaven', or a deceiving god, to which can be added the character of a seducer of 'the Human Will'. Hence the image of the snaky fibres appearing in Blake's illustrations (e.g. in *Jerusalem, WBIB* 1: Pl. 74),[24] and particularly the netting image used in Plate 45 of *Jerusalem* (*WBIB* 1: Pl. 45)[25] should be reinterpreted in reference to the figure of Typhon, though in Blake studies it has only been mentioned that the serpent of the Fallen World is a biblical allusion, or a symbolic implication of the net associated with Urizen, i.e. 'the net of Urizen' (pl. 28: 11.13 E 83).[26] This interpretation prompts us to redefine the fibre nets in Plate 25 of *Jerusalem* (*WBIB* 1: Pl. 25). Though this torture scene has only been considered in the context of either Druidical sacrifice, or of the Martyrdom of St Erasmus,[27] and it is true that the figure can be identified with Vala,[28] yet as for the female whose fingers resemble snaky fibres, the Typhonic figure should also be considered in our interpretation. Further, and much more intriguingly, I would like to suggest that the sun/moon image on Albion's thighs can be associated with a Master-Mason's apron.[29] Interestingly, when we superimpose the image of a Freemasonry apron onto the position of Albion's thighs, it can be interpreted that he is forced to wear an apron of repression and materialism, which on a deeper level emphasizes his suffering with the snaky fibre of Typhon. Actually, in terms of the masonic backgrounds of the age, it is widely known that Freemasonry society was secularized; for example, Hogarth's *Night*, though slightly early for Blake's time, provides us with a satirical depiction of such Freemasons. In the picture, the two figures are drunk, wearing Master-Masons' aprons in addition to other peculiar belongings such as the square in a neck, the hats and the swords. Such materialistic displays, according to Blake, epitomize souls. Seen in the similar satirical view of the principles of Freemasonry, the struggling figures of Urizen in the elements, i.e. Water or Earth (*WBIB* 6: 83, 1 87), should be regarded as Blake's ironic depictions of Urizen attempting to overcome Masonic initiations – the trials by Fire, Water and Air.

In the illuminated plate of *Jerusalem* 37/[33] (*WBIB* 1: Pl. 37) the female body of Jerusalem lies under a similar hovering figure with the same ominous features.[30] In contrast, Albion is held by a Christ-like man just above, 'between the Palm tree & the Oak of weeping'.[31] Though few critics have discussed it from this point of view, this particular plate clearly contains several Egyptian allusions,[32] and it is significant that the literary text accompanying the plate contains flood images which might well be connected with the deluge of the Nile. As Damon comments, 'Blake placed Beulah as an intermediary between Eternity and Ulro (this world of Matter)' (Damon 1965: 43); hence the death of Jerusalem in the plate should be considered as the symbolic destruction caused by the yielding to the seduction of the material world (cf. *WBIB* 1: Pl. 58). From the same view, similar hovering forms should be understood as variants of the figure which are juxtaposed with ominous images such as a corpse in Blake's work, e.g. *The Marriage of Heaven and Hell*, Copy E, Plate 14 (*WBIB* 3: 167), by which I believe Blake symbolizes spiritual death or destruction. Indeed, although it needs further investigation, I propose that Blake's hovering figure, especially when combined with the snakelike images, should be reconsidered as infused with his concept of, or rather his own intention to connote, Egypt as the Orient. It may be argued that in giving the figure these connotations Blake might have made use of his own reworking of Typhon, the Egyptian god. I believe the significance lies more deeply than has yet been recognized in his concept of Egypt, as an analogue of the fallen world, or the seductive Orient; in this particular case, i.e. *Jerusalem* 37, the Nile. Moreover, this realization of the significance of Blake's reworking of Typhon, and Egyptian mythologies in general, will lead us to recognize the importance of the question of Egypt as the Orient in Blake. Consequently, we will be in a better position to comprehend Blake's intention in placing the pyramid behind the Orc-like new man figure.

Much remains to be done in reinvestigating the status of Blakean idiosyncratic figures and their assigned functions in relation to his understanding of Egyptian mythological figures. There remain several areas within which Blake might have integrated, (re)formatted or intertextualised concerning the matter of the Orient, yet the core issue in this discussion is rather, I believe, closely related with Egyptian backgrounds in Blake's time. Let me end with these reflections on Blake's Egypt as the Orient by suggesting that the most that may safely be claimed is that Blake probably was aware of the danger, and insecurity, of Imperialistic domination. For him, Albion, i.e. England, should not be involved with the Empire as a Western sickness; i.e. she should not become another Egypt. Thus the question also strongly evokes, and is involved with, political and historical contexts. Therefore, how Blake's mythology can be reconstructed in relation to Egyptian genealogies should be more carefully investigated, in order to relate Blake's imagination with how he embraced Egypt as the Orient, an identification which I believe we can understand in the light of persistent explorations of Egyptian mythological figures.

## Notes

1  Hall (1937: 120).
2  Cited in Roe (1969: 193)
3  Most recently Leask 2002 (especially chapters 2 and 3).
4  Essick suggested that 'Blake's image in *Jerusalem* of Egypt as a "perverted" Eden . . . includes the perversion of Adam's universal language into the "many tongued / And many mouthd" ' (Essick 1989: 23).
5  Blake texts are quoted from the Erdman edition, cited as E followed by the page numbers.
6  The plate is reproduced in *William Blake's Illuminated Books* (hereafter *WBIB*), 5 vols (London: The William Blake Trust/The Tate Gallery, 1991–5), Vol. 3, p. 203. Subsequent references to the illuminated works of William Blake will be designated by the volume number, followed by the page, or plate, number, as in (*WBIB* 2: Pl. 3), or (*WBIB* 3: p. 23).
7  The image is reproduced in Hall 1937 (opposite 41).
8  These illustrations are reproduced in Tayler 1971 (the frontispiece of 'The Bard' and the first page of 'The Triumphs of Owen').
9  See also the reproduction in Tayler 1971 (the first page of 'The Bard').

10  The engraving can be found in Darwin 1791 I, opposite 145. Most recently, Priestman's argument about this engraving (Priestman 1999: 102–5) complements Mee's analysis of the engraving (Mee 1992: 157–9). Apart from those studies, there have been ardent discussions regarding this plate: see Beer 1993: 35, 259.

11  See also Paley (1978: 175). The point to be emphasized is that the hovering figure in the engraving can be compared with a similar figure in the plate from *Visions of the Daughters of Albion* in which Oothoon is running towards her lover (*WBIB* 3: p. 243).

12  *Visions of the Daughters of Albion*, pl. 5, ll. 3; E 48.

13  The engraving is reproduced in Beer (1993: 42). Also see Hilton (1983: 229–30).

14  See Darwin's view of these phenomena; 'in their most violent state, raising water from the ocean in the west or sand from the deserts of the east'; or 'in less violent degrees they only mix together the two currents of north-east and south-west air, and produce by this means incessant rains' (Darwin 1791: I. 392).

15  For the same theme in Coleridge's work, Beer argues: 'the Typhonic, destructive fountain of *Kubla Khan* stands in the same relation to the stately fountain of immortality as the burning Typhonic sun of *The Ancient Mariner* to the harmonious ideal sun of the Mariner's vision' (Beer 1970: 241).

16  I believe the icon of a winged ark can be specified in the discourse of Typhon and Osiris in the traditional Egyptian mythologies, though critics have connected it with Bryant's other moon icon, Moon-ark (cf. Paley's comment about the 'house boat-like moon-ark' (*WBIB* 1: p. 161, 168). My interpretation is that, though it has not yet been pointed out, the ark image connotes a tomb of Osiris killed by Typhon, which can symbolize the death of the imaginative world, destroyed and spoiled by the material world. See also Raine (1968: I. 232–3).

17  Cf. Beer (1969: 373); 'The theme of Isis and Osiris is repeated in the design which Blake takes over from Fuseli, representing "The Fertilization of Egypt" . . . [T]he dog-priest Anubis lifts his hands towards the distant light of the dogstar Sirius, while in the background the jealous god Typhon covers with his wings the springs of the Nile'. Also, Roe (1969: 172), Todd (1972: 176–7) and Damon (1965: 116).

18  The illustration is reproduced in Warner (1984: 141).

19  Blake's Spectre is enthusiastically studied in Hilton (1983), Chapter 8 (especially the illustration of *For the Sexes: The Gates of Paradise*, see pp. 166–7). To elaborate such an inference, it is helpful to follow the suggestion of John Beer whose discussion provides us with a key to a proper understanding of the significance of Egyptian traditions, including the sun/moon imagery depicted in the wings of the winged figure in the plate of *The Gates of Paradise*. 'The tradition of Isis, Osiris and Typhon', Beer says, 'with the destructive heat-demon Typhon and yearning light-goddess Isis enacting a fruitless struggle as Isis tries vainly to recreate the Osiris who would reconcile both principles, bears a curious resemblance to one of the central principles of Swedenborgianism, where heat and light are seen as separated elements of the lost, true sun. The favourite Egyptian hieroglyphic of sun, serpent and wings could easily be aligned with this myth, which is, moreover, linked to one of the most powerful of traditional images: that of the ambiguous Nile, sometimes flooding its country with dangerously destructive force before being swallowed up in a deathly sea, but also a necessary power of fertility . . .' (Beer 1993: 34).

20  This is of course related to the role of Los in the myth-poetics, who is a creator, carrier, occasionally maintainer of, the material sun, the imitation of the real sun and possession of Urizen. Raine (1968) also rightly comments that 'the name "Los" is "Sol" spelled backward.' (I. 223); see also Priestman (1999: 113), Damon (1965: 246–7). Damon further emphasizes '[Los] creates the *material* sun.' Blake might have been influenced by the Swedenborgian principle of the sun: 'The Sun of the natural World is perfectly dead, but the Sun of the spiritual World is alive' (Cited in Raine 1968: I. 225).

21  Warner suggests this resemblance (1984: 14–15, 18–20). The traditional image of the Nile mud, which we have seen towards the beginning of the discussion, is certainly remembered for this snake/egg image.

22  The engraving is reproduced in Hall (1937: 123).
23  Warner comments on the relationships between Blake and Fuseli/Swedenborg/Jacob Boehme; 'Blake . . . at the time he met Fuseli was absorbed in the work of Swedenborg and probably of Jacob Boehme' (Warner 1984: 138).
24  The literary text reads: 'Albion is here being forced to sacrifice his potentially infinite Energy to the creation of a limited, materialistic universe'. As for the umbilical cord, see Mitchell (1978: 200), also cf. Mellor (1974: 295).
25  Erdman sees Vala netting Albion (Erdman 1974: 319). In contrast with this image, the net image to be released in *Jerusalem* 85 should be considered, in my opinion, to be redeemed from destruction and seduction, since in the plate the real sun is back shining in the sky, symbolic of the redemption attained.
26  Cf. Hilton's account of Blake's 'fibres' (Hilton 1983, Chapter 5).
27  E.g. Erdman (1974: 304).
28  For example, Erdman sees 'the veil which Vala holds up as an operating tent', and 'the intestine-veil' (1974: 304).
29  A good example of it is reproduced in Peterfreund (1998: 69). As for Blake and Freemasonry, see Peterfreund 1998 (Chapter 3), Schuchard (1992; 1999; 2000) and Sutherland (1970).
30  As for the design of *Jerusalem* 33/37, see Erdman (1974: 312), Paley (*WBIB* 1: p. 188), Paley (1983: 204), Roe (1969: 179–80); Hilton (1983: 162–3). It has been pointed out that the 'blue death' in 'Albion's feet' can be identified as Druidic human sacrifice (e.g. Paley 1983: 204). Most recently, Grant (1999: 84).
31  Paley has pointed out that 'the palm is the victorious symbol of Christ's entry into Jerusalem' (*WBIB* 1: p. 188). As for the association of a palm tree linking the design and Blake's watercolour of 1806, *The Repose of the Holy Family in Egypt* (Butlin 1981, Cat. 472, Pl. 543) see Grant 1999: 94: 'Sturdy palms do, of course, signify Egypt, as in the late water colour *Moses Placed in the Ark of the Bulrushes* (Butlin 1981, Cat. 774, Pl. 968) and in the print evidently related to it, *The Hiding of Moses* (Bindman 1978, Pls. 624a and 624b). But the positioning of palms at the exit gate of the Garden of Eden is more explicitly ominous, as in the 1803 *Angel of the Divine Presence Clothing Adam and Eve with Coats of Skins* (Butlin 1981, Cat. 436, pl. 513)'.
32  See Paley's annotation: 'The winged disk that supports these events derives from one of the most ancient symbols of divinity, found on Sumerian cylinder seals. An engraving of such a winged disk, signed "Basire Sc", appeared in the first volume of Jacob Bryant's *New System*, plate VIII' (Paley, *WBIB* 1. p. 188).

# 4 Rebekah Bliss: Collector of William Blake and Oriental Books

## Keri Davies

Every person who bought Blake's work in his lifetime is of significance to Blake scholarship. The importance of book-collecting is that it is a cultural practice by which the collector learns what his or her culture's ethos and his or her private sensibility look like. The serious study of private libraries, and of the lessons that can be learned from book ownership, can elucidate the interests and tastes of the owner, and the texts that may have influenced his or her thinking.[1] This chapter is concerned with one such person, the collector once known simply as 'Mrs Bliss'. Her library exemplifies a culture of book-collecting in which precious books of East and West, works by Blake and rare Oriental manuscripts, are juxtaposed. The Bliss library is an important indication of the intellectual and cultural context of Blake's circles of friendship, one that challenges some long-held assumptions about Blake and the milieu in which he worked.

Blake scholarship has found the identity of Mrs Bliss difficult to unravel; an 1826 sale catalogue was long our sole source of information.[2] But the Bliss library is of such importance, both to Blake and to the history of book-collecting in Britain (being that of one of the earliest female collectors) that it would seem appropriate to know more about her and about the extent and nature of her collection. And as we shall see, it will compel a reconsideration of Blake's original context of reception. As well as works by Blake, Mrs Bliss was also a prominent collector of Oriental books, of Arabic, Sanskrit and Turkish manuscripts, of Persian and Mughal miniatures, and of Chinese watercolours. Mrs Bliss's library resembles that of another collector of Blake and Oriental books, William Beckford, in not conforming to the standard book-collecting model of the time – the Dibdinian type of the Bibliotheca Spenceriana.[3] Her library does not include long sets of Aldines or tall Elzevirs; there is no enthusiasm for incunabula, for Wynkyn de Worde or Pynson; there are no classics in *editio princeps*. Instead, there is an insistence on the beauty of individual books – of fine illustrations and handsome bindings. De Ricci's comments on the Beckford collection could equally apply to Mrs Bliss': 'less a library, in the proper sense of the word, than a cabinet of bibliographical rarities and freaks, each one a gem of its kind'.[4] One might indeed argue that for Bliss, like Beckford, the unorthodoxy of her collecting parallels that of her social mores.[5]

A clue to the identity of 'Mrs Bliss' emerged with the discovery of a letter written in September 1794, from the book-collector Richard Twiss to his friend Francis Douce, that:

A Lady here has just shown me . . . two curious works of Blake N° 13 Hercules Build' Lambeth. One 'the gates of Paradise', 16 etchings. 24$^{mo}$ the other 'Songs of Innocence' prin[*ted in*] colours. I suppose the man to be mad; but he draws very well <u>have</u> [*you*] <u>any thing by him?</u>[6]

This is the earliest reference to either of these books by Blake and the 'Lady here' the first person known to have possessed any work by him. She is therefore of considerable importance to our understanding of Blake's contemporary audience, not just for her chronological priority but also for her completely unexpected class and gender profile.

There are only five extant copies of *For Children: The Gates of Paradise* and one of them belonged when it was sold in 1826 to 'Mrs Bliss'.[7] The 1826 sale catalogue also indicates that she owned a copy of *Songs of Innocence and of Experience*. The coincidence is so striking that one must consider whether the 'Lady here' and Mrs Bliss are not the same person.

The copy of the *Songs* is described as 'printed in colours', and Richard Twiss was a careful bibliographer, at least by the standard of his times.[8] Blake experimented with colour printing of the *Songs* — rather than printing in a single colour with later hand-colouring — just for a brief period around 1794.[9] The little emblem book *For Children: The Gates of Paradise* is also dated 1793. We can be confident that the 'Lady here' in September 1794 had recently acquired these two little books; probably from the poet–printer himself since there was little time for them to have circulated within the book trade. Richard Twiss wrote, 'I suppose the man to be mad'.[10] Is that an opinion that could reasonably be formed from sight of the books alone? Alternatively, Twiss may have had some report of Blake's eccentricities from the 'Lady here' herself?

In an essay printed in Clark and Worrall, *Blake in the Nineties*, I told how I identified the 'Lady here' as Rebekah Bliss (1749–1819), noted the Blake works in her library, and tentatively suggested her personal acquaintanceship with Blake and his possible access to the other books in her library.[11]

Rebekah Bliss was born in London in a house on the Strand, in 1749. Her birth is recorded in the Register of the Independent Chapel at Carey Street, New Court.[12] Of her father, William Bliss, little is known. He died in November 1763.[13] Her mother, born Sarah Gorham, died five years later and is buried in Bunhill Fields, the Dissenters' burial ground.[14] Rebekah Bliss was only fourteen when her father died and nineteen when her mother died. The Register of the Independent Chapel at Carey Street New Court additionally recorded the births of Anne Bliss in 1750, John Bliss in 1751 and William Bliss in 1753, but none of her siblings seems to have reached adulthood. She found herself, at an early age, not quite alone in the world, because her bachelor uncle, John Gorham, and her Maitland cousins were part of the same Independent Chapel congregation, but perhaps with a freedom to determine her own future denied to most of her female contemporaries.

In 1801, the *Gentleman's Magazine* recorded the death of Rebekah Bliss's maternal uncle:

In King's road, near Bedford row, Mr. John Gorham, an eminent surveyor and builder, who lived in habits of the strictest œconomy, though reputed to be worth upwards of 200,000 l.[15]

The role of John Gorham, her oldest close relative, must have been crucial in her young life and there are a number of striking aspects to his will.[16] The estate is shared more or less equally amongst his nephews and nieces: the Maitland brothers, Robert, Ebenezer, John and Alexander, their sister Ursula Ware (the five children of Gorham's sister Ursula), and Rebekah Bliss (the sole surviving child of his sister Sarah). All four Maitland brothers are men of business, and one, Ebenezer, is a director of the Bank of England. Nevertheless, John Gorham is sufficiently convinced of his niece's abilities to make her his sole executrix: 'And I do hereby nominate constitute and appoint my said Niece Rebecca Bliss Executrix of this my last Will and Testament'.[17]

Ordinarily, the pressures to marry would have been considerable, but Rebekah Bliss remained a spinster. (The 'Mrs' is an honorific title applied to unmarried women of sufficient age, wealth and social status.) Some time before 1780, she met another orphan heiress, Ann Whitaker, and the two women set up home together in Church Street, Kensington, in a house built by John Gorham. They lived together for nearly forty years. Rebekah Bliss died in 1819, aged 70, and was buried at Loughton, in Essex, where Ann Whitaker had a country house, and was lady of the manor.

It is clear from the wills both of John Gorham and of Ann Whitaker that they had an awareness of women's (particularly married women's) subservient legal status and made attempts to remedy matters. Before the Married Women's Property Act came into force in 1883, married women were technically barred from land-owning and there were other restrictions as to what a married woman could legally possess. The elderly bachelor John Gorham leaves:

> an annuity of One hundred pounds for the life of Elizabeth the wife of my said Nephew Robert Maitland to be paid to her for her separate use half yearly at Lady Day and Michaelmas free from all deductions whatsoever.[18]

And similarly Ann Whitaker:

> Also I give to Mrs Mary Palmer wife of John Palmer of Chancery Lane London one hundred pounds life annuities her own separate use and benefit exclusive and independent of her said husband.[19]

Note the emphasis on providing a married woman with an income of her own.

Lillian Faderman (in her wonderful book *Surpassing the Love of Men*) has shown that passionate friendships with other women were a crucial part of the lives of middle-class women in the eighteenth century.[20] Through correspondence and memoirs, she has pieced together stories that corroborate how ubiquitous the ideas of romantic friendship were among literate eighteenth-century women. Bliss and Whitaker were able to resist the heterosexual imperative, and find fulfilment as a couple, partly because they had no close male relatives to force them into marriage, and partly because their background respected female autonomy. The domestic arrangements of their Kensington home were shaped according to their own inclinations.

Our earliest source for reconstructing Rebekah Bliss's library is her will of 1816.[21] It makes numerous bequests of books and manuscripts – not always described with the nicest bibliographical exactitude. I shall mention just a few, to give a flavour of her collection. She leaves to

M[rs] Walker Southgate the Minerals & Case with Contents standing in Chimney recess also a Book of Chinese Drawings of Flowers Folio & 6 v[ols] of Flora Danica a Persian Manuscript contain[g] 5 Poems & a smaller one of the Turkish Wars of the Emperor Babur & Gulistan to M[r] Walker the three latter Books.

John Walker, the Quaker partner of Robert Owen in the development of New Lanark, was born in 1765; his wife Sally in 1774. His father Isaac had bought the Arnos Grove estate in Southgate, part of Edmonton parish, in 1777.[22] Mrs Bliss makes bequests that must have been intended to meet the intellectual interests of her friends the Walkers. These bequests also exemplify some of the themes of the Bliss collection. There are natural history specimens ('the Minerals & case with Contents') and books – of Chinese drawings and *Flora Danica* – and Persian manuscripts – still unidentified copies of the *Five Poems* of Jami, the *Baburnama*, and the *Gulistan* (or 'Rose Garden') of Sa'di.

The 'Chinese Drawings of Flowers Folio' is a superb volume of nineteen botanical paintings, executed by a Chinese artist but on European paper, and now in the Victoria and Albert Museum.[23] *Flora Danica* is one of the great monuments of botanical illustration.[24] Not completed until 1883, it eventually consisted of 17 folio volumes (Mrs Bliss had acquired the first six) with over three thousand plates depicting Scandinavian plants. When Mrs Bliss, as I presume, showed her Blake books to Richard Twiss at Bush Hill, was she visiting her friends the Walkers at the neighbouring estate of Arnos Grove? And thereby confirming that she was indeed the 'Lady here' who owned Blake books in 1794?

Here is another typical sequence of bequests, this time to her Maitland relatives:

> I Also give to M[rs] Fuller Maitlands Daughters 2 Vol[s] of L Oiseaux dorees & 2 Vol[s] of Le Vaillants Birds as a Token though a small one of my Remembrance to them. List of Books with the Parlor Book Case for M[r] Ebenezer Maitland to have at mine or M[rs] Whitakers decease as she shall direct . . . I give him of my own purchasing S[ir] W[m] Hamiltons Roman and Grecian Antiquities in 4 Vol Folio . . .

Rebekah Bliss's interest in science reflects a widespread female interest in natural philosophy that developed during the eighteenth century.[25] What is noteworthy is that her wealth enabled her to fill her library with some of the grandest publications in the field. *Les Oiseaux dorées* is a spectacular book on birds of Paradise, printed in gold and the iridescent plumage hand-coloured. Le Vaillant's work on exotic birds, *Histoire naturelle des Oiseaux de paradis et des rolliers, suivie de celle des toucans et des barbus*, is printed in colour and finished by hand. Apart from their undoubted beauty, these books display a scientific accuracy that few ornithological artists have matched since.[26] They are also technically innovative in printing and colouring, and would surely have been of interest to William Blake on these grounds alone. Her will makes further bequests of the natural history specimens:

> Mr John Maitland the Shell case with its contents of Shells & Minerals Stuft Birds at top in back parlour & all the other Stuft Birds that are undevis'd – Mrs Chambers a Mineral Case standing in window of Library.

We also see from her will that her cousin, Ebenezer Maitland, is left 'Sir Wm Hamiltons Roman and Grecian Antiquities'.[27] This publication is of very great importance in the development of neo-classical design.[28] Moreover, we know that Blake saw it, because the British Museum has two sheets of drawings by Blake which are careful copies of designs in this book.[29] In view of the value and rarity of these volumes, their presence in the Bliss library represents strong evidence that William Blake knew Mrs Bliss and copied these designs from the book in her possession. (Bindman, who first recognized the Blake drawings as copies from the *Hamilton Collection*, makes no suggestion as to where Blake could possibly have seen this rare book.)[30] I would add that there is another aspect to the designs from the Hamilton vases. In the more complex images, such as Plate 68 (Figure 4.1, 4.2) and some others, I would suggest we see the kind of placing of images on the picture plane, ignoring vanishing-point perspective, that Blake was to use in the Arlington Court picture.[31]

Since Rebekah Bliss died in 1819, why did it take until 1826 for her library to be put up for sale? A codicil to the will makes it clear:

> I give and bequeath the Use and Enjoyment of all my Library of Books Book-Cases Cabinets of Shells Minerals Pictures and all other Articles of Furniture Glasses &c. which belong to me and are standing in the House at Kensington to M[rs] Ann Whitaker for and during her Life and after her Death I give and bequeath them as under written unless she chooses to give them in her Lifetime.

Mrs Bliss's library was thus kept substantially intact, even though so many books are bequeathed in her will. It was the death of Ann Whitaker in 1825, aged 83, which precipitated the sale, not that of Rebekah Bliss, who died in 1819. Some of Rebekah's books are indeed later listed in Ann's will, as in this bequest to her physician:

**Figure 4.1** Plate 68 of *Antiquités Etrusques, Grecques et Romains*. Tirees du cabinet de M. Hamilton. Collection of Etruscan, Greek and Roman antiquities from the Cabinet of the Hon. Wm Hamilton. (Naples: [Francesco Morelli], 1766–1767.)

**Figure 4.2** William Blake, 'The Apotheosis of Bacchus' after *Antiquités Etrusques, Grecques et Romaines*, Plate 68. (British Museum) Butlin: 174.

> Sir Henry Halford Bar[t] Hamiltons Egyptia with plates Brittons Antiquities Duppas Life Mich[l] Angelo Oriental Drawings Folio late Mrs Bliss's as a mark of respect for his attention.[32]

I have tentatively identified the 'Oriental Drawings Folio' with a collection of Chinese export watercolours in the Victoria and Albert Museum.[33] Chinese export painting remains a paradox. The art establishments of both East and West have thought the genre unworthy of serious consideration. Produced from the seventeenth to the nineteenth century, largely in the artisan workshops of Canton (now Guangzhou), export painting tends to evoke two principal, deeply-entrenched attitudes. Students of Chinese art view it as the work of mere artisans, inferior to the painting of the literati and the court. In the West, it has been seen as a mere decorative adjunct to European art and architecture of the period. These competing prejudices ignore the fact that Chinese export of artefacts (porcelain as well as painting) grew from international trade and, consequently, can be seen as a form of dialogue between two aesthetic systems. In no area of this trade are the differences more fundamental and the ensuing compromises more interesting than in painting. The value that Mrs Bliss placed on her Chinese drawings is manifested in the superb bindings she gave them – exemplified in the 'Oriental Drawings Folio' where a panel of French printed silk with a *chinoiserie* design has been set into an elaborately gilt morocco frame.

The major source for reconstructing the Bliss Library is an auction catalogue: *BIBLIOTHECA SPLENDIDISSIMA: A CATALOGUE OF A SELECT PORTION OF THE LIBRARY OF MRS. BLISS, Deceased, Removed from her Residence at Kensington*, whereby the bulk of her library was auctioned in April 1826 in 814 lots sold over four days.[34] The Bliss library contained a large collection of natural history books and more than seventy illuminated manuscripts: missals, psalters and Books of Hours.

Anthony Blunt has stressed the importance of Blake's apprenticeship years, exploring and recording the monuments of Westminster Abbey: 'It gave him his first contact with medieval art, which was to remain a powerful influence and source of inspiration for the whole of his life'.[35] To these possibilities must now be added the medieval illuminated manuscripts in the library of Mrs Bliss. Blake himself saw a connection between Books of Hours and his illustrated pages for he called his works 'Illuminated Books' (1793 Prospectus E 693). Several modern scholars have detected resemblances in design between Blake and his medieval exemplars.[36] The manuscripts in the Bliss collection include some of quite early date, unfashionable and barely collected by Bliss's contemporaries. Here, as elsewhere, Bliss commands our respect for her recognition of quality in unfamiliar areas of connoisseurship.[37]

To return briefly to her natural history books, even here one can trace Blakean resemblances. They included as lot 305: 'Merian (M. S.) Dissertation sur la Generation et les Transformations des Insectes de Surinam, Lat. Et Fr. 71 *coloured plates, calf gilt Haye* 1726'.[38] Madame Merian's illustrations of caterpillars and spiders seem to me to prefigure Blake's marginal decorations and in particular those of the 'entomological' plates 12 and 14 of *Europe*. Rodney M. Baine has commented that 'no other English poet or artist used biological images and symbols − beast, bird, insect, reptile, fish, tree, and plant − more often or more meaningfully than did William Blake'.[39] The question of Blake's knowledge of and acquaintanceship with the great outpouring of natural history books in the late eighteenth century must regretfully be left for the moment. The rest of this chapter will be concerned with establishing the likelihood of William Blake's personal friendship with Rebekah Bliss, and the access to Oriental books, manuscripts and drawings this would have made possible.

The five Blake lots in the 1826 sale were:

10 Blake's (W.) Gates of Paradise, 16 *plates, red morocco, gilt leaves*
11——Songs of Innocence and Experience, 2 vols, *coloured engravings, red morocco, gilt leaves*
. . .
41 Blair's (Robt.) Grave, a Poem, *illustrated by 12 etchings, by Schiavonetti, from designs by W. Blake, calf extra, gilt leaves* 1808
. . .
370 Young's (Edw.) Night Thoughts, *with engravings from Blake's designs, half bound, red morocco* 1797
371 Young's (Edw.) Night Thoughts, *with engravings from Blake's designs, coloured calf extra, marble leaves* 1797

The 'Bliss Blakes', as we might call them, were collected from 1794 (*For Children: the Gates of Paradise*), through 1802 (the supposed date of her copy of the *Songs*) and at least up to 1808 (Blair's *Grave*). The presence of so many Blake books in the Bliss collection − *Bibliotheca splendidissima* − does not in itself suggest any close acquaintanceship, but when we look at individual titles, the inference is hard to avoid.

Mrs Bliss's *For Children: The Gates of Paradise* (Lot 10 of the 1826 sale) is a proof copy before Blake and Johnson's imprint was added to the title page. It would have been strange for her to acquire this particular copy from Johnson when the rest of the edition specifically bears his name as publisher. This lends credence to the view that she must have acquired it directly from Blake himself.

Her copy of the *Songs* (Lot 11, which Bentley identifies as Copy P, the Sir Paul Getty copy) is again distinctive with, unusually, *Innocence* and *Experience* separately paginated in Blake's hand, to correspond to its binding in two volumes as though Blake knew beforehand Mrs Bliss's intentions as to binding.[40] As I noted above, books from the Bliss library are often characterized by their fine bindings. Even more significantly, Copy P is the only copy of the *Songs* carrying a textual correction in Blake's hand. Line 12 of 'The Tyger':

What dread hand & what dread feet

is altered to read:

What dread hand formd thy dread feet[41]

An interesting comparison is with the text as given by B. H. Malkin in *A Father's Memoirs of his Child*:

What dread hand forged thy dread feet[42]

In both cases, these corrections are attributable to Blake himself. Moreover, if the correction supplied to Malkin is evidence of his and Blake's close personal relationship, the correction for Mrs Bliss's *Songs* may surely be regarded likewise. I would suggest that Blake made these careful amendments for close acquaintants that he knew would actually read the *Songs* – not just want the work for the sake of the illustrations.[43]

There is also the instance of her two copies (Lots 370 and 371, plain and coloured) of Young's *Night Thoughts* with the Blake designs. There are just twenty or so copies of *Night Thoughts* hand-coloured by William and Catherine Blake. Bentley suggests that these copies of *Night Thoughts* were sold directly by Blake himself; and that they derive from the copies supplied to Blake by Richard Edwards as part of a customary arrangement between publisher and engraver.[44] Thus, even in the example of Bliss's ownership of a relatively extensively-produced work like *Night Thoughts*, circumstances still suggest a purchase made directly from Blake.

The copy of Blake's *Songs of Innocence and of Experience* (Copy P), which appeared in the 1826 sale, is dated by Bentley and Viscomi as *c.* 1802, and could not have been the book shown to Twiss in 1794.[45] However, Rebekah Bliss's cousin, Ebenezer Maitland, was one of the joint executors of her estate and, by a curious coincidence, his great-grandson J. A. Fuller Maitland owned some leaves of the *Songs* (the colour-printed Copy G).[46] It is tempting to assume that these leaves came from the Bliss library.[47] She may thus have owned two copies (G and P) of *Songs of Innocence and of Experience* to put with her two copies of *Night Thoughts*. Given that Viscomi allots Copy G a date of 1794, this could have been the one Twiss saw that year.[48] The evidence is meagre, but the implication is that Bliss possessed a second copy of the *Songs*, perhaps Copy G.

There is another member of the Maitland family who owned work by Blake, and that is William Fuller Maitland, grandson of Rebekah's cousin Ebenezer and uncle of J. A. Fuller Maitland.[49] In 1887, Christie's sold *Jerusalem* (E), *Thel* (A) and coloured *Night Thoughts* (E) from the collection of William Fuller Maitland.[50] He also owned at least two Blake drawings and the large colour print 'Pity' now in the Metropolitan Museum.[51] Can there be a connection between at least some of these Blakes and Mrs Bliss? The only one of William Fuller Maitland's Blakes for which we have a clear history, the coloured *Jerusalem* (Copy E), was in Blake's possession at his death – and he died after Rebekah Bliss. Nevertheless, it is certainly possible that Fuller Maitland's *Book of Thel* and the Blake drawings in his collection came from Mrs Bliss. It is clear that our knowledge of the full extent of Rebekah's collection is still incomplete.

What overlap might there have been between Rebekah Bliss's circle and that of Blake? Blake, perhaps, might have been a fellow-worshipper at the Carey Street chapel. New Court is conveniently near Lincoln's Inn Fields and Blake would have known the chapel from his apprenticeship days with Basire when he lived at Great Queen Street.[52] Blake could perhaps have met Rebekah Bliss through the social circle of the congregation.[53] Robert Winter, the minister at New Court, was born in 1762 at Brewer Street, Golden Square, just around the corner from the Blake family.[54] Blake then might have known him from childhood.[55]

In her will, Rebekah Bliss left Robert Winter her copy of 'Magna Charta in Gold Letters a token of Remembrance in boards'.[56] This is perhaps the most sumptuous book published in England during the nineteenth century and probably the first book printed in gold. The title page, dedication and text leaves are vellum, printed in letters of gold, all with splendid hand-painted decorated borders and emblazoned arms richly illuminated in gold and colours.[57] This, and one or two other books in Rebekah's library, suggests her sympathy with radical politics.

If William Blake and Rebekah Bliss had some personal acquaintanceship, then this would help explain Blake's distinctive use of the word 'bliss' (as a common noun, not as a surname). It appears forty-four times in the *Blake Concordance*, including four times in the *Visions of the Daughters of Albion*, once in *America*, four times in *Europe*, three in the *Book of Ahania*, and nine times in *Jerusalem*. Blake does not use the word 'bliss' in *Thel*, the *Songs*, in *The Marriage of Heaven and Hell*, in the *Book of Los*, the *Song of Los*, nor in *The Book of Urizen*, nor in *Milton*. However, he uses it no fewer than twenty times in *The Four Zoas*. There seems to be some pattern here. I am not suggesting that every instance of Blake's use of the word 'bliss' refers to Rebekah, but the term occurs consistently in those books which feature a female protagonist (Ahania, Oothoon, Enitharmon, Jerusalem, Vala), excepting the *Book of Thel* (which may have been written before Blake made the acquaintance of Mrs Bliss). For Blake, 'bliss' often seems to signify not just sexual pleasure, as in *Visions of the Daughters of Albion*, Plate 6:

> Take thy bliss O Man! (6: 2 E 49)

or in *Jerusalem*, Plate 79:

> . . . the Visions of the Night of Beulah
> Where Sexes wander in dreams of bliss among the Emanations
> Where the Masculine & Feminine are nurs'd into Youth & Maiden (79: 74–6
> E 236)

but specifically women's experience of sexual pleasure. This meaning is surely implicit in *America*'s 'sweet valleys of ripe virgin bliss' (pl. 6: 30 E 59) and the Book of Ahania's 'babes of bliss' (pl. 5: 19 E 89) and 'mother-joys, sleeping in bliss' (pl. 5: 38 E 90) among many other instances.

'Bliss' was, too, a favourite word of Milton's, as thus in *Paradise Lost*: 'These two | Imparadis't in one anothers arms | . . . shall enjoy their fill | Of bliss on bliss.' (IV: 505–9) These lines are drawn on in *Visions of the Daughters of Albion*:

I'll lie beside thee on a bank & view their wanton play
In lovely copulation bliss on bliss with Theotormon:
Red as the rosy morning, lustful as the firstborn beam. (pl. 7: 25–7: E 50)

Alicia Ostriker has drawn our attention to Blake's stylistic feature of repeating favourite words and parallel phrases throughout the *Songs*;[58] and Northrop Frye long ago commented, 'Behind the pattern of images in poetry . . . is a pattern of words.'[59] (I might add, however, that I see no 'pattern' to Blake's use of another favourite word: 'terrific', of which there is a similar number of occurrences, thirty-eight in all, variously in *America*, *The Book of Los*, *The Book of Thel*, *Descriptive Catalogue*, *The Four Zoas*, *Jerusalem*, *The Marriage of Heaven and Hell* and *Milton*.)

How did Blake view the romantic friendship of Rebekah Bliss and Ann Whitaker, these two virgin daughters of Albion? (In London society, it is their perceived virginity that protects them, where they are known and accepted as a couple.) They are not the only female couple in Blake's circle. After the death of Blake's one-time business partner, James Parker, in 1805, his unmarried sister Sarah, who had kept house for her brother in Kentish Town, promptly added her friend Ann Shout to the household. The two women remained together until Sarah Parker's death in 1825.[60] Christopher Hobson notes that, in *The Four Zoas* manuscript, 'a series of visual images presents lesbianism as an alternative to male domination, even a component of apocalypse'.[61] When Blake follows Milton in using 'bliss' as signifying sexual pleasure, is he connecting the romantic friendships of Bliss–Whitaker and Parker–Shout to the 'lesbian' entanglements of the marginal drawings to the *Four Zoas*? It might be argued that the *Four Zoas* marginalia are voyeuristic if not perverse; and thus difficult to relate to any respect for stable same-sex relations. We should not forget the cruel edge to Blake's humour as when, in *An Island in the Moon*, he mocks his friend John Flaxman's spinal curvature by nicknaming him 'Etruscan Column' (E 449).

It is not uncommon to find Oriental books in the libraries of Blake's friends and collectors. Samuel Boddington, who owned a number of important Blakes[62] (probably acquired through his friendship with John Linnell), also owned a small book of Chinese watercolours now in the Victoria and Albert Museum.[63] Blake's friend Alexander Tilloch (Blake was one of the eighteen engravers who in 1797 signed a testimonial in Tilloch's favour)[64] owned a few Oriental manuscripts including one of great beauty – a copy of Jami's *Yusuf u Zulaykha*, now in the John Rylands Library.[65] However, these are isolated and exceptional items in collections of very different aspect; Boddington is best known for his collection of prints after Stothard; Tilloch's library is strong on alchemy, chemistry and theology. In the Bliss library on the other hand, the Chinese and Indian drawings, the Persian and Turkish manuscripts form a coherent collection – Mrs Bliss's Oriental books are directed to one end: to document the natural history and peoples of these far-off lands. There is also with Bliss an aesthetic choice – of the exotic, the beautiful, the strange – which informs the wider aspects of her collecting, whether of printed books, Western manuscripts, books by William Blake, or of Oriental books.

The 1826 sale included thirty lots of Indian drawings, none of which I have been able to trace. The printed books on India include works by Thomas Daniell (Figure 4.3), Edward Moor (Figure 4.4) and Balthazard Solvyns.[66]

Thomas Daniell and his nephew William were in India from 1785 to 1794, and William's journals record their travels round the subcontinent. The greatest fruit of their endeavours was *Oriental Scenery* (1795–1807), Lot 70 in the 1826 sale, which has been described as the finest illustrated work ever published on India.[67] Mrs Bliss must have bought it at the time of publication, when it was offered at 200 guineas. It is at the very least possible that the Daniell's illustrations of monumental Indian architecture stand behind the overwhelming scale of the trilithon illustrated on *Milton*, Plate 4.

Lot 408, Edward Moor's *The Hindu Pantheon* (Figures 4.7 and 4.9), published by Joseph Johnson in 1810, has long been recognized as a source used by Blake. It contains 105 plates engraved by J. Dadley and by Raddon from line drawings of Hindu deities by Moses Haughton. *The Hindu Pantheon*, praised by Flaxman both in his lectures and in his encyclopaedia article, gives a wealth of information, both pictorial and verbal, about Indian sculpture.[68] On Plates 44 and 45 are views of the elephant-headed Ganésa. Blake drew a similar figure perhaps intended as a caricature of John Varley (Figure 4.5).[69] The caricature alludes to John Varley's well-documented heavy build and imposing physique.[70] Perhaps Blake has also picked up the humorous aspect of the god in Hindu mythology.

**Figure 4.3** Thomas Daniell, *Oriental scenery: . . . views in Hindoostan drawn and engr.* By T. Daniell. (London: [T. Daniell], 1795–1807.)

**Figure 4.4** Plate 105 ('Garuda') of Edward Moor, *The Hindu Pantheon*. (London: printed for J. Johnson, 1810.)

Moor's Plates 10 and 105 portray the eagle-headed Garuda, of whom Moor writes:

> He is sometimes described in the manner that our poets and painters describe a griffin, or a cherub, and he is placed at the entrance of the passes leading to the Hindu garden of Eden, and then appears in the character of a destroying angel, in as far as he resists the approach of serpents, which in most systems of poetic mythology, appear to have been the beautiful, deceiving form that sin originally assumed.[71]

To Blake this would surely have been reminiscent of the Covering Cherub, a symbol originally derived from Ezekiel 28.13, which Blake takes to represent the tyrannical Law that blocks man's way back to Paradise. Very similar to the Garuda of Moor's Plate 105 are the winged, bird-headed riders of *Jerusalem* Plate 46 (Figure 4.6). Of course this is not to deny Blake's originality or inventiveness; it is rather to indicate the way in which his knowledge of Indian sculpture contributed to his inventiveness.

Blunt suggested that one of the engravings in Moor's *Hindu Pantheon* (Figure 4.7) provides us with a source for the design at the head of Chapter III of *Jerusalem* (Figure 4.8), sometimes called 'Beulah Enthroned on a Sun-Flower'.[72] And Moor's drawing of Durga, the consort of Shiva (Figure 4.9), is surely echoed in Blake's 'Lucifer' from the Dante watercolours (Figure 4.10).[73]

**Figure 4.5**  William Blake, *Jerusalem*. Plate 46 (detail).

**Figure 4.6**  William Blake, *Jerusalem*. Plate 78 (detail).

**Figure 4.7** Edward Moor, *The Hindu Pantheon*. (London: printed for J. Johnson, 1810.)

**Figure 4.8** William Blake, *Jerusalem*. Plate 53 (detail).

**Figure 4.9** ('Durga') Edward Moor, *The Hindu Pantheon*. (London: printed for J. Johnson, 1810.)

To conclude this summary view of Indian sources for Blake, let us look at Lot 345, Balthazard Solvyns, *Les hindoûs* (Paris, 1808), elaborately bound in four volumes.[74] A plate in Vol. I shows the expiatory festival of *Neela Pooja* (Figure 4.11).[75] The participants burn incense in the palms of their hands. Plate 1 of *Milton* shows a figure in a vortex of billowing smoke (Figure 4.12). The smoke, as Nelson Hilton has pointed out, emanates from the figure's left palm and, to a lesser extent, from his right wrist.[76] I should like to suggest this image of 'smoke' emerging from Milton's hands derives in part from Solvyns's image.

If Mrs Bliss's printed books can be traced bibliographically, very few of the manuscripts and Oriental books can be so identified. Of the following bequest:

> Mrs Whitaker Maintenon Missal and any other Book or Books she chuses to have selected for her own use. The Remainder I would have divided with the Book Cases to Mrs Ware & Mr Alex[r] Maitland making an amicable and equal division as I wish her Sons to possess them & recommend the Hindoo collection of Books and drawings to be parted with also the Missals as none of the Family perhaps may like them

**Figure 4.10** William Blake, 'Lucifer': Illustrations to Dante's *Divine Comedy*. (National Gallery of Victoria, Melbourne) Butlin: 812.69.

neither the 'Maintenon Missal' nor the 'Hindoo collection of Books and drawings' has so far been traced.

Some others of her books and manuscripts were inherited by her cousin Alexander Maitland, from whom they descended to his son, the Rev. Samuel Roffey Maitland.[77] Part of Maitland's collection was sold at auction in 1842:

> VALUABLE BOOKS AND MANUSCRIPTS. A Catalogue of the Very Select and Elegant Library, Printed & Manuscript, of a Private Gentleman, together with Another Collection, including The most beautiful and valuable collection of Missals, and other richly illuminated Manuscripts, which have been offered for sale during many years; some of the delicately and highly finished Paintings in which, have been engraved in Dr. Dibdin's Decameron. Also some splendidly illuminated Manuscripts in the Hebrew, Chinese, Arabic, Persian, Burmese, Hindostan, Sanscrit, Singalese, Japonese, Russian, Italian, French, and English Languages, with curious specimens of Ancient Music. . . . Which will be Sold by Auction, by Mr. Fletcher, at his Great Room, 191, Piccadilly, on Thursday, April 21st, 1842, and 3 following Days, (Sunday excepted.) at Twelve o'Clock.

A copy of this 1842 sale catalogue, now in the British Library Department of Manuscripts, has been marked up by Sir Frederic Madden with price, seller and buyer, sometimes adding further notes on the ultimate destination of the lot.[78] Madden marked thirty lots as originating in the Bliss collection: 'Those MSS. to

**Figure 4.11** Detail of Vol. 1, 11th No.; No. 1 from F. Balthazard Solvyns, *Les hindoûs.* 2 vols. (Paris: chez l'auteur, place Saint-Andre-des-Arcs, no. 11, et chez H. Nicolle, rue de Seine, no. 12, à la librairie stèrèotype, de l'imprimerie de Mame frères, 1808.)

which M. is prefixed belonged to the Rev. S. R. Maitland, Librarian to the Abp. of Canterbury. He inherited them from his father, who had them from a Mrs. Bliss the widow [*sic*] of a Collector of that name of Kensington.' Of the three lots acquired by Madden for the British Museum, just one came from among her Oriental books:

> 698 Chinese costume. A volume containing upwards of forty figures, representing the costume etc. of the Natives, with descriptions in Chinese, finely executed[79]

Where did Rebekah acquire her books? Thomas Dibdin (who illustrates one of her manuscripts in his *Bibliographical Decameron*) tells us that Lot 720 of the 1842 sale 'was purchased at the sale of Mr. Edward's library' and adds:

> My respectable neighbour, (and indefatigable collector of 'rich and rare' gems, in the department of book illuminations) Mr. [*sic*] Bliss, is the present possessor of the volume here alluded to. . . . It is a thick broad duodecimo of HOURS OF THE VIRGIN; containing 13 larger illuminations . . . and thirty one borders of fruits and flowers, &c. . . . The condition of this curious little volume is most desirable. It was sold for 56l. 15s.[80]

Perhaps Rebekah did indeed frequent James Edwards' shop in Pall Mall, who, according to William Beloe, a contemporary commentator:

**Figure 4.12**  William Blake, *Milton*. Title page (detail).

was the first person who professedly displayed in the metropolis shelves of valuable books in splendid bindings, and having taken a large house in one of the most frequented and fashionable streets, it soon became the resort of the gay morning loungers of both sexes. At the same time also invitation was held out to students and scholars, and persons of real taste, from the opportunity of seeing and examining the most curious and rare books, manuscripts, and missals.[81]

When Dibdin refers to a manuscript from the Bliss collection, he writes of 'my neighbour . . . Mr. Bliss', evidently pretending to more knowledge than he had. He had presumably seen no more than the name 'Bliss' against an entry in the sale record and assumed the purchaser to be male. Since few collectors, and no women, bought openly at auction, to mistake Rebekah's sex is, I suppose, understandable. Dibdin's account presumably led Madden astray.

Apart from the volume of Chinese drawings acquired for the British Museum, all the Oriental books in the 1842 sale were acquired by the noted Persian scholar Nathaniel Bland.[82] Following his suicide in 1866 (apparently because of his gambling debts), the Bland collection was acquired *en bloc* by the Earl of Crawford, and the Crawford collection itself purchased in 1901 by Mrs John Rylands. The Oriental books from the Bliss collection should now be in the John Rylands University Library, Manchester.[83]

Frederic Madden notes on the sale catalogue that the following lots were purchased by Bohn on behalf of 'Mr. Bland':

690 ORIENTAL MS. – The adventures of Krishna, in Sanscrit, written in a most minute character, on a Roll 45 feet 7 inches long, ILLUMINATED WITH NUMEROUS BEAUTIFUL PAINTINGS IN GOLD AND COLOURS, by Native artists, mounted on rollers in a mahogany case
691 ALCORAN, a beautifully written MS., in Arabic, the divisions of the chapters and verses marked in gold, in the original Oriental binding
691★ ORIENTAL MS. – written upon 26 leaves of the Talipot, by Native Artists, richly illuminated in gold
692 Beautiful MS. – in the Singalese Character, upon the Talipot leaf, by Native Artists. A very fine and perfect specimen
693 Divani Hafiz, or the Poems of Hafiz, one of the most eminent of the Persian Poets, a beautifully written MS., in the original Oriental binding
693★ ORIENTAL MS. – Divanagair Gheeta, or Adventures of Krishna in Sanscrit, A MOST BEAUTIFUL MANUSCRIPT in the Sacred Language of Hindostan, executed at Cashmire, containing 101 MINIATURE PAINTINGS, most exquisitely finished in the richest gold and colours, bound in crimson velvet, 8vo.
This exquisite volume was formerly in the collection of James Edwards, Esq. at whose sale it was purchased for £25. 5. 0
695 ORIENTAL MS., Sirnah Baghueen, A MOST BEAUTIFUL MANUSCRIPT, WITH ONE HUNDRED AND FORTY PAINTINGS, executed by a Native Artist, in gold and colours, bound in crimson velvet folio
One leaf of this remarkably fine and beautiful Oriental Manuscript, is unfortunately damaged.
696 Book of Fishes, printed in Colours, with descriptions and a prefatory treatise in the Japanese Language
697 Book of Plants, Reptiles and Insects, printed in Colours, with descriptions in Japanese
698 Chinese Costume. – A volume containing upwards of forty figures, representing the costume etc. of the Natives, with descriptions in Chinese, finely executed
699 Chinese Habits. – A volume printed on paper made from silk by Native Artists, containing representations of the Habits of the Chinese, morocco folio
700 PERSIAN MANUSCRIPT. – Works of Nizami one of the most admired Persian poets, A MOST BEAUTIFUL Persian MS, written about the year 1630, WITH THIRTY SEVEN PAINTINGS, executed by a Native Artist, in the richest gold and colours, and each page ornamented with borders of gold, a remarkably fine Manuscript, in the Oriental binding, with beautifully painted sides folio

In the Bliss library, the books that were the most far-flung in their origin, the most difficult to procure in Rebekah Bliss's lifetime, the most unexpected in an Englishwoman's library of *c.* 1800, were the two Japanese books that appeared in that 1842 sale:

696 Book of Fishes, printed in Colours, with descriptions and a prefatory treatise in the Japanese Language
697 Book of Plants, Reptiles and Insects, printed in Colours, with descriptions in Japanese

Lot 696, the 'Book of Fishes', can be identified as *Umi no sachi* ('The Wealth of the Sea').[84] This rare two-volume encyclopaedic work was published in 1762.

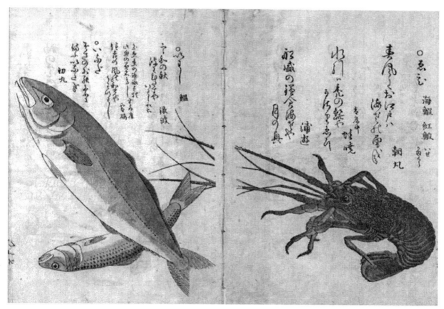

**Figure 4.13** *Umi no Sachi.* An album of fish and other animals of the sea, compiled by Sekijuken Shūkoku and illustrated by Katsuma Ryūsui. This edition was first published in 1762, but this copy was printed in 1778. (JRULM Catalogue, 100)

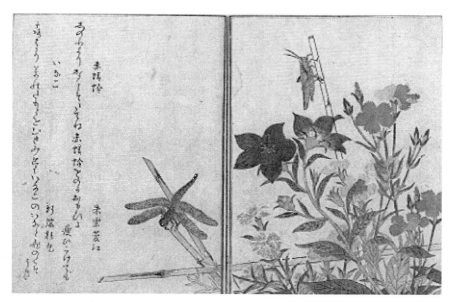

**Figure 4.14** *Ehon mushi erami.* The famous album of insects illustrated by Utamaro with text by Yadoya no Meshimari (Ishikawa Masamochi); first volume now missing. Published in 1788, but this copy is a later reprint. (JRULM Catalogue, 115)

The superb colour woodcuts are by Katsuma Ryūsui (1711–96). Over seventy species of fish, turtles, crustaceans and shellfish are represented (Figure 4.13).

Lot 697, the 'Book of Plants, Reptiles and Insects', is *Ehon mushi erami* ('Picture book of selected insects', Figure 4.14). Published in 1788, it is a poetry anthology in two volumes, illustrated by Kitagawa Utamarō (1753–1806), one of the most important masters of the Japanese print. In the early 1780s, Utamarō moved into the residence of the publisher Tsutaya Juzaburo (1750–97), who helped to develop and promote Utamarō's talent. During the 1780s, the two co-operated in producing collections of humorous 31-syllable verses known as *kyoka*, which contained verses by *kyoka* poets with finely produced woodblock-print designs by Utamarō, such as the *Ehon mushi erami*, which deals with insects, frogs, snakes and flowers. Mica or gold dust, and powdered mother of pearl were sometimes used to give a special sheen to his pictures. Blake perhaps responded to their technical innovation in his later printings of the *Songs* where gold and silver enrich the already elaborate colouring.

Japan is always used by Blake to indicate the eastern termination of the world. Thus the wings of the covering cherub 'spread from Japan / Where the Red Sea terminates the World of Generation & Death' (*Jerusalem*, pl. 89: 48–9; E 249). It is extraordinary to observe that in the library of Rebekah Bliss, William Blake, the greatest English printmaker, could have encountered the work of the great Japanese master, Utamarō.

Up to the mid-nineteenth century, Rebekah Bliss still had some posthumous reputation as a collector of Indian drawings. The most recent mention of Mrs Bliss occurs in the 1850 sale by Puttick and Simpson of the final part of the Library of the Rev. S. R. Maitland.[85] Lot 736 is 'INDIAN DRAWINGS. A volume containing thirty-two very beautifully finished Drawings of Mythological Subjects, Portraits, &c. / ∴ From Mrs. Bliss's well known collection.' It sold for £3. After that, all memory of her library and her friendship with Blake was lost. She was not known to Blake's younger friends, Linnell and Palmer. She was unknown to Gilchrist when he came to write the *Life of William Blake* (1863). In the wider field of book-collecting, she was unknown even to those collectors and libraries (Chester Beatty, the Earl of Crawford, the British Museum, the Pierpont Morgan Library, the Victoria and Albert Museum) that acquired drawings and manuscripts from her collection.

Ever since the publication of Gilchrist's *Life* with its subtitle 'pictor ignotus', there has been a widely held assumption that Blake lacked any significant contemporary audience. This chapter has presented the empirical evidence for a hitherto unrecognized feminine audience. Blake's work can now be seen as having a particular appeal to women collectors such as Elizabeth Aders, Rebekah Bliss, Hannah Boddington, Maria Denman, Nancy Flaxman, Elizabeth Iremonger, Harriet Jane Moore, Miss C. L. Shipley and the women subscribers to Blair's *The Grave*.[86] Some long-held assumptions associating Blake exclusively with a male radical intelligentsia are implicitly undermined and arguably wholly refuted.

I have suggested that Blake and Bliss had some personal acquaintanceship and that Rebekah Bliss acquired most of her Blakes directly from the artist. Blake may have thus had access to the collection of which his books formed a part and have known the precious Oriental books in Mrs Bliss's possession. We can see in the Bliss library a plentiful source of Oriental images available to Blake.

Whether one considers bibliophiles, book collectors, or simply people who buy books, there can be little doubt that most of them are, and in the past were, men. Until relatively recently, for economic and social reasons, few women have left important collections of books. I have been concerned in this chapter with one example from a category of lost libraries — the private libraries of women collectors of the late eighteenth and early nineteenth centuries — lost because dispersed and attributed in later accounts to husbands or male heirs. As a forgotten bibliophile, contemporary of Wollstonecraft and Austen, Mrs Bliss's collection of sumptuously-bound printed books and illuminated manuscripts provides an extraordinary example of a dissenting, woman-centred, female connoisseur. Correspondences between Blake's art and the art of India and the East are not coincidental but may derive from the library of his friend and collector, Rebekah Bliss.

## Notes

1 Recent studies can be found in Rivers 1982; Myers and Harris 1991; Myers, Harris and Mandelbrote 2000; Rivers 2001.
2 See Bentley 1977: 654.
3 Dibdin, *Bibliotheca Spenceriana*, 1814–15. The *Bibliotheca Spenceriana* provides a model for the collecting of early printed books.
4 De Ricci 1930: 85.
5 It has been suggested to me that Beckford may have acquired, for instance, Indian drawings from the Bliss sales.
6 Bodleian Library, MS. Douce d. 39 fol. 70v.
7 Bentley 1977: 191.
8 On Richard Twiss, 1747–1821, antiquary, see DNB.
9 Viscomi 1993: 267.
10 This is, I believe, the earliest imputation of madness to Blake, and it comes just ten years since Blake was a respectable printshop owner in partnership with James Parker. (For Parker's worthy and profitable career, see Bentley 1996: 208–31.)
11 Davies 1999: 212–30.
12 National Archives, RG 4/4228 (London: Carey Street, New Court (Independent): Baptisms, 1707–57).
13 National Archives, PROB 11/893 (Will of William Bliss of Saint Olave Southwark, Surrey).
14 National Archives, RG 4/4633, Vol. 11, p. 99 (Bunhill Fields Burial Ground: Authenticated registers of burials).
15 *Gentleman's Magazine*, Vol. 71 (1801), p. 768 (Entry for 28 April). £200,000 would be more than £9 million in present-day values (source: Grahame Allen, 'Inflation: the value of the pound 1750–2002. Research paper 03/82. London: House of Commons Library, 2003).
16 National Archives, PROB 11/1361, ff. 288r–91v (Will of John Gorham). Probate was granted for the estate of John Gorham in August 1801.
17 National Archives, PROB 11/1361, ff. 288r–91v (Will of John Gorham). In my experience, a sole executrix would normally be appointed where there was no male close relative or friend to share the responsibility. To do so here, when there are adult Maitland nephews, is striking and unusual.
18 National Archives, PROB 11/1361, ff. 288r–91v (Will of John Gorham).
19 National Archives, PROB 11/1709, ff. 172–81 (Will of Ann Whitaker).
20 Faderman 1985. For recent criticism of this pioneering book, see Duberman et al. 1991: 4–7; and Donoghue 1993. Moore (1992) offers a valuable critique of Lillian Faderman's 'reliance on the category of gender to the exclusion of a systematic consideration of sexuality'.

21 National Archives, PROB 11/1614 (Will of Rebekah Bliss, Spinster of Kensington, Middlesex).

22 Garnier 1998: 122–34; Baker 1976: 159; Newby 1949; Owen 1920: 247–50 et passim.

23 Victoria and Albert Museum, 8102. My assertion of a Bliss provenance here and elsewhere in this paper is necessarily tentative. On paintings executed by Chinese artists for the European market, see Clunas 1984.

24 On *Flora Danica*, see Buchheim 1979: 161–78; Haase 1965: Vol. 2, 1–58 (includes an extensive bibliography of the *Flora Danica*).

25 See, for instance, Rousseau 1982: 197–255.

26 Sitwell, Buchanan and Fisher 1953.

27 *Antiquités Etrusques, Grecques et Romaines* 1766–7.

28 On its designer, Pierre Hugues, Baron d'Hancarville, see Haskell 1987.

29 Butlin 1981: 174, 175.

30 Bindman 1977.

31 Butlin 1981: 803.

32 National Archives, PROB 11/1709, ff. 172–81 (Will of Ann Whitaker).

33 Victoria and Albert Museum, D.14 to D.63–1903. Illustrated, with the binding, in Clunas 1984.

34 . . . / COMPRISING / An extensive, rare and valuable Collection of Original / Persian, Chinese, Turkish, Hindostan, and other Drawings, / exquisitely finished, representing the Manners, Amuse- / ments, Customs, Dress, Trades, Architecture, Manufactures / and Costumes of the Eastern Nations, richly Illuminated / Missals, Expensive Works on Botany and Natural History, / the Various Galleries, Books of Processions, National / Works of Art, and An Assemblage of Fine Drawings and Prints. . . . the Whole in the Finest Condition, Many on Large Paper, with Proof, and Early Impressions of the Plates, the Works on Natural History and Botany Most Beautifully Coloured, Sumptuously and Tastefully Bound in Morocco and Russia, by Kalthoeber, Staggemeier, C. Lewis, Bohn, Welcher, C. Smith, Murton, and Other Eminent Binders, Regardless of Expence, and Finished in Their Best Style. / Which will be Sold by Auction, / BY SAUNDERS & HODGSON, / At Their Great Room, 'The Poet's Gallery,' 39, Fleet Street. On Wednesday, April 26th, 1826, and Three Following Days, At Half-Past Twelve O'clock Precisely. To Be Viewed, Three Days Preceding, and Morning of Sale, and Catalogues had (price 1s. each)

35 Blunt 1959: 4.

36 For example, Hagstrum 1964: 31–3.

37 Munby (1972) discusses the changing attitude to Gothic illumination between the reigns of George II and Victoria, and mentions many of the pioneering names (Beckford, Douce etc.) in the collecting of illuminated manuscripts, but not, of course, Rebekah Bliss.

38 Merian 1726.

39 Baine 1986: 3.

40 Bentley 1977: 419. Illustrated in colour in Woof, Hebron, with Woof 2000.

41 Erdman (1982: 794) relegates the handwritten emendation to a textual note alongside notes on the earlier manuscript readings even though its editorial status is entirely different. Lincoln in his otherwise exemplary edition of the *Songs* (1991: 187–8) ignores it entirely.

42 Malkin 1806: xxxix.

43 Cf. Blake's letter (9 June 1818) to Dawson Turner: 'Those I Printed for Mr Humphry are a selection from the different Books of such as could be Printed without the Writing, tho' to the loss of the best things' (*Letters* E 771).

44 Bentley 1988: 302.

45 Bentley 1977: 368; Viscomi 1993: 305–6, 377.

46 Bentley 1977: 415.

47  See Bentley 1977: 412–25, for details of how the copies of the *Songs* have been variously bound, disbound and rebound. Bentley's 'Table' (365–72) indicates in summary the fragmentary nature of many surviving copies of *Innocence* or the *Songs*.
48  Viscomi 1993: 376.
49  On William Fuller Maitland, 1813–76, connoisseur, see DNB.
50  Bentley 1995: 64, 86, 271.
51  Butlin 1981: 92, 311, 363.
52  Bentley 2004a: 739–40.
53  I am aware that J. T. Smith claimed that Blake attended no public worship for the last forty years of his life (Bentley 2004a: 606–7), but this is a round figure and may not exclude church attendance in the early 1790s.
54  Black 1990.
55  Robert Winter was christened on 25 April 1762, at Carey Street New Court Independent Nonconformist, London, the son of John.
56  Magna Carta Regis Johannis, 1816.
57  Lowndes 1864: '[T]he most magnificent edition of Magna Carta was printed in letters of gold by John Whittaker in 1816, and dedicated to the Prince Regent, afterwards George IV. The ordinary copies were on thick glazed card-board, some white, others tinted of various hues, and these were published at 10l. 10s. Others had decorated borders and emblazoned arms, with portraits in colours, and these were much more expensive. Others, again, were printed on white or purple satin or vellum, in super-royal folio, highly decorated with heraldic emblems and armorial bearings, chiefly under the direction of Mr. Thos. Willement. Some copies have in addition finely-painted portraits of King John, Roger Bigod, and the Prince Regent; these were published at from fifty to one hundred guineas. Some few copies were even more expensive than this, and by means of paintings, jewelry, and gorgeous binding, reached a cost of two hundred and fifty guineas.' (1450)
58  Ostriker 1965: 56.
59  Frye 1947: 427.
60  National Archives, PROB 11/1433, ff. 342r–43v (Will of James Parker); PROB 11/1695, fol. 301 (Will of Sarah Parker).
61  Hobson 2000: 50.
62  Bentley (1977: 105, 137–8, 160, 202, 260, 426, 644) records Samuel Boddington as owning *America* (P), Descriptive Catalogue (E), *For the Sexes* (C), *Songs* (C), *Jerusalem* (H), *Europe* (M) and a coloured *Night Thoughts* (T).
63  Victoria and Albert Museum, D.895 to D.922–1898.
64  Bentley 2004a: 78.
65  Tentatively identified as JRULM Persian MS 23. For an illustration from this manuscript, see Robinson 1980.
66  Weir (2003) puts Blake's references to Hinduism, long since brought to our attention by the scholarly intuitions of Damon, Frye and Raine, into their contemporary context of late-eighteenth-century knowledge of Hinduism. Unfortunately, in developing his theme that comparative studies into Eastern religion 'found a ready audience among members of London's dissenting community' (87), Weir takes on trust E. P. Thompson's versions of 'antinomianism' and 'dissent', defined so broadly as to become entirely meaningless.
67  Daniell 1795–1807.
68  Flaxman 1829.
69  Butlin 1981: 690.
70  Kauffmann 1984: 17.
71  Moor 1810: 340.
72  Blunt 1959: 38.
73  The suggestion comes from Burke 1973: 290.
74  Solvyns 1808.

75 Vol. I, 11th No; No 1: NILA-PAYAH [1re Section Livraison IIme]: NYLAR-POUDJAH = NILA POUJA / VARIOUS EXPIATIONS OF THE HINDOOS.

76 Hilton 1983: 214. I should add that Hilton sees a source for this image in Emblem I of Michael Maier's Atalanta fugiens (Oppenheim H. Gallieri and J. T. Bry: 1617).

77 On Samuel Roffey Maitland, 1792–1866, antiquary and librarian, see DNB.

78 British Library. Department of Manuscripts: P.R.2.c.14(3).

79 Formerly Egerton MS 1055, it is now in the collection of the British Museum, Department of Asia.

80 Dibdin 1817.

81 [Beloe] 1817.

82 Bodleian Library. Diary of Frederic Madden.

83 I have checked *Bibliotheca Lindesiana* (1898), but can make only guesses at identifying the Bliss lots in the 1842 sale with titles in the handlist.

84 The two Japanese books were identified with the aid of Kornicki 1993. I am grateful to Professor Kornicki (private communication) for confirming my initially tentative identifications. A puzzle is how Rebekah Bliss acquired her Japanese books. Not only are they immensely rare in European libraries of this date, but also she has managed to acquire Japanese works that fit her collecting interest in natural history.

85 CATALOGUE / OF / THE GREATER PART OF THE / VALUABLE LIBRARY / OF THE / REV. S. R. MAITLAND, D.D., / IN WHICH WILL BE FOUND / . . . / BIBLIOGRAPHICAL WORKS, / AND BOOKS IN GENERAL LITERATURE, / A VOLUME OF INDIAN DRAWINGS, / . . . / ETC. ETC. / WHICH WILL BE SOLD BY AUCTION, / BY MESSRS. / PUTTICK AND SIMPSON, / AUCTIONEERS OF LITERARY PROPERTY, / AT THEIR GREAT ROOM, 191, PICCADILLY, / On Monday, April 29th, 1850, and three following days, / AT ONE O'CLOCK MOST PUNCTUALLY. / – / May be viewed on Friday and Saturday before the Sale.

86 Names identified with difficulty from Bentley 1977.

# 5 Blake and the Chinamen

Mei-Ying Sung

Blake often portrayed himself, particularly after 1800, as an engraver whose skills were held in low general esteem, his 'Graver' neglected. In a letter to George Cumberland, 26 August 1799, Blake claims, 'For as to Engraving in which I cannot reproach myself with any neglect yet I am laid by in a corner as if I did not Exist & Since my Youngs Night Thoughts have been publishd Even Johnson & Fuseli have discarded my Graver' (E 704). The decline of engraving as a practice in the eighteenth century has sometimes been narrated as a surrogate of the story of Blake's own decline. Morris Eaves in *The Counter-Arts Conspiracy* (1992) says the craft of engraving is today in 'oblivion', and that 'methods of reproduction more efficiently coordinated with the printer's press and painter's palette replaced engraving as Blake knew it' (Eaves 1992: 188). Scholars such as Eaves have established how Blake didn't – or couldn't – fit in with increasingly elaborate engraving projects typified by Boydell's Shakespeare Gallery of the early 1790s.

In other words, the picture we tend to get both from Blake himself and from modern scholars is that engraving itself was reaching the end of an era and that Blake's experience of decline was paralleled elsewhere. In fact, the opposite is true. In Britain, the use of copper-plate engravings at the end of the eighteenth century was accelerating and expanding. For the first time, prints made from engraving were reaching mass audiences not just in Britain but also in overseas consumer markets of a previously unimaginable size. During the course of Blake's own lifetime, engraving and copper-plate printing were in demand in an unprecedented quantity.

The problem for Blake, living in London's Lambeth and South Molton Street, was that this rise in demand for engraving skills and copper-plate printing came from the potteries of Stoke-on-Trent, Staffordshire, in the Midlands region of England. The crucial innovation which established the mass production of decorative domestic pottery for a growing population was the introduction of the transfer-printing method of printing designs onto ceramics before firing.

In this chapter, I would like to show that in Blake's time there was a prospering business in pottery using copper-plate engraving techniques, but from which Blake failed to benefit. Neither does Blake seem to have been interested in developing his professional association with this burgeoning new area despite plenty of evidence that he was well positioned, through networks of friendship and patronage, to be able to obtain further employment opportunities for his engraving or designing skills.

That the techniques and technologies of engraving employed by Blake for book illustration, and those used by the Stoke-on-Trent transfer-printing manufacturers are similar, can be easily demonstrated. The industrialized scale of manufacturers such as the Spode factory of Stoke-on-Trent has ensured that large amounts of information, much of it contemporary with Blake's lifetime but also having significance for the present day, can be deduced from their production of transfer-printed ceramics. If one takes *Illustrations of the Book of Job* (1826), a work demonstrating Blake's virtuoso skills in the engraving method and arguably the high-point of nineteenth-century engraving, the techniques look very similar, particularly in their relegation of etching. If we compare Blake's *Job* copper plate, recto and verso, with a copper plate for transfer-printing, it is evident that the same skills have been employed. The plate-maker's marks and 'knocking-up' marks (*repoussage*) on both copper plates show the same materials and techniques were used both by Blake and by the Spode factory (see Figures 5.1, 5.2, 5.3 and 5.4).[1] The engraving tools used in both prints for paper and for transfer-printing onto pottery are also the same (Hind 1908: Fig. 1; Drakard & Holdway [1983] 2002: 19). More remarkably, both Blake and the Spode factory sourced their copper plates from the same copper-plate makers. G. Harris of 31 Shoe Lane in London, who supplied plates both for Blake's engraving of *Canterbury Pilgrims* (1810) and *Illustrations of the Book of Job* (1826), Plate 1, also supplied many surviving plates used by Spode for transfer-printing between 1808 and 1827 (Drakard &

**Figure 5.1** Blake's copper plate for the *Illustrations of the Book of Job* (1826), Plate 13 recto. Author's photograph with permission of the British Museum.

**Figure 5.2** Blake's copper plate for the *Illustrations of the Book of Job* (1826), Plate 13 verso. The hammer marks are from the technique of knocking-up (*repoussage*) to correct engraving mistakes, which correspond to the mended lines on the recto. Author's photograph with permission of the British Museum.

Holdway 1983: 28). The stamping of plate-makers' marks, giving the name and address of their maker, is clearly visible on the backs of these Blake and Spode factory copper plates.

The title of my chapter on 'Blake and the Chinamen' is intended to signal something of the complexity of the diverse cultural routes which influenced the history of British engraving. There was rather more that needs to be understood about Blake's perception of the fate of engraving than the effect of its relegation by the Royal Academy or the practical and commercial obstacles which faced Boydell's print enterprises.[2] At the height of the Chinese fashion in England around the 1750s, the trade in porcelain was a prosperous business.[3] As the Chinese had developed over several centuries a much more advanced technology of porcelain-making, the English had admired and tried to imitate them with enthusiasm. The interest in Chinese style and objects, especially porcelain, was the prevailing fashion in mid-eighteenth-century England. It was popular not only to collect Chinese exported ceramics but also 'chinoiserie' style furniture and images, the application of this adjective being itself an indicator of the prevalence of the popular taste. William Hogarth's *Marriage à-la-Mode*, Plate II, published in a widely disseminated engraving made in 1745, shows the luxuries of an aristocrat's house including a range of Chinese porcelain prominently displayed above the

**Figure 5.3** Copper plate recto for transfer-printing on pottery at the Spode Factory & Museum, *Temple Pattern, c.* 1798. Reproduced by kind permission of the Spode Museum Trust; copyright Spode.

fireplace (O'Connell 2003: 246, 249). This indeed represents the fashion of the eighteenth-century British wealthy household, where Chinese ceramic figures, porcelain jars and vases were highly valued and extremely desirable objects for rich collectors. Although by Blake's time much of this chinoiserie had been replaced by neo-classical purity, china remained a favourite English house-hold decoration. Curiously, it was Josiah Wedgwood, one of the most notable popularizers of the newly-fashionable neo-classical style in domestic ornamental ceramics, whose pottery business best exemplifies how the connections between china ceramic wares and transfer-printing involved the transposition of engraving skills from book illustration to pottery production.

Right the way through the eighteenth century, there had been close con-nections between English china dealers (or 'chinamen' as they were known) and the criss-crossing of Chinese imports and Midlands domestic manufactures involving the engraving and print trades. Trade cards issued by chinamen dealers are particularly interesting in indicating the development of the industry. English china dealers often had their engraved or etched trade cards designed in a Chinese or chinoiserie style, an advertising technique meant to hint to the customer that their ceramic wares were of the highest quality. John Dobson, a London china and earthenware merchant (*c.* 1750s–1760s), had a Chinese ginger jar depicted on his trade card, and the inscription: 'John Dobson / at the China Jarr / In St. Martins Court near Leicester Fields / LONDON: / Sells all sort of China Earthen-/ Ware, Stone and Flint-Glass, at / the Lowest Prices' (Young 1995: 12, Pl. 3).

**Figure 5.4** Copper plate verso for transfer-printing on pottery at the Spode Factory & Museum, *Temple Pattern, c.* 1798. As in Figure 5.2, the hammer marks are caused by the technique of knocking-up (*repoussage*) to correct engraving mistakes. Reproduced by kind permission of the Spode Museum Trust; copyright Spode.

Interestingly enough, from these trade cards we can see that the china trade was associated with other kinds of trade in ceramics. Despite the hint of a Chinese association, Dobson perhaps represents the lowest form of chinaman, selling the cheaper mass-produced earthenware ceramics in imitation of their high-quality Chinese porcelain original. At the other end of the commercial spectrum would be those manufacturers and dealers trading in porcelain of high quality and price, merchants such as Josiah Wedgwood, who were also associated with highly developed networks of printmakers and artists. More significantly, other china-men doubled their role as dealers in ceramics with engraving and print-selling. For example, Richard Coffin (active 1759–70), who had his trade card designed with two large Chinese figures and a small cathedral, added the inscription: 'TEA / COFFEE / Chocolate / China & Glass / Sold by / RICH^D: COFFIN / Engraver & / Print-Seller / near BROAD GATE / in the / Church Yard / EXON' (Snodin 1984: 274). In other words, the trade of 'Engraver & Print-Seller' was sometimes combined with the role of 'chinaman', in this instance dealing not only in ceramics and glassware but also the highly prized beverages they were designed to contain.

The development of a relationship between pottery and print-making was an important innovation of the eighteenth-century English chinamen. The commercial impetus was driven by the possibility of distributing scarce Chinese imported ceramics, together with the much sought after commodities of coffee, chocolate and tea, to new customers on a larger scale. As hand-painting onto ceramics after the Chinese manner was an expensive and time-consuming process, the English potters developed transfer-printing techniques to cater for this eager new market. Inevitably, transferring copper-plate engraving to ceramics first began with chinoiserie patterns and then quickly developed into depictions of English pastoral scenes or portraiture.

With the possibility of such valuable markets being available to the first innovators, it is not surprising that there were many craftsmen simultaneously involved whose work was often carried out in isolation. For this reason, the exact origin of transfer-printing onto ceramics is not certain, but it was greatly improved in 1751 by John Brooks, an Irish mezzotint engraver who came to England in the 1740s, working at Battersea in London (Leary & Walton 1976–7: 13–14; Drakard 2002: 28). John Sadler of Liverpool, possibly working independently with similar methods, patented a transfer technique in 1756 and did most of the transfer-printing for Wedgwood from 1761 to 1770 before his partner, Guy Green, took over until 1799 (Drakard 2002: 45). However, Robert Hancock had also practised transfer-printing onto porcelain in Worcester in the 1750s. These pioneers were later joined by Enoch Wood & Sons (1783–1846) and the Ralf Stevenson and Williams company (1825–7) in Stoke-on-Trent, all of whom were also producing transfer-ware, as well as many other English pottery factories.[4] The now famous Willow pattern (still being sold) on transfer-printed pottery was designed in 1780 by Thomas Minton, once apprentice to Spode, with much of this pottery becoming widely known as Staffordshire Blue.

Although chinoiserie as a part of rococo fashion had been replaced by the neo-classical style in the late eighteenth century, there were many books and designs circulating at Blake's time that distributed knowledge of these tastes. *A New Book of Chinese Designs, Calculated to Improve the Present Taste*, published and engraved by Mathew Darly and George Edwards in 1754, was one of the finest of the chinoiserie pattern-books. It included designs of architecture, flowers, furniture, people, costume, landscape and so on (Snodin 1984: 271, 275). Much early transfer-printed pottery shows patterns taken from this book (Roberts 1998: 43).[5]

Starting out as an engraver, Mathew Darly went into partnership with George Edwards, publishing a series of political and satirical prints. There is a direct Blake connection to their work. The anonymous *A Political and Satirical History of the Years 1756 and 1757* (1757), in which appear several caricatures published by Darly and Edwards, not only combined text and image in a combination similar to Blake's illuminated books, but a number of Blake's autograph signatures bearing the date 'May 29 1773' are inscribed in one copy of the edition, now in Michael Phillips's collection and displayed at the 2000 Blake exhibition at Tate Britain (Hamlyn & Phillips 2000: 108–9). If Blake had seen Darly and Edwards' prints on political and satirical history, he may have also seen their chinoiserie book and known something of the prospering transfer-printing business for ceramics.

Added to this range of developments which might be related to Blake are two other important factors. The first is that the Spode factory in Stoke-on-Trent today still uses techniques of transfer-printing which are not only based upon their eighteenth-century originals but also directly employ copper plates manufactured in the nineteenth century bought from the same copper-plate makers

Blake was familiar with. The second factor is that the Midlands potteries were not only keen to use pattern books such as those published by Darly and Edwards but adapted political designs drawn from the caricature print trade. In David Drakard's study, *Printed English Pottery: History and Humour in the reign of George III 1760–1820* (1992), the eighteenth-century process of black on-glaze printing, the so-called 'glue bat method', is demonstrated by the modern ceramic historian and engraver Paul Holdway using a Spode copper plate originally engraved in 1803 entitled *A STOPPAGE to a STRIDE over the GLOBE*, showing Napoleon restrained by John Bull. The use of a contemporary political caricature print demonstrates the close relationships between the pottery factories and the print trade.

The technique of transfer-printing for porcelain is worth describing in order to emphasize its similarities to printing on paper.[6] During the early process of on-glaze transfer-printing, the engraved intaglio copper plate is first charged with a fine-boiled linseed oil and cleaned off so that the oil is retained only in the engraving. The transfer medium is formed by pouring onto flat dishes warm, liquid, gelatinous animal glue which, on cooling, becomes firm but flexible and resilient sheets of jelly about 3mm thick. A section of this glue jelly, called a 'bat', is cut to the size of the engraving. Supported by a soft cushion, the bat is firmly pressed onto the copper plate. The oil in the engraving is picked up on the surface of the glue bat which is then carefully stripped from the copper plate and placed on the cushion with the oily side on top. The pottery is rolled onto the bat: this adheres to the surface and is then stripped away leaving the almost invisible oil on the glazed surface. A very finely ground powder is lightly dusted over the transferred oily impression for colouring. The powder sticks to the oil, then, with careful cleaning, it is removed from the glazed surface to reveal the transferred design.

As the technique was improved, the on-glaze method was replaced by under-glaze and the glue by a thin sheet of tissue paper. The copper plate was inked and the design pressed onto the tissue by running them together under a roller. At the preparatory stage of taking proofs, the engravers used a rolling press similar in type to the one Blake would have owned. This is the basis of the technique still used by Spode. Illustrations in Copeland (2000: 10) show such processes. Firstly, the ink is applied to the copper plate and worked into the engraving with a dabber. Subsequently, the ink is scraped off from the surface of the copper plate leaving ink in intaglio-engraved lines. Soap and water are applied to soften the tissue paper which is then laid onto the copper before the copper plate, with the tissue on top, is passed through a roller press. The tissue is then peeled away and, with the impression taken from the copper plate still wet, placed on the pot.

An alternative method involved the use of a colourless oily liquid instead of ink. The design was applied to the pot as described above, and then defined by dusting with powdered colour in the same way as the 'glue bat method'. Lady Shelburne saw this method when she visited the Birmingham enamelling factory of John Taylor in 1766. She described in her diary how Taylor:

> made and enamell'd a landscape in the top of a box before us which he afterwards gave me as a curiosity from my having seen it done. The method of doing it is thus; a stamping instrument managed only by one woman first impressed the picture on paper, which paper is then lain even upon a piece of white enamel and rubbed hard with a knife, or instrument like it, till it is

marked upon the box. Then there is spread over it with a brush some metallic colour reduced to a fine powder which adheres to the moist part and, by putting it into the oven for a few minutes the whole is completed by fixing the colours.[7]

The woman who 'impressed the picture on paper' would have been using an engraved copper plate. The all-important addition of powdered colour for the enamelling process is a reminder of how Blake was using parallel technologies in developing his method of colour printing onto paper from 1794 onwards. Another way was to cut down the part of the print needed to be transferred from the tissue paper, then place the tissue in position, followed by rubbing down the transfer with a brush.[8]

Instead of painting pieces by hand, the English transfer-printing process from copper-plate engraving allowed fine lines to be applied onto ceramics. The process enabled mass reproduction in a cheap and rapid manner. Artists' designs such as those by John Flaxman, Angelica Kauffman and James Gillray quickly became popularized by the chinamen and the commercialization of art and print further expanded in the ceramic industry.[9] Apart from the use of pattern books, the sources for transfer-printing were largely from existing prints available on the contemporary market. For example, Wedgwood's transfer-printer John Sadler would ask Wedgwood to go to the print shops in London to choose suitable designs and to post them to him. Sadler then made alterations and re-engraved the designs, adapting them for printing decoration onto the company's creamwares.[10] Copyright was not an issue at this time, as there were pattern books for everyone's use such as Edwards and Darly's *A New Book of Chinese Designs* (1754). On 9 July 1756, the book was advertised in the *Liverpool Chronicle*: 'Drawings in the Chinese, Gothick and Modern Taste for any manufactory business, and Engravings of any kind in Architecture, Ornaments, Landscapes, Heraldry & c.' (my emphasis).[11] In other words, such books were clearly designed to assist the production of ceramics and other manufactures which required patterns to work from.

Indeed, the success of the entire process of transfer-printing on ceramics depended heavily upon the engravers' skills. Their fees could be quite high. To engrave a set of plates suitable to transfer-print five or six ceramic jugs, the charge would be around £30 (Price 1984: 47). The established engraver of prints Valentine Green – who engraved from paintings by Royal Academicians such as Benjamin West – also completed transfer-engravings for Worcester potters (Leary & Walton 1976–7: 16; William-Wood 1981: 165). By contrast, Blake never did any engraving for transfer-wares; neither were his designs ever used for transfer-printing. However, it is worth considering the links Blake most certainly had with Josiah Wedgwood and to use them as a context for trying to understand why Blake did not avail himself of the opportunities afforded by an industry which was using copper-plate engraving on a massive scale.

Blake's only certain connection with the English chinamen was the engraving he did for the Wedgwood factory catalogue (Essick 1991: 96–100, Figs. 217–34). Probably as a result of John Flaxman's introduction, Blake made drawings and engravings of creamware, or Queen's Ware, for Wedgwood at some time around 1815. For the eighteen plates, Blake was paid £30 (Wedgwood's account file; Bentley 2004a: 810). Despite their being signed 'd & sc' (designed and engraved), it is clear Blake did not design the plates himself but took them from Flaxman's designs. Geoffrey Keynes noted in *Blake Studies* in 1971 that eight of Blake's Wedgwood copper plates survived although they have not since been traced (Keynes 1971: 65). Blake's plates were never published and sold in a conventional manner as a catalogue for customers but were used by Wedgwood and his salesmen as a pattern book. They were later much altered and had Blake's signatures removed (Essick 1991: 96–7).

Let us compare this amount of labour and payment with the 22 plates Blake engraved for *Illustrations of the Book of Job* for John Linnell about ten years later, which is probably the best payment Blake ever received for engraving, the latter was around £175 including copyright, for a job on which Blake spent over two years of endeavour (see Bryant 1987). This payment seems quite substantial in comparison with the £30 for the eighteen Wedgwood plates but the *Job* plates were not commercially successful. According to John Linnell's account book, the subscriptions hardly covered the expenditure for Blake's labour, the cost of copper plates, printing paper, binding and so on. In other words, because Wedgwood would have been able to bear the expenses of production and commission more readily, there was every incentive for Blake to have developed this line of his trade.

Neither was the commission for the 1815 creamware Blake's first encounter with the Wedgwood family. Nearly thirty years earlier, around 1784 or 1785, there appears to have been another commission, once again probably through the agency of John Flaxman's introduction. A Wedgwood company ledger of 1784–5 records the payment of £3. 17s. to Flaxman's account for 'Blake for painting on Ceiling pictures' for Etruria Hall, the Wedgwood family estate at Stoke-on-Trent.[12]

Etruria Hall was built between 1768 and 1771. Between 1781 and 1787 John Flaxman completed drawings for ceilings, ornamental friezes and chimney pieces although it is not clear whether all of his designs were implemented. Flaxman might have spared at least one ceiling design for Blake.

Although Blake's ceiling painting for Etruria Hall has now been lost, a fan-shaped watercolour (approx. 11.5 × 38.1 cm) in the Prints and Drawings Room in the British Museum attributed to Blake appears to be the work Flaxman refers to (see Figure 5.5). Martin Butlin's catalogue (1981: Cat. 223A, Pl. 256) names it *Design for a Fan (?): The Corinthian Maid, The Origin of Painting*, dated *c.* 1795.

The picture is on the verso of a sketch for a title-page, probably an early idea for *America: A Prophecy* (*c.* 1793) (Butlin 1981: 116–7, Cat. 223A recto, Pl. 255). While the recto image has been identified in detail because of its allusion to *America* dated to 1793, the subject of the verso cannot be so clearly attributed.[13] Although there has been some doubt whether the painter was Blake, it has been described as 'a perfectly genuine example of Blake's Stothard-like decorative neo-Classicism of the 1790s' (Butlin 1981: 117). Indeed, as Butlin says, the Greek legend of the origin of painting was a commonplace in the neo-classical revival of the later eighteenth century (see Rosenblum 1967; Levitine 1958). However, the real significance of this design lies in its connection with Wedgwood and the development of pottery manufacture.

The story on the fan-shaped painting tells of a Corinthian maid who was moved by love to invent the art of portraiture. Knowing that her lover was to leave the country, she traced the shadow of her lover's silhouette cast on the wall by lamplight. This mimetic image was improved by the maid's potter father, Butades,

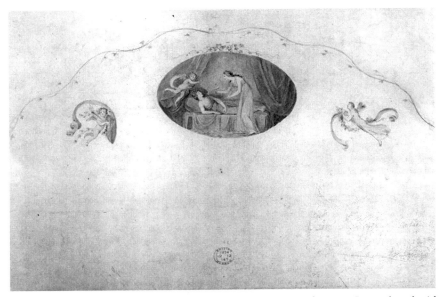

**Figure 5.5** William Blake, *The Corinthian Maid, The Origin of Paining*. Reproduced with permission of the British Museum. © The Trustees of The British Museum.

who filled in the outline with clay and baked it with his other pottery. The legend passed into literature and was included in such influential reference works as Diderot's *Encyclopédie* (1751–72).

The theme of the central panel of Blake's fan-shaped design, similar in some ways to the composition of the title-page of *Songs of Experience* (1794), can be accurately identified as 'The Origin of Painting', the same subject as Joseph Wright of Derby's *The Corinthian Maid* painted around 1782–5 (National Gallery of Art, Washington DC), almost the same time as this ceiling design by Blake. According to his correspondence, Wright painted *The Corinthian Maid* for his patron Josiah Wedgwood particularly because of the legend's association with Butades's role in creating ceramics at the same originating moment as the inception of painting (Rosenblum 1967: 21 n. 59; Egerton 1990: 132–4). The subject of a potter's daughter obviously appealed to Wedgwood who could claim pottery-making as almost a sister art of painting. To increase the evocation of pottery lying behind the story, and to flatter his patron's interests, Wright added two large pottery vases and introduced a glowing kiln into the picture.

Although Wright's painting owes some debt to David Allan's earlier oil painting, *The Origin of Painting* (1775; National Gallery of Scotland), his chief inspiration was from a poem *An Essay on Painting* (first published in 1778) by his friend William Hayley, Blake's later patron. Wright wrote to Hayley in 1784: 'I have painted my picture from your Idea.'[14] This is possibly the year Blake was first introduced by Flaxman to Hayley, who was already by then a popular poet (Bentley 2004a: 30–1).[15] Indeed, Flaxman seems to have been quite busy spreading Blake's reputation in this year, not only bringing him to Hayley's attention but also to Wedgwood's. Blake's idea for the ceiling painting might have been meant to parallel Wright's painting, with them both having common allusions to and familiarity with Hayley's *Essay on Painting*. This type of network of sociability, patronage and common interest between literary and artistic circles, with Wright referring to Hayley's poem and Wedgwood in a position to make further commissions to Blake via Flaxman's introduction, is indicative of the type of professional associations Blake had available to him, even by the mid-1780s. In other words, as early as 1784, there was almost certainly the potential for Blake to have developed a more permanent and financially rewarding relationship with a man, Josiah Wedgwood, who was emerging as an important employer of engraving skills, at a period during which transfer-printing methods, which depended on copper-plate engravers, were becoming more and more fashionable.

What were the obstacles to Blake developing such an association with the Staffordshire pottery industry? During 1784, Blake had formed a print-selling business partnership with James Parker, who had also been one of James Basire's apprentices. William and Catherine Blake moved to Broad Street and lived with Parker and his wife (Bentley 2004a: 33). The business was not a great success. Blake recalled later in a letter that, at that time, 'a Print shop was a rare bird in London' (letter to George Cumberland, 2 July 1800; E 706). The partnership with Parker was shortlived. By the end of 1785, Blake had moved to Portland Street when the partnership formally ended and, presumably, his one-man workshop started with Blake seeking commercial engraving work and taking the first steps towards developing the relief etching techniques of the illuminated books.

At the same time as running his print-selling business with Parker, however, Blake also exhibited four drawings, including three illustrations to the biblical story of Joseph: 'Joseph making himself known to his brethren', 'Joseph's brethren bowing before him', 'Joseph ordering Simeon to be bound', and a picture of 'The Bard, from Gray' (untraced) for the Royal Academy annual exhibition opening on 28 April 1785 (Bentley 2004a: 39). In other words, even in 1784 Blake's ambition was to be an original painter but he was constrained to operate in the print business because he might be able more readily to capitalize on his apprenticeship skills as a copy-engraver. The print-shop partnership with Parker was a logical way of trying to extend the reach of those skills into London's art market.

Within this context, it can be considered that the ceiling painting Blake made for Wedgwood's house combines both his commercial and his artistic aspirations. As a young artist and engraver, Blake had the potential and opportunity to become successful in both spheres. The reputation of Wedgwood's pottery firm had reached both a national and international height by the 1770s. Not only were Wedgwood's so-called Queen's Wares appealing to King George III and Queen Charlotte, but Wedgwood also received commissions from Catherine the Great of Russia for a dinner and dessert service for 50 people with a decoration of views of Britain, which has become known as the Frog Service (Young 1995: 134). Flaxman's introduction of Blake to Wedgwood was an ideal opportunity for Blake to become Wedgwood's designer or engraver in the newly developing practice of transfer-printing. By the 1780s, the technique of transfer-printing was greatly improved from John Sadler's first developments with Josiah Wedgwood's creamware in 1761. Unfortunately, Blake's relations with Wedgwood's business were not to develop any further until nearly thirty years later in 1815, when Blake engraved the pottery shapes for Wedgwood's catalogue.[16]

Between the two encounters with the Wedgwood business, the first time with Josiah Wedgwood I (1730–95) and the second time with Josiah Wedgwood II (1769–1834),[17] Blake engraved many other commercial plates, invented the relief-etching process for his illuminated books, and made many paintings and drawings on religious and literary themes. None of them made any great profit. He was especially frustrated in trying to follow his profession as an engraver. In a letter to William Hayley of 7 October 1803, Blake wrote, 'Art in London flourishes. Engravers in particular are wanted. Every Engraver turns away work that he cannot Execute from his superabundant Employment. Yet no one brings work to me' (E 736). Although Blake doesn't refer to it, this flourishing employment of engraving also included the accelerating use of engraving in the technologies of transfer-printing onto pottery. Despite the opportunities offered by the involvement of Flaxman (and possibly Hayley and Wright of Derby) in the 1780s, Blake's despondent letter was written following his return to London after the three years living alongside Hayley in Felpham. There is other evidence of Blake rejecting attempts to advance his material well-being. Another letter of early 1803, this time to his brother James Blake (E 725–7) complained about William Hayley's attempts to turn him into a portrait painter. While there is little to suggest Blake would have relished the close proximities that would have been required for the portraiture of clients, the advantages of working – at least intermittently – for Wedgwood on a straightforward commission basis might have been usefully followed. At the very least, the presence of a burgeoning Midlands pottery industry which sourced its copper plates from the same suppliers Blake used himself, and their requirement to gather new designs from London rather than provincial Stoke-on-Trent, helps us balance our sense of the actual conditions of the engraving profession during Blake's lifetime. The truth may be that Blake did not recognize the potential of transfer-printing on pottery, but kept to his endeavours of achieving success in the high-art market typified by the Royal Academy exhibitions. The result may have been Blake's commercial failure in both the engraving and painting professions.

Neither is it the case that transfer-printing proved to be a temporary phenomenon. A personal visit to the Spode Factory at Stoke-on-Trent in 2005 enabled me to see their collection of 25,000 copper plates, and to witness Spode's continuing use of what are basically eighteenth-century transfer-printing techniques still employed in the highly commercialized world of twenty-first-century pottery manufacture. Spode's last commercial engravers, including Paul Holdway, demonstrated to me their engraving techniques which are clearly very similar to those of the eighteenth century. Indeed, many copper plates now used by Spode date from the nineteenth century. The present-day engravers simply do what it is known Blake did many times in his relief-etching, recycling old plates by using their verso or by using areas of unmarked surface for small decorative designs. Blake would also have recognized a system of apprenticeship which only died out in very recent times. Compared to Blake's time, when commercial engraving was still thriving, the modern Spode engravers are only now reaching the end of engraving history. While even now, in the early twenty-first century, the Spode engravers in Stoke-on-Trent are working full-time in a respectable career, Blake seems to have struggled fully two hundred years ago to earn a living in Britain's capital city through commercial engraving.

The reason why Blake was comparatively unsuccessful in following an engraving career probably lies in his lack of awareness of the developments in this market. He may have struggled not because he was a marginalized enthusiast but because he did not read market trends well enough. In an emerging scientific age, while experiments were taking place in many different art-related crafts, such as Wedgwood's pottery-making (see Young 1995), George Stubbs's enamel painting on pottery (see Vincent-Kemp 1986), Gainsborough's soft-ground etching (Rosenthal & Myrone 2002: 236), etc., Blake's invention of relief-etching or experiments of fresco painting and monotype for his large colour prints were not successful in terms of their commercial purpose. Transfer-printing on pottery was a successful innovation made by Sadler and Wedgwood and followed up by several other pottery manufacturers – including Spode – who had a better awareness of its business potential. In quantitative terms, there was no decline in engraving employment during Blake's lifetime and it is misleading to think that opportunities for availing himself of the engraving employment potential of the transfer-printing process, even as early as the mid-1780s, were not available to him through his friendship and association with Flaxman, Hayley and the fringes of Wedgwood's patronage.

## Notes

1 Similarly to Figs. 5.3 and 5.4, another Spode copper plate in Drakard & Holdway (2002: 48–9) shows the knocking-up marks of *repoussage* for mending mistakes of engraving. For studies on Blake's copper plates, see Sung 2005.

2 See Eaves 1992 and Dörrbecker 1994.

3 For the Chinese taste in eighteenth-century Britain, see Kerr 2004a & b; Parissien 2004: 44–51, 222–31, 348–59; 'Chinoiserie and Gothic' in Snodin 1984: 271–6.

4 For the history of transfer-printing on pottery, see Price 1984; Drakard 1992; Leary and Walton 1976–7; William-Wood 1981.

5 For engravings used as decoration for eighteenth-century English pottery, see Watney 1966.

6 Illustrations of process, see Drakard 1992: 31–2.

7 Cited in Leary and Walton 1976–7: 13.

8 See illustrations in Copeland 2000: 13, 14.

9 For the artists and engravers involved in transfer-printing on pottery, see Drakard 1992: 17–21.

10 Drakard 1992: 6.

11 Price 1984: 44.

12 Josiah Wedgwood founded his manufactory at Etruria in Stoke-on-Trent (while his partner Thomas Bentley lived in Liverpool). It is situated on the road from Cobridge to Newcastle-under-Lyme. The name of Etruria was given by Wedgwood in memory of an ancient state in Italy, once celebrated for the exquisite taste of its pottery. Wedgwood also built a village near his factory, the Etruria Village, to accommodate his workers. See Young (1995), Wedgwood (1980) and http://www.wedgwoodmuseum.org.uk/factories.htm.

13 Wilton (1973–4) identifies the painting as a fan design, but has no supporting evidence.

14 The letter from Wright to Hayley dated 22 December 1784, currently in a private collection, was exhibited at the Tate Gallery, London from 7 February to 22 April 1990. See Egerton 1990: 132–4.

15 A letter of 26 April 1784 (?) from Flaxman to Hayley says, 'I have left a *Pamphlet of Poem* with Mr. Long which he will transmit to Eartham; they are the writings of a Mr. BLAKE you have heard me mention, his education will plead sufficient excuse to your Liberal

mind for the defects of his work & there are few so able to distinguish & set a right value on the beauties as yourself, I have before mentioned that Mr Romney thinks his historical drawings rank with those of Mi. Angelo; he is at present employed as an engraver, in which his encouragement is not extraordinary – Mr Hawkins a Cornish Gentleman has shewn his taste & liberality in ordering Blake to make several drawings for him, & is so convinced of his uncommon talents that he is now endeavouring to raise a subscription to send him to finish [*his*] studies in Rome [;] if this can be done at all it will be determined on before the 10th of May next at which time Mr Hawkins is going out of England – his generosity is such he would bear the whole charge of Blakes travels – but he is only a younger brother, & can therefore only bear a large proportion of the expence [.]' Bentley 2004a: 30–1.

16  See illustrations in Essick 1991: figs. 217–34.
17  For the Wedgwood family business, see Wedgwood 1980.

# 6 Colour Printing in the West and the East: William Blake and Ukiyo-e

Minne Tanaka

## 1 Introduction

The main objective of this chapter is to discuss how colour printing developed independently in Europe, with specific reference to Britain, and in Japan in the eighteenth century, and to suggest certain points of convergence between these geographically distant traditions. Before the age of colour photography, colour printing from a copper or wooden plate was the only means of reproducing, colour images for book illustrations or for art. The basic problem of keeping the different colours separated proved to be an enormous, almost insuperable, challenge for eighteenth-century engravers and printers in both West and East. The danger was that the colours would blend or blur and outline or form would be lost. In a world of black-and-white engraving or etchings, colour printing was an attractive proposition if only a cheap and reliable process could be invented. As such, now largely obsolete practices of colour printing, although highly important in the age before colour photography, have been a neglected area of research with few scholars attempting to reconstruct the relevant historical methods.

William Blake invented at least two methods of colour printing, one from copper and one from millboard. However, the exact details of how he worked are still an area of some controversy even though the Blake collector Graham Robertson, the majority of whose collection is in Tate Britain, had experimented with Blake's supposed methods as early as 1907. This chapter will show how Blake's endeavours came at the end of a period of searching for such a technique, a goal sought by European as well as by Japanese artists.

William Blake's characteristics as artist and printer have been attracting more attention recently, but still much is left unstudied. Robert N. Essick's *William Blake, Printmaker* in 1980 was followed by two influential works: Morris Eaves' *The Counter-Art Conspiracy: Art and Industry in the Age of Blake* (1992) and *Blake and the Idea of the Book* (1993) by Joseph Viscomi. A large exhibition on Blake was held at Tate Britain in 2000–1 where the co-curator Michael Phillips's two-pull theory of colour printing caused a controversy between him and Essick–Viscomi,[1] which has not been settled yet. Their dispute is about Blake's method of making the illuminated books. I will not go into the details of this controversy here, but the vigorous debate that it has produced shows the importance and timeliness of this issue.

In this chapter, in order to examine Blake's method, I would like to trace the preceding history of colour printing up to his lifetime. Also, as there flourished, right here in Japan, an art of colour printing contemporary to Blake, I would like to trace the history and technique of Ukiyo-e, in order to compare it with Blake's colour printing and to shed new light on both.

## 2   History of Colour Printing in Europe

The history of colour printing in Europe begins almost at the same time as the history of printing itself. In 1456 Gutenberg's 42-line Bible was printed with the rubrics painted by hand. The first colour-printed Psalter came out the next year. The same publisher, Fust and Shoeffer of Mainz, produced colour-printed books in the following years. They cut the metal into interlocking sections so that each section could be inked separately and put together for printing. This laborious method did not suit commercial purposes and was abandoned for centuries until it was reintroduced in Britain in the nineteenth century to prevent forgery in bank notes.

At the end of the fifteenth century, Erhard Ratdolt, a printer of Augsburg, attempted colour printing from wood blocks. This was a technique with which I am familiar because it developed in China and Japan in the seventeenth and eighteenth centuries and then became of great importance in Europe in the nineteenth century. In Japan, as we shall see later, it developed and culminated in the flourishing tradition of Ukiyo-e in the eighteenth century, but the differential between its labour and costs and those of hand-colouring meant that its potential remained unexplored in Europe.

During the sixteenth century, many prints were made from chiaroscuro woodcut, using two or three wood blocks and a narrow range of colours to imitate the effects of wash and highlights in drawings. This method was widely practised to disseminate the drawings of the Mannerists. In *A Descriptive Catalogue*, Blake writes scathingly of this method:

> These Pictures, among numerous others painted for experiment, were the result of temptations and perturbations, labouring to destroy Imaginative power, by means of that infernal machine, called Chiaro Oscuro, in the hands of Venetian and Flemish Demons; whose enmity to the Painter himself, and to all Artists who study in the Florentine and Roman Schools, may be removed by an exhibition and exposure of their vile tricks. They cause that every thing in art shall become a Machine. They cause that the execution shall be all blocked up with brown shadows. They put the original Artist in fear and doubt of his own original conception. The spirit of Titian was particularly active, in raising doubts concerning the possibility of executing without a model, and when once he had raised the doubt, it became easy for him to snatch away the vision time after time, for when the Artist took his pencil, to execute his ideas, his power of imagination weakened so much, and darkened, that memory of nature and of Pictures of the various Schools possessed his mind, instead of appropriate execution, resulting from the inventions; like walking in another man's style, of speaking or looking in another man's style and manner, unappropriate and repugnant to your own

individual character; tormenting the true Artist, till he leaves the Florentine, and adopts the Venetian practice, or does as Mr. B. has done, has the courage to suffer poverty and disgrace, till he ultimately conquers. (E 547)

As G. E. Bentley Jr. points out in *The Stranger from Paradise* (2001), Blake seemed to use 'Demon' as a synonym for 'villains', and Blake's outraged theological treatment of these technical issues led many to conclude that the author was mad.[2] Blake's bigotry and strength of language might have confused his readers, yet at least it shows his familiarity with the technical idiom involved.

In the latter half of the seventeenth century, there lived in the Netherlands the prominent colour printer, Johannes Teyler, who used intaglio plates for the first time, and inked *à la poupée*; that is to say, he put various coloured inks on a copper plate and printed at a single impression. He accomplished a very high quality of prints, unrivalled for several decades. I assume his method shared basic common features with Blake's colour printing method. Although he produced many exquisite prints, Teyler's elaborate and expensive methods could not find any immediate successors. Blake's techniques of illuminated printing were later to meet a similar fate.

In the eighteenth century, the reproduction of drawings in an intaglio tradition produced much more convincing results than the relief methods of the earlier chiaroscuro printers. At the end of the seventeenth century the mezzotint method was discovered, which enabled the printers to gain a range of tones, even with a single black ink.

In 1704, Isaac Newton's *Opticks* had put into the public domain the idea that there are three primary colours, red, yellow and blue, from the balance of which all others may be achieved. Although this is a gross simplification, and the primaries are not the same for pigments as they are for light, it was sufficient to give a few pioneering printers the stimulating idea that the ideal colour printing process might be achieved with just three carefully balanced mezzotint plates. Foremost among these printers was Jakob Christophe Le Blon, who applied Newton's theory of colour to printing inks. In his method, he carefully analysed the proportion of each primary colour and prepared the mezzotint copper plates according to those results.

Le Blon's method was extremely laborious. Not only did the printmaker have to judge by eye the right balance for yellow, blue and red in creating a separate image on each of the three copper plates, he then had to hold a near-perfect register in printing the plates. The piece of paper went through the press three times, once for each colour. By the use of pinholes at the corners of the image, the paper was laid as accurately as possible on the inked plate before rolling through the press. This technique was developed out of the necessity to ink the plates quickly. Basically, the aim of multiplate printing is to make this process easy. In Japan, where the printers became extremely skilful in registration, they prepared up to 20 plates according to the colours required. In the West, Le Blon's theory restricted the number of plates to only four, including black for outlines.

The years before and during the French Revolution saw intaglio colour printing in France enter its most brilliant phase. With the arrival of the Directoire and the Consulate, the newly-ascendent group of printers destroyed the revolutionary plates of the preceding generation and printed subjects more suitable to the new taste of the age. The role the printers played before and after the French Revolution shows a typical characteristic of the medium: its radical and speculative nature. Throughout the history of printing, we find not only intense political engagement, but also financial risk, indicated by the unusually high number of bankruptcies, or near bankruptcies. In some cases, like with Teyler and, later, Robert Thornton, rich investors ended up exhausting their entire wealth. Blake's lifelong complaints about suffering poverty and neglect, therefore, may be seen as indicating his representative rather than marginal status.

Eighteenth-century English colour printing arises after a period of inertia when Edward Kirkall, a Yorkshireman who came to London, started producing colour prints. He was contemporary with Le Blon, who had moved to London in 1720. Kirkall used one metal plate to mezzotint the shadows and etch the outlines. Then he added tones with one or two wood blocks engraved in the chiaroscuro manner. The result was a compound print, executed with both relief and intaglio methods.

No printer in England directly followed Kirkall's example, but John Baptist Jackson, who had worked under Kirkall in his youth, went to Paris and brought the technique to the Le Sueurs brothers before returning to England in 1754. There, seeing his prints did not sell very well, he set up a factory at Battersea for the production of pictorial paperhangings; he also published an *Essay on Engraving and Printing in Chiaroscuro* (Jackson 1754). A copy of this book is in the King's Library in the British Library with an inscription denoting that it was the first work published in England that was illustrated using colour printing.

Le Blon, who started his career as a printer in the Netherlands, moved to London in 1720 and stayed until 1732. While in the city, he set up a 'Picture Office', aiming to distribute cheaper but good quality prints to decorate people's houses, instead of more expensive paintings, as part of the general expansion of the consumer economy. Although his invention was a landmark in the history of colour printing, this project ended up as a financial failure, leaving the company in bankruptcy.

By this time, the main stream of commercial colour printing in England moved on to newly-acquired methods; aquatint and stipple engraving, a chief practitioner of which was William Wynne Ryland. Ryland was later appointed engraver to the king and used his skill of engraving in the crayon manner for the *Collection of Prints in Imitation of Drawings* (1788) compiled by Charles Rogers. His partnership to sell prints ended (yet again) in bankruptcy, but his engravings after Angelica Kauffman in mezzotint, and later in stipple, brought him great success. In 1780 he held an exhibition of prints after pictures by Kauffman, possibly the first exhibition by a London print-seller. He lived an extravagant life, which led him to eventual execution for forging bills to the value of £7,000.[3]

In Blake's own time, the chief practitioner of stipple engraving was Francesco Bartolozzi, to whom Blake refers scathingly in his *Public Address* of 1809 when he complains that 'Engraving . . . has Lost all Character & all Expression' (E 572). This technique, which had won such popularity, was brought into England from France by Ryland, but the printing method adopted in England was different from that used in France. Ryland did not bother to prepare multiple plates according to the number of the colours required; instead printers used a single plate. Often they inked the plate in black or another single colour (a reddish-brown tint was common), but they also produced multicoloured prints by inking the plate *à la poupée*. This became the method generally practised in England throughout the eighteenth and nineteenth centuries, when the print industry was at its peak. Invented by a London engraver, Robert Laurie (1749–1804) in 1776, it required much skill and care on the printer's part, because no matter how well the plate was engraved, if it had been blotted in the printing process, the impression could have been destroyed. Much caution was required when wiping, as well as inking, the plates.

The next intaglio method introduced into colour printing was aquatint, the latest development before the introduction of photography in preparing the plates. This is a method to 'stop out' the biting of acid using resin or alcohol, and often printed in black or single-colour ink but, as in the case of stipple engraving, we find some examples printed in multicolours. Again, in England, the technique of *à la poupée* was used, whereas in France multiple plates were prepared in a method invented by Jean Baptiste Le Prince (1733–81), a French painter and engraver.

The earliest adaptation of aquatint to colour printing seems to have been at least as early as 1768, in Amsterdam. Its introduction into England was by the Hon. Charles Greville, who purchased the details of the method from the inventor Le Prince and communicated them to his engraver friend, Paul Sandby (1730/1–1809), who seems to have modified and improved the process. Sandby was a topographical watercolourist and graphic artist who was born in Nottingham but came to live in the London area, both in Windsor and in Great Pulteney Street on the edge of Soho in 1752. He was a founder member of the Royal Academy and his brother was its first Professor of Architecture. Blake was born just around the corner in 1757, so he might have known the older artist as a neighbour in his childhood.

In the early days, aquatints in England were executed only in monochromes. We have to wait some thirty years, for the days of F. C. Lewis, to see English multicolour aquatints, which appeared just after the heyday of their French equivalents, though without matching their exuberance. Usually they were printed in monochrome ink or two or three colours at most, and were often combined with other techniques such as engraving or etching. Still, there were some examples of multicolour aquatint prints. One of the most beautiful examples was by Dr Robert John Thornton (1765–1832) in his *Temple of Flora*, as it was first announced in 1799, or *The New Illustration of the Sexual System of Carolus von Linnaeus*. Dr Thornton, when he inherited the family fortune in 1797, left his medical practice to pursue his lifelong passion for botany. He commissioned a few artists who specialized in botanical works to execute the plates, and wrote down the most allegorical and fanciful explanations of the plants to accompany them himself. He had to give up this ambitious project of 90 images when it went bankrupt at only one-third of the way through. Yet this is an outstanding work in the history of colour printing in England, and the individual prints are still much sought-after objects among the collectors. It is interesting to note that this project was contemporary with Blake's experiments in colour printing although they do not seem to have collaborated or exchanged ideas, even though they did have a connection later on, when, through the introduction of John Linnell, Thornton commissioned a series of illustrations of Virgil's *Pastorals*. Blake finished them in wood-block printing, which did not please the commissioner, although they were destined to be admired by the young followers of

Blake later on. This was the only time Blake employed the method of wood-block printing. Geoffrey Keynes describes the situation:

> Dr. Thornton was not an imaginative man. He was enterprising and prolific where botany and medicine were concerned, and employed recognized artists to illustrate his works, sometimes on a lavish scale. Unrecognized genius, however, left him unimpressed, and Blake's woodcuts only prompted him to jeer. When they were laid before him he was horrified by such rough and amateurish work, and immediately gave directions that the designs should be re-cut by a professional wood-engraver. This would have been done but for the intercession of Linnell, and, it is said, of Sir Thomas Lawrence and James Ward, whom Thornton happened to meet at the house of a common friend. Though these artists warmly praised the woodcuts, Thornton remained uneasy, and felt that he had to apologize for the inclusion of such work in his book. Accordingly he caused the following note to be printed below the first woodcut. 'The Illustrations of this English Pastoral are by the famous BLAKE, the illustrator of *Young's* Night Thoughts, and *Blair's* Grave; who designed and engraved them himself. This is mentioned, as they display less of art than genius, and are much admired by some eminent painters.'[4]

The style of these prints was imitated by Blake's later followers who called themselves 'the Ancients'. The chief members of the group included Edward Calvert, Samuel Palmer, George Richmond and Frederick Tatham.

## 3    Blake's Method of Colour Printing

Blake's earliest experiment with colour printing was executed around 1794, using his unpublished early plates of *There is No Natural Religion* and *All Religions are One*. He combined his method of relief etching and colour printing, and developed his techniques in printing his illuminated books in colours. Blake's friend the miniaturist Ozias Humphry was so impressed by this method that he persuaded Blake to select and compile some designs, giving birth to *Large and Small Books of Designs*, which developed into the Twelve Large Colour Prints.

The set consists of twelve colour prints, each having up to three pulls extant. They are basically printed from sheets of millboard, finished by hand in watercolour and ink. Although these pictures can be counted among the most exuberant and original works executed by the artist, surprisingly the study of these Large Colour Prints is relatively undeveloped.

Most of the study so far has been done by Martin Butlin, who, in an article written in 1989, places the pictures as following:

> The prints are . . . as a group, the first really mature individual works in the visual arts that Blake created. Moreover they are, as a group, probably the most accomplished, forceful, and effective of Blake's works in the visual arts. Even a work like *Lamech and his Two Wives*, that may seem at first sight rather awkward and ungainly in its forms, can be seen to exhibit these qualities precisely because of its content: this is not always the case with Blake.[5]

The originality of the technique explains the eloquence of the Large Colour Prints. It stemmed not from the individual pictures painted earlier, but developed from his own illuminated books of the early 1790s.[6]

The method of Blake's colour printing was recorded by D. G. Rossetti as informed to him by Tatham (who, presumably, heard it directly from Blake):

> Blake, when he wanted to make his prints in oil, . . . took a common thick millboard, and drew in some strong ink or colour his design upon it strong and thick. He then painted upon that in such oil colours and in such a state of fusion that they would blur well. He painted roughly and quickly, so that no colour would have time to dry. He then took a print of that on paper, and this impression he coloured up in water-colours, re-painting his outline on the millboard when he wanted to take another print.[7]

In his *Catalogue*, Butlin quotes a letter from Tatham of 6 November 1862 to William Rossetti to complement the above account:

> They were printed in a loose press from an outline sketched on paste-board; the oil colour was blotted on, which gave the sort of impression you will get by taking the impression of anything *wet*. There was a look of accident about this mode which he afterwards availed of, and tinted so as to bring out and favour what was there rather blurred.[8]

But then Butlin points out two possible errors made by this direct witness of Blake:

> Tatham, who was not born until 1805, seems to have erred in several respects. Blake did not use oil paint but rather 'fresco', a medium much like that of his temperas. Nor does he seem to have actually repainted his millboard 'plate' before taking further impressions, which were therefore weaker in intensity, requiring more finishing in pen and watercolour. Repetition of each design was therefore limited, none being securely traced in more than three examples, and each version is unique. In fact, Blake seems to have used this technique more for its textual qualities than as a means of reproduction.[9]

Subsequently, its accuracy has often been questioned; and indeed most contemporary testimony as to Blake's technical methods is equally suspect.

The Twelve Large Colour Prints developed from the *Small and Large Books of Designs*, which were compilations of full-page images in colour printing from copper plates gathered from his earlier illuminated books. After printing this series in 1795 and 1804, Blake never returned to this method, but moved on to his 'temperas' instead. Yet the Large Colour Prints cannot be overlooked as a merely transitional project, because their procedures of composition provide a key to understanding both his earlier illuminated books and later temperas as well. In other words, Blake's experiments in methods of colour printing, together with those of his predecessors such as Le Blon and John Baptist Jackson, represent a European solution to printing colour which was a problem that equally challenged artists in the Japanese Ukiyo-e tradition.

A few decades after Blake's experiments, the situation of colour printing changed dramatically. By the mid-nineteenth century the innovative method of lithography, together with the technology of photography, enabled colour printing to enter the modern age. Therefore Blake's experiments must be understood as the culmination of a tradition rather than as a new beginning.

## 4    History of Colour Printing in Japan

This history of colour printing in Western Europe was paralleled by a similar quest to print colours in Japan where technologies of reproduction revolved around wood blocks rather than the copper plates which were the European norm. Of course, from 1635 until 1854 Japan was closed to Europeans except for limited access for Dutch traders, so that widespread exchange of culture was not possible. However there are intriguing patterns of parallel development.

The history of printing in Japan begins well before the period of Ukiyo-e. The earliest example of wood-block printing goes back to the mid-eighth century, and even in the fourth century Chinese prints had been introduced into Japan. There can be found some examples of Korean books in the fifteenth century, and *Ise-monogatari*, printed in 1608, is the oldest extant book printed in Japan with illustrations. These illustrations were hand-coloured on black and white prints, but in 1667 a book of designs for kimonos was colour printed using four colours, although each print was in monochrome.

Yet it was with the arrival of the form of Ukiyo-e that Japanese colour printing achieved outstanding popularity and rapid progress. The term 'ukiyo-e' is often wrongly identified as the artistic form of colour printing, but it also includes painting. Still, the majority of the form was colour printing. Ukiyo-e is a form of popular art which saw its golden age in the late eighteenth and nineteenth centuries. Its main subjects were: depictions of popular beauties, actors and sumo-wrestlers; scenes from plays or historical stories; landscapes; birds and flowers. Many schools flourished and masters held large workshops with many apprentices, but we have to understand that in this art the horizontal influences, such as the trends of masters working contemporarily, may have been stronger than traditions inherited vertically through chronological succession.

Ukiyo-e printing started from black and white prints in the last few decades of the seventeenth century. The earliest known artist is Hishikawa Moronobu who died in 1694. These black and white prints were called *Sumi-zuri-e*, meaning pictures printed in Chinese ink. In the first half of the eighteenth century, this developed first into *Tan-e*, and then *Beni-e* and *Urushi-e*. *Tan-e* means pictures of '*tan*', an orange pigment traditionally used in Japan made from lead, sulphur and nitre. This was a method of painting orange as a chief colour, with some other colours such as green and yellow, over *Sumi-zuri-e*. Later on, the pigment '*tan*' was replaced by '*beni*', which was a red pigment taken from safflowers, and this method was *Beni-e*. '*Urushi*' means Japanese lacquer, and the name comes from the lacquer-like effect caused by the Chinese ink mixed with fish glue. *Urushi-e* is included in *Beni-e*.

The early colour printing method called *Beni-zuri-e* was introduced in 1744. This was a method using two to three colour plates apart from the black plate, and colours such as green, indigo and yellow were used together with red. This technique flourished for twenty years, until an innovative method called *Nishiki-e* was invented by Suzuki Harunobu and dominated the scene for more than a century.

The beauty of the prints was so striking that they were called *Nishiki-e*. '*Nishiki*' means Japanese brocade or just splendour. This is a method of multicolour print-ing invented in 1765 and practised by countless masters. One thing we have to bear in mind is that these artists were regarded as mere artisans and their social ranking was among the lowest. Although their prints were highly sought after when the Western world discovered them in the late nineteenth century, they were executed and treated merely as a form of popular art. Also they were mass-produced and the labour was strictly divided between designer, engraver and printer. There are many suggested parallels to the ambivalence of Blake's own status as commercial engraver excluded from the domain of the fine arts.

Ukiyo-e colour printing can be said to be a form of art typical of 'Edo' in two ways: as the place name and the name of an era. The Edo period, which lasted for about 260 years from the beginning of the seventeenth century until the mid-nineteenth century, coincided with the flourishing of Edo, the former name of Tokyo before Japan opened. Some Ukiyo-e artists took active parts in Kamigata, which is in the Kyoto–Osaka area, but this art can be counted as the popular culture which flourished in Edo under the government of shogun. Interestingly, the peak of Ukiyo-e printing is considered to be the 1790s, when Kitagawa Utamaro and Toshusai Sharaku produced their masterpieces. This exactly coincides with Blake's execution of his Large Colour Prints.

## 5   Press, Pigments and Technique of Colour Printing

Basically, the technique of engraving plates can be divided into three categories: intaglio, relief and planography. To print intaglio plates, a very strong pressure is required, which can be gained from a rolling press. Images can be printed with less pressure, such as that of a letterpress or even just rubbing by hand, from relief or plane plates. As a commercial engraver, Blake engraved and etched a lot of intaglio plates, and owned a rolling press for proof-printing. Yet, as he developed his own art of colour printing, he moved from intaglio plates to relief and plane plates. His Twelve Large Colour Prints are, with one possible exception, mostly planography, and I assume that he used a letterpress to print this series. Ukiyo-e wood blocks are typical examples of relief engraving, and they were printed without a press, rubbing forcefully from the back using a tool called a *baren*.

The methods of multicolour printing can be categorized into two groups: inking a single plate *à la poupée*, and preparing plates to the number of colours required. As I mentioned before, *à la poupée* was the dominant method used in England, and Blake employed it as well. Ukiyo-e printing is a typical example of multiplate printing, where the blockcarvers prepared as many as twenty wood blocks if required. In the West, Le Blon's technique of analysing every colour into the three primary colours reduced the number of plates to three, or four with the use of an additional plate for black. In any case, registration comes into question with this method. When a print is made from multiple plates, printers need some clues or devices to put together the different parts into the original image of the design. With a printing press, this is not so difficult, but with a rolling press, pins were used as indicators. In Ukiyo-e printing, the blockcarver carved a mark called *kento* on every plate, and the sizes of paper were regulated.

Until the nineteenth century, whatever the form of art – say, painting, printing, even to glazing glass or porcelain – the artists themselves had to prepare the colours by mixing pigments and binders. In Japan, black *sumi* was prepared by dissolving a bar of Chinese ink into water, and sometimes adding *nikawa* fish glue for gloss. Other pigments were placed dry on the plate itself, and mixed with rice starch glue with a brush right there on the plate. What Blake used for binders is not recorded, but interesting research is going on among paper conservationists and technical art historians. It is generally accepted that Blake did not use oil, but is likely to have used some kind of gum, sugar, egg tempera and animal glue. Apparently he used the same mixture as he printed with when finishing the prints with a brush.

The technical requirements of colour printing make it virtually impossible for a working printer to ink the same plate twice. There are only two options: a single plate printed *à la poupée*; or plural plates, designed to simplify the inking, printed separately with registration to reconstruct the original design. Blake's own experiments must always have remained within the limits of working practicability: therefore I conclude that he printed most of his designs *à la poupée* from one plate.

In this chapter, I have compared the history of colour printing in the West and the East. We cannot assume any direct influence between the techniques of the West and the East. Probably Blake knew nothing about Japanese Ukiyo-e prints, though some of the essays in this volume suggest possible routes of transmission. Yet considering their separate development, what is most striking is not the differences between Ukiyo-e and Blake's colour printing but their similarities.

### Notes

1  Essick and Viscomi, 'An Inquiry into William Blake's Method of Color Printing'. The first online draft of the essay appeared on 15 October 2001, followed by the published online version (February 2002) and the print version published in *Blake: An Illustrated Quarterly* 35 (Winter 2002a). See also Butlin (2002a) and Essick and Vicomi (2002b).
2  Bentley 2001: 330.
3  One anecdote repeated in Gilchrist's nineteenth-century life of Blake is that Blake's father brought his son, when he was fourteen, to Ryland for an interview, thinking about apprenticing him to this fashionable engraver. Blake is alleged to have said that this man had a face to be hung, predicting the master engraver's future and refusing to apprentice under him (Gilchrist 1998).
4  Blake 1937 (introduction by Keynes).
5  Butlin 1989.
6  Butlin 1969.
7  D. G. Rossetti, 'Supplementary' in Gilchrist 1998: I 376.
8  Butlin 1981: *Text*, 156.
9  Ibid.

# 7 Representing Race: The Meaning of Colour and Line in William Blake's 1790s Bodies

Sibylle Erle

Discussions about Blake's conceptualization of racial difference usually start from the skin-colours of 'The Little Black Boy' in *Songs of Innocence* (1789)[1] and the noble bodies of the slaves in his engravings to John Gabriel Stedman's *Narrative of a Five Years' Expedition* (1796).[2] In the late eighteenth century 'race' underwent a paradigmatic shift. It became more and more associated with Buffon's idea of degeneration. The concept of the Great Chain of Being, as used to justify the set position of each species within the natural world, was still invoked in the life sciences, but it coincided with the acknowledgement of evidence which suggested that the notion of a graded, unchanging ladder of life was wrong.[3] The late eighteenth century also saw a notable increase in the taxonomical energy expended on humans. Indicators of race, especially skin-colour and physical appearance, became established tools for characterizing human types; types which were at the same time perceived as dependent on climate and modes of living. The growing awareness of variety within each racial type, however, resulted not in greater tolerance but in more sweeping racial generalizations. Looking at Blake and the context of racial science, helps us to understand how theories of human origin, and especially the discourse on race, affected artistic responses to chosen and attributed aspects of human identity.

The concept of race had been associated with monogenetic theories of human origin, formulated in the works of naturalists such as Linnaeus, Buffon and Blumenbach: Linnaeus first included humans as the most perfect animal in his ascending hierarchy of perfection, and Buffon, followed by Blumenbach, rejected taxonomic systems in favour of comparative approaches to the different manifestations of the human.[4] The landmark of these non-theological and rigidly scientific analyses of the human form is Buffon's *Histoire Naturelle*, published in 44 volumes between 1749 and 1804, and translated into English from 1780. Particularly relevant to the 1790s debate is Blumenbach's *Generis Humani Varietate Nativa* (1775). His enormous skull collection, *Collectionis Suae Craniorum Diversarum Gentium Illustratae Decades*, was published between 1790 and 1828. With the advent of racial science, biological difference was explained in terms of social hierarchy. Despite an initial resistance to this European debate, and especially to Linnaean thinking, the paradigms of racial research took root in Britain. The principal disseminator was surgeon John Hunter, who lectured on comparative anatomy. The most important British publication inspired by Hunter is Charles White's *An Account of the Regular Gradation in Man* (1799). Although citing 'gradation' as the cardinal principle of all animal life, White arranged the European and the African into polar opposition, claiming the African 'seems to approach nearer to the brute creation than any other of the human species'.[5]

William Blake is part of a tradition which identifies race within faces. The close link between art and facial anatomy was made in racial science, propagated through the Dutch anatomist Petrus Camper whose *Works . . . on The Connexion between the Science of Anatomy and The Arts of Drawing, Painting, Statuary* was published in London in 1794.[6] From 1758 onwards, and propelled by religious belief substantiated by apparent empirical evidence, Camper argued that variation in skin-colour or bone shape could be explained through adaptation. Acclimatization could mean that a black person literally turned into a white person.[7] The same monogenetic and environmentalist argument concerning the material effects of human migration is put forward in *Observations Made During A Voyage Round the World* (1778), written by John Reinhold Forster who together with his son George accompanied Captain Cook as official naturalists on his second voyage.[8] We can assume that Blake was aware of the different attempts at human taxonomy, because he used skin-colours along with skeleton shapes as variable co-ordinates of the human body in his work in the early 1790s. Environment in Blake contributes to identity, especially to the dynamic of the interplay between body and soul, but never in a categorical way. In the *Continental Prophecies*, Blake develops allegorical relationships between America, Europe, Africa and Asia but associates all of these continents with the same kind of darkness.[9] Not only in the coloured plates but also in the texts, some of Blake's figures change both in shape and colour. This chapter will explore the belief systems – both religious and scientific – which contributed to the identities of some of Blake's 'raced' and 'animalized' figures.

The representation of character or type in the human face had been popularized within the debate about body–soul relationships, discussed and illustrated in *Physiognomische Fragmente* (Physiognomical Fragments) (1775–8), written by the Swiss pastor Johann Caspar Lavater.[10] The publication history of his physiognomy project is complicated, because Lavater continued to accumulate new material, and further complications arose from the publication of abridged editions, the first appearing in the early 1780s, and from the various translations of the amended and abridged editions into Dutch, French and English. In the late 1780s Blake made four engravings for one of the English translations, Lavater's *Essays on Physiognomy* (1789–98). Before joining the team of engravers working on the so-called Hunter translation, Blake had already engraved a portrait of Lavater for the radical publisher Joseph Johnson in 1787.[11] The link between Blake, Lavater and late-eighteenth-century physiognomy is Henry Fuseli, Lavater's London-based childhood friend, as well as future Professor and Keeper of the Royal Academy.[12] Blake engraved the frontispiece to Fuseli's translation of Lavater's *Aphorisms on Man* (1788), owned the book and annotated it.[13] Even though *Essays on Physiognomy* did not include many close analyses of outer-European individuals – indeed, some of the material was never translated into English[14] – Lavater's physiognomical doctrines had a strong influence on contemporary characterizations of race. The degree of Blake's awareness of Lavater's work may be gauged from the register of his annotations to *Aphorisms on Man*:

I hope no one will call what I have written cavilling because he may think my remarks of small consequence For I write from the warmth of my heart. & cannot resist the impulse I feel to rectify what I think false in a book I love so much. & approve so generally (E 600)

According to Blake-biographer Alexander Gilchrist, *Aphorisms on Man* was one of Blake's favourite books, which he kept all his life.[15] Reading Blake in the context of physiognomical theory is an attempt to get to grips with Blake's understanding of human character and its representation.[16]

Before Lavater, physiognomy was mostly associated with magic, astrology and divination. Lavater not only attempted to bring scientific rigour to the pastime of face-reading, he launched his new approach with a motto from the Bible: 'God created man after his own image.'[17] The theme of true identity and disclosed inner nature is further accentuated in Blake's annotations to *Aphorisms on Man*. In response to Lavater's 'Know that the great art to love your enemy consists in never losing sight of the MAN in him: the most inhuman man still remains man, and never CAN throw off all taste for what becomes a man', Blake writes: 'None can see the man in the enemy if he is ignorantly so, he is not truly an enemy if maliciously not a man. I cannot love my enemy for my enemy is not man but beast & devil if I have any. I can love him as a beast & wish to beat him' (E 589). At this point it is useful to think of *The Marriage of Heaven and Hell* in which Blake has Isaiah say: 'My senses discover'd the infinite in every thing, and as I was then perswaded. & remain confirm'd; that the vioice [*sic*] of honest indignation is the voice of God, I cared not for consequences but wrote' (E 38). For Blake 'honest indignation' is justified because once anger and vengeance are released, a man's ability to discern what is true and to do what is right is restored. The extreme version of this is his rather dubious advice to 'Sooner murder an infant in its cradle than nurse unacted desires' (E 38). With regard to physiognomy, being like a 'beast' implies a loss of human qualities and eventually of likeness to the divine being. In Blake, this is a process of individual choice and inner growth: it does not mean 'beast' and inferior races are interchangeable. Indeed, mainstream Enlightenment thought may reasonably be summarized as having no fixed scale defining racial hierarchy. It is possible to speak of a relative openness in the attitudes to otherness, since the discoveries in comparative anatomy acknowledged both differences and similarities. Moreover, due to the scope of its theoretical venture comparative anatomy put off closure of its area of study. Theories of transmutation and the belief in the inheritance of acquired characteristics were not uncommon. Evolution by natural selection was only made plausible after Mendel's discovery that heredity was particulate. Then, the idea of European superiority was mostly a moral argument, considering sociological stages, degrees of civilization, refined behaviour, customs, traditions and, finally, recommending the practice of Christian faith. The biological determinism of today's neo-Darwinism may have been intuited.[18]

Evidence for Blake's interest in facial bone-shape is in the margin of Fuseli's preliminary drawing to the frontispiece of *Aphorisms on Man* (Figure 7.1): two heads sketched in profile. Because of the differences between design and finished engraving it is generally held that Blake and Fuseli collaborated.[19] David Weinglass pointed out that it was common practice with Fuseli to give the engravers working for him 'rough visual hints to work up'.[20] What is unusual

**Figure 7.1**  Henry Fuseli's preliminary drawing to Johann Casper Lavater's *Aphorisms on Man* (1788). (Collection of Robert N. Essick.)

about the *Aphorisms* frontispiece is that instead of giving a portrait of Lavater, the author of the impending *Essays on Physiognomy*, it pictures a moment of divine inspiration.[21] Looking at Fuseli's two profile drawings, it is tempting to speculate that they were part of a conversation about physiognomy and the representation of likeness.[22] Because whether or not they depict Lavater and/or Fuseli at different times of their lives,[23] the two lines or compasses connecting the foreheads with the chins via the noses indicate that the portrayed shared the same facial angle.[24] It is also worth bearing in mind that there is yet another different sketch of a Lavater-like face. It is on the back of Fuseli's Michelangelo drawing, originally designed for the frontispiece to his own *Aphorisms on Art* (1789–1831).[25] This third sketch could be Lavater at an even later stage of his life. The nose is too big for the face and the line marking it is very prominent. Considering the importance which Lavater attributed to the nose, this sketch is possibly a caricature.[26] When reading these sketches against physiognomical theory, it becomes clear that what is being put to the test is likeness itself.

Blake's pondering of the representation of body and soul is set against the backdrop of a wider enthusiasm for physiognomy and the British reception of Lavater. A more generalized theory, identifying moral integrity as physically manifest in the face, was also appropriated into contemporary print culture and, in particular, in the widely available work of popular cartoonists such as James Gillray and John Nixon. This process proved a problem for the representational repertoire, of which Lavater was acutely aware. The caricaturists tended deliberately to flout the rules of proportion and combined fashion with physiognomical expression to produce politically critical – possibly anarchic – statements as visually codified representations. Lavater deplored any kind of deviation, because it challenged a truthful representation of human spirituality, and held that the caricaturist was potentially dangerous: a caricature could come to replace the true, physiognomical portrait.[27] M.E. Reisner and more recently Alexander Gourlay have convincingly demonstrated that some of the pilgrims of Blake's *Sir Jeffery Chaucer and the nine and twenty pilgrims on their journey to Canterbury* (c. 1808) were caricatures of well-known contemporary figures such as William Pitt and the Prince Regent, frequently portrayed by Gillray.[28] The pilgrims are an exception, because Blake, like Lavater, preferred to represent the naked body and to do so as accurately as he was able. Most of his figures are clothed in semi-transparent and clinging garments as if to emphasize Blake's point, as he expresses it in *A Descriptive Catalogue* (1809), that they are 'the physiognomies or lineaments of universal life, beyond which Nature never steps' (*DC* 10, E 532–3).

Lavater, when talking about the resemblance between humans and animals, was confident that standard proportions enabling precise classification of humans and animals would one day be accurately determined: researchers of the calibre of Petrus Camper would, no doubt, make possible scientific distinction between skulls.[29] Camper was interested in beauty and perfect form, as well as the dividing line between man and animal, and employed an anatomical argument which emphasized spiritual and intellectual equality. His approach was comparative which suggests that nothing in his work was either immediate or absolute. Throughout, readers are invited to *compare* the given illustrations. His translator stresses that everything Camper criticizes in the 'most distinguished painters' is 'founded upon comparative anatomy'.[30] Linking his work to Buffon's *Histoire Naturelle*, and while trying to evolve a definitive description of the human form,

Camper not only revised Galen, he concentrated – followed by Blumenbach – on bone-structures and eventually resorted to sawing through skulls to determine the profile of human facial bones.[31] He worked with Charles Le Brun's facial angle and claimed that he was able to measure the degrees of humanity from the skull of an ape to that of a classical statue:

> When in addition to the skull of a Negroe, I had procured one of a Calmuck, and had placed that of an ape contiguous to them both, I observed that a line, drawn along the forehead and the upper lip, indicated this difference in national physiognomy; and also pointed out the degree of similarity between a negroe and the ape. By sketching some of these features upon a horizontal plane, I obtained the lines which mark the countenance, with their different angles. When I made these lines to incline forwards, I obtained the face of an antique; backwards, of a negroe; still more backwards, the lines which mark an ape, a dog, a snipe, &c. – This discovery formed the basis of my edifice.[32]

The likeness between the two heads in Fuseli's preliminary drawing seems to have been determined according to Camper's 'discovery'. Whereas Camper claimed that the face changed with age,[33] Fuseli's drawings though representing different ages have the same facial angle. This means that he must be measuring a constant. In the section on 'National Physiognomy', Camper inaugurates a taxonomy which stretches from animal life and different ethnic groups to human perfection sculptured into marble – implying that, in his view, the human form culminates in inanimate matter. Underlying this transposition is the Platonic idea of ideal form which only truly exists in an immaterial world. This notion was crucial to the theory of representation developed by the German art historian Johann Joachim Winckelmann (1717–68), first translated into English by Fuseli in 1765,[34] who argued that the unfigurable in art could only be expressed through allegories. Consequently, the statues of Greek Gods are representations not of the Gods but of the idea of a God.[35] The attempt to trace the perfect human body through from animal to unanimated – which signifies ideal form – is a typical feature in the thinking of both Lavater and Camper, as if the ideal could only ever be encoded according to a superior sign-system. Blake's genealogy of the ideal body is different. Instead of isolating his examples, he offers an overview which includes geographical context. In *The Song of Los* he installs 'heart-formed Africa' as the reference point of the continental prophecies, where ultimately everything originated:

> Adam stood in the garden of Eden:
> And Noah on the mountains of Ararat:
> They saw Urizen give his Laws to the Nations
> By the hands of the children of Los.
> Adam shuddered! Noah faded! black grew the sunny African
> When Rintrah gave Abstract Philosophy to Brama in the East.
> [. . .]
> To Trismegistus. Palamabron gave an abstract Law:
> To Pythagoras Socrates & Plato.
>
> (*The Song of Los*, Plate 3:3, 6–19, E 67)

The link between these territories – in a world beyond Eden and a life after the Flood – is the 'Laws' of Urizen.[36] It has been argued that for Blake the African, or 'fallen child of the sun', was 'one of the central symbols of the oppression of fallen man' and Detlef Dörrbecker in his splendid Blake Trust edition argued that Blake might have associated Pythagoras with sun-worship.[37] Just as Lavater or Camper, Blake happily juxtaposes images or figures into causal relationships: while Los, the voice of the *Song*, is portrayed as a sun-god and Pythagoras as a priest of the sun, the African is affected by it. Now, if we return to Pythagoras and geometry, we might want to acknowledge a metaphorical system in Camper's European vantage point; or rather in the central survey point of Camper's charts which, based on their superimposed grids, would always indicate what a living European being lacked. (This, according to Winckelmann, is 'edle Einfalt und stille Grösse'; as translated by Fuseli, 'noble simplicity and sedate grandeur'.)[38] Blake not only turns the family tree of the human race upside down, but also makes each body within his taxonomy susceptible to change.

In 1994 David Bindman had already identified a Lavaterian influence in Blake's 'Song of Liberty', a poem appended to *The Marriage of Heaven and Hell* (1790–3): 'O African! Black African! (go. winged thought widen his forehead.)' (E 44).[39] 'The Song of Liberty' projects a flexible body, or at least one which approaches ad infinitum an absent ideal. In terms of comparative anatomy's premise that the connection between all races manifests itself in geometrical proportions, it is crucial that what Blake here demands is a change of mind: if the Jew stopped counting money his face would literally expand.[40] Gradually bulging foreheads are at the core of Camper's measured system. In Blake, the advice to both Jew and Black African is 'Look up! look up' (E 44). This echoes Lavater who took the *imitatio Christi* quite literally.[41] Christ's incarnation meant redemption because through his exemplary life-story man had been given the opportunity to re-establish his own relationship to God. By imitating Christ, man would return to what had originally been intended for him:

> Suppose a man who had got a near view of an Angel – of a God – of the Messiah [. . .] such a man must be entirely destitute of imagination and sensibility, if an aspect so august did not imprint on his countenance some of the traits which must have struck him. His physiognomy must infallibly have borne sensible marks of the Divinity who filled his soul, the *Deum Propiorem*.[42]

Lavater's concern for salvation and the redemption of his fellow human beings verges on anti-Semitic sentiment. His belief in perfectibility was so strong that he publicly challenged the Jewish philosopher Moses Mendelssohn. In the dedication to his translation of Bonnet's *La palingénésie philosophique* (1769) he declared that Mendelssohn – if he really aspired to the next higher stage of existence – had no choice but to convert to Christianity. Lavater pointed out that if Mendelssohn did convert his features would become more refined, because they would in due course lose their Jewishness.[43] When and if such categories as nationality or race were transcended by adopting different beliefs or changing habits, according to Lavater, physiognomy would also alter.[44]

Camper's views of comparative anatomy, in print from 1784 and translated into English in 1794,[45] had been filtered into Lavater's analyses of human profiles. These differentiate between European types, such as Mediterranean or Nordic, and even outline the influence of religion: while he claims 'Englishmen have large, well defined, beautifully curved, lips', he makes an exception for the Quakers and Moravians 'who, wherever they are found, are generally thin-lipped'.[46] Even though he gives environmental explanations for ethnic variety – 'there will always be something mutually local and common between the beautiful and the deformed' – he ends the 'National Physiognomy' section on the understanding that some are inferior: 'Yet ought not the lowest of the human race to be discouraged. They are the children of one common father, and their brother is the first born of the brethren.'[47] Lavater's approach was, no doubt, culturally biased, because it reiterated the cultural superiority of a white and European perspective. Charles White, for example, quotes Lavater on German skulls in 1799 to emphasize his point about its superiority: 'Everything about it bears the impress of an European head, and it sensibly differs from the three which follow.'[48] In this respect, Blake's obsession with the human body and its different – racially coded – manifestations makes sense. His approach, however, is different: Albion, the first or whole English man, is the pivotal point of his creation myth. He is both country and man, and he is the origin of mankind. Blake's scale of ethnic variety seems – throughout – to refer to pre-Enlightenment models of essence. According to Blake's comment, in his annotations to *Aphorisms on Man*, evil men being like beasts, individuals can either cut themselves off and turn into beasts, or seek redemption and ascend towards a purer likeness of their creator. A good example of this process, producing different shapes at different times, is Orc in *America: A Prophecy* (1793), who, as the personified 'Revolution in the material world',[49] argues with Albion's Guardian Angel (England) after raping the 'shadowy daughter of Urthona':

> Dark virgin; said the hairy youth, thy father stern abhorr'd;
> Rivets my tenfold chains while still on high my spirit soars;
> Sometimes an eagle screaming in the sky, sometimes a lion,
> Stalking upon the mountains, & sometimes a whale I lash
> The raging fathomless abyss, anon a serpent folding
> Around the pillars of Urthona, and round thy dark limbs,
> On the Canadian wilds I fold, feeble my spirit folds.
> For chaind beneath I rend these caverns; when thou bringest food
> I howl my joy! and my red eyes seek to behold thy face
> In vain! these clouds roll to & fro, & hide thee from my sight.
> (*America*, Plate 1:1, 11–20, E 51)

This confrontation between Orc and the personification of America has been interpreted by Dörrbecker and others as a war between Britain and its former colonies and, in particular, the taking possession of the American land by the European settlers. Orc represents revolution as well as violence. While Dörrbecker discusses his 'animal metamorphoses' in relation to their possible symbolic frames of reference, it is also useful to think about their function within the plot of the poem. In view of the Ovidian tradition of transformation it is important to realize that they are neither instigated by a God, nor are they the consequence of a reward or punishment. Orc is in charge of his identity. When he gets really excited, his shape changes. He assumes power, does evil and turns into something less than human. Part of the ambiguity of *America*'s ending is the question of our attitude to Orc. Part of him is a beast.[50]

Judith Wechsler in her seminal article 'Lavater, Stereotype, and Prejudice' (1993) pointed out that Lavater's judgements about ethnic groups are the more differentiated the closer they are to Switzerland. Georg Christoph Lichtenberg, a

Göttingen Professor of Physics and one of his foremost critics, wrote into his London travel diary that the portraits of Lavater's blacks were wrong. What Lichtenberg contradicts here are his generalizations and more importantly his allegorizing of individuals.[51] Lavater reasoned that:

> It is probable we shall discover what is national in the countenance better from the sight of an individual, at first, than of a whole people; at least, so I imagine, from my own experience. Individual countenances discover more the characteristics of a whole nation, than a whole nation does that which is national in individuals.[52]

In what follows Lavater extrapolates his own opinions before he moves on to consider other authorities on national character. He abstracts from the features of individual faces to then generalize about nations. As emphasized by Wechsler, it is often unclear whether Lavater wrote about particular images or simply reiterated what he thought to be characteristic of a certain type or group.[53] In volume IV of *Physiognomische Fragmente* (1778) Lavater, in response to Lichtenberg's attack *Über die Physiognomik; Wider den Physiognomen* (1778) (About Physiognomy; Against the Physiognomist), insisted on a causal relationship between physical beauty and moral integrity. His moral viewpoint is a direct consequence of confident generalization about universal attitudes towards race.[54] In *Essays on Physiognomy* this imaginary exchange between Lavater and Lichtenberg appears at the beginning of Volume I:

> But first of all let us rectify a mistake, which I should hardly have expected in a Geometrician. 'Why,' demands our Author, 'might not the soul of Newton inhabit the scull of a Negro? an angelic mind dwell in a hideous form? Belongs it to thee, feeble mortal, to constitute thyself a judge of the works of God?' The question under discussion by no means is, 'What God *can* do?' We are only examining, 'What we have reason to expect from Him, after the knowledge already attained of his nature and his works.' – 'God, the author and the principle of all order, what *doth* He?'[55]

It is interesting to see that in arguments about racial hierarchy the 'Negro' is used as a recurring benchmark for human achievement. Kant in his *Observations on the Feeling of the Beautiful and the Sublime* (1763) draws on Hume's argument about non-biological, continental or essential human types to stress the point about underachieving ex-slaves.[56] In Kant's work, moral universalism coexists with racial coding. As a result, the gulf between blacks and whites is identified as enormous: 'So fundamental is the difference between these two races of man, and it appears to be as great in regard to mental capacities as in colour.'[57] Especially with Camper and Lavater, skin-colour in these generalizations about ethnic groups becomes secondary because greatness is perceived as materialized in the shape of the human skull. In these kinds of philosophical argument, Newton is used as the embodiment of greatness. The other side of the coin of generalization is that Lavater compared the allegorical 'Negro' with the individual 'Newton'.

Until now I have argued that Blake probably subscribed to the ideas of physiognomical theory and the belief that the soul or mind influenced, perhaps even initiated, physical change. In view of the later dualism with figures casting off their fallen bodies to assume their 'human forms divine', Blake's conception of body–soul relationships in the 1790s is quite remarkable. In *The Marriage of*

*Heaven and Hell* (*c*.1790–3) he provides us with famous formulations roughly contemporary to his annotations to Lavater: 'Man has no Body distinct from his Soul for that calld Body is a portion of Soul discernd by the five Senses. The chief inlets of Soul in this age' and 'Energy is the only life and is from the Body and Reason is the bound or outward circumference of Energy' (E 34). These resolutions have been reworked from standard religious premises about man's existence: 'That Man has two real existing principles Viz: a Body & a Soul' and 'That Energy. calld Evil. is alone from the Body. & that Reason. calld Good. is alone from the Soul' (E 34). Blake here breaks with the body–soul dualism which is the basis for Lavater's arguments. Possibly in response to Lavater he creates a triangular situation: the material body has to be transcended and judgements about it are always only of a preliminary nature. Body and soul are one; and this one is all energy. Problems arise from how one man perceives another, because statements about human identity are derived from the material body and determined by the methodological tools used in visual analysis. Blake warns us against abstracting generalizations and the fallacy of the five senses, because they can only ever discern a 'portion of Soul' – though he himself has a tendency to generalize, especially in the 'Proverbs of Hell' from *The Marriage of Heaven and Hell*.

So what does a body based on energy and indistinguishable from the soul look like? Blake's use of colour is emblematic of inherent preliminary states and flexible bodies. Traditionally, skin-colour in Blake has been regarded as part of a system of racial classification. David Bindman argued that black in Blake is a metaphor for sin. Skin-colour, moreover, changes across the different versions of 'The Little Black Boy':

> In the terminal design there are however significant differences in the coloring from one copy to another. The Black Boy is seen to be freed from the cloud of his blackness but in most early copies he is shown as white whereas in some later copies he is emphatically colored black by Blake's hand.[58]

Black does not always signify sin. Dark skin-colour is not only part of the slavery theme in 'The Little Black Boy' or *Visions of the Daughters of Albion* (1793); it can also be associated with resurrection, redemption or liberation, that is escape from darkness, as for example in *America*[59]:

> Let the slave grinding at the mill, run out into the field:
> Let him look up into the heavens & laugh in the bright air;
> Let the inchained soul shut up in darkness and in sighing,
> Whose face has never seen a smile in thirty weary years;
> Rise and look out, his chains are loose, his dungeon doors are open.
> [. . .]
> They look behind at every step & believe it is a dream.
> Singing. The Sun has left his blackness, & has found a fresher morning
> (*America*, Plate 6:6–13, E 53)

'The Little Black Boy' shifts the metaphor of the body being a 'cloud' to a simile: the body is 'like a shady grove' (E 9). In the Tate Trust edition of the *Songs* this line is glossed with a reference to idol worship.[60] Thinking in terms of body–soul relationships, the 'shady grove' may be an allegory, describing a certain kind of human existence. A reference to the body as 'cloud' can be found in Blake's annotations to Emanuel Swedenborg's *Divine Love and Divine Wisdom* (1778), possibly written in the same time-frame as 'The Little Black Boy' and *Essays on Physiognomy*: 'Think of a white cloud. as being holy you cannot love it but think of a holy man within the cloud love springs up in our thought. for to think of holiness distinct from man is impossible to the affections. Thought alone can make monsters, but the affections cannot' (E 603). Why should a 'shady grove' be less abstract than a 'cloud'?

> And we are put on earth a little space,
> That we may learn to bear the beams of love,
> And these black bodies and this sun-burnt face
> Is but a cloud, and like a shady grove.
> ('The Little Black Boy', Plate 9:13–16, E 9)

A 'grove' is less abstract than a 'cloud' because it concretizes a certain kind of human existence. Lauren Henry has argued that the poetic combination of a black body with a 'cloud' (transient and abstract) is a comment on the 'African speaker's struggle to construct an identity [. . .] the image of the protected grove is set up in opposition to the sun and to Christianity'.[61] The black boy is taught under a tree and watches the rising sun from the shade. He envisages a seemingly happy future:

> For when our souls have learn'd the heat to bear
> The cloud will vanish we shall hear his voice.
> Saying: come out from the grove my love & care,
> And round my golden tent like lambs rejoice.
>
> Thus did my mother say and kissed me,
> And thus I say to little English boy.
> When I from black and he from white cloud free,
> And round the tent of God like lambs we joy:
> ('The Little Black Boy', Plate 10:17–24, E 9)

However, both 'cloud' and 'shady grove' are metaphors for the body. What makes 'The Little Black Boy' a problematic statement about human relations is voiced in the poem's final stanza: its protagonist has internalized a social role:

> Ill [*sic*] shade him from the heat till he can bear,
> To lean in joy upon our fathers knee.
> And then I'll stand and stroke his silver hair,
> And be like him and he will then love me.
> ('The Little Black Boy', Plate 10:25–28, E 9)

Both the 'cloud' and the 'shady grove' can be, once again, transposed to the act of casting or providing shadow. The black boy will give shade and thus subordinate his own needs to those of the white boy. In return he will be loved. The voice of the final stanza is – to use Althusser's term – a fine example of interpellation. It articulates happily the socio-political situation of a slave whose body may be used for comfort and shelter. Nothing will change any time soon, because all that can be done is to wait until God calls for both of them.

The notion of a universal connection between human beings is emphasized in Samuel Stanhope Smith's *Essay on the Causes of the Variety of Complexion and Figure in the Human Species* (1787), reviewed by *The Analytical Review* in December 1788.

While physiognomical diversity could be recorded according to geography, climate and behaviour, the similarities between individuals were down to universal like-heartedness. In relation to sentimental psychology this establishes understanding as based on emotion and more specifically simple, innocent feeling:

> An acquaintance with the human heart has ever been thought important [. . .]; those who feel lively emotions wish to know if the same string vibrates in another bosom – if they are indeed tied to their species by the strongest of all relations, fellow-feeling – in short, if the world without resembles that within. [. . .] But observing the human heart, we may be said to work under ground [. . .]; the jealousy or ambition that actuates our antipodes is not supposed to differ from the passions which agitate us, – nor can the fortitude of an Indian [. . .] be distinguished from the pride or virtue which made many heroes endure grievous calamities.[62]

Even earlier than Smith, Thomas Clarkson and James Ramsay argued that skin-colour depended on climatic conditions.[63] For these environmentalists colour is a variable in human identity. It connotes a state of human existence and physically manifests itself on the surface of the body. For Blake the bond between individuals and across ethnic groups is established as a spiritual rather than a physical resemblance.

Blake's fascination with Africa tends to be now discussed in connection with Blake's relationship with the Swedenborgians. Indeed, abolition and Swedenborgianism go hand in hand. One founding member, the Swede Carl Bernhard Wadström, together with Augustus Nordenskjölk developed a plan to set up an African colony, a community of blacks and whites in Sierra Leone on the West Coast of Africa.[64] David Worrall has now drawn our attention to the possibility that Blake was especially attracted to the 'theological foundation' of the Swedenborgian venture, its emphasis on conjugal love and the idea that Africa was an uncorrupted Eden-like country.[65] In the poem, Blake has the black boy remember the teachings of his mother: 'Look on the rising sun: there God does live / And gives his light. and gives his heat away' (E 9). This suggests that Africans are better adjusted to the sun and thus are closer to God but further away from rational intelligence.[66] Blake allows the black boy to project the idea that the African can be shield or mediator to the European: 'For when our souls have learn'd the heat to bear / The cloud [the body] will vanish we shall hear his voice' (E 9). The boy's longing for equality, based on the whiteness or purity of the soul, has a sad ring to it: judging, as Bindman did, from the illustration, the positioning of the two boys still suggests or rather reaffirms racial hierarchy: 'Ill [*sic*] shade him from the heat till he can bear, / To lean in joy upon our fathers knee' (E 9).[67] But is this giving 'shade' to the disadvantaged white body a permanent arrangement? Blake's point here is that bodies change by adapting to their respective environments: in this instance, through the tanning which means that the white boy will become black eventually. All is well, as long as the soul is white. The fundamental difference between the three characters of 'The Little Black Boy' is how they project the connection between their white souls and black bodies. In contrast to the mother, seemingly unaware of her privileged though heathen situation, the son has doubts as well as thoughts about Christianization. He wants to be *like* the English boy. Instead of appealing to the universally human, Blake has a victim of racial discrimination re-emphasize a limiting belief system. In 'The Little Black Boy' he flaunts the paradox of the European soul within an African body. What is sad about this poem from *Songs of Innocence* is that although Africa is closer to God, the black boy cannot be happy in Africa.[68] Such a combination of 'European soul within African body' is compelling, especially in connection with *The [First] Book of Urizen* where Blake again identifies Africa with the cradle of civilization. Does he suggest that the European type comprises all those who have been able to redeem themselves since the Fall? The features of this type approach neoclassical perfection but is the spiritual body of the white European also superior? Swedenborg's remarks on race and, in particular, Africans are in *The True Christian Religion* (1781). He considers the English to be in need of spiritual 'Moderators':

> With respect to the People of England, the better Sort amongst them are in the Centre of all Christians, in consequence of possessing an interior intellectual Light; [. . .]. That light however is not active of Itself, but is rendered active by others, particularly by Men of Note and Authority, and shines with peculiar Brightness whensoever such Men declare their Sentiments. For this Cause the English in the spiritual World have Moderators set over them, and Priests allotted them, of distinguished Character, and great Talents, in whose Judgment they acquiesce by reason of this their natural Disposition.[69]

According to Swedenborg the Africans have no problems following his theological deliberations: the Africans are 'as sun-worshippers' ('He who is the Sun of the Angelic Heaven') and are equipped with 'interior Rationality' and 'interior Vision'.[70] Next to thematic links there is a strong argumentative parallel between Swedenborg and Blake's ideas of embodied ethnic relationships: the African is closer to the idea of primordial man and his faculties, because his ability to endure love is superior. Yet he cannot be happy. We have come full-circle, because part of any discussion about Africa and in particular Sierra Leone is colonial speculation. With speculation comes missionary work and not necessarily false exploitation since the initial impulse of the Sierra Leone scheme was idealistic.[71]

While points of view and attitudes to Africa seemed well defined, it is curious that those to Asia were amorphous. Camper, for example, concerned with the characterization of human types, divided mankind into four categories: Negro, Calmuck, European and Antique. He started with the skull of a Negro, arranged animal skulls to its left and put the skulls of a Calmuck, a European and a sculpture of an antique to its right.[72] To explain the absence of a representative of the Americas in his ascending scale of human beauty, Camper explains – and he has a point – that the American is really only a variation of the Asian type. They crossed the Bering Strait and wiped out the original American people: 'The many journeys also taken from Russia, through Siberia; and more particularly the celebrated voyage of the late Capt. Cook, afford additional proofs of the fact.' He decided to use the Calmuck as an example of 'all Asia (from Siberia to New Zealand) and also North America'. South Americans, according to Camper, were mostly descendents of Europeans.[73] Reinhold Forster, on the other hand, claimed that there existed 'two great varieties of people in the South Seas'.[74]

Dignified gestures involving the noble black body are a much contested point.[75] A plate which has sparked constant critical commentary is the one which juxtaposes three ethnic groups: 'Europe supported by Africa & America'. These figures have often been compared to the three goddesses of joy, charm and beauty from classical mythology, Rubens's painting of three voluptuous white women with different hair-colour and Raphael's same-looking women with apples. The most obvious difference is that Blake's three women face the viewer. The black and the white girl hold hands, while holding onto a rope or ribbon, and the American, whose head is significantly lower, seems to bear the brunt of Europe's weight. We might have expected Blake and Stedman to idealize the Europe-figure and to Europeanise Africa and Asia,[76] and yet we are confronted with a face-triptych with deeply embedded sentiment about a given inequality.[77] Stedman, in his verbalization of this allegory about ethnic harmony, justifies the absence of Asia: 'I might have included Asia, but this I omitted, as having no connection with the present narrative.'[78] The development away from the goddesses towards three idealized women of different ethnic origin, once again, raises the question about reification and control.[79]

Asia does not escape idealization. While Blake was apprenticed to James Basire in the 1770s the Basire workshop produced exquisite engravings after William Hodges for James Cook's *A Voyage towards the South Pole, and Round the World* (1777).[80] Part of the images illustrating the Cook expedition was a portrait of Omai (Mai), a native of Polynesia brought back from the South Pacific. When Omai stepped offboard the *Adventure* he was adopted by Joseph Banks and quickly became a London celebrity.[81] In 1775–6 he was painted by William Hodges, William Parry and Joshua Reynolds.[82] In 1776 *Omai* by Reynolds was exhibited at the Royal Academy and in 1777 an engraving after Hodges, done by James Caldwell, was published with Cook's *Voyage to the South Pole*. Omai, according to Cook's first description, was not perceived as either happy or beautiful. While Reynolds and Parry's paintings, commissioned by Joseph Banks and probably based on a sketch by Nathaniel Dance, generalized Omai's facial features by giving him a somewhat 'oriental' or orientalized dignity,[83] Hodges's painting, commissioned by John Hunter,[84] as well as Caldwell's engraving, nicely exemplify the ideological gap between sitters and their portraits: even more than Hodges, Caldwell renders the image according to the neoclassical taste of the Royal Academy. In many contemporary satires, however, Omai was used to embody what society was lacking.[85] Reification and control, within the context of the Royal Academy, meant that bodies underwent cultural appropriation, just as in Camper's combination of national physiognomy with the idea of human perfection.

A comparison of Blake's illuminated works with plates he was commissioned to engrave is problematic and has at least limited potential. As Morris Eaves in 'On Blakes We Want and Blakes We Don't' (1996) pointed out, to understand 'The Little Black Boy' we need to read it alongside 'The Chimney Sweeper'.[86] I have argued that we need to look at the commercial engravings, the situation of their production as well as their protoscientific medical contexts. While in the 1790s Blake argues that man has 'no Body distinct from his Soul', anatomists, anthropologists as well as physiognomists, struggle with a theoretical model which prescribed causal body–soul relationships. At the core of it all is a belief in a common human origin. What is at stake here is how human identity can be determined. To appreciate fully the degree to which Blake's notion of the 'Human form divine' (E 13) may be regarded as a liberating notion it is important to understand the various attempts at man-made human forms.

## Notes

1  'The Little Black Boy' is a two-plate poem. On the second plate the skin-colours of the little black boy range from pink, light and dark brown to the slightly purple color of Jesus's gown (copy Z, 1826, Library of Congress).
2  The noble body is much argued about in Mellor 1994: 69–94, Wood 2002: 94–106, Youngquist 2003: 70–86.
3  Tim Fulford, Peter J. Kitson and Debbie Lee have worked extensively on the concept of race in the Romantic Age and within the context of British colonialism. See Kitson 1999; Fulford and Kitson 1998; and Lee 2002.
4  Hudson 1996: 247–64; Curtin 1965: 28–57, 227–43.
5  White 1799: 42.
6  Camper 1794: 1.
7  Camper 1794: 16–17, 22, 59; Robert Paul Willem Visser 1985: 97, 100–3.
8  Forster 1778: 252–84. Charles White, who uses Camper's gradation argument, is more realistic about the skin's potential to change and adapt to different climates (for example White 1799: 130–3).
9  It was common practice in Enlightenment racial science to associate each continent with different skin-colours; see Hudson 1996: 255. Camper, on the other hand, argued that the influence of food and climate on body shape was relative (1794: 17, 28).
10  Graham 1979; Johnson 2004: 52–74.
11  Essick 1983: 150–7.
12  Allentuck 1967: 89–112; Hall 1985.
13  Essick 1991: 40–1.
14  Thomas Holcroft's 1789 translation of the abridged German edition (1783–7) gives four types of national physiognomy in its chapter on skulls: German, East-Indian, African and Calmuc or Tatar; Lavater 1789: I: 224–6. National physiognomy and those who wrote about it – among them Camper – are in Volume 3. This chapter has no illustrations (Lavater 1789: III: 85–127. Henry Hunter's translation of the new and revised French edition (1781–1803) has the same four categories as the Holcroft translation. The four skull-types, both in profile and front view, are arranged on one plate and thus easier to compare (Lavater 1789–98: II: plate facing 165. This Hunter translation makes only two references to Camper: Lavater 1789–98: III: 106, 160. The extensive visual material is in Volume 4 of the French edition published as late as 1803. This volume was never translated into English.
15  Gilchrist 1998: 63.
16  Barbara Stafford discusses the connection between engraving and dissection (1991: 54–72). Tristanne Connolly has emphasized the importance of life drawings from corpses for Blake and in relation to William and John Hunter (2002: 34–9, 79–81).
17  See King James Bible, Genesis 1. 27.
18  Hudson 1996: 250.
19  Todd 1972: 173–81 (175); Essick 1980: 51.
20  Weinglass 1994: 91.
21  Essick 1991: 40–1; Todd 1972: 174.
22  Stemmler 1993: 164–5.
23  Essick 1991: 41.
24  Le Brun 1701: 45–7. Blake was familiar with Charles Le Brun, one of the painters and body-theorists revised by Lavater. While working in the library of the Royal Academy in

1779 and when being offered advice by its Keeper George Moser, Blake resolutely rejected the paintings of Le Brun and Rubens; see Gilchrist 1998: 30.

25  Todd 1972: 176.
26  *The Monthly Review* 66 (1782): 489. 'If the nose, as our author observes, is the distinctive mark of a LUMINOUS UNDERSTANDING, he has, without perceiving it, composed his own panegyric in this assertion; for to judge from three profiles which lie now before us, M. Lavater has one of the largest, most humane and fine-turned noses which we have met with.' *The Monthly Review* 70 (1784): 142.
27  Lavater 1789–98, trans. Hunter, I: 108. Holcroft annotated: 'By *Caricature*, the Author appears to mean nothing more than an imperfect drawing.' Lavater 1789, trans. Holcroft, I: 107.
28  Reisner 1979: 481–503; Gourlay 2002: 97–147.
29  Lavater 1789–98, trans. Hunter, II: 106, 159–61.
30  Camper 1794: viii.
31  For racial science see Kitson 2001 and for trade in skulls see Fulford 2001: 91–116, 117–33.
32  Camper 1794: 9.
33  Camper 1794: 70–4.
34  Hall 1985: 27–9.
35  Winckelmann 1766: 2–31. See also Potts 2000: 96–101, 108–12.
36  Tannenbaum 1982: 191.
37  Frye 1947: 212; Blake 1995a: 127–8, 347–8.
38  Winckelmann 1765: 30.
39  Bindman 1997: 97–106 (103). For 'transcendent communication', see Bindman 2002: 100.
40  For possible anti-Semitism in Blake, see Shabetai 1996.
41  Pestalozzi 1975: 286–7.
42  Lavater 1789–98, trans. Hunter, III: 182.
43  Wechsler 1993: 119.
44  Lavater 1789–98, trans. Hunter, II: 407–8.
45  Bindman pointed out that Camper knew William Hunter, Professor of Anatomy to the Royal Academy from 1768 to 1783. Both William and his brother John were interested in comparative anatomy; Bindman 1997: 104.
46  Lavater 1789, trans. Holcroft, III: 86.
47  Lavater 1789, trans. Holcroft, III: 124–5, 127.
48  White 1799: 47.
49  Damon 1988: 309.
50  Blake 1995a: 27–35, 40–2.
51  Lichtenberg 1967–72, II: 688; Fischer and Strumpp 1989.
52  Lavater 1789, trans. Holcroft, III: 85–6.
53  Wechsler (1993) foregrounds Lavater's anti-Semitism (107, 114).
54  For the 'generalizing trend in European writing during the eighteenth century', see Hudson 1996: 251.
55  Lavater 1789–98, trans. Hunter, I: 237.
56  In 'Of national characters' David Hume essentializes racial difference. In a footnote he elaborates on the inhabitants of the northern and southern hemispheres: 'I am apt to suspect the Negroes [. . .] to be naturally inferior to the whites. There never was a civilized nation of any other complexion than white, nor even any individual eminent either in action or speculation. [. . .] Not to mention our colonies, there are negroe slaves dispersed all over Europe, of which none ever discovered any symptoms of ingenuity; tho' low people, without education, will start up amongst us, and distinguish themselves in every profession. In Jamaica indeed they talk of one negroe as a man of parts and learning; but 'tis likely he is admired for very slender accomplishments, like a parrot, who speaks a few words plainly.' (Hume 1758: 125).

57 Kant 1960: 111.
58 Bindman 1997: 98. See also Easton 2005.
59 Blake 1995a: 57–8; Blake 1993: 138–9.
60 Blake 1991: 150.
61 Henry 1998: 80.
62 *The Analytical Review* 2 (1788: 7. 431).
63 Ramsay 1784, pl. 9; Clarkson 1786: 211; Smith (1787: 23).
64 Paley 1985: 17.
65 See Chapter 2 of this volume.
66 Blake 1991: 148–50; Coleman 2005: 104–5.
67 Bindman 1997: 101.
68 See also Richardson 1990: 233–48.
69 Swedenborg 1781, II: 437 (para. 807).
70 Swedenborg 1781, II: 453, 455–6 (paras 837, 838, 839).
71 Curtin 1965: 88–119.
72 Camper 1794: 9.
73 Camper 1794: 15, 20–1.
74 Forster 1778: 228.
75 For the clashing opinions of Stedman, Johnson and Blake, see Rubinstein and Townsend 1998: 273–98. For Blake's friendship with Stedman, see Bentley 2001: 115–16. Essick has stressed further that 'the dignified postures and expressiveness of the figures' were most likely Blake's stylistic improvements. Similar alterations can be argued for New South Wales aborigines, engraved for John Hunter: Essick 1991: 64–5, 71.
76 Mellor 1994: 82.
77 Apart from the noble bodies and dignified gestures, the faces of these three figures could be in accord with the scale of national physiognomy (as expounded by Camper 1794: 4–9).
78 Stedman 1796, II: 395, illustration facing page 394.
79 Mary Louise Pratt has pointed out that Stedman's *Narrative* became a European success because of its account of European jungle warfare next to Stedman's romance with the mulatto slave Joanna (1992: 90–102).
80 Thomas 2004: 27–34.
81 Omai was dark but not black or like a 'negroe'. His skin-colour may have been 'copper'. For practices of racial categorization see Douglas 1999.
82 In the Archive of the National Portrait Gallery there is yet another portrait, engraved by a J. Page after an unknown artist in 1774. See NPG D9162.
83 Guest 1992: 105, 107, 112.
84 Joppien and Smith 1985: 64–6.
85 Smith 1985: 80, 81–5.
86 Eaves 1996: 413–39.

# 8 Africa and Utopia: Refusing a 'local habitation'

## Susan Matthews

Reading Swedenborg's *Heaven and Hell*, Blake is provoked by an annotation already written on his copy, the famous line from *A Midsummer Night's Dream*: 'And as Imagination bodies forth y[e] forms of things unseen – turns them to shape & gives to airy Nothing a local habitation & a Name.' Blake's response is: 'Thus Fools quote Shakespeare The Above is Theseus's opinion Not Shakespeares You might as well quote Satans blasphemies from Milton & give them as Miltons opinions' (E 601). Blake's irritation at first seems puzzling: wasn't he the one who suggested that Satan spoke for Milton? And surely giving form to things unseen is a perfect account of his commitment to an embodied imagination. In this chapter I am going to suggest that Blake's argument with this line derives from his fear of territorializing the imagination, of finding 'a local habitation'. It may be no accident that the comment is written on Swedenborg's *Heaven and Hell* as the involvement of the London Swedenborg Society with utopian schemes in Africa could provide a case in point of the danger of attempting to locate Utopia.[1] In the plan for a settlement at Bulama, as in the plan to resettle British blacks in Sierra Leone, Africa is imagined as an empty space rather as in earlier utopian fantasies set in Africa, such as Berington's *Signor Gaudentio*: 'They made for the highest hills they could see, from whence they perceived an immense and delicious country every way; but to their greater satisfaction, no inhabitants' (Berington 1763: 52). This place with 'no inhabitants' is also one which can be seen as a vast prospect, laid out to the traveller. This chapter asks whether Blake's Africa is a place with no inhabitants, a utopian land to be constructed as the imagination dictates.

Even if he disapproves of Theseus's account of the imagination, Blake remembers the line: it is echoed by the voice of the emanations at the opening of *Milton*, Book 2:

> But the Emanations trembled exceedingly, nor could they
> Live, because the life of Man was too exceeding unbounded
> His joy became terrible to them they trembled & wept
> Crying with one voice. Give us a habitation & a place
> In which we may be hidden under the shadow of wings (pl. 30 [33]: 21–5: E 129)

Here the desire for 'a habitation & a place' is associated with femininity, limitation, and with retreat from 'the life of Man'. Fear of the 'unbounded' thus produces Beulah, a state which perhaps embodies some of the qualities of utopian writing: it is a place separated from the conflicts of the wider world. Whereas the forest in *A Midsummer Night's Dream* fails to provide an escape, replicating the social hierarchies of the court from which the lovers flee, Beulah is seen as moony, feminine, contained. Perhaps it could be equated with Fuseli's lament for the loss of a public culture of art: 'The ambition, activity, and spirit of public life is shrunk to the minute detail of domestic arrangements – every thing that surrounds us tends to show us in private, is become snug, less, narrow, pretty, insignificant.'[2] In this chapter, however, I want to propose a wider meaning: that Blake's dislike of Theseus's formulation lies in its attempt to translate the universal into the specific, individual or local. We are familiar with Blake's belief in minute particulars. But to particularize is not the same as to locate. Local identities are here rejected by an imagination that refuses to know its own place: it is Urizen who will proclaim: 'Let each chuse one habitation:/ His ancient infinite mansion:' (E 72). The 'ancient infinite mansion' sounds all too Burkeian, a place in which identity is fixed by inherited estate. Blake's angry annotation suggests hostility to the idea of a fixed identity, one rooted in place, race, station or inheritance.

Writing on civic humanist art theory, John Barrell insists that Blake's use of the word 'individual' has been comprehensively misunderstood. Instead of representing a belief in the uniqueness of the individual, he argues, it belongs with Milton's older idea of an identity which cannot or should not be divided from its source: 'as the OED defines it – "that cannot be separated, inseparable"; "forming an indivisible entity; indivisible" '.[3] Barrell also quotes Johnson's definition: 'undivided; not to be parted or disjoined', and comments: 'It is not so much that an "individual soul" cannot be, it should not be divided, from other souls, or from Christ' (Barrell 1986: 242). I want to explore here what such a sense of identity might mean for Blake's writing on place and on race. If the work of the poet is not to provide 'a local habitation & a Name', what kinds of meanings can we give to his writing about specific places?

Given that Blake's poems are full of place names – deriving one of their most distinctive effects from lists – it is perhaps strange to claim that they are not about place. Compare, though, how his friend Fuseli, strongly aware of being a foreigner in England, writes in his 1767 *Remarks on Rousseau* of Rousseau's unhappy experiences in England:

> He should have known that the *English* have no compliments for their friends; – hence the pretended neglect of salutations: – that they are extremely shy to address, or to enter into conversation with a foreigner, even if he speaks the language – that their shyness increases in proportion, if he does not.[4]

It makes sense, then, that Erasmus Darwin's description of a nightmare in his poem *The Botanic Garden* should not only draw on Fuseli's famous 1781 painting *The Nightmare* but also praise the work through an allusion to the lines from *A Midsummer Night's Dream*:

> –Such as of late amid the murky sky
> Was mark'd by FUSSELI'S poetic eye;
> Whose daring tints, with SHAKSPEAR'S happiest grace,
> Gave to the airy phantom form and place. –[5]

The comparison of a Swiss artist to the national poet Shakespeare is highly flattering, and the lines endorse Fuseli's ability to give form to the imagination.

The refusal of Blake's visual images to illustrate in this sense, running in counter-point to the words rather than providing a literal visualization, is one of the clichés of Blake criticism. But it is also both true and an expression of his refusal of Theseus's concept of the imagination.

As a writer who left London only for a brief stay on the Sussex coast, Blake has no reason to distinguish a national from a universal identity. Despite a scheme to send him to Rome in 1784, he never travelled. Whereas the dual functions of Albion as Britain and eternal man might sound like the grandiose ambitions of empire, one of the reasons why it is not is that Blake has no concept of otherness: Englishness as national character only exists abroad. His failure to travel is one key to the absence of a sense of place, or of national identity: Blake's writing about Africa (or the Orient) exists in a different mode from that of contemporary travel writing – like for example Stedman's or the work of James Bruce which Blake's patron William Hayley so much admired.[6] Perhaps the closest that Blake comes to travel writing is in *The Marriage*, where he provides a parodic account of a travel writer exploring and recording the customs of hell: 'As I was walking among the fires of hell, delighted with the enjoyments of Genius; which to Angels look like torment and insanity. I collected some of their Proverbs: thinking that as sayings used in a nation, mark its character, so the Proverbs of Hell, shew the nature of Infernal wisdom better than any description of buildings or garments' (E 35). Once again, the Swedenborgians, about whom he is thinking in *The Marriage*, are the butt of the hostile account of the traveller. Maps, of course, do not feature in Blake's writing: he is willing to comment politely on the fantasy cartography of Malkin's six-year-old son, Thomas, who invented 'a visionary country, called Allestone', and recorded the towns and rivers of the island kingdom in a detailed map.[7] But maps are replaced by diagrams in Blake's illuminated poetry in which the points of the compass become parts of a pattern, the individual element subjugated to the meaning of the whole.

Recently a number of writers have suggested that Blake's writing reveals a particular interest in Africa. This is the implication of Lauren Henry's ' "Sunshine and Shady Groves": what Blake's "Little Black Boy" learned from African writers'.[8] Henry traces links between the language of 'The Little Black Boy' and a poem by Phillis Wheatley, 'An Hymn to the Morning', through the shared phrase 'shady groves'. Henry argues that 'Wheatley's intense preoccupation with the sun . . . can be traced to African origins' reflecting a memory of African ideas of God (Henry 1998: 75–6). Via this link, Blake's poem is made to reveal its roots in African culture, bearing out Nelson Hilton's perception that Blake identifies 'particularly with "black" '.[9] And yet, much as we might like to wish this pun on Blake, blackness in his writing often appears to be the result of the Fall. In the *Song of Los*, the imposition of Urizenic law is followed by what sounds like a fall into blackness: 'Adam shudderd! Noah faded! black grew the sunny African' (E 67). If the verbs work in parallel, then the negativity of 'shudderd' and 'faded' prepare us to read 'grew' as an equally negative process. It seems likely that blackness here reads as a move away from the perfection of the eternal body. I am persuaded by Alan Richardson's reading of 'The Little Black Boy' which finds the negative account of blackness voiced by the boy to be the false consciousness imposed by a missionary culture.[10] But, for the moment, I want to remember that at the end of the poem, the boy loses his blackness in heaven. In 'A Song of Liberty' a form of limitation seems to afflict not only the 'citizen of London' and the 'Jew', but also the African: 'O African! black African! (go. winged thought widen his fore-head)' (E 44). Just as the Jew is seen as conventionally a money-lender, the black African here is denied intellect.[11] We might wonder whether the 'Song of Liberty' fails to liberate its own concepts.

Is it therefore appropriate to bestow on Blake's writing the glow of authenticity derived from a link with African culture, and indeed is authenticity a valid source of authority? Does it matter that Blake should value blackness, and is his writing better if it acknowledges African roots? The recent debate over Equiano's account of his African childhood provides a parallel: his use of white-authored texts to construct his own memory of his childhood in Africa has been used to support the claim that that his account is fictional, a necessary part of his abolitionist narrative which conceals his true birthplace in South Carolina.[12] It is understandable that Henry wishes to root the familiar eighteenth-century poetic formula 'shady groves' in an African reality as a means of restoring a lost Africanness to the culture of Wheatley and via her to Blake. But perhaps Africa rightly belongs in the *Song of Los* to the Little Black Boy, to Phillis Wheatley and to Olaudah Equiano in whose *Interesting Narrative* Africa is a lost Eden, lost to memory and laboriously reconstructed through the white texts about the continent. If this is so, then it is the diaspora of the slave trade which turns Africa into a lost land, threatening to destroy even its memory. In *The Song of Los* as in *The Book of Urizen*, Africa is associated with the heart: 'heart-formed'. Yet the lack of recognizable punctuation also allows us to conclude that Africa is in England:

> And on the mountains of Lebanon round the deceased Gods
> Of Asia; & on the desarts of Africa round the Fallen Angels
> The Guardian Prince of Albion burns in his nightly tent (19–21 E 68)

As in the *Visions of the Daughters of Albion*, Blake seems aware that when writing of other continents and cultures, he is writing about the imaginations, fears and sympathies of the British: 'Africa' and 'Asia' tell of the imaginings of the mental traveller, imaginings that confuse geographic categories.

## 1 Addressing the Sun

In his own copy of *The Marriage of Heaven and Hell*, Blake's friend George Cumberland added the title 'Satan's Address to the Sun' to Plate 21, the image of a man looking upwards. In doing so, Cumberland reads the image as an illustration to *Paradise Lost IV*, where Satan's sense of exile turns to anger at the sun:

> to thee I call,
> But with no friendly voice, and add thy name
> O sun, to tell thee how I hate thy beams
> That bring to my remembrance from what state
> I fell (IV: 35–39)

This is a role that Equiano had already taken in *The Interesting Narrative* of 1789 where he quotes the words of Beelzebub in *Paradise Lost* II: 232–40, words which threaten revolt: 'What peace can we return? / But to our power, hostility and hate; / Untam'd reluctance, and revenge, tho' slow'. As Equiano warns the British reader: 'Are you not hourly in dread of an insurrection?'[13] Blake reuses the image of a man looking up to the sun for Plate 6 of *America* but his lines reverse the meaning, telling not of exile but of a return to a lost paradise, imaged in the act of seeing the heavens. Since looking is being for Blake, this action enacts liberation:

> Let the slave grinding at the mill, run out into the field:
> Let him look up into the heavens & laugh in the bright air; (pl. 6: 6–7: E 53)

But the trope of the address to the sun can also take on a meaning which is specific to the abolition campaign. One of the justifications for slavery lay in the argument that only negroes could work effectively in the torrid zone. Stedman, for instance, claims that: 'The quantum of sugar, &c will be had, and must be provided by negroes, natives of Africa, who alone are born to endure labour under the vertical sun.' (Stedman 1796: 1, 203). We can hear an echo of this argument, significantly changed in meaning, in the voice of the mother in Blake's 'The Little Black Boy' who tells her son:

> And we are put on earth a little space,
> That we may learn to bear the beams of love . . . (E 9)

Here blackness is proof of direct exposure to God: looking up to heaven is the ability to see the divine. Blackness is not the result of being 'bereav'd of light' (E 9) as her son has come to believe, but proof of an ability to withstand the sun's beams. Yamba in Hannah More's 1795 *Cheap Repository* tract poem believes in her own inner darkness, the guilt of man's sinfulness that is part of evangelical Christianity: 'Oh ye slaves whom massas beat, / Ye are stained with guilt within'.[14] In Blake's versions, the sun is equated with the 'beams of love', with access to God. Blackness therefore is proof not of lack of light or of sin but of an ability to 'look up into the heavens & laugh in the bright air'.

Lauren Henry argues that 'The Little Black Boy' draws on Phyllis Wheatley's 'An Hymn to the Morning', a poem quoted by Thomas Clarkson in *An Essay on the Slavery and Commerce of the Human Species* (1786) as evidence of the intellectual powers of the African mind.[15] But Clarkson's respect for Wheatley's 'Hymn' probably derives from its ability to use a familiar poetic language derived from Milton's *Paradise Lost*, although her version of the address to the sun echoes not Satan's angry lament, but Adam's morning hymn of praise, a hymn which explicitly sets God above the sun: 'Thou sun, of this great world both eye and soul, / Acknowledge him thy greater' (V:171–4). By contrast, Wheatley's poem sets the sun above all, and just as in Blake's poem, shows his rays too strong for the onlooker:

> But Oh! I feel his fervid beams too strong,
> And scarce begun, concludes th'abortive song. (32)[16]

Allusion to Milton does not necessarily bring with it his theological position: it is common in the period both to invoke the address to the sun and to find in the passage a pre-Christian, pagan or universalist form of worship. The most famous passage in Ossian was the address to the sun which ends *Carthon*, and Macpherson's note points to the similarity with Satan's speech in *Paradise Lost*. This version, spoken by the blind poet Ossian, links Satan with Milton, drawing on both Satan's address to the sun and Milton's invocation to Light: 'Whence are thy beams, O sun! thy everlasting light?' The anger of Milton's Satan here turns to melancholy: 'But to Ossian, thou lookest in vain; for he beholds thy beams no more.'[17] The new emphasis is on transience, the mortality of the poet and the contrast between age and youth, a meaning which may have a specific resonance in the politics of Scotland.

We might assume that a key meaning of the sun is that it signals the universal: it is impossible to locate within one discourse or debate. But to stress the universal force of the image at this period is also potentially to signal an interest both in pagan religions and in comparative mythography. Both Payne Knight and Erasmus Darwin were fascinated by the idea that primitive religions included sun worship. As Marilyn Butler explains, they 'believed that the key lay in a universal sexual myth. Critics of Christianity's claim to unique revelation had picked out the host of rituals and fables from all cultures which appeared to imitate the action of the sun impregnating matter – and thus implied that early man worshipped the driving force in nature, the principle of life itself.'[18] Similarly, contemporary utopian tales set in Africa feature sun worship. In George Cumberland's 1798 *Captive of the Castle of Senaar*, the worship of the sun is not presented as a pagan religion, but as a supremely enlightened celebration of the life force, of Holy Energy. The inhabitants of Sophis see the sun as 'one of the eyes of the universe, through which the eternal Energy emits what light it is pleased to bestow on us'.[19] Cumberland's utopia is interesting both because it was warmly received by Blake, a lifelong friend, but also because his network of friendships helps to define a set of interests and associations with Africa. Cumberland was also a friend of the naturalist Henry Smeathman, whose advice was instrumental in the selection of Sierra Leone as the site of an attempt to relocate poor London blacks in 1786.[20] This was a project which Cugoano viewed with some scepticism, despite initial support. Cumberland, like William Hayley, was also interested in James Bruce's African travel writing, and it is clear that he sets his African utopia just beyond the limit of Bruce's own exploration of the sources of the Nile, beyond Sennaar and beyond the mountains of the moon.[21]

Another source, identified by G. E. Bentley, is the earlier African utopia *The Adventures of Signor Gaudentio*, first published in 1737 as the work of Simon Berington, but republished many times, including in *The Novelist's Magazine* of 1785.[22] Cumberland's utopian community sees in the sun 'that glorious body of fire now above us, the origin and support of all natures here' (Cumberland 1798: 82). In *Signor Gaudentio*, sun worship appears as a pagan religion, but he describes how the action of the sun images a Shaftesburyan model of 'systematic benevolence', a sociability that is 'reciprocal, and regulated' (ibid. 82). Cumberland's utopian fantasy clearly also draws on Swedenborg. Cumberland was a friend of the Swedenborgian sculptor John Flaxman, the man who probably introduced Blake to Hayley and, in *The Wisdom of Angels*, Swedenborg uses the sun to explain the nature of divinity: 'Some Idea of Love, as being the Life of Man, may be had from the Heat of the Sun in the World'.[23] But whereas the sun functions as a simile for men, it is the image of God for angels: 'Divine Love, appears before the Angels in Heaven as a Sun' (Swedenborg 1788: 5). Kathleen Raine quotes Swedenborg's comment that 'The Worship of the Sun is the lowest of all Kinds of Worship of a God' and argues that at the ending of 'The Little Black Boy' sun worship as a primitive pagan religion has been displaced by a belief in God.[24] But much of Blake's work from the mid 1790s suggests by contrast that the sun is a valid image of God; to the eye of vision (as in the last plates of *Jerusalem*) everything is human anyway. If blackness is fallen in the *Song of Los*, the epithet 'sunny African' reasserts the closeness of the African to the divine. In calling him 'sunny' he is linked with one meaning of the title character, Los, whose name is (amongst other things) a backwards image of Sol, the Sun (perhaps particularly obvious to Blake as he wrote on the plate in mirror writing). Blake's poetry and his art repeatedly use the sun to figure the divine. In the 1805 watercolour, *The River of Life* (Figure 8.1), illustrating lines from the Book of Revelation, the throne of God is represented simply as the sun ringed with angels, the source of the river of life. The river lined with classical buildings seems to belong to a world like that of Cumberland's utopian city of Sophis; a neoclassical civilization set just off the map drawn by James Bruce. The river here is an idealized version of the Nile, freed from the darkness, tyranny and superstition implied in Fuseli's *Fertilization of the Nile*:

Neither Cumberland in his utopian city of Sophis nor Swedenborg in his visionary account of heaven present sun worship as a form of pagan African religion. For Cumberland it is worship of a first cause, of Holy Energy; for Swedenborg it allows the imagination of the divine. Yet for both of them, the African setting is significant. Africa is seen as the source of a lost wisdom, one which Europe, the 'corrupted continent' in Cumberland's tale, needs to recapture.[25] According to Swedenborg, it is Africans who recognize most clearly

**Figure 8.1** William Blake, 'The River of Life', *c.* 1805. Pen and ink and watercolour on paper. [The Tate – Tate, London 2005.]

the nature of God: 'The Gentiles, particularly the Africans, who acknowledge and worship one God the Creator of the Universe, entertain an Idea of God as of a Man, and say that no one can have any other Idea of God' (Swedenborg 1788: 11). In all of these examples, the African setting is important not as difference, but as retaining a lost wisdom.

## 2 Utopian Africa

In an Ode addressed to the explorer James Bruce, William Hayley imagines the 'Social Arts' waiting on Bruce's yet unpublished account of his travels:

> They ask what Afric's unknown genius taught,
> Lost knowledge to revive, or aid inventive thought.[26]

Hayley, along with the Swedenborgians, was interested in a particular piece of 'lost knowledge' that Bruce had recovered. This was a manuscript of the Book of Enoch, a work that had survived in the West only in fragments in Greek translation. Already by 1785, when he published *An Essay on Old Maids*, Hayley was aware of the most famous story that Enoch tells, the love of the fallen angels for the daughters of men. Enoch's story is a longer version of a story in Genesis 6, telling of events which led up to the flood, of a time in which erotic love as a form of miscegenation produced a race of giants. The full manuscript was discovered by Bruce in Abyssinia, brought back to Europe and described by him in his *Travels to Discover the Source of the Nile* in 1790. Perhaps this is one model for the work of the traveller to hell in *The Marriage* who collects proverbs and sayings (E 35). The story is particularly important for ideas about Africa since the most familiar account described the Africans as the descendants of Noah's son Ham (in *The Song of Los*, the sons of Har). The flood with which God punished human sinfulness brought to an end a time in which 'There were giants in the earth' (Gen 6.4). For Blake and a number of other writers it seems that the Genesis story, elaborated in the lost Book of Enoch, of an antediluvian world of imagination and sexual desire carried a power which could not be contained by the wrath of a God who judges that 'every imagination of the thoughts of [man's] heart was only evil continually' (Gen 6.5). Through this association, the Nile takes on an association with erotic love for Hayley and others. It is an indication of the continuing connection between the sun and the Enoch story that Byron uses it in *Manfred* (1817), in another address to the sun:

> Glorious orb! The idol
> Of early nature, and the vigorous race
> Of undiseased mankind, the giant sons
> Of the embrace of angels, with a sex
> More beautiful than they, which did draw down
> The erring spirits who can ne'er return. (III.II: 4–9)

Just as the events that Enoch describes precede the biblical flood, so Fuseli's illustration 'The Fertilization of Egypt' for Darwin's poem *The Botanic Garden*, which Blake engraved (Figure 8.2), takes on an association with the erotic. The flooding of the Nile brings fertility in both human and agricultural senses. In Cumberland's African utopia, erotic love is celebrated as 'the chief link of our society . . . the root of our morals, and the object of our silent devotion'

**Figure 8.2** Henry Fuseli, 'The Fertilisation of Egypt', in Erasmus Darwin, *The Botanic Garden; a poem, in two parts*. London: printed for Joseph Johnson, 1791. [Reproduced with permission from the British Library.]

(Cumberland 1798: 37). Doctors prescribe sexual healing: 'it is no uncommon thing for one of these sages to prescribe a sexual connection, as a remedy for the apparent disorders of the mind' (ibid. 69–70). Young people cohabit freely: 'for they are fully sensible of the dangers arising from the suppression of the natural fires' (ibid. 44). Cumberland also imagines a society in which polygamy is acceptable (even if not a frequent practice, due to the requirement that it is accepted by the first wife). Cumberland is careful, however, to distinguish the sexual freedoms of his imaginary utopia from the fabled sexual tyranny of the harem; his narrator tells of growing up in Turkey and of the death of one of the women in the seraglio who is implicated in an affair. Africa is used to construct a fabulous land distinguished from the associations of particular geographical places. His Sophians are unlike the surrounding Africans, light in colour and modelled in many respects on Cumberland's idea of Greece, reflecting his enthusiastic neoclassicism.

Nevertheless, the African setting for his sexual utopia is not accidental. Polygamy was one of the African practices that the evangelicals involved in the Sierra Leone Company aimed to eradicate. As Hannah More's friend and collaborator, Henry Thornton, wrote: 'Every measure will be taken for laying a foundation of happiness to the native, by the promotion of industry, the discouragement of polygamy, the setting up of schools'.[27] In contrast, Bruce's *Travels* contains a lengthy defence of polygamy in 'Mahometan' society, arguing that it 'secured civil rights to each woman, and procured a means of doing away that reproach, of *dying without issue*, to which the minds of the whole sex have always been sensible.'[28] David Worrall has recently argued that Blake in *Thel* provides a critique of the sexualized role of women in Swedenborgian plans for colonization. James Bruce, however, sides with the controversial pro-polygamy argument of Martin Madan's *Thelyphthora*, a work which produced a storm of discussion, parody and refutation on its publication in 1781.[29]

## 3 Climate and race

'Black grew the sunny African' seems to fit with theories which argued that human beings belonged to one race, differentiated in skin tone (and perhaps in behaviour) through climatic influences. This belief would fit with the monogenetic beliefs common amongst abolitionists in the period. Even though there are limits to his abolitionism, Stedman is explicit in his belief that human beings form one race, distinguished simply by the effect of climate and the sun's rays:

> These are the most probable reasons why the Americans are of a copper-colour or red, and the inhabitants of Africa, called Negroes, are black, *viz.* the one being more burnt by the sun than the other, and not because they are two distinct races of people: since no person who examines and reflects, can avoid seeing that there is but one race of people on the earth, who differ from each other only according to the soil and the climate in which they live. (Stedman 1786: 380)

Similarly, Cugoano, the black London writer Blake is most likely to have known (since he worked as a servant to the artist Richard Cosway) and whom he mentions in his notebook fragment *An Island in the Moon*, is explicit in his statement that all men belong to one race: 'For God who made the world, hath made of one blood all the nations of men that dwell on all the face of the earth.'[30] The question then is whether Blake's writing shares the assumptions about the effect of climate on character that mark, say, Adam Ferguson's 1767 *Essay on the History of Civil Society*. Ferguson associates particular human characteristics with the extremes of hot and cold climates, of south and north. In some ways, his model of climate and geography seems to fit the mapping of the north and the south lands on to the human body which is implicit in the figures of Urizen and Orc in the 1790s prophecies. Ferguson claims that the north is associated with a lack of passion, with a fear of change, with sluggishness, and that the south is marked by sexual passion. Blake's association of Urizen with the frozen north, with the caverned head and with rationality; and Orc with the fires of desire, the loins, the southern lands, seems to fit this model. According to Ferguson, the northerner (here the Laplander) is 'dull rather than tame; serviceable in a particular tract; and incapable of change' (Ferguson 1767: 173). The southern lands are associated with heightened passions and with sexuality, with 'The burning ardours, and the torturing jealousies, of the seraglio and the haram, which have reigned so long in Asia and Africa' (ibid. 176–7). But Ferguson also argues that the influence of the sun is to depoliticize, to make people too easily content to challenge tyranny. Mary Wollstonecraft's 1792 *A Vindication of the Rights of Woman* seems to mirror

Ferguson's ideas, assuming like him that the torrid zone is a place which tends to make for political quiescence:

> But, if from their birth men and women be placed in a torrid zone, with the meridian sun of pleasure darting directly upon them, how can they sufficiently brace their minds to discharge the duties of life, or even to relish the affections that carry them out of themselves?[31]

For Wollstonecraft and for Hannah More, it is only in the temperate zone that people are likely to find a balance between reason and passion, to be capable (respectively) of romantic love or of Christian devotion. In *Coelebs* (1809), Hannah More imagines the moderation of true Christianity in climatic terms:

> 'How many men have I known', replied Mr Stanley, smiling, 'who, from their dread of a burning zeal, have taken refuge in a freezing indifference! As to the two extremes of heat and cold, neither of them is the true climate of Christianity; yet the fear of each drives men of opposite complexions into the other, instead of fixing them in the temperate zone which lies between them, and which is the region of genuine piety'. (II: 258–9)[32]

Although More believes that Christianity can be exported to torrid zones by missionary work, the temperate zone nevertheless functions as her image of true judgement. Zeal and indifference (the climatic extremes of Christian devotion) are equally available to 'men of opposite complexions': More, like Blake, uses the language of race in a way which is irrespective of location.

Stedman's *Narrative of a Five Years' Expedition* for which Blake engraved a number of illustrations in 1793 parallels some of Ferguson's assumptions about the relationship between climate, race and sexuality. Arriving in Surinam, Stedman is struck by the free sexual mores of the white settlers, concluding that: 'Dissipation and luxury appear to be congenial to the inhabitants of this climate' (Stedman 1786: 27). Whilst Surinam often appears Edenic in the *Narrative*, the climate is often invoked at moments of fear, not only in his vivid account of the dangers and suffering he encounters in his mission to repress slave revolts, but also in the Kurtz-like warning he receives from a settler, Mr Klynham: 'But the climate, the climate will murder us all' (ibid. I: 135). The fear of imminent abolition tips Stedman over into a view of slaves as savage: 'The national character of these people [negroes], as I have remarked it, where they are as free to act by their own will and disposition as in Africa, is perfectly savage' (ibid. 203). Yet Stedman's narrative also at times resists the assumption that knowledge and civilization come from Europe, as in the eloquent put-down of an Indian to a Swedish missionary: 'Do you then really believe, that we and our forefathers are all, as you would teach us, condemned to suffer eternal torments in another world, because we have not been taught your mysterious novelties?' (ibid. I: 382). As an attack on religious imperialism this seems to parallel the statement in *The Marriage*: 'For all nations believe the jews code and worship the jews god, and what greater subjection can be' (E 39).

If Blake's monogenetic model of race is indeed modified by ideas about climate, then the meanings associated with north and south are significantly changed. Wollstonecraft's implicit valuation is reversed and Ferguson's preference for the balanced exertion of the temperate zone forgotten in favour of the clash of contraries exerted by the extremes of climate. If Urizen is sent by the Eternals to 'the north' (pl. 2: 3 E 70) and fights his vain battle for control 'In his hills of stor'd snows, in his mountains / Of hail & ice' (pl. 3: 32–3 E 71), the sexualized Orc of the Preludium to *America* is identified by the Shadowy Female with Africa:

> Thou art the image of God who dwells in darkness of Africa;
> And thou art fall'n to give me life in regions of dark death. (pl. 2: 9–10 E 52)

His effect is to bring about a revolution of sensual awareness in which the females will be 'naked and glowing with the lusts of youth' (pl. 15: 22 E 57). A conventional representation of the Last Judgement, with heaven at the top and hell at the bottom, overlays the geographical model. But if Africa becomes hell the conventional valuation is reversed.

## 4 Art and Eden

In contrast to the climatic model of Ferguson, Wollstonecraft and More, which favours the temperate zone, is one which imagines Africa as the location of Eden. Instead of defining the 'torrid zone' as the place where 'the vertical rays of the sun' destroy the capacity for intellectual resistance to oppression, the sun figures as the source of energy and of political liberation in Blake's writing. The slave here labours indoors, the free man escapes to the light of the sun. It is the little black boy, who can 'learn to bear the beams of love', and the little girl lost, who can 'Naked in the sunny beams delight' (E 29) that show the possibility of political and sexual liberation.

Despite the problems that Stedman encounters, the *Narrative* often describes the flora and fauna in Edenic terms: 'To use the figurative language of the sacred book, Surinam was a land that flowed with milk and honey' (Stedman 1786: 75–6). It is like a 'large and beautiful garden, stocked with everything that nature and art could produce, to make the life of man both comfortable to himself, and useful to society'. Stedman's Surinam is not just a garden but a place which contains 'art' and 'all the luxuries, as well as the necessaries of life'. Annotating his copy of Reynolds' 1798 *Works* Blake finds himself arguing with the assumption that civilization moves from 'necessaries to accommodations'. Reynolds claims that: 'The regular progress of cultivated life is from necessaries to accommodations, from accommodations to ornaments.' Blake answers:

> The Bible says That Cultivated Life. Existed First – Uncultivated Life. comes afterwards from Satans Hirelings[.] Necessaries Accomodations & Ornaments [are Lifes Wants] <are the whole of Life> (E 637)

Whereas Reynolds assumes a Fergusonian stadial model of progress, Blake's utopian vision refuses this model: it is Satan's hirelings that destroy 'Cultivated Life' and 'Ornament'. The portrayal of Surinam as Eden fits within the conventions of abolitionist writing of the time – familiar from Equiano's *Interesting Narrative*, as from the writing of white abolitionists. The trope is a rejection of the pro-slavery argument that the slave trade released African prisoners from a life of hardship in Africa. But Stedman also refuses the notion of Surinam as a primitive utopia in his insistence on the presence of art and of luxury. Similarly, Cumberland's Sophians cultivate art and luxury, though using commerce only for 'immediate barter' (Cumberland 1798: 79). Strikingly he refers to 'innocent luxury': 'We ate out of bowls of fine porcelain; reposed on exquisitely soft yellow mattresses; and, in a word, partook of much innocent luxury, amid such magnificence as is unknown in Constantinople' (ibid. 61). 'Ornament' is a key word for Cumberland, as for Blake, signifying the means by which art dignifies existence. Cumberland's, Blake's and Stedman's Eden is therefore one which borrows from a neoclassical ideal of the civilized city of art, located, in Cumberland's imagination, beyond the source of the Nile, and representing a civilization which is free from the political tyranny associated with Egypt and with Sennaar, the African places known through the narratives of travellers. But then Cumberland does not portray his Sophians as black Africans. Although they live in the heart of Africa they are imagined as being of Greek descent and they are separate from the 'simple Africans' of the surrounding community. Berington's African utopia, like Cumberland's, imagines a community who settle in an uninhabited part of Africa. Berington's Mezzorainians are racially pure: 'they have neither wars, nor traffick with other people, to adulterate their race' and are 'brown, but their features are the most exact and regular imaginable; and in the mountainous parts, towards the line, where the air is cooler, they are rather fairer than our Italians' (Berington 1763: 61). Berington's African utopia seems in many ways like the 'southern clime' of Blake's 'A Little Girl Lost' and 'The Little Girl Found' of *Songs of Experience*, in which Lyca (a name strikingly like Cumberland's Lycas) sleeps 'in desart wild':

> Leopards, tygers play,
> Round her as she lay; (E 21)

Isaiah, rather than the Africa of European travellers such as Bruce, returns in Blake's and Berington's utopias as a place of wildness without threat. Gaudentio sees a 'large lion come out of the grove, about two hundred paces below me, going very quietly to the spring to lap: when he had drank, he whisked his tail two or three times, and began to tumble on the green grass' (Berington 1763: 33). In its utopian mode, Blake's writing refuses geographical specificity. The lions and tygers in the *Songs* belong to the familiar imagined world of childhood, which for Wheatley, Equiano and Cugoano is Africa, even if that Africa is constructed from the Bible, from Milton and from the writing of white travellers. But the conventions of climate theory are also resisted. Urizen is placed in the north, but he also has 'dark deserts' (pl. 5: 14 E 73), in *The Book of Urizen*, Los throws 'his right Arm to the north, / His left Arm to the south'. Perhaps his attempt is to put the separated qualities of north and south back together again. The association between Orc and Africa is made by the Shadowy Female, but I would like to argue that she is wrong on all counts: Orc is not a god, nor does God live in specific geographical places. She sees him as living 'in darkness of Africa' in America (pl. 2: 8 E 52), yet the association of darkness with Africa is a sign of her own failure to recognize the closeness of Africa to a knowledge of the divine lost to Europe. The poem describes Orc not as black or white, but red. Blake's figures of the Ancients in the *Descriptive Catalogue* were seen by contemporaries as oddly red in colour. According to Blake, this redness is due to 'The flush of health in flesh exposed to the open air' (E 545).[33] In insisting on the reddish colour of healthy skin, Blake echoes a debate in Cumberland's *Captive* where pictures also represent flesh as surprisingly red: 'The picture was much applauded – but to my then weak judgment it seemed, though pleasing in one respect, preposterous –

every flesh protuberance being so warm that I called it a red woman' (85). Lycas is told that 'The fleshy parts of muscles are red, porous, and consequently are the warm parts of the body'. Blake links the red colour to the circulation of blood, and in doing so shows his preference for transparency, revealing the internal organs of the body – muscles, blood – which are shared by all human beings, rather than the surface of the flesh. Indeed translucence seems to be an important quality for Blake: it is characteristic of the watercolour which is used to add colour to many of his illuminated books. In *The Four Zoas*, Night the Seventh, the work of Enitharmon is to colour in the lines drawn by Los 'with beams of blushing love' (E 370): this description of watercolour links the method with the words of 'The Little Black Boy' where the beams of the sun are 'beams of love'. Translucence is the quality of watercolour that allows the beams of sunlight to pass through. As Tristanne Connolly stresses, Blake's ideal is 'of a transparent body like a transparent garment which reveals rather than covers' (Connolly 2002: 15). Engraving Stedman's illustration of the arrival of the slave ship after the middle passage, Blake uses the same technique of cross-hatching for the skin of the slaves and for the jacket of the slave-driving sailor. Skin-colour thus becomes a garment, something which is not inherent in the individual. Blake again follows Cugoano, who writes:

> It does not alter the nature and quality of a man, whether he wears a black or a white coat, whether he puts it on or strips it off, he is still the same man. And so likewise, when a man comes to die, it makes no difference whether he was black or white, whether he was male or female, whether he was great or small, or whether he was old or young; none of these differences alter the essentiality of the man, any more than he had wore a black or a white coat and thrown it off forever. (Cugoano 1999: 41)

Cugoano, baptized like Blake at St James's Piccadilly, shares with Blake a similar conceptualization of racial difference. Oothoon's colour in *The Visions* has thoroughly confused Blake's readers, causing problems for those who want to see the poem as 'about' slave-rape. In his highly literal reading in *Slavery, Empathy and Pornography* Marcus Wood insists on Oothoon's whiteness, arguing that she is a white English woman who takes a journey to America and is raped by a slave-owner.[34] But Oothoon could also be read as an example of a blindness to race and colour in Blake which stands at the opposite extreme to Stedman's careful delineation of degrees of racial intermixture. Blake sees blackness as a result of the Fall in precisely the same way as north is separated from south in *The Book of Urizen*, or masculinity from femininity. To this extent, Blake's writing (as Saree Makdisi has argued) (2003a) seems to require a universalist perspective which ignores racial and geographical definitions.

## 5 Political Africa

According to Vincent Carretta, up to 20 per cent of London's population in the late 1780s may have been black.[35] For London's blacks, the choice of an African identity seems to have been a political act, as when some of the most prominent and politically active black campaigners against the slave trade wrote as 'Sons of Africa'. Whereas Blake writes the voices of the daughters of Albion, these writers choose identities which are not those of a particular African nation, but that of the continent itself. Ottabah Cugoano is described as 'a Native of Africa' on the 1787 title page of *Thoughts and Sentiments*; Equiano is 'Olaudah Equiano, or Gustavus Vassa, the African' in 1789. If Englishness only exists abroad, African-ness, similarly, is the product of exile. But it is a different conception of Africa from that of English travellers to the continent. James Bruce's expensive five volume set of *Travels* ends with maps which specify location in terms of degrees from a Greenwich meridian: 'all laid down by actual survey with the largest and most perfect instruments now in use. By His Majesty's most dutiful and faithful servant James Bruce.'[36] Bruce is much preoccupied in his journeys with the instruments he takes with him to help him to map new lands. In doing so he contributes to a sense of Britishness, not only through his exploration, but also through situating African places in relation to Greenwich. The larger scale map, showing the whole of the Nile, represents Jerusalem centrally, at the top, whilst Nubia, the mountains of the moon and Sennaar are at the bottom. The disposition of the map can be read once again as a version of the Last Judgement, showing the ascent from the 'darkness of Africa' to the heavenly city. As Marcus Wood points out: 'Cartographic theorists increasingly see maps and myths of national power as intertwined'.[37] In 1798, an anonymous caricature 'The Night Mare or the Source of the Nile' uses Fuseli's famous painting to represent Nelson sitting on Emma Hamilton lying on a huge round bed and lifting up her flimsy nightdress.[38] The chamber pot carries the words: 'Source of [the] Nile' and the book on the bedside chair is 'Bruce's / Travels etc'. Africa becomes the feminized place of conquest, the prize which Britain has just won from France in the Battle of the Nile at Aboukir on 1 August 1798, which allowed the British to cut the French army off from France. Thomas Clarkson made a rather different use of the river image to portray the abolitionist campaign as the work of European campaigners in his *History of the Rise, Progress, and Accomplishment of the Abolition of the African Slave-Trade by the British Parliament*.[39] His book opens with a map of an imaginary river, in which the campaigners against slavery form the tributaries that flow into the great sea of abolition. Despite his sense of humanity as one race, Blake's conception of the imagination rejects the idea of a single source, suggesting that the imagination of any individual can access inspiration. In his image of the River of Life, the figures swim, or fly, upstream towards the source of light. In *The Book of Urizen*, creation is not the work of one man, but a binding of the multiple and shifting identities of eternity.

    If Blake is worried about providing 'a local habitation & a Name', his writing is also continuously aware of the limitations of utopian thinking: there are times at which the specificities of politics and power require the writer to use names in a sense quite other than the neoclassical world of civic humanism that Barrell describes. In *Milton* Book One it is the sons of Los who 'surround the Passions with porches of iron & silver . . . / Giving to airy nothing a name and a habita-tion / Delightful!' (pl. 28 [30]: 1, 3–4 E 125). Blake in any case is not always of the civic humanist world of public art. He is also a traveller within his own culture, a mental traveller for whom London and Felpham are some of many contact zones. Blake is well aware of the internal boundaries of England, ones which mark off individual identities within the nation. Hannah More's sister, Patty, chronicling the sisters' attempt to bring education, religion and conformity to the Mendips in the year 1798 to 1799 in *The Mendip Annals* (More 1859), compares the villagers to blacks. To the sisters it is clear that it represents a kind of internal missionary work. The parodic travel writing of *The Marriage* hits home in its recognition that England, like Africa, contains multiple worlds.

At times (perhaps determined by political contingency) it is clear that there is a place called Africa that is not located in the Mendips, a place with its own history. In *Jerusalem* Africa seems to carry out Equiano's threat of 'imminent insurrection':

> When Africa in sleep
> Rose in the night of Beulah, and bound down the Sun & Moon
> His friends cut his strong chains, & overwhelm'd his dark
> Machines in fury & destruction, and the Man reviving repented
> He wept before his wrathful brethren, thankful & considerate
> For their well timed wrath. (pl. 40 [41]: 19–24 E 187–8)

Here, anger resists the limitation of Beulah's 'local habitation'. If black skin seems like a garment in the engraving to Stedman, there is surely something more sinister in the statement that Albion's 'machines are woven with his life'.

The concept of states (places like Beulah, which are not located) allows Blake to escape the association of places with fixed identities. Perhaps it is the lack of a concept of individual identity that makes Blake believe that he can write from the identities of those in his own culture, Londoners from Africa, who are travellers: Los reflects the sun (and their experience of loss) as a mirror image. Whether this is possible is not for me to judge.

## Notes

1  See Deirdre Coleman's account of utopian schemes in *Romantic Colonization and British Anti-Slavery* (2005). David Worrall also discusses Swedenborgian schemes in Chapter 2 of this book.
2  *The Life and Writings of Henry Fuseli*, ed. John Knowles, 3 vols, London, 1831, 3: 45–9.
3  Barrell 1986: 242.
4  Fuseli 1768: 116–17.
5  Darwin 1991: 93
6  See Stedman 1796 and Bruce 1790. Stedman's title belongs to the same genre as Bruce's in its claim to scientific accuracy.
7  Malkin 1806: 93.
8  Henry 1998.
9  Nelson Hilton, 'Blake's Early Works', 191–209 in Eaves, 2003, 200.
10  Richardson 1994: 153–66.
11  See Lauren Henry's discussion of the contemporary debate about African intellectual potential, Henry 1998: 72.
12  See Vincent Carretta, 'Introduction' in Equiano 1995: x–xi.
13  Equiano 1995: 112.
14  See Richardson (2002), who demonstrates conclusively that this element of self-loathing is added by More to a poem originally by Eaglesfield Smith.
15  Henry 1998: 74.
16  Phillis Wheatley (2001), *Complete Writings*, ed. Vincent Carretta, Penguin: New York and London.
17  *The Poems of Ossian* (1896), trans. James Macpherson, introduction by William Sharp, Edinburgh: Geddes, 184.
18  Butler 1981: 129.
19  Cumberland 1798; 1991: 62.

20  Ferguson 1992: 199.
21  See G. E. Bentley, 'Introduction', Cumberland 1991: xiv. Cumberland's Commonplace Book contains an anecdote about James Bruce.
22  As Bentley points out, one of Blake's projects as a commercial engraver was for *The Novelist's Magazine*, though he did not work on the 1785 issue that includes *Signor Gaudentio*, xxviii.
23  Swedenborg 1788: 3.
24  Raine 1968: 13.
25  Cumberland 1991: 36.
26  Bruce 1790.
27  Henry Thornton, Report of the Sierra Leone Directors, 1791, pp. 49–50, quoted in Ferguson 1992: 209.
28  Bruce 1790: I, 286.
29  Worrall (see Chapter 2) follows Helen Bruder in reading Thel's rejection of sexuality as endorsed by the poem, a reading that, whilst it may make Blake's account of sexuality more palatable, seems difficult to sustain in relation to other of Blake's texts of the 1790s.
30  Cugoano 1999: 29. According to Carretta, this is an imagined quotation.
31  Wollstonecraft 1994: 124.
32  More 1809.
33  My argument here is suggested by Jon Mee's study of the role of blood in *Blake Nation Empire* (2006), ed. Steve Clark and David Worrall.
34  Wood 2002: 183.
35  Vincent Carretta, introduction to Cugoano 1999: x.
36  Bruce 1790: Volume V, map.
37  Wood 2000: 5.
38  See Weinglass 1994: 63.
39  Wood 2000: 1. See Clarkson (1808), facing page I, 258.

# 9 An Empire of Exotic Nature: Blake's Botanic and Zoomorphic Imagery

## Ashton Nichols

In numerous Romantic literary works, the exotic East is represented in complex, multivalent terms. Asia in these texts is described as inviting yet mysterious, beautiful yet fearful, alternately beguiling and terrifying in the diversity of its natural and human riches. The very concept of such natural riches became a crucial part of the discourse of empire. Ever since Edward Said's *Orientalism*, scholars have debated the extent to which Western culture misrepresented Asia in the production of these varying discourses of domination. These analyses of Western attempts to construct textual versions of the East have, however, produced less attention than we might expect to one of those discourses, the discourse of natural history. While many scholars have noted Mary Louise Pratt's linkage of travellers' descriptions of nature to the ideology of empire, fewer have elaborated on the way that poetic metaphors drawn from nature are directly appropriated into the language of politics. Likewise, Saree Makdisi argues that 'the "civilizing mission" of modern British imperialism can be seen as one of planetary "domestication," through which [. . .] the entire world could be absorbed into the bosom of gentle English domesticity' (Makdisi 1998: 118), yet little subsequent discussion has developed links between such 'domestication' of the 'wilds' of exotic nature. Critiques of Orientalism have focused on the effects of naturalistic discourse on human culture, yet it is clear that the details of these representations of the natural world were also a crucial source for Western constructions of the East.

Most recently, Tim Fulford, Debbie Lee and Peter J. Kitson have linked the global study of botany and natural history to the rise of British imperialism. In *Literature, Science and Exploration in the Romantic Era*, they examine the 'Indian botany' of Sir Joseph Banks and, more importantly, 'its effects on imperialist thought and its influence on literature'; according to Fulford, Lee, and Kitson, Banks helped to 'precipitate new kinds of Orientalist scholarship and the new forms of verse that have come to be called Romantic' (2004: 71). In an earlier edited volume, *Romanticism and Colonialism: Writing and Empire, 1780–1830* (1998), Fulford and Kitson brought together essays that reveal the British Empire and Romanticism evolving along similar, if not always supportive, lines on issues such as race, Orientalism and the cultural construction of 'nature', human and otherwise. As Fulford and Kitson note in their introduction to this collection, 'Romanticism cannot be properly questioned without an investigation of its complicity with, and its resistance to, the colonialist discourses of a Britain becoming steadily more imperialist as the nineteenth century progressed' (1998: 12).

Just as numerous European writers sought to provide a history for those parts of the world that seemed to lack a history, natural historians from the mid-eighteenth century onwards offered textual accounts of previously undescribed versions of nature. Like descriptions of the human cultures of Asia seen through the eyes of Occidentals, nonhuman nature produced a Westernized narrative (Where had these apparently alien aspects of nature originated? How had they done so?); Western taxonomic categories (kingdoms, classes and species); and textual and visual records (here is what I saw in Japan; here is what a tiger or a panda looks like) of a world far beyond European society. Visions of the Eastern world took shape in the West, first in order to be described, later in order to be classified, and finally in order to be appropriated or conquered. Theresa Kelley, for example, notes the attraction of 'exotic' plants among the natural history illustrators of the late eighteenth and early nineteenth centuries. In many cases, the illustrated plants are 'made to look larger than the landscape features depicted behind them' (Kelley 2003: xi). In such instances, an ostensibly objective naturalist – in Kelley's example, Dr Robert Thornton – resorts to personification of an aggressive kind to convey the strangeness of the exotic Eastern plant:

> This extremely foetid poisonous plant will not admit of sober description. [. . .] She comes . . . with mischief fraught; from her green covert projects a horrid spear of darkest jet [black], which she brandishes aloft: issuing from her nostrils flies a noisome vapour infecting the ambient air [. . .] on her swollen trunk are observed the speckles of a mighty dragon; her sex is strongly intermingled with its opposite! Confusion dire! (Kelley 2003: xii [*Temple of Flora*, 1801]).

As this example suggests, even the natural world of new-found plants can quickly become a battleground for ideological and cultural discourse tied to the expansion of empire.

William Blake's poetry and visual images provide an excellent source for a discussion of these issues. As is often the case with Blake, however, the rhetorical situation is complex and oppositional. Famously, 'I must Create a System or be enslav'd by another Man's,' and yet, Blake's system creates an aesthetic empire in the process of speaking out against almost all forms of human empire-building: 'Empire is no more!' (*The Marriage of Heaven and Hell* 25: 20 E 45). In *Jerusalem*, according to S. Foster Damon, Blake refers to English acquisitions in Asia when he describes 'On the Euphrates Satan stood: / And over Asia stretch'd his pride' (*Jerusalem* pl. 27: 48–9 E 172). In the same work, during the imagined time of Blakean innocence, 'the skiey tent' of mankind 'reached over Asia' (60: 17). It is clear that Blake's naturalistic imagery is drawn not only from his understanding of British and European natural history, but also from his emerging sense of the exotic plants and animals that were making their way, literally and in textual accounts, from the four corners of the earth to London. By the time Blake is writing in the 1790s, tigers and rhinoceroses could be found in British zoos and menageries, and countless species of tropical and Asian plants were growing and reproducing in English gardens and hothouses. In this regard, Blake can be positioned as part of the shift, recently analysed by Robert J. Richards (2002) in *The Romantic Conception of Life: Science and Philosophy in the Age of Goethe*, from earlier paradigms of Linnaean taxonomy towards later Romantic and vitalist models of biology.

Blake's botanic imagery is filled with a sense that the plant and animal kingdoms intermingle in numerous, often interdependent, ways. If we doubt the importance of botanic imagery to Blake, we need only consider this passage from his prophecy *Milton*:

Thou perceivest the Flowers put forth their precious Odours!
And none can tell how from so small a center come such sweets
Forgetting that within that Center Eternity expands [. . .]
               [. . .] listening the Rose still sleeps
None dare to wake her. soon she bursts her crimson curtaind bed
And comes forth in the majesty of beauty; every Flower:
The Pink, the Jessamine, the Wall-flower, the Carnation
The Jonquil, the mild Lilly opes her heavens! every Tree,
And Flower & Herb soon fill the air with an innumerable Dance
Yet all in order sweet & lovely . . . (pl. 31 [34]: 46–8, 56–62 E 131)

The best way to establish the impact of natural history on Blake's botanical images, however, is through several direct comparisons.

Blake's plants, in many of his descriptions and illustrated plates, bear interesting connections to more strictly scientific natural history illustrations of the period. Erasmus Darwin's plate of the Amaryllis (*Amaryllis formosissima*) (Figure 9.1) and

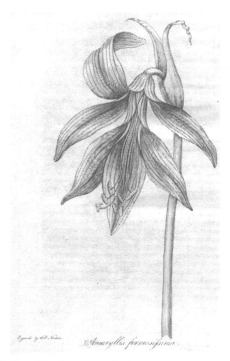

**Figure 9.1** *Amaryllis* from *The Botanic Garden* by Erasmus Darwin (1791), grandfather of Charles.

Gloriosa flower (*Gloriosa superba*) (Figure 9.2) from *The Botanic Garden* (1791) provides accurate botanical renderings of two lush and lavish plant species. The blossoms are anatomically correct down to their stamens and pistils, and the petals and leaves curl with a careful naturalistic irregularity. Blake's comparable plates from 'The Blossom' (Figure 9.3) and 'Infant Joy' (Figure 9.4) in *Songs of Innocence* (1789) reveal the extent to which Blake's imagery was directly affected by natural history illustration. His compositions echo the page layout and designs of works like Darwin's and seek to achieve the same sort of 'regular' irregularity often found in botanical drawings. At the same time, Blake's plants in both plates are clearly products of his imagination; neither are actual specimens that could be found in nature. The illustration of 'The Blossom' actually lacks a blossom; Blake renders a more leaf-like exfoliation designed to frame the poetry and hold the humanized angel figures at the top of the plate. 'Infant Joy' offers a somewhat more realistic image, but the leaves here suggest no actual species, and the flower is clearly designed to hold the human figures rather than to reflect any literal blossom from the natural world.

One of Blake's strangest images is also drawn directly from his awareness of contemporary works of natural history. The frontispiece to *For the Sexes: The Gates of Paradise* (1793) (Figure 9.5) depicts a curious image that accompanies a later aphoristic verse: 'The Catterpiller on the Leaf / Reminds thee of thy Mothers Grief' (E 268). Blake depicts a plump caterpillar munching its way through a leaf and hanging over the larval body of a second bizarre creature, an

**Figure 9.2**  *Gloriosa* from *The Botanic Garden*, 'The Loves of the Plants' (1791).

**Figure 9.3** A visionary plant from Blake's *Songs of Innocence* (1789), Plate 11. (Lessing J. Rosenwald Collection, Library of Congress. Copyright © 2005 the William Blake Archive. Used with permission.)

insect pupa with a beatific human face. The image echoes the page design of many insect natural history illustrations of the period. A beautiful plate by Jacob L'Admiral (1694–1770), first published in Amsterdam in 1774, for example, presents the precise relationship between caterpillars and leaves used by Blake (Figure 9.6). It matters little to my argument if Blake knew of L'Admiral's specific image. What a comparison of the two images suggests is the way styles of imagery drawn from scientific illustrations made their way into the visionary realm of Blake's imaginings.

Blake's well-known image of 'A Poison Tree' in *Songs of Experience* (E 28) provides another example of the discourse of natural history appropriated for poetic purposes. As so often, the natural object becomes an analogue for the human mind: 'And I waterd it [my anger] in fears, / Night & morning with my tears: / And it [my anger] grew both day and night. / Till it bore an apple bright.' Blake's 'poison tree' kills his foe, even though the location of this powerful plant is all in the mind: 'The Gods of the earth and sea, / Sought thro' Nature to find this Tree / But their search was all in vain: / There grows one in the Human Brain.' ('The Human Abstract' 21–4 E 27). Blake based these powerful images on a real tree. The species (the *upas* tree, *Antiaris toxicaria*) can still be found in Indonesia, where it was used traditionally as the source of a powerful toxin applied to spear tips and arrow points. But the tree on which Blake bases his poem is an Orientalist

**Figure 9.4** Humans in a blossom from *Songs of Innocence* (1789), Plate 25. (Lessing J. Rosenwald Collection, Library of Congress. Copyright © 2005 the William Blake Archive. Used with permission.)

invention, a powerful symbol that arrived in the West via one fallacious account, magnified through the words of a scientist, poet, and natural historian.

Here is Erasmus Darwin, describing the poison tree in 1791:

> Fierce in dread silence on the blasted heath
> Fell Upas sits, the Hydra tree of death.
> Lo! From one root, the envenom'd soil below,
> A thousand vegetative serpents grow;
>             [. . .]
> A thousand tongues in quick vibration dart;
> Snatch the proud eagle towering o'er the heath,
> Or pounce the lion as he stalks beneath;
> Or strew, as marshalled hosts contend in vain,
> With human skeletons the whiten'd plain.
>                         *(Botanic Garden* 2: 115)

Erasmus Darwin did not just invent this horrifying fantasy. He poetically and imaginatively recorded a 'scientific' account of the poison tree that had appeared in the *London Magazine* of 1783. Darwin's note records his source: 'There is a poison-tree in the island of Java, which is said by its effluvia to have depopulated the country [. . .] in a district of 12 or 14 miles round it, the face of the earth is quite barren and rocky, intermixed only with the skeletons of men and animals;

**Figure 9.5** Blake produced a plate clearly inspired by natural history illustration as the frontispiece to *For the Sexes: The Gates of Paradise*. The caption for this curious image ('What is Man! The Suns light when he unfolds it / Depends on the Organ that beholds it' E 260) is less cryptic than the couplet he wrote on the same subject: 'The Catterpiller on the Leaf / Reminds thee of thy Mothers grief.' (E 268) (Plate 1. Pierpont Morgan Library. Copyright © 2005 the William Blake Archive. Used with permission.)

affording a scene of melancholy beyond what poets have described or painters delineated' (Darwin 1791: 2: 115). Darwin's details derive from a text ostensibly produced by one N. P. Foersch, a Dutch surgeon. Foersch, about whom, somewhat mysteriously, virtually nothing else is known, describes his own natural history of this tree as 'simple unadorned facts, of which I have been an eyewitness' (ibid: 2: 188). He adds that, of the hundreds of malefactors who have been sent to collect the toxic gum resin that runs out between the bark and the tree, scarcely ten per cent have ever returned. He also describes a miasma from this tree that is carried on the wind and results in miles and miles of barren country: 'Not a tree, nor a shrub, nor even the least plant or grass is to be seen' (ibid: 2: 188). Finally, Foersch provides a powerfully Orientalist account of the origins of this tree, an account which he attributes to an old 'Malayan priest': 'The country around the tree was inhabited by a people strongly addicted to the sins of Sodom and Gomorrah; when the great prophet Mahomet suffered them not to lead such detestable lives any longer, he applied to God to punish them; upon which God caused this tree to grow out of the earth, which destroyed them all, and rendered the country for ever uninhabitable' (ibid: 2: 190). So a common species

**Figure 9.6** Caterpillars on leaves by Jacob L'Admiral (1774). (Copyright © 2005 University Rare Books, Special Collections Research Center, North Carolina State University Library. Used with permission.)

of Indonesian tree with poisonous sap, related to the mulberry and the breadfruit tree, becomes a quasi-demonic, devouring, Asiatic vegetative monstrosity. Here is another perfect example of the way Romantic Orientalism grew from its textual origins, even when those origins appeared in the apparently innocent discourse of natural history. In these examples, and others like them, Blake appropriates and imaginatively reconstructs a version of the East for purposes of his own poetic, painterly, often anti-imperialist critique of Western exoticism.

Consider, finally, representations of the Asiatic tiger. By the time William Blake imagines his own 'Tyger Tyger, burning bright, / In the forests of the night' in *Songs of Experience* (E 24–5) (1794), the European imagination is already saturated with descriptions of a mysterious and bloodthirsty creature that is often identified with wider characteristics of the regions in which it dwells. George Louis Leclerc, Comte de Buffon, had, by 1750, called the tiger 'the scourge of every country he inhabits', having 'no characteristics but those of the basest and most insatiable cruelty. Instead of instinct he has nothing but an uniform rage, a blind fury; so blind indeed, so undistinguishing, that he frequently devours his own progeny, and, if she offers to defend them, he tears in pieces the dam herself' (Buffon 1791: 132–3). A creature that sometimes kills its offspring and mate? Beware of any country that produces such an animal. As is stated earlier, 'the degree of fierceness' in certain creatures 'depends on the degree of heat in the land that produced them', and so the tiger is 'chiefly confined to the warmest provinces of the East' (Buffon 1791: 133). Beware also of warm provinces, this 'scientific' text implies. Buffon even goes so far as to offer an account of the tiger's ferocity based on class structure. The tiger is more vicious than the lion, says Buffon, because of his second-class status in the hierarchy of the cat family: 'The first class [the lion] is less tyrannical than the inferior classes, which, denied so full an assertion of authority, abuse the power with which they are entrusted' (ibid: 132). If this is true of animals, then perhaps Europeans should also beware of the ferocity of any humans who find themselves members of 'inferior' classes. Here we can see precisely how the seemingly neutral discourse of natural history might shade into the ideology of European colonial and imperial powers.

Oliver Goldsmith, whose *An History of the Earth and Animated Nature* drew many of its details from Buffon, adds that the tiger's 'disposition is as mischievous as its form is admirable, as if Providence was willing to shew the small value of beauty, by bestowing it on the most noxious of quadrupedes' (Goldsmith 1795: 2: 233–4). Goldsmith agrees with Buffon that the tiger 'seems to partake of all the noxious qualities of the lion without sharing any of his good ones [. . .] the tiger is fierce without provocation, and cruel without necessity' (ibid: 2: 235). This creature, 'though glutted with slaughter, is not satisfied [. . .] but levels all with indiscriminate cruelty, and scarce finds time to appease its appetite while intent upon satisfying the malignity of its nature' (ibid: 2: 235). Of course, tales of maneaters among this species stretch back to antiquity. But by the time of Buffon and Goldsmith, traits of the tiger are identified with more generalized claims about eastern culture and about the human beings that inhabit the same region: this creature, like the lands it comes from, is described as mysterious, sinister, ferocious and insatiable.

Goldsmith's 1795 plate of the tiger presents the creature in a very accurate naturalistic rendering (Figure 9.7). The size and scale of the animal is clearly

**Figure 9.7** A tiger from Oliver Goldsmith's *An History of the Earth and Animated Nature* (1795) (Engraved by Scot and Allardice. Archives and Special Collections, Dickinson College, Carlisle, PA. Used with permission.)

suggested. The eyes are vivid and intensely focused; the mouth is open slightly as if panting or preparing to strike. The strongly muscled body is evident, as are the prominent whiskers and the wide ruff around the sides of the face. The plate seems almost photographically realistic, even by today's standards of illustration. Blake's 'tyger', by comparison, is an unrealistic creature that seems unlikely to have been drawn from life. Surely the layout of Blake's page was influenced by his viewing of contemporary works of natural history, but everything else in this image seems drawn from the visionary realm (Figure 9.8). The tree that looms overhead is out of scale and unrealistic. Its branches come out from too low a spot along the trunk. Its size also seems wrong if we conceive of the tiger as a ten to twelve-foot long beast. Blake's has more of the look of an overgrown kitty-cat. In fact, the shape of the skull looks more like the head of a teddy bear than of a ferocious beast. The ears are almost panda-like. The creature looks scrawny and underfed as its broad chest tapers to an almost greyhound-like waist. The facial expression is dazed, in part because of the wide-open rendering of the eyes, but also because of the sad or confused straight line of the mouth.

We know very little about actual tigers in London in the 1790s, but it seems unlikely that Blake had seen the single haggard specimen that was apparently still alive in the menagerie of the king at the Tower of London in the 1790s. Henry I had begun the first royal British menagerie; his collection found its way eventually into the Tower of London where it remained until 1831. Stamford Raffles founded the Zoological Society of London in Regent's Park in 1826, but the grounds were not formally opened to visitors until 1828 and not to the general public (that is, without invitation or subscription) until 1846 (Altick 1978: 317). Lord Byron saw a tiger that 'talked too much' at the Exeter 'Change [Exchange] menagerie in the Strand in 1813 (*Journals* 1973–83: iii, 14 November 1813). Blake's tiger plate is more likely drawn from his own awareness of other illustrations of such creatures in natural history works such as Goldsmith's or Buffon's, but the actual animal we see depicted in the *Songs of Experience* (1794) is clearly also a product of Blake's naturalistic imaginings and has seemed to many viewers somehow inappropriate as a visual depiction of 'fearful symmetry' (24 E 25).

Blake may also have learned some of what he knew about tigers from the work of Thomas Bewick. When Bewick published his own *History of Quadrupeds* in England in 1790, he was clearly drawing on well-established accounts of the tiger. He notes that it is 'the most rapacious and destructive of all carnivorous animals' and 'is even said to prefer human flesh to that of any other animal' (Bewick 1790: 171). Bewick links the creature with precise geographic locations: 'The Tiger is peculiar to Asia; and is found as far north as China and Chinese Tartary: It inhabits Mount Ararat, and Hyrcania of old, famous for its wild beasts. The greatest numbers are met with in India' (ibid: 171). Bewick also emphasizes tigers' interactions with humans; this animal 'does not seem sensible to the attention of its keeper; and would equally tear the hand that feeds, with that by which it is chastised' (ibid: 172). His diction reminds us that creatures with keepers are always in cages, and that hands that feed often also chastise. Bewick includes an additional narrative in which a colonial party subdues this naturally rapacious feline in a surprising way: 'Some ladies and gentlemen being on a party of pleasure, under a shade of trees, on the banks of a river in Bengal, were suddenly surprised at seeing a tiger ready to make its fatal spring: One of the ladies, with amazing presence of mind, laid hold of an umbrella, and unfurling it directly in the animal's face, it

**Figure 9.8** 'Tyger Tyger, burning bright' (E 24). Blake's tiger from *Songs of Experience* (1794) seems gentler than Goldsmith's plate, but the pose of Blake's creature has surely been drawn from natural histories of the period. (Copy Z, Plate 42. Lessing J. Rosenwald Collection, Library of Congress. Copyright © 2005 the William Blake Archive. Used with permission.)

instantly retired' (ibid: 172). A second dinner party was not so lucky: 'A Tiger darted among them whilst they were at dinner, seized on a gentleman, and carried him off in sight of his disconsolate companions' (ibid: 172). In such cases, we see the human culture of a region linked to the natural environment in ways that will gradually allow imperialist assumptions to emerge from the apparently neutral discourse of naturalistic observation.

By the time G. A. Henty wrote his Victorian history of Tippoo Sahib, Sultan of Mysore, the discourse of natural history and human history had merged in powerful ways. Tippoo, like his father Haidar Ali, had fought against colonial domination of the Indian state of Mysore for decades. Tippoo was well known for his ruthlessness and his uncompromising military tactics. He had been called 'The Tiger' throughout his career fighting against the British, and he apparently referred to himself as 'The Tiger' as well. He was reputed to have actual tigers guarding his palaces. The word 'tiger', we should recall, had been used to describe a 'person of fierce, cruel, rapacious, or blood-thirsty disposition' (*OED*) since the sixteenth century. By the time Henty's boy's-book *The Tiger of Mysore* appeared in 1896, descriptions drawn from natural history had merged almost completely with descriptions of the human subject. Tippoo 'is a human tiger; he delights in torturing his human victims, and slays his prisoners from pure love of bloodshed. He is proud of the title of "Tiger"; his footstool is a tiger's head, and the uniforms of his infantry are a sort of imitation of a tiger's stripe' (Henty 1896: 83). The trappings of tigerhood are clearly assumed to be the most appropriate outward signs of the human tiger within. Tippoo, the veritable human tiger, however, was killed in 1799 by British soldiers, soldiers whom Henty would no doubt have us believe must have acted much more like gentlemen than like tigers during their own military engagements. From the vantage point of history, of course, the Tiger of Mysore appears to be a very different sort of 'creature'. As Tara Chand notes in *The History of the Freedom Movement in India*, ' 'Tipu refused to surrender and died bravely fighting in defence of his fort' (Chand 1965: I: 226–7). So is this human tiger a villain or a hero? From our postcolonial perspective it is clearly up to the reader to decide.

In conclusion, William Blake is a particularly complex figure in terms of the empire of exotic nature he builds within his own imaginative system. On the one hand, Blake was hostile to 'vegetable' nature in all its forms. He saw the natural world as a sign of our 'fallen' condition, and his anti-materialism disdained all forms of embodied 'spirit', a category that includes humans and all other aspects of 'animate nature' as well: botanical, zoological, even insectivorous. At the same time, Blake makes powerful use of natural imagery throughout his poems and plates. To be in nature is to be always removed from the idealized world of visionary imagination, but that does not prevent him from suggesting inter-connections among all living beings. As a result, his caterpillars and butterflies often have human faces, while his human figures sometimes sprout roots and branches. His birds' tails and wings echo flower stalks and vines, while his mythic figures often connect the 'human form divine' (E 13) with the botanic or the bestial.

Blake may have distrusted 'nature' in visionary terms, but he celebrated its physical beauty, its sensuous details and its crucial role in our awareness of our human place in the cosmos. In *Auguries of Innocence*, for example, he reveals the cost of human ignorance of those connections that unite all aspects of creation: 'The wanton Boy that kills the Fly / Shall feel the Spiders enmity' and 'He who shall hurt the little Wren / Shall never be belovd by Men' (*Auguries of Innocence* 33–4, 29–30 E 490). In many of his songs and short lyrics, Blake suggests that only human beings upset balances that exist throughout the rest of the natural world. *The Book of Thel* presents a cloud, a lily, a clod of clay and a worm that all accept their roles in a cycle of organic life and death in a way that the humanized Thel cannot. *The Four Zoas* imagines an idealized future state in which the fallen aspects of human psychic integrity are reunited with themselves and with the rest of animate creation. 'The Sick Rose', by contrast, suggests that nature employs destructive processes that are at odds with all human hopes and optimism: 'And his dark secret love / Does thy life destroy.' (7–8 E 28) At his most cryptic, of course, Blake understands that 'nature' is a category created by us, even as we are creatures bound up in its material reality: 'Where man is not, nature is barren' (*The Marriage of Heaven and Hell* E 37).

# 10 Blake, Hayley and India: On *Designs to a Series of Ballads* (1802)

Hikari Sato

For about 150 years, William Hayley (1745–1820) was stigmatized as a second-rate poet, a meddlesome patron and a worldly-wise biographer in the context of Blake studies. This is partly because contemporary poets and authors, such as Byron, Hunt, Hazlitt and Southey, relentlessly piled disparagement on the works of Hayley while he was still alive.[1] Their judgements certainly influenced Alexander Gilchrist when he wrote *Life of William Blake* (1863; 1880). This biography tried to rescue Blake from oblivion and misunderstanding so enthusiastically that it took an adamantly aggressive attitude to anyone considered an enemy of Blake and, for that matter, particularly to William Hayley. Mona Wilson also repeats the stereotyped image of Hayley in her *Life of William Blake* (1927; 2nd edn. 1948), although she admits that Blake obtained new knowledge of the country life and the open sea at Felpham, which gave him inspiration for his later works. Blake, she says, must have had a 'fruitful' three years at Felpham.[2] One of the more significant works concerning the reassessment of Hayley is *Blake's Hayley: The Life, Works, and Friendships of William Hayley* (1951), in which Morchard Bishop closely examines the relationship between Blake and Hayley on the basis of their correspondence and makes it clear that they were in more than just a business relationship. In 1957, 'the immediate effect of Hayley on Blake' was confirmed in Northrop Frye's 'Notes for a Commentary on *Milton*', which suggests that Blake learned a lot about the epic tradition from Hayley who was familiar with modern European literature as well as the classics (Frye 1957: 102). He even says that Hayley was as liberal as Cowper.[3] Frye's opinion was highly valued by Joseph Anthony Wittreich, Jr whose ' "Domes of Mental Pleasure": Blake's Epic and Hayley's Epic Theory' argued in 1972 that Blake wrote *Milton* under the direct influence of Hayley and his works, such as *An Essay on Epic Poetry* (1782) and *The Life of Milton* (1796). Two years later in 1974, his vindication was forcefully challenged by Judith Wardle, who insisted that Hayley was fundamentally a conservative, basically apolitical, country gentleman in contrast to Blake's continuous commitment to social, political and religious satire in support of the idea of freedom. In 1994 the compromise position was suggested that Blake might have been influenced by Hayley's epic theory even if this 'appears to be an act of poetic homage to the status quo rather than the product of such "visionaries of public virtue" as Milton and Blake' (Cox 1994: 441).

On the two premises that Blake spent a 'fruitful' and 'rewarding' three years at Felpham and that Blake had access to classical and contemporary literature through Hayley, I would like to propose a hypothesis that Blake acquired knowledge about India during his Felpham years.[4] Focusing on *Designs to a Series of Ballads* written by Hayley and published by Blake in 1802, I will work from the initial premise that Hayley used Indian motifs in the *Designs* to commemorate his son who had died in 1800 and that Blake became familiar with India through the collaboration with his erudite patron. The following argument is structured in two parts. First, I will discuss briefly the significance of *Designs* (Hayley 1802), referring to the biographical facts concerning William Hayley and Thomas Alphonso Hayley, and then I will examine Blake's engravings for the *Designs* to explore a possible intervisual and intertextual relationship between Blake and eighteenth-century Indian literature.

## 1  *Designs to a Series of Ballads* (1802)

According to the preface to the *Designs*, Hayley wrote the ballads to amuse 'Mr. Blake, the Artist, who has devoted himself, with indefatigable spirit, to engrave the plates intended to decorate the volumes, in which I hope to render affectionate justice to the memory of Cowper.'[5] He planned to write one ballad every month, accompanied by three engravings, to be sold at half a crown. The series was to be completed with 15 ballads, which would constitute a quarto volume and contain 45 engravings. The first ballad, 'The Elephant', was published in June 1802, 'The Eagle' in July and 'The Lion' in August. The production date of 'The Dog', the fourth ballad, is unknown. Each ballad was printed by Blake and the copies were sent to the friends of Hayley together with a letter in which the author asked them to distribute them further to their acquaintances. Because of this unusual way of selling the ballads, the project of the *Designs* did not attract much attention and was abandoned after the issue of the fourth ballad.[6]

Three years later, the unfinished project was properly completed when *Ballads Founded on anecdotes relating to animals* (1805) was published by Richard Phillips, a publisher in London. It acquired a much wider readership than the previous edition and was reviewed in some journals: it was favourably commented on in *The Eclectic Review* while dismissed as an 'incomparably absurd' piece of mediocrity in *The Annual Review*.[7]

Negative judgements have frequently been passed on the literary value of the ballads: 'empty productions, long-winded, bald, devoid of every poetic virtue save simplicity, – in the unhappy sense of utter insipidity' (Gilchrist 1863, I: 165). The fact remains that Hayley produced the *Designs* in 1802 and further enlarged it to the *Ballads* in 1805, both of which were accompanied by the engravings of Blake. The clue to this continued attention may be found in the frontispiece to the *Designs*.[8] The plate of a young man sitting at the foot of a tree in the middle of a group of animals is often referred to as 'Adam naming the beasts', but, as Hayley himself writes in a letter to John Johnson on 16 May 1802, Adam is not naming but is just 'surrounded' by animals.[9] Adam and the animals are relaxed in a calm, warm and friendly atmosphere, which is difficult to associate with the biblical implication that man is the lord of all creation.[10] On the contrary, the plate reminds us of the wolf and the lion that live peacefully with the lamb and the calf in an ideal world, as is described in Isaiah.[11] The biographical context allows us to read the young man in the frontispiece not only as Adam but also as

Hayley's son Thomas Alphonso, who died a premature death at the age of twenty in 1800.

The four ballads of the *Designs* have the common theme of saving life. In 'The Elephant' and 'The Dog' animals rescue their benefactors from danger while in 'The Eagle' and 'The Lion' a devoted mother and a brave wife fight with a wild creature to save their child or husband respectively. Apart from the shared theme, biographical references to Thomas Alphonso are embedded in various guises in each sentimental story.

The first ballad, 'The Elephant', is a story of a sagacious elephant that saves someone in return for his kindness. Led by his attendant, the elephant walks to water every day, passing beside the hut of a gardener, who gives him vegetables whenever he comes. One day the elephant, who has previously often let children play on his back, suddenly captures the gardener with his trunk and lifts him up so high in the sky that everyone thinks that the animal has gone mad. The elephant carries him away wildly, and then gently releases him at a high window of the upper floor of a building. The shivering gardener sees a tiger wandering around, looking for prey, and understands that he has been rescued by the elephant. The scene is set in India.

It is not difficult to trace the bibliographical background of this ballad. According to *A Catalogue of the Very Valuable and Extensive Library of the Late William Hayley, esq* (1821), Hayley owned the 1774 edition of *An History of the Earth, and Animated Nature* by Oliver Goldsmith, and its fourth volume includes a chapter entitled 'Of the Elephant'.[12] It says, for example, that elephants often seize a man with their trunks, hurl him in the air and crush him under their feet when they are angry. Although they are dreadful when offended, elephants are usually gentle and obedient and they even stroke and fondle their keepers with their trunks to show affection. The 'Indians and Negroes' are mentioned as people who hunt and tame wild elephants and 'Their chief food is of the vegetable kind, for they loath all kind of animal diet' (Goldsmith 1774, IV: 257). The following episode is particularly relevant to the ballad:

> An elephant in Adsmeer, which often passed through the bazaar or market, as he went by a certain herb-woman, always received from her a mouthful of greens. Being one day seized with a periodical fit of madness, he broke his fetters, and running through the market, put the crowd to flight, and, among others, this woman, who in her haste forgot a little child at her stall. The elephant recollecting the spot where his benefactress was accustomed to sit, took up the infant gently in his trunk, and conveyed it to a place of safety. (Goldsmith 1774, IV: 280)

'The Elephant' and the passage quoted above share common components, such as a benefactor who gives an elephant vegetables, an elephant that suddenly becomes violent, and a rescue scene in which the elephant saves someone with its trunk. It is likely that Hayley wrote the ballad referring specifically to this encyclopaedic work of Goldsmith.[13]

In 1795 when Hayley wrote *An Elegy on the Death of the Hon. Sir William Jones*, Thomas Alphonso started his apprenticeship to John Flaxman, then engaged on a commission for making a monument to Sir William Jones for St Mary's Church, Oxford. In a letter to his father on 4 January 1796, Thomas Alphonso mentions the project in progress at the workshop of his master as follows:

Mr. Maurice (author of the Indian Antiquities, and an Elegy on Sir William Jones,) called at our house a few days ago, to see the monument of Sir William, and he has honoured it with a very handsome present, a copy of his Elegy, and of his Indian Antiquities. He has also very politely invited me to drink tea with him in Norton-street, and look over his library, which consists of valuable books chiefly on art and antiquities. (Hayley 1823, Thomas: 154)[14]

It is conceivable that Thomas Maurice, the author of the first elegy on Sir William Jones, had an interest in Thomas Alphonso, the son of the author of the second elegy on the same oriental scholar. Although we do not know what books Thomas Alphonso found in his library, he certainly had a chance to read Maurice's *Elegy* and *Indian Antiquities* and would subsequently himself be engaged in modelling for the memorial sculpture of Sir William Jones on behalf of his master (Hayley 1823, Thomas: 222–3).

Ironically, a fatal disorder of the spine made him give up studying art in London and retire to Sussex just after he became interested in India. His father often visited London to acquire new medicines and the latest knowledge of the malady and in a letter to Thomas Alphonso on 1 December 1798 he wrote about a present for his disabled son of 'admirable prints' by Daniel (a mis-spelling of Daniell) (Hayley 1823, Thomas: 431). These were probably either the first series of *Oriental Scenery: Twenty-Four Views in Hindoostan*, which were published between March 1795 and January 1797, or the second series of the collection of aquatints with the same title, which were published between August 1797 and December 1798. Thomas Daniell (1749–1840) and William Daniell (1769–1837) sailed for India in 1785 to make a career as landscape painters and returned to England in 1794 to publish commercial prints of Indian scenery. They immediately had great success and subsequently issued the third and fourth series of *Oriental Scenery*.[15] Since Hayley's letter is dated 1 December 1798, the prints that he mentioned could be those of the second series, which were completed in the same December.

A further link between Thomas Alphonso and India may be in a 'favourite engraved elephant' on an ancient gem. On page nine of the ballad, 'The Elephant', the figure of the engraving 'From an Antique Gem' is printed; the plate clashes with other illustrations which are faithfully based on the plot of the ballad.[16] The jewel appears to have become an 'emblem' of Hayley's son's 'long and severe trial – mildness of spirit, and energy of mind' (25 April 1799: Hayley 1823, Thomas: 458).

The fourth ballad of the *Designs*, 'The Dog', is also a sentimental life-saving story, which consists of three characters: Lucy, the owner of the dog; Edward, a young officer of the British army; and the faithful Fido (whose name derives from a favourite spaniel of the Hayleys). The story begins with a farewell scene in which Edward tells Lucy that he is to be engaged in military service in India. Suffering from the sorrow of parting, she orders Fido to accompany and protect him. In India Edward makes a habit of swimming in a river after he finishes his daily work. One day, when he is taking off his clothes to plunge into the stream as usual, Fido runs noisily around him, making every effort to prevent him. Edward beats the dog and hurries to the water. Fido overtakes him and throws himself into the river, where an open-mouthed crocodile awaits. To soothe the sorrow of Lucy when the death is reported, an anonymous sculptor makes a statue of the dog, which is placed in her chamber. Edward finally returns to England and is married to Lucy.

This story is also based on a factual episode, or to be more precise, the dialogue between William and Thomas Alphonso. In May 1796, Hayley planned to build a tower at his estate in Felpham and told his son that he had an idea of decorating the entrance with 'a stone image of the sleeping Fido'. (Although the ballad does not tell us which type of dog Fido is, it is drawn as a spaniel with a black and white wavy coat, just as the real Fido was, in the illustration – see Figure 10.1.) Apparently, Edward has nothing to do with Thomas Alphonso. The former is a young man who goes to India, enjoys swimming and is married to his fiancée while the latter never went abroad and died of illness at the age of twenty. Fido, however, connects both and the portrait of Edward, a healthy and vigorous military officer, paradoxically corresponds with Thomas Alphonso, an artist with a weak constitution.

An important fact is that Hayley settled in Chichester near Portsmouth. His *Memoirs* contain several passages concerning young officers who left for India and whom Hayley knew well as friends, such as the eldest son of Jeremiah Meyer (1735–89), a certain Captain Howell to whom he gave financial support for some reason or other, and a son of Charlotte Smith (1749–1806).[17] When Hayley wrote in a letter to his son that 'She [Charlotte Smith] has a very natural maternal wish to send a copy of our dear Romney's admirable sketch of her head, to a worthy son in India', Thomas Alphonso replied that he would willingly make a copy of her portrait (Hayley 1823, I: 365). Obviously the Hayleys were familiar with young people who went to India to start their career.

Hayley was fond of swimming and firmly believed in the goodness of sea-bathing, which, to his disappointment, Thomas Alphonso did not like at all (Hayley 1823, Thomas: 143). Edward, a brisk and healthy officer who is dispatched to India, enjoys swimming there, both features directly opposite to those of Thomas Alphonso. In other words, the father revived his son in the most desirable form, by giving him health and a future which Thomas Alphonso had never enjoyed. Thus 'The Dog' may be read as a personal and private elegy dedicated by the father to his son, which is why it was placed at the beginning of the *Ballads* when the *Designs* was revised and enlarged in 1805. I will now go on to consider the degree to which Blake allowed himself to become involved in the process of mourning dramatized in the *Designs*.

## 2  Illustrations for *Designs to a Series of Ballads* (1802)

The plates for the first ballad of the *Designs* are dated 1 June 1802 when Blake and Hayley were still in a honeymoon period.[18] As Hayley repeatedly mentions in his letters, Blake made the engravings for them, sitting side by side with his patron. The library of Hayley was a store-house of contemporary knowledge and it is conceivable that Blake had full access to his collection of books and prints. In fact he was commissioned by Hayley to make engravings of the portraits of great authors to decorate the library and in his letter to Thomas Butts on 11 September 1801 Blake wrote: 'I must express my wishes to see you at Felpham & to shew you Mr Hayleys Library. which is still unfinishd but is in a finishing way & looks well' (E 716).[19] In addition to this circumstantial evidence, the plates for the

**Figure 10.1** William Hayley, *Designs to a Series of Ballads*, 1802, 'Man with dog falling into water' ('The Dog'), op. p. 26. (This item is reproduced by permission of *The Huntington Library, San Marino, California*.)

*Designs* themselves give us hints as to how Blake acquired knowledge of the exotic animals, plants and landscape described in the ballads. There are two possible channels – Hayley's personal advice and reference books in his library.

It is highly probable that Hayley influenced Blake in his conceiving the composition of the illustrations, a possibility that has already been discussed by Peter Tomory. In his essay on the design for 'The Lion', Tomory compares Blake's sketch and the engraved version. He observes that the braveness of the heroine is foregrounded in the sketch while the lion is made bigger and nobler in the engraving and concludes that 'Hayley himself may have had something to do with these changes' (Tomory 1975: 378).[20] I would agree with his argument, but where does the lion come from in the first place? It has no resemblance to an image of a lion faithfully drawn in the illustrations of either *An History of the Earth, and Animated Nature* by Goldsmith or *A General History of Quadrupeds* (1790) by Thomas Bewick, both of which were available in Hayley's library. The portrait of the formalized lion for the ballad has something in common with the image of the lion designed by Thomas Alphonso from an antique gem, which Hayley mentions in his letter when he writes about the elephant.[21] In Blake's original sketch the lion is realistically drawn as a beast, which implies that the formalized one was preferred to the real one when it was engraved, probably on Hayley's instigation.

The second channel is Hayley's library and it is probable that he gave Blake advice on which books he should refer to when he drew the illustrations. The frontispiece of 'The Lion' (Figure 10.2), which depicts the mother shooting at the formalized lion, is a curious illustration in the sense that the scenery is unlikely to be found anywhere in the world. The lion lives in grassy plains and open savannah, but in the illustration it stands on a cliff which overhangs a valley. The palm tree, at the foot of which the lion is shot, cannot be found in any of its preferred habitats. The plate consists of a curious combination of an African animal and the landscape of the West Indies. Undoubtedly, Blake had little correct knowledge of the African beast, and the reference book, which he might have consulted in Hayley's library, did not contain correct information about the lion either. According to *An History of the Earth, and Animated Nature*, the lion lives in mountainous areas as well as plains:

> Such, however, of these animals, as are bred in a more temperate climate, or towards the tops of cold and lofty mountains, are far more gentle, or, to speak more properly, far less dangerous than those bred in the torrid vallies beneath. The lions of Mount Atlas, the tops of which are covered in eternal snows, have neither the strength nor the ferocity of the lions of Bildulgerid or Zaara, where the plains are covered with burning sands. (Goldsmith 1774, III: 214)

The landscape of 'the torrid vallies' was drawn behind the lion probably because the author wanted it to be understood as a dangerous and ferocious kind of beast. Although both Blake's engraving and Goldsmith's description are wrong, their common error in natural history indicates a possible intertextual connection between Goldsmith and Blake.

The plates for 'The Elephant' and 'The Dog', both of which are relevant to India, include the same design of buildings crowned with three domes and, obviously, their peculiar combination reminds us of the Taj Mahal. It is worth remembering that Hayley bought several prints from the Daniells for Thomas Alphonso in December 1798, as we have already seen, and that Thomas Daniell published two large aquatints of the Taj Mahal with a descriptive booklet in 1801. It is highly probable that the prints by the Daniells, which Hayley collected for his son, gave Blake some hints about the scenery in India.

Another crucial work of literature concerning India is *Travels in India* (1793), whose author, William Hodges (1744–97), was a landscape painter and a friend of Hayley.[22] He spent a week with the Hayleys at Eartham in 1793 and 'being very

**Figure 10.2** William Hayley, *Designs to a Series of Ballads*, 1802, 'Hunters' ('The Lion'), op. p. 26. (This item is reproduced by permission of *The Huntington Library, San Marino, California*.)

fond of children, and struck with the various accomplishments of the little Alphonso, encouraged him to exercise his infantine pencil' (Hayley 1823, Thomas: 58–9). In the same year Hayley proposed a project in which William Cowper, George Romney and William Hodges might engage together, although this 'considerable work', as Hayley puts it, was in fact abandoned because of the health problems of the members.[23] When Hodges died utterly destitute in 1797, Hayley wrote that 'Death delivered him from a scene of unmerited distress' (Hayley 1809: 259).

Hayley had a copy of *Travels in India* and some of the passages in the book correspond to the visual images on the plates for the *Designs*. In the frontispiece of 'The Elephant' a marketplace is drawn with a background of the three domes of the Taj Mahal. According to Chapter 7 of *Travels in India*, 'Adjacent to this monument [the Taj Mahal] there was a great bazaar, or market for the richest manufactures of India, and of foreign countries, composed of six courts, and encompassed with great open porticoes; but scarcely a vestige of this building is now remaining' (Hodges 1793: 124). In the fourth chapter, Hodges makes an argument about the Hindu, Islamic and Gothic architecture, which he ends with the following observation:

> The Grecian confessedly was suggested by the primitive form of a rural hut in a champaign woody country; and the Oriental and Gothic I conceive has derived its form and its ornaments from those suprizing excavations which are found in rocky and mountainous regions. (Hodges 1793: 77)

In the headpiece of 'The Elephant', the building, to which the man is carried by the elephant, has an entrance with a Gothic arch. The porch has four columns, two of which are highly decorated. The pillars consist of a combination of square parts and round parts with ornamented top and bottom parts. The pillar shows a strong resemblance to the illustration, 'A Column taken from the Temple of Vis Visha at Beneres', inserted in *Travels in India*.[24]

The third possible reference work for Blake the engraver is the third volume of *The Asiatick Researches* (1792), which was also available in Hayley's library. In the illustration for the 'The Dog' (Figure 10.1) the crocodile opens its jaws as widely as possible, showing half of its head above the water. It does not resemble the reptile that we know as a crocodile but looks almost like a monster with a huge pair of V-shaped jaws. *An History of the Earth, and Animated Nature*, one of the possible reference books in the library of Hayley, does contain an illustration of a crocodile, but the creature, whose side view is drawn on the plate, resembles a shabby lizard lying on a rock rather than the predatory semiaquatic reptile. A realistic picture of a crocodile could be found in the illustrations for *Narrative of a Five Years' Expedition against the Revolted Negroes of Surinam* (1796) by John Stedman, only if we ignore differences between the crocodile and the alligator. According to Stedman, however, the two reptiles are different from each other 'not merely in the name, but in the shape and in the nature also', and it is likely that Blake accepted the explanation, never thinking of their affinities.[25]

The third volume of *The Asiatick Researches* includes an essay entitled 'On Egypt and Other Countries adjacent to the Ca'li' River, or Nile of Ethiopia. From the Ancient Books of the Hindus', in which Francis Wilford describes a crocodile which matches the visual image of the monstrous creature in Blake's engraving. His imaginative rather than scientifically accurate picture of the creature goes as follows:

> Ra'hu is represented, on account of his tyranny, as an immense river-dragon, or crocodile, or rather a fabulous monster with four talons, called *Grába*, from a root implying *violent seizure*. The word is commonly interpreted *bánger*, or *shark*; but in some dictionaries it is made synonymous to *nacra*, or *crocodile*; and in the *Puránas* it seems to be the creature of poetical fancy. (Wilford 1792: 333)

The reptile with surprisingly big jaws drawn on the plate for the 'The Dog' represents not so much a real crocodile as the 'immense river-dragon' or 'the creature of poetical fancy' described in the passage quoted above. The association of a crocodile with a shark makes sense in Blake's illustrations in which the monster is visualized as a creature living in a huge expanse of water.

We have so far explored the possibility that Blake had access to contemporary literature on India through Hayley and confirmed the validity of the following three assumptions: that Hayley wrote a series of ballads for the *Designs* to console himself for the loss of his son; that Thomas Alphonso had great interest in India; and that Blake was deeply involved in the publication of the private project of his patron. From these observations, we can conclude that Blake acquired his knowledge of Indian scenery and culture under the guidance of Hayley who had a good collection of Oriental literature in his library. After his three-year stay at Felpham, Blake suddenly starts to mention India, China, Japan and other nations, which do not appear in his earlier prophecies. Undoubtedly Blake had sufficient knowledge on the diversity of religions and cultures to shift his perspective from a regional view of the world to a global one. Not as a flattening process of homogenization but as this implies an equal respect for a wide range of people, values and ways of life, accompanied by mutual tolerance; and, if so, Hayley and his library must have had a great significance in the progress of Blake's thoughts.

## Notes

1 See lines 309–14 in 'English Bards and Scotch Reviewers' (Byron 1973–83: 117); 'The Feast of the Poets' (Hunt 1814: 48–9); *Lectures of the English Poets* (Hazlitt 1930, V: 145–6); and Southey's review of *Memoirs of the Life and Writings of William Hayley, Esq.* (1823) in *The Quarterly Review* XXXI (1825). According to *The Gentleman's Magazine*, XC (November 1820), 'Mr. Hayley may, perhaps, be better appreciated as the Poet of the drawing-room, [. . .] than as an author whose works will go down to posterity as elevating the character and displaying the vigour of our national genius' (470). In his unfinished *Essay on Fashionable Literature*, Thomas Love Peacock points out that literature, whose only aim is to amuse, not to instruct, was prevalent in the country, referring to Hayley as a typical example of that form: 'In these publications, the mutual flattery of "learned correspondents" to their own "inestimable miscellany" carries the "Tickle me, Mr. Hayley" principle to a surprising extent' (Peacock 1934, VIII: 270).
2 Wilson 1927: 163, 178–9.
3 Frye 1957: 102.
4 For Blake and India in the early 1790s, see, for example, Makdisi 2003a: 204–59 and Weir 2003.
5 The Preface to the *Designs* cited in Bentley 2004a: 125.
6 Bentley suggests that Blake sent a few copies of 'The Dog' to booksellers in London (2004a: 143).
7 *The Eclectic Review*, I (1805) 921–3; *The Annual Review*, IV (1805) 575–6. In his review of Hayley's *Memoirs* in *The Quarterly Review*, XXXI (1825), Southey mentions the *Ballads* sarcastically, quoting the nonsense refrain: 'He published also a little volume of "Ballads founded on Anecdotes relating to Animals", and if any person collects books, which are curious for their absurdity, this volume is well entitled to a place in such a collection. Some one upon reading it quoted the burden of one of O'Keeffe's doggerel songs, Hayley-gayly, gamborayly, higgledy, piggledy, galloping, draggle-tailed dreary dun' (310).

8  For the plates, see Bindman ed. 1978.
9  See Fitzwilliam Hayley-Johnson letters cited in Bentley: 'He [Blake] is at this moment by my side, representing on Copper an adam [*sic*], of his own, surrounded [by] animals, as a Frontispiece to the projected Ballads' (Bentley 2004a: 128). For 'Adam naming the beasts', see also Essick 1989.
10  'Each naming proclaims a further separation between the human and the divine; each calls into existence another error, a new bane rather than a new blessing' (Tannenbaum 1982: 219–20).
11  Isaiah 11.6–9; 65.25.
12  The *Catalogue* is reprinted in Munby ed. 1972: 83–171.
13  A possible source for 'The Eagle' is also to be found in *An History of the Earth, and Animated Nature* (Goldsmith 1774, V: 91).
14  *Memoirs of Thomas Alphonso Hayley* is bound together in Hayley's *Memoirs* with independent page numbers and hereafter cited as 'Hayley 1823, Thomas'.
15  Archer 1980: 9, 13, 219–21.
16  For the plate, see Essick 1991: 82.
17  Hayley 1823, I: 307; Hayley 1809: 282. See also Hayley 1823, Thomas: vi–vii.
18  Bentley 2004a: 129–30.
19  All quotations from Blake are from David V. Erdman (ed.), *The Complete Poetry and Prose of William Blake* (New York: Doubleday, 1988), hereafter cited parenthetically, giving page number with a capital letter 'E'. For the plan to decorate the library with portraits of great authors, see Bentley 2004a: 91–2.
20  Tomory also argues that there is a noteworthy parallel between the archer in 'The Lion' and the Fuseli drawing of *Odysseus Killing the Suitors*, which was completed in July 1802. For the sketches of Blake for the ballads, see Butlin 1981: *Plates*: 467–74.
21  The engraving of a lion 'From an Antique' is signed 'T. H. del', which suggests that the plate was designed by Thomas Alphonso. For the plate, see Essick 1991: 82.
22  For Hodges and Hayley, see Bonehill 2004.
23  Hayley 1809: 198–9.
24  Hodges 1793: 62–3.
25  Stedman 1796, I: 145. Plate 15 on page 144 gives a faithful description of 'The Alligator or Cayman of Surinam'. Blake made engravings for the *Narrative* and was 'Stedman's most trusted friend in London'. For Blake and Stedman, see Bentley 2004a: 61, 66.

# 11 The Authority of the Ancients: Blake and Wilkins' Translation of the *Bhagvat-Geeta*

Tristanne J. Connolly

William Blake's sole mention of the *Bhagvat-Geeta* refers to a painting now lost. The description is frustratingly brief and tangential. Among the many things it does not explain is the lag between the publication of Charles Wilkins' translation in 1785 and Blake's exhibition in 1809: it is unclear when in this time span Blake produced the painting, or read the *Geeta*. Probably because there is so little to go on, few critics pursue the connection between Blake and the *Geeta*, and those who do tend to compare Blake's 'myth' with Hindu 'myth'. In the process, Hinduism is often made equivalent to other traditions: anything Blake might have found in it could equally come from classical, biblical or hermetic sources.[1] Demonstrating the *Geeta*'s influence by seeking identical structures and concepts in Blake, critics also make Hindu and Blakean myth equivalent in content.[2] These critics operate like Enlightenment mythographers, working from principles shared by figures as different as Jacob Bryant (whom Blake mentions in the *Descriptive Catalogue*) and William Jones. Their syncretism, based on the Judeo-Christian idea of a singular origin, enables them to find continuities between different systems; those continuities arise from connection to the pure source from whence all other systems spring. There is the temptation to place one's own views in this crucial original position, but there is also the threat of discovering that one's own system cannot claim this ultimacy.[3] William Jones struggles with the convincing claim the 'primeval fountains of Indian literature' have for chronological precedence over the Judeo-Christian tradition: 'Either the first eleven chapters of *Genesis*, all due allowance being made for a figurative Eastern style, are true, or the whole fabrick of our national religion is false' (in Shaffer 1975: 122). Jones can put the authority of the Bible in question, and give Christianity the limited, local name of 'our national religion', but he questions it without abandoning its own terms, hinting that those terms themselves cause the conflict: the narrative of origins must be true for the rest to stand, and that narrative must itself be original, not borrowed from an older source.

P. J. Marshall accuses the writers he surveys in *The British Discovery of Hinduism in the Eighteenth Century* of an 'inability . . . to describe a religious system except in Christian terms'. It is understandable, perhaps inevitable, to approach an unfamiliar system of thought by analogy with a familiar one, but along with the benefits of mediation can come the dangers of distortion. A particular selective vision has been found at work among eighteenth-century Western writers who made a distinction between popular Hinduism, which they condemned, and philosophical Hinduism, in which they discerned similarities to Christianity and Western thought (Marshall 1970: 20). Such a distinction enables universalism, and disposal of difference and detail under the devalued category of the popular; it allows a generalized mysticism to float untethered by history and actual practice. Similarly, by separating the 'myth' from the writings, critics can discuss Blake's connection with the *Geeta* philosophically, apart from its context: a *Descriptive Catalogue* of paintings dominated by 'patriotic grandeur' (Erdman 1977: 448), and a translation published by the East India Company. From the majority of Blake criticism, one would never know that this *Geeta* bore an introduction by Warren Hastings, Governor-General of Bengal then of India, whose trial was 'the high point of public interest in Company affairs' (Teltscher 1995: 157) and a turning point for British power in India.

Two Blake critics who address such issues are David Weir and Saree Makdisi. Their arguments are predominantly opposed. Weir holds that Blake's understanding of Hinduism was formed exclusively in a republican and dissenting context, sympathetic to Indians in a shared opposition to empire and state religion (Weir 2003: 13, 22). Makdisi, on the other hand, argues that British radicals contributed to imperial discourse by displacing on to the East luxury, despotism and all that was contrary to their self-disciplined individualism (Makdisi 2003a: 214–15). Nonetheless, both conclude that Blake is a champion against empire, and for hybrid collectivity.[4] Almost as much as the ahistorical critics, Weir and Makdisi protect Blake from complicity in any imperialistic relationship between knowledge, power and profit. On the contrary, I find Blake not so much an opponent of empire as a proponent of an Orientalism outmoded by the time of his exhibition in 1809, but exemplified in the 1785 *Geeta*. Blake's affinity becomes clear when his references to 'Hindoo' culture in the *Descriptive Catalogue* are placed alongside Wilkins' and Hastings' introductions to the *Geeta*. Like Wilkins and Hastings, Blake shows genuine interest in and respect for Indian cultural productions as contributing to collective human knowledge, revealing portions of divine truth and ultimate reality. At the same time, all three see in Hinduism manifestations of the one true religion, Christianity (or their own personal versions of it); and all three attempt to turn knowledge of India to personal profit and the glory of Britain.

It would have been impossible for Blake as a Londoner not to notice the trial of Warren Hastings, which began in 1788 and continued for seven years, placing it between the publication of the *Geeta* and the *Descriptive Catalogue*. Hastings was represented as responsible for crimes involving excessive violence and financial corruption in dealings with Indians.[5] Initially, the trial was a blockbuster: 'By eight o'clock in the morning the avenues leading to [Westminster] Hall, through New and Old Palace Yards, were filled with ladies and gentlemen of the most respectable appearance . . . who stood in the street for upwards of an hour' then rushed in for the best seats (*The History of the Trial of Warren Hastings* [1796] i. 74, quoted in Teltscher 1995: 157). It was a media event, reported in the popular press (Musselwhite 1986: 92), and suitably spectacular with the lurid rhetoric of Burke and the theatrics of Sheridan who, after one speech (tickets for which went for fifty guineas) fainted in Burke's arms (Suleri 1995: 53–4). The trial's length, and ambivalent outcome (Hastings was acquitted, but his reputation and finances ruined [Musselwhite 1986: 91]) reflect the slow but certain death of the attitudes it represented. Sara Suleri considers that Hastings' 'guilt or innocence' was 'an obsolete issue' since 'the transgressions of which Hastings was guilty conform perfectly to the extortionism upon which the East India Company was based' (Suleri 1995: 52). She views Burke as attempting to try the East India Company and colonialism itself by trying Hastings. But the Company and colonialism were outstripping the terms on which both Burke and Hastings understood them. Both believed that India should be ruled according to its own traditions (Suleri 1995: 51–2). The question was whether Hastings had done this, but his successor as Governor-General, Cornwallis, had already begun 'the dismantle- ment of the legal system based on the Indian laws that Hastings had instituted and replaced it with a system that followed British practices' (Weir 2003: 28). After all of this, to display a painting depicting Hastings-sponsored interactions with Indians would be to take part in a controversy, but an inconclusive and outdated one.

If Hastings was a suitable candidate to be blamed for the East India Company's sins, and if Wilkins' work was funded and published by that major imperialist organization, still, neither of them shows the explicit racism and superiority which can be found in later works. The starkest example is Macaulay's well- known statement that, having consulted 'the Orientalists themselves', he has not found 'one among them who could deny that a single shelf of a good European library was worth the whole native literature of India and Arabia' (Macaulay 1972: 241). James Mill's *History of British India*, which became an East India Company textbook, affords another comparison, and an especially suitable one because Mill was writing it at the same time that Blake was writing the *Descriptive Catalogue*.[6] Mill shares with Macaulay a utilitarianism which goes along with a contempt for mythology. Both mock Indian 'History, abounding with kings thirty feet high, and reigns thirty thousand years long' (Macaulay 1972: 242–3), which Mill calls 'the offspring of a wild and ungoverned imagination' which 'mark[s] the state of a rude and credulous people . . . who cannot estimate the use of a record of past events' (Mill 1975: 33). Macaulay questions whether the government should continue to fund anything, whether construction of a building or study of a language, which has proven itself useless (Macaulay 1972: 239). In contrast, Hastings had directly or indirectly supported the work of British and Indian scholars on diverse topics including both Islamic and Hindu law, Bengali grammar, and Indian history, as well as the *Geeta* (Brockington 1989: 92– 7). Arguing for the establishment of a professorship in Persian at Oxford, he considered preparation of students for Company service, but also argued that 'the manners of the various inhabitants of the earth' should be studied for their own sake, since such study 'cannot fail to open our minds, and to inspire us with that benevolence which our religion inculcates, for the whole race of mankind' (in Brockington 1989: 92). His appreciation of other cultures involves, but is not restricted to, practical use. Intellectual and spiritual gains from other cultures do not entail any reduction of Christian importance; indeed, they are motivated by a specifically Christian benevolence. In the introduction to the *Geeta*, Hastings concedes that 'the study of Sanskreet cannot, like the Persian language, be applied to official profit, and improved with the official exercise of it' (14). He emphasizes that 'barren applause' is the only incitement to such study – to persuade Nathaniel Smith, Chairman of the Company, that diligent scholars like Wilkins 'can only derive [their] reward, beyond the breath of fame, in a fixed endowment' (14). He flatters Smith as having 'a mind too liberal to confine its beneficence to such arts alone as contribute to the immediate and substantial advantages of the state' (14). Although Blake of course could not have been a candidate for Hastings' patronage, he may have been attracted by his liberal diversion of Company funds toward mythological studies, considering that Blake styled himself a quasi-antiquarian (of a most impractical sort), and did not consider creative intellectual pursuits to be ennobled by poverty.[7] C. A. Bayly sees the increase of racism, 'the notion of "native depravity" . . . generalized to all Indians', as connected to larger changes in attitudes to finance in which the trial of Hastings played an influential role: 'Hastings and his coadjutors had been corrupted by the "big money" of the East India Company, but also by the "petty cash" of the Indian commercial classes' (Bayly 1989: 149). He adds that 'the idea of an uncorrupt and virtuous civil service was coming into being at the very same time as money-making and commerce became increasingly despised by the gentry' (Bayly 1989: 50). What Brockington calls Hastings' 'cavalier approach to accounting' was evident both in the offences he was tried for, and his patronage of scholarship.[8] Hastings' comfort with money, and his willingness to spread it around, contrasts with Macaulay's version of concern for how scholars will make a living: those educated in impractical Oriental knowledge emerge as unemployable burdens on the state (Brockington 1989: 245–6). Makdisi pinpoints the kinship between the irrational history of the Hindus abhorred by Mill, and the 'improbable' and 'impossible' kind of history Blake advocates in the *Descriptive Catalogue* (Makdisi 1998: 3). The *Catalogue* also lobbies for state support of public art with a mythological bent. Hastings stands for an administration that funded such useless pursuits.[9] With Hastings' style of Orientalism, then, Blake can reject increasing utilitarianism without having to sacrifice hopes of personal advantage. He can retain British and Christian centrality without having to ally himself with an obtuse and unimaginative bigotry. Instead of the growing imposition of British culture on Indians, he opts for outdated syncretism which allows him to see Indians and Britons as originally alike.

Blake's description of 'The Bramins' reveals little about how the lost painting depicted the relationship between Wilkins and his Hindu advisors, if it did at all. Nanavutty pictures Wilkins 'seated cross-legged on the floor with the Bramins grouped around him in the traditional Indian manner' (Nanavutty 1957: 167). She picks up on the description's suggestion that Wilkins is central to the painting by placing him at the centre of the group. (Is this position traditional for receiving, or giving instruction?) Weir imagines 'Wilkins in some kind of Indian costume that accorded with Blake's idea of the "manner" of a Brahmin, even though he had no sense of what such a costume would look like' (Weir 2003: 21). He combines the only two definite contents of the painting: Wilkins and incorrect costume. The title could then refer to Wilkins himself, as a Bramin. Only the plural suggests another presence, and for all we know it could be his patron Hastings in similar clothing. In both conjectural scenes there is a British core and a Bramin exterior. The title is 'The Bramins' but 'The subject is, Mr. Wilkin [*sic*], translating the Geeta' (E 548).[10] The description concentrates on Blake's sources more than on the Bramins: it turns out to be about how the *Geeta* is translated or imported into Blake's world and world view. Wilkins is in India, in communication with Indian pundits, and can read Hindu scripture. Felpham was the furthest Blake ever got from London (physically, anyhow), and though he boasted of his Hebrew and Greek (E 727) he never claimed the same of Sanskrit. Blake's authority on the *Geeta* must come from reading books like Wilkins', and, of course, from imagination. He calls 'The Bramins' 'an ideal design, suggested by the first publication of that part of the Hindoo Scriptures, translated by Mr. Wilkin.' For Blake, this authority is enough to override actual practice, just as a philosophical Hinduism assimilable to Christianity can override devotional Hinduism. Blake writes, 'I understand that my Costume is incorrect, but in this I plead the authority of the ancients, who often deviated from the Habits, to preserve the Manners, as in the instance of Laocoon, who, though a priest, is represented naked' (E 548). Blake places Hindu and classical traditions side by side, considering 'the instance of Laocoon', an ancient Greek priest depicted in statuary, to be applicable to live eighteenth-century Bramins. 'The authority of the ancients' is Blake's excuse for changing the Bramin 'Costume'. Given the vocabulary, it becomes difficult to tell whether he is changing the costumes or the customs, the habits or the habits, of the Hindus to fit his imaginative vision. Wilkins' connection to the authority of the *Geeta* may have encouraged Blake to clothe him as a Bramin, but Blake's connection to the authority of the Laocoon definitely encourages him to clothe the Bramins any way he wants. He can turn them into ancient Greeks, or even ancient Britons. The reference to Laocoon suggests that the incorrect 'costume' is nakedness. Describing another lost painting, 'The Ancient Britons', Blake claims 'the three general classes of men' [the Beautiful, Strong and Ugly] 'could not be represented by any historical facts but those of our own country . . . without violating costume. The Britons (say historians) were naked civilized men' (E 542). In this case, Britons are the best choice for a representation of archetypes, and Blake is concerned not to violate custom or costume, but present the Ancient Britons in their accurate historical nakedness. The naked truth of the Bramins, then, is a European fabrication. It clothes the Bramins in the antiquity of the Britons and the Greeks.

When Hastings depicts a translator-among-the-Bramins scene, he adds a third presence. Against the accusation of introducing 'the knowledge of Hindoo literature into the European world, by forcing or corrupting the religious consciences of the Pundits, or professors of their sacred doctrines', he claims, 'Very natural causes may be ascribed for their reluctance to communicate the mysteries of their learning to strangers, as those to whom they have been for some centuries in subjection, never enquired into them, but to turn their religion into derision, or deduce from them arguments to support the intolerant principles of their own. From our nation they have received a different treatment' (14–15).[11] While Hastings advocates tolerating different beliefs and valuing the mysteries of another religion, he takes the opportunity to contrast British colonial rule, European and enlightened, with Mughal rule, Oriental and despotic, and ascribe to the Bramins a confiding trust and respect for the benevolent British. Beyond this bias, though, the comparison is accurate: British rule was more favourable to Hindu traditions. The change from Mughal 'derision' to British study rescues Hindu scriptures from inaccessibility and lack of authority. Making study of Indian antiquities part of the East India Company's business, and looking to Hindu traditions as guides for rule, benefits the Bramins as cultural interpreters to the British: both gain a share of knowledge and power. Hastings mentions this process: he remarks that the Bramins who contributed to Nathaniel Brassey Halhed's translation of the 'Hindoo laws' did so 'cheerfully and gratuitously'; they 'refused to accept more than the moderate daily subsistence of one rupee each . . . nor will it much redound to my credit, when I add, that they have yet received no other reward for their meritorious labours' (15). It is in his interest to represent Indians as not wanting much in return from the English, but he seems surprised, even shamed, by the Bramin disregard for material profit, implicitly in contrast to imperialistic cashing in. This contrast may be hidden because of anxiety of empire; or, it may suggest that there are different kinds of profit, and a different kind of exchange here. By emphasizing the pecuniary rewards they ascetically forgo, Hastings calls attention away from the temporal power they gain through laws being based on texts their caste has authority to interpret. Bayly finds that 'hierarchy and the Brahmin interpretation of Hindu society which was theoretical rather than actual over much of India as late as 1750 was firmly ensconced a century later'; one cause was that 'British law began to dispense to all castes and communities the high Brahminical and scholarly traditions derived from the seminaries' (Bayly 1988: 158).[12] Hastings' picture of the Bramins could be part of the good treatment by which he made them allies: underneath the good Public Relations for both the benevolent British and the selfless Bramins, a tacit understanding of mutual interest.

Wilkins expresses similar sentiments on the Bramins' trust in the British but, unlike the diplomatic Hastings, is more blunt about the power games involved.

> The *Brahmans* esteem this work to contain all the grand mysteries of their religion; and so careful are they to conceal it from the knowledge of those of a different persuasion, and even the vulgar of their own, that the Translator might have fought in vain for assistance, had not the liberal treatment they have of late years experienced from the mildness of our government, the tolerating principles of our faith, and, above all, the personal attention paid to the learned men of their order by him [Hastings] under whose auspicious administration they have so long enjoyed, in the midst of surrounding troubles, the blessings of internal peace, and his exemplary encouragement, at length happily created in their breasts a confidence in his countrymen sufficient to remove almost every jealous prejudice from their minds. (23–4).

A different picture appears here. Reticence about secret traditions is not the natural result of subjection and derision. These learned men enjoy and can be swayed by personal attentions, and are prone to jealous prejudices which can be almost, not entirely, removed. Hastings is interested in endorsing his style of British rule; Wilkins is suspected by Marshall of being a deist (Marshall 1970: 29), and as he uses the Bramins as an excuse to get on the priestcraft hobbyhorse, it seems likely he is. For this purpose he adds a fourth presence: the vulgar, through whom he at once vindicates and condemns the Bramins. Wilkins asserts that though the Bramins 'believe but in one God, an universal spirit, they so far comply with the prejudices of the vulgar, as outwardly to perform all the ceremonies inculcated by the *Veds*, such as sacrifices, ablutions, &c. They do this, probably, more for the support of their own consequence, which could only arise from the great ignorance of the people, than in compliance with the dictates of *Kreeshna*' (24). The convenient separation of philosophical and popular is at work here. The Bramins' philosophy is pure, but they do not rise above the vulgar. They cater to popular belief and practice for their own prestige, and this makes them hypocritical and disloyal to their god. As if it is not already clear that he is using the Bramins as material for his own quarrels with Christianity, he adds, 'the superstition of the vulgar is the support of the priesthood in many other countries' (24). Wilkins finds reflected in Hinduism not only the Christian doctrines he admires, but also the Christian corruptions he condemns. Even though he sees not just Bramins but all priests as self-interested deceivers of their people, this is not exactly that British respect that wins Bramin confidence. Wilkins' frank judgement might win over those of the vulgar who are undeceived, but it is not likely to endear the ones who hold and manipulate the knowledge he needs for his studies; that takes Hastings' willingness to work with the Bramins' desire for 'consequence'. Wilkins is associated with liberality, mildness, tolerance, and above all, personal attention, as a countryman of Hastings: his Britishness, more than his actual attitude, gives him credibility with the Bramins. Wilkins does not mention his own Sanskrit scholarship as potentially giving him an entrée. This could be humility, but it could also be a comment on the philosophical confounded with the practical, academic pursuits embroiled in petty politics: perhaps he thinks his knowledge and interest would hold little sway over these Bramins, without Hastings' diplomatic manoeuvrings.

Hastings is concerned to combat English prejudice against 'the inhabitants of India' who 'not very long since . . . were considered by many, as creatures scarce elevated above the degree of savage life'. He wishes to replace this misconception with an accurate picture from Indians themselves, but for this to work, the popular must again be devalued in favour of the philosophical: 'Every instance which brings their real character home to observation will impress us with a more generous sense of feeling for their natural rights, and teach us to estimate them by the measure of our own. But such instances can only be obtained in their writings' (13). Though Hastings, unlike Blake, is in the midst of Indian culture, he still displaces it on to writing, and since this is an introduction to the *Geeta*, the writings in question are not contemporary. Present-day Indians will be respected not in their own right but because of their more illustrious ancestors, who were closer to the source which unites all religions and cultures, and whose writings can, more easily than current practices of devotional Hinduism, be seen by Hastings as 'accurately corresponding with . . . the Christian dispensation, and most powerfully illustrating its fundamental doctrines' (10). Such correspondence is the necessary basis for English appreciation of Indian rights: they are 'natural rights' (arising from the origin, the state of nature) and are estimated 'by the measure of our own'. Hastings' argument is also an affirmation of Braminical importance. The 'real character' of Indians is not found in the activities or opinions of the lower castes, but in the texts and textual authority associated with the highest caste, the philosophers.

Hastings goes on to say that these ancient writings 'will survive when the British dominion in India shall have long ceased to exist, and when the sources which it once yielded of wealth and power are lost to remembrance' (13). Considering what was at stake in the question of which culture was oldest, it is impressive to hear Hastings characterize 'British dominion' as historically insignificant, and India as enduring eternally. As daring as the statement is, it is also carefully qualified. Hastings predicts the demise of British power: not altogether, but in India. The British will depart when wealth and power have been yielded, which is only economically logical, and the same logic would suggest moving on, indefinitely, to greener pastures. If Britain is a young, opportunistic upstart, it will act like one. However, grammatically, it is not India that yields wealth and power to Britain, but 'British dominion in India' that yields to an unspecified object: Hastings leaves room to interpret British rule as generally profitable, to India as well. The 'sources of wealth and power' on both sides will be 'lost to remembrance' on both sides. This makes British dominion transient and unimportant in its greatness, but also in its transgressions. It engages in exchange of wealth and power with India and can move on without attachments or regrets, because, in the long run, both will get over any damage, and use up any gains. Not specifying who yields or who forgets, Hastings need not measure which side prospers or suffers most. As with the 'real character' of Indians, valuing the ancient writings allows the present to be written off. It also extends mutual benefit beyond material wealth and power. Indian writings will endure beyond the memory of British dominion, and the East India Company, by publishing the *Geeta*, contributes to, and partakes of, that longevity.

It is not, however, ultimate longevity in the case of the *Geeta*. The Hindu scriptures which can make the claim of greatest antiquity are the Vedas, but they were almost inaccessible. Wilkins admits he has not read the Vedas, because they are hard to come by and difficult to study, for Bramins as well: 'there are but few men in *Banaris* who understand any part of them' (26). Yet, Wilkins is nonetheless able to make an observation about them that had 'escaped all the commentators, and was received with great astonishment by the *Pandeet*, who was consulted in the translation' (26). Because the *Geeta* 'mentions only three of the four books of the *Veds*', Wilkins contests 'the present belief that the whole four were promulgated by *Brahma* at the creation' (25). It turns out that Wilkins was correct, that the fourth Veda is later (Hinnells 1995: 547), but he astonishes his pandeet who was going on the authority of his own tradition. Of course, the sheer antiquity of Hindu writings was astonishing to those who considered Judeo-Christian tradition to be the most ancient and authoritative, with an exclusive claim to divine inspiration. Here, Wilkins strikes an equivalent outsider's blow, but it does not have an equivalent effect. Questioning the age of a Veda does not damage Vedic authority which is not based on the Judeo-Christian assumption of singular origin, but it makes a move toward saving Biblical authority on its own terms. It also allows Wilkins to participate in the study of the Vedas, even though he has not read them. Their ancientness may threaten the status of the Bible, and their difficulty and rarity obstruct Wilkins' scholarship, but though he cannot completely solve these problems, his discovery makes a dent in them.

Wilkins vindicates his attention to a later text by casting the *Geeta* as a more refined development. He associates the Vedas with superstition and priestcraft, and considers 'the principal design' of the *Geeta*'s dialogues 'to unite all the prevailing modes of worship of those days; and, by setting up the doctrine of the unity of the Godhead, in opposition to idolatrous sacrifices, and the worship of images, to undermine the tenets inculcated by the *Veds*.' He has chosen a text more admirable and worthy of study than the most ancient, apparently because it has caught on to the correct (Judeo-Christian) idea of denouncing polytheism and idolatry. Although such commonalities exist between Wilkins' variety of Christianity and the *Geeta*, he still asks 'the reader' to 'have the liberality to excuse the obscurity of many passages' from which the efforts of his notes have been 'insufficient to remove the veil of mystery' (24–5). This is nothing to apologize for; Wilkins underplays his accomplishments here. As the first Westerner to produce any extended translation from Sanskrit (Marshall 1970: 5, 12), he faced, and removed, enormous obscurities. He describes the difficulty of the *Geeta* by Christian analogy: 'small as the work may appear, it has had more comments than the Revelations.' Although Oriental scriptures do not have an exclusive monopoly on inscrutability, they out-obscure the most obscure book of the Bible; not only that, but their commentaries are yet 'more obscure than the original'. While contextualizing the *Geeta* in terms a Christian reader would understand, Wilkins gets in another dig at his Christian opponents. The remarks on interpretations of the *Geeta* could apply to interpretations of Revelation as well, and generally to the right way to approach Christian scripture: 'it was thought better to leave many of the most difficult passages for the exercise of the reader's own judgment, than to mislead him by such wild opinions as no one syllable of the text could authorize' (25). Applied to *Geeta* or Bible, his recommendation renders priestcraft superfluous while skewering its sophistry.

Hastings spends much of his introduction creating an apology for the *Geeta's* 'sublime' and 'obscure' style in terms which, incidentally, seem suitable to describe Blake's prophecies: 'Many passages will be found obscure, many will seem redundant; others will be found cloathed with ornaments of fancy unsuited to our taste, and some elevated to a track of sublimity into which our habits of judgment will find it difficult to pursue them' – yet he asserts 'few . . . will shock either our religious faith or moral sentiments' (7). For all the cultural alienation he feels he has to mediate, he somehow finds that the *Geeta* constitutes 'a single exception, among all the known religions of mankind, of a theology accurately corresponding with that of the Christian dispensation, and most powerfully illustrating its fundamental doctrines' (10), such niggling exceptions as polytheism, monism and reincarnation aside. Clearly, a certain selectivity allows Hastings to take this view, and he recommends the same for other readers: he asks them to allow for 'obscurity, absurdity, barbarous habits, and a perverted morality' and recommends that 'where the reverse appears', it should be received 'as so much clear gain' (7). While he recognizes that the *Geeta* cannot be properly judged by 'rules drawn from the ancient or modern literature of Europe', nor its 'sentiments or manners', nor its 'tenets of religion, and moral duty' (7), those parts of it which are valuable to Christian readers are those that coincide with Christian views.

In the *Descriptive Catalogue*, Blake also finds value in difference by making it the same:

> The antiquities of every Nation Under Heaven, is no less sacred than that of the Jews. They are the same thing as Jacob Bryant, and all antiquaries have proved. How other antiquities came to be neglected and disbelieved, while those of the Jews are collected and arranged, is an enquiry, worthy of both the Antiquarian and the Divine. All had originally one language, and one religion, this was the religion of Jesus, the everlasting Gospel. Antiquity preaches the Gospel of Jesus. (E 543)

He begins by asserting the equal sacredness of all cultural traditions, but the singular verb ('antiquities . . . is') signals what comes next: 'they are the same thing'. Their sacredness relies on their similarity, not to each other but to Christianity. Perhaps it is to be a 'reasoning historian', such as he rails against in the next sentence, to point out that it is difficult to have Christianity before Christ. It is possible to reduce the anachronism by taking Blake to mean that the Gospel of Jesus is one of many later embodiments of the ancient religion but, still, it is the version given attention here. If it is worthy of enquiry why the Jewish antiquities are collected and others neglected, it is also worth enquiring why Blake neglects them here by not naming them.[13] Some specificity would have served the point that they are 'no less sacred'; if this is so, then the original religion would be reincarnated just as faithfully in an everlasting *Geeta* as an everlasting Gospel. Blake's choice of Jacob Bryant to represent 'all antiquarians' only emphasizes that Blake considers all mythologies to be different versions of the one he favours, and he will not let anachronism or faulty scholarship deter him. Bryant's motivation is 'confirmation of the Mosaic account'; he promises 'it will be found, from repeated evidence, that every thing, which the divine historian has transmitted, is most assuredly true', other world mythologies being less accurate accounts of the same history (Trawick 1967: 171, 176). As has frequently been observed, Bryant's 'textually myopic methods and pious assumptions' were out of date in 1774 when his *New System* was published, and ridiculed by contemporaries such as Fontenelle (Feldman and Richardson 1972: 241). Even more outdated than Wilkins' and Hastings' variety of Orientalism, this reference emphasizes that Blake's comparative mythography is rather less than current, or that he prefers older models because they are more conducive to his purposes.[14]

The *Descriptive Catalogue* offers an early history of art parallel to its history of religions. Blake discusses

> those Apotheoses of Persian, Hindoo, and Egyptian Antiquity, which are still preserved on rude monuments, being copies from some stupendous originals now lost or perhaps buried till some happier age. The Artist having been taken in vision into the ancient republics, monarchies, and patriarchates of Asia, has seen those wonderful originals called in the Sacred Scriptures the Cherubim, which were sculptured and painted on walls of Temples, Towers, Cities, Palaces, and erected in the highly cultivated states of Egypt, Moab, Edom, Aram, among the Rivers of Paradise. (E 530–1)

He adds that Greek art and mythology are copied 'from greater works of the Asiatic Patriarchs' (E 531). Though the originals are 'Asiatic', Blake places them in the Biblical Near East: they are done by 'Patriarchs', they are called 'Cherubim', and they are 'erected in' Biblical lands connected to Eden. The origin of art and mythology is placed inside Judeo-Christian tradition and made even more exclusive because Blake's access to the 'wonderful originals' is through vision; the ones which are 'still preserved on rude monuments' for anyone to see are, though excellent copies, still mere copies. Vision gives nineteenth-century English Blake direct access to the original and superior works of the ancients, after which he models his own productions. He uses the ancient world, then, as a mine of inspiration. Blake has a monopoly through vision, the unique trade route he has discovered; it also allows him to represent his ancient East as he pleases, because who could travel there, in the same way to the same place, to verify? What works or voices could come from the visionary East, unmediated by Blake, to contradict? The disadvantage is that if the monopoly is imaginary, so are the profits.

The context of this discussion of 'wonderful originals' is Blake's description of 'The Spiritual Form of Pitt Guiding Behemoth'. 'The two Pictures of Nelson and Pitt are compositions of a mythological cast, similar to those Apotheoses of Persian, Hindoo, and Egyptian Antiquity.' As Blake admits, he wishes to 'emulate the grandeur' of ancient heroes and 'apply it to modern Heroes, on a smaller scale' (E 531), borrowing not only the 'grandeur' of temporally and geographically distant cultures for Englishmen of the present day, but also the mythological ability of heroes to approach godhead, 'apotheoses': Blake produces smaller-scale euhemerism for Pitt and Nelson. There are straight and ironic possibilities here: is he explicitly making these leaders into gods, and implicitly making them into false gods, mere humans with exaggerated reputations, while linking them to the principles of comparative mythology and histories of religious error? In the next paragraph he writes, 'The Artist wishes it was now the fashion to make such monuments [as the "wonderful originals"], and then he should not doubt of having a national commission to execute these two Pictures on a scale that is suitable to the grandeur of the nation, who is the parent of his heroes' (E 531). Blake borrows grandeur more for himself as an artist than for Pitt and Nelson, making it more understandable that he calls them 'his heroes': they are the 'heroes' he has created in these pieces.

'The Ancient Britons' offers a similar list of 'Ancient Sculpture and Painting, and Architecture, Gothic, Grecian, Hindoo and Egyptian'. These, along with 'Milton, Shakespeare, Michael Angelo, Rafael . . . are the extent of the human mind. The human mind cannot go beyond the gift of God, the Holy Ghost' (E 544). This is another example of the syncretism I have argued most Blake criticism on the *Geeta* shares with comparative mythography. In a sort of collective unconscious, all of these different cultural productions are not only equated, but traced back to Christian inspiration: the Holy Ghost. The human mind is defined, its limits set by the Holy Ghost; therefore, all human minds must be Christian. An earlier point in the same argument suggests Blake's motivation for using this scheme of exclusive origin:

> He knows that what he does is not inferior to the grandest Antiquities. Superior they cannot be, for human power cannot go beyond either what he does, or what they have done, it is the gift of God, it is inspiration and vision. He had resolved to emulate those precious remains of antiquity, he has done so and the result you behold; his ideas of strength and beauty have not been greatly different. (E 544)

In protesting that his art cannot be inferior to antiquities, Blake may be dealing with insecurity about the quality of his art, or fear of artistic failure. His aggrandizement of Pitt and Nelson − and his wish that antiquity would revive so that he could be a public artist − show an intense desire for success and recognition, which we know was not met: 'The exhibition' the *Descriptive Catalogue* was written for 'was a complete failure. No works appear to have been sold and only one, hostile, review has been traced' (Butlin 1981, 2:472). But if Blake's present day did not confirm the value of his art, the connection to antiquity he creates ensures that on some level his works achieve the limits of human power; they can partake of the primacy of the original.

The work of the Orientalists began to reveal that the ultimate source was not Judeo-Christian; antiquarian searches for ultimate origins were pushing those very origins out of Western reach. 'A kind of rationalist pathos' has been discerned in Jones: 'the Bible as accurate history . . . was doomed to extinction, in part by his own researches' (Shaffer 1975: 121). Still, Jones, Hastings and Wilkins all take this with equanimity. Jones is secure enough to consider the possibility that Moses drew from Indian fountains, even though he dismisses it in the end.[15]

Hastings freely admits the mortality of the British Empire, in India at least, compared to the eternal duration of Hindu literature. Wilkins intrepidly subjects the Vedas to some textual criticism, despite the impenetrable obscurity of these oldest of scriptures. As though admitting that the origin is inaccessible to them, they approach as close as they can, finding ways to displace the power and longevity of the ancient, ways for it to rub off by association since they cannot wholly claim it. But if the single, pure origin is suspected to be not historical fact but Judeo-Christian fantasy, then it can be fantasized, and this is just what Blake does: he imagines the wonderful originals according to his desires. Although in 1809 this claim is outdated, and endangered by the impending devaluation of mythology seen in Mill and Macaulay, Blake had staked it in the 1790s in his first explicit reference to Hinduism in the *Song of Los*. He apparently advocates equal sacredness (or lack thereof) for all religions when he writes that 'Rintrah gave Abstract Philosophy to Brama in the East' while 'To Trismegistus. Palamabron gave an Abstract Law: / To Pythagoras Socrates and Plato'; 'Jesus . . . recievd / A Gospel from wretched Theotormon;' 'Antamon . . . to Mahomet a loose Bible gave' and 'to Odin, Sotha gave a Code of War' (3:11–30) (E 67). In each case, a Blake-invented personage is credited with revealing the world's philosophies and religions to their founders: not only Hindu philosophy to Brama, but also Christianity to Christ. Through syncretism, its strengths and weaknesses combined, Blake's own mythology can be the origin of all.

## Notes

1  Northrop Frye lists Krishna's chariot, along with Venus', Juno's, Bacchus', and Ezekiel's, as inspiration for Blake's chariot symbolism (Frye 1947: 273). Kathleen Raine claims that the Hindu and Greek concepts of reincarnation and cyclical time are the same (Raine 1969, 1: 252–3, 324). As recently as 2000, Joseph Denize similarly envisions a circle closing as Blake opens the *Geeta*: Indian philosophy meets up with one who has already encountered it through hermeticism, gnosticism, neoplatonism and alchemy (Denize 2000: 382–3).

2  Piloo Nanavutty enumerates the 'points of resemblance' between Blakean and Hindu accounts of creation, and finds 'complete agreement' between Blake's contraries and the concept of *Samsara* as developed in the *Gita* (Nanavutty 1957: 173). Charu Sheel Singh argues that the Four Zoas are conceived 'on the basis of the Gita's hierarchical idea of the human faculties' (Singh 1981: 180). He also considers Rintrah to be Indra because of their associations with thunder and with justice, and links Krishna in his totality with Albion as cosmic man (Singh 1988: 28, 30, 36). John Adlard stands out for arguing that Blake opposes the *Geeta*'s abdication of desire and closure of perception, but still demonstrates these differences through similarities in vocabulary, and adds evidence to Frye's association of the 'three classes' of *Milton* with the three 'Goon' or qualities of the *Geeta* (*satwa*, truth; *raja*, passion; and *tama*, darkness, according to Wilkins [107]) even though Elect, Redeemed and Reprobate seem quite clearly to be Protestant terms (Adlard 1964: 461–2).

3  Marshall shows that while comparative mythology was based on a Christian world-view, it could also be used to undermine Christian authority. If other religions were shown to contain elements of, and also predate, the Judeo-Christian tradition, that would prove it derivative, with no claim 'to be the unique instrument of God's providence' (Marshall 1970: 25). As he tellingly puts it, 'Hinduism was . . . used as a stick to beat Christianity' (Marshall 1970: 33). Even these sceptical arguments centre on Christianity and operate on its logic of a single, ultimate origin.

4  The arguments summarized here are focused on the 1790s. However, Makdisi, as part of these assertions, and Weir, elsewhere in his book, both draw on the *Descriptive Catalogue*, and my conclusion here argues that the tendencies of the *Catalogue* are apparent in the *Song of Los*.

5  For a full analysis of the 20 charges brought against Hastings, see Marshall 1965.

6  Makdisi emphasizes that though it was published 1817–36, 'Mill launched his project as early as 1806, when the first generation of romantic poets was still in its prime' (Makdisi 1998: 4).

7  In the 'Ancient Britons' section of the *Descriptive Catalogue*, Blake writes, 'The British Antiquities are now in the Artist's hands; all his visionary contemplations, relating to his own country and its ancient glory, when it was as it again shall be, the source of learning and inspiration' (E 542). Thomas Griffiths Wainewright plays on Blake as visionary antiquary, caricaturing him as 'Dr. Tobias Ruddicombe, MD' working on 'an account of an ancient, newly discovered, illuminated manuscript, which has to name "Jerusalem the Emanation of the Giant Albion!!!"' (in Bentley 1969: 371). On art and affluence, Blake argues, in *A Vision of the Last Judgment*, 'Works of Art can only be produced in Perfection where the Man is either in Affluence or is Above the Care of it . . . Some People & not a few Artists have asserted that the Painter of this Picture would not have done so well if he had been properly [patr[onized]] Encouragd Let those who think so reflect on the State of Nations under Poverty & their incapability of Art. tho Art is Above Either the Argument is better for Affluence than Poverty & tho he would not have been a greater Artist yet he would have produced Greater works of Art in proportion, to his means' (E 561).

8  Brockington's example is the payment of the pandits who advised Halhed on the Hindu law code, as mentioned in Hastings' *Geeta* introducion. Apparently, Hastings paid Halhed for these expenses 'after the Code was finished', so they must have been used towards Halhed's next project, the Bengali grammar. Then, according to the minutes of the trial, Hastings asked to be reimbursed for these and other out-of-pocket expenses 'on the eve of his return' to Britain. Brockington also mentions the 'preferment in Company service' and 'financial help from the agency for the Nawab of Oudh' Hastings arranged for Halhed, who in return defended Hastings 'in a whole series of pamphlets . . . after his return to London' (Brockington 1989: 93, 95–6). Hastings' financial involvement with the Begams of Oudh was the subject of the speech that ended in Sheridan's fainting fit.

9  That Blake would not reject imperial wealth as dirty money, and may rather have associated it with a desirable kind of patronage, is suggested by his relationship with Thomas Butts. As well as being his most reliable source of cash, Butts was, as Bentley notes, 'the only one of Blake's correspondents . . . to whom he spoke of his mythological characters by name' (Bentley 1956: 1052, 1065). As Chief Clerk of the Commissary General of Musters, responsible for keeping track of soldiers and equipment as well as paying the troops, he helped run the military arm of the empire. Like Hastings, he combined shady finances with forwarding others' interests. He was 'adept at finding places for his relatives and friends in his office' (possibly including Blake's brother James); one of various income supplements detailed by Bentley was approval of exorbitant overtime pay for his sons. The Commissary also ran foul of the rising concern for efficiency: it was abolished after a parliamentary inquiry ('Thomas Butts' 1053, 1057–8, 1064).

10  Blake consistently drops the s, perhaps creating a pun, and more disguises: Wil kin, Will Blake's kin or alter ego allowing him to be present in India among the Bramins. One reason for Blake to identify with Wilkins is that they were both involved hands-on in the mechanical as well as intellectual production of books. Besides the *Geeta* translation, the other great accomplishment associated with Wilkins is that he 'was the first to discover and, in 1778, personally use methods of engraving, casting and setting Bengali characters' (Schwab 1975: 37). According to Marshall, Wilkins 'personally made' all tools required for casting the font, 'with the sole assistance of Indian craftsmen' (Marshall 1970: 11),

somewhat like Blake producing engravings with the sole assistance of Catherine, the extent of her interest and contribution uncertain.

11  Unless otherwise specified, all quotations from Hastings and Wilkins are taken from their introductions to the *Geeta*.

12  The dispersal of power widens with this dissemination of Braminical traditions to all castes. At the same time as it puts the Bramins in the position to influence the law, it also takes away their exclusive hold on this knowledge – part of the jealously secretive priestcraft Hastings and Wilkins discuss, and break through.

13  Even when Blake makes specific references to India, Hindus and Hinduism, it is always as one item in a list of nations. India serves to represent the East, or the whole world in its vast extent. *Milton* adds personification and description, but it draws on the Oriental stereotypes of indolence and opulence: 'India rose up from his golden bed: / As one awakened in the night' (31:14–15). The other references appear in *The Song of Los* (3:11, discussed below), *Milton* (14:7, 35:16), and *Jerusalem* (58:39, 67:40, 72:39, 80:47, 82:28).

14  Makdisi bases his argument that Blake's purposes are anti-imperialist on the same concepts from the *Descriptive Catalogue*: the irrational and anachronistic approach to history, and the original oneness of diverse religions and cultures. He finds in these the liberating potential to multiply possible pasts, presents and futures, and allow contradictions such as a world unity which preserves national identity (Makdisi 1998: 3, Makdisi 2003a: 257). I agree that these concepts could be profitably turned to such 'utopian' purposes (Makdisi 1998: 171), but I do not find that Blake uses them in this way.

15  Shaffer emphasizes Jones' 'rejection' of 'the revolutionary implications of his work on the antiquity of Hindu civilization' (Shaffer 1975: 117), while Weir accents his 'courage to question the authority of the Bible' (Weir 2003: 83).

# PART II

Blake in the Orient:
The Early–Twentieth–
Century Japanese Reception

# 12 Blake's Oriental Heterodoxy: Yanagi's Perception of Blake

Ayako Wada

When we consider the history of Blake's reception in Japan, no one will dispute the vital importance of Muneyoshi Yanagi (1889–1961). His name, now predominantly known as a religious philosopher and father of the folk craft movement in Japan, is deeply engraved in the hearts of the subsequent Japanese students of Blake for the publication of his monumental work, *William Blake*: it extended over seven hundred and fifty pages and was published in 1914 when the author was only 25. This is the first serious book-length study of Blake in Japan and the achievement is incomparable in terms of the level of devotion to Blake as well as the depth of study with Yanagi's Japanese predecessors.[1] Although Lafcadio Hearn (1850–1904) lectured at the Imperial University of Tokyo on Blake first in 1899 and twice more in the subsequent years and the lecture notes were posthumously published,[2] his coverage of Blake's works did not extend beyond those contained in the 1893 Muse's Library edition by W. B. Yeats, nor did it leave any traceable influence on the mind of the listeners (see Yano 1957: 535).[3]

Yanagi's enthusiasm for Blake – not only exemplified in his book but also demonstrated by his energetic activities as a member of the school of *Shirakaba* or White Birch,[4] the major ones of which are the Blake exhibitions in 1915 and 1919[5] – was certainly stirred by his British predecessors, and in terms of its evangelical devotion even rivalled theirs.[6] Although Yanagi's work has so far been mostly discussed in the context of Blake's reception in Japan, his achievement can never be fully appreciated unless it is compared to Blake's reception in Britain, both by contemporaries, and through to the early decades of the twentieth century. While Yanagi's highly comprehensive annotated Blake bibliography lists 57 academic works altogether, seven names are chosen as those to whom he is deeply indebted: they are Alexander Gilchrist, A. C. Swinburne, (William Michael and Dante Gabriel) Rossetti,[7] W. B. Yeats, Arthur Symons, John Sampson and A. G. B. Russell (Y xiii–xiv).[8] Among them, special attention ought to be given to Gilchrist and Swinburne: they are not only the first two names Yanagi listed but also those whose works he emphasized that every student of Blake must read (Y 740,743). Although Yanagi had already had a most important encounter with Blake when he first read *The Marriage of Heaven and Hell*, a copy of which he had borrowed from his friend Bernard Leach around 1911 (Y ix–x), his enthusiasm for Blake was all the more fuelled by the works of Gilchrist and Swinburne. In what follows, after the chronology of Blake's reception in Britain is briefly delineated, their achievements are examined so that Yanagi's kinship with them may be gradually made clear. In so doing, this chapter will expound how Yanagi 'loved the East in the West' in Blake, as Leach commented 12 years after Yanagi's death (Hisamori 1977: 176), and also seek to suggest what made Blake for him, if not a simple figure, at least a reasonably accessible one.

In order to delineate the relationship between Gilchrist, Swinburne and Yanagi, the focus must be on the period between 1827 and 1920. This can be divided into three stages just as G. E. Bentley broke down the longer period including Blake's lifetime between 1757 and 1920 in *Blake Books* (Bentley 1977: 15–32): works which serve as landmarks to distinguish the one stage from the other are Gilchrist's *Life of William Blake* (1863) and E. J. Ellis and W. B. Yeats's *The Works of William Blake, Poetic, Symbolic, and Critical* (1893). The period is marked by the gradual ascendancy of Blake: during the first stage (1827–63) Blake was saved from oblivion; during the second stage (1863–93) Blake's reputation was crucially revitalized; during the third stage (1893–1920), serious efforts were made to present Blake's works to the public in a more accessible form. Although numerous publications during the period are often bewilderingly anomalous by present–day standards, they are, nevertheless, the foundation of subsequent Blake studies,[9] without which, for instance, Sir Geoffrey Keynes's definitive edition of *The Writings of William Blake* would never have emerged in 1925. The perspective now glimpsed by the introduction of these three divisions into the period is that Gilchrist dominates the second stage and that Swinburne also belongs to it; Yanagi's work produced during the cradle of Blake's reception in Britain belongs to the end of the third stage as one that received their influence.

Gilchrist's work is analogous to what T. S. Eliot called in 'Tradition and the Individual Talent' 'the new work of art' (Eliot 1920; 1928: 41) that vitally destabilizes the order of the preceding works. Indeed, it exhibited an almost unprecedented power to renovate truth and reject the ungrounded speculations respectively shown in the preceding biographies of Blake: i.e. one in *Nollekens and his Times* (1828) by John Thomas Smith; the other in *Lives of the Most Eminent British Painters, Sculptors, and Architects* (1830) by Allan Cunningham. Smith was the first who attempted to appeal to the public on the basis that Blake was unjustly stigmatized as a man of deranged intellect due to the controversy between him and Robert Hartley Cromek/Thomas Stothard concerning the origin of Blake's tempera painting entitled *Sir Jeffery Chaucer and the Nine and Twenty Pilgrims on their Journey to Canterbury*. In Smith's eyes, Blake's design was clearly perceived as genuine as his conviction was betrayed in his statement that 'I most firmly believe few artists have been guilty of less plagiarisms than he [Blake]' (Bentley, *Blake Records* 2004a: 607).[10] Smith directed the public's attention to the panoramic view of the incident starting from the Blair's *Grave* illustrations and showed how Blake was exploited by Cromek. By adding similar accounts from Stothard's side also, Smith further testified to the unreliability of Cromek, who, to him, is 'a man who endeavoured to live by speculating upon the talents of others' (*BR* 613).[11] Cunningham's 'Life of Blake', in spite of its significance of numbering Blake as one of the most eminent British painters and thereby saving Blake's name from oblivion due to its wide circulation,[12] was far from serving in favour of Blake in the most critical point. Cunningham not only declared that Blake's design to the Canterbury Pilgrims was 'a failure' (*BR* 644)[13] but also attributed the cause of the Blake/Cromek controversy to Blake's confounding vision with reality, endorsing Cromek's response that 'the order had been given in a vision'

(*BR* 693). Cunningham ascribed the origin of the design to Stothard's *The Procession of Chaucer's Pilgrims to Canterbury* by claiming 'Blake's visit to Stothard during the early progress of his picture' as the 'startling testimony' (*BR* 643).[14] To Cunningham the engraver Cromek was 'a man of skill in art and taste in literature' (*BR* 642), whereas Blake was an untrustworthy two-fold figure – 'a man of sagacity and sense' during the day and one who 'gave a loose to his imagination' during the night (*BR* 639–40).

To Gilchrist, who discerned unmistakable genius in Blake, it was imperative to save Blake from the imputation of madness. The controversy concerning the design to Chaucer's Canterbury Pilgrims was crucial, as Gilchrist says:

> This squabble with Cromek was a discordant episode in Blake's life. The competition with Stothard it induced placed him in a false position, and, in most people's eyes, a wrong one . . .
> Now, too, was established for him the damaging reputation, 'Mad,' by which the world has since agreed to recognize William Blake. (Gilchrist 1945: 248)

Indeed, Blake's serious attempt to let the public judge whose design to the Canterbury Pilgrims is genuine between his and Stothard's by his 1809 exhibition and *Descriptive Catalogue* was given a most hostile review by Robert Hunt in *The Examiner* (dated 17 September 1809) and the reviewer publicly denounced Blake as 'an unfortunate lunatic, whose personal inoffensiveness secures him from confinement' (*BR* 283). To Gilchrist the question of Blake's sanity was presented as hanging on how his opponent was judged when the entirely opposite views on Cromek were introduced by Smith and Cunningham. Although Gilchrist could not entirely blame Cromek for showing 'bolder discernment of unvalued genius' (Gilchrist 1945: 218) and also for his sagacity in choosing the most fashionable and commercially successful engraver for Blake's designs to reach a wider public (ibid: 219), nevertheless, he uncovered the fact that 'Cromek jockeyed Blake out of his copyright' (ibid: 219–20) of Blair's *Grave* designs both by paying an insignificant amount of money for them and by transferring the task of engraving the designs from Blake to Schiavonetti. In addition to this, Cromek's highly insulting letter dated May 1807 to Blake was quoted as evidence to throw 'a flood of light' into the nature of the writer as the 'predacious Yorkshireman' (ibid: 254), who, far from gaining earthly fame for Blake, drove him to utter neglect and poverty.

In 1988, modern readers of Blake experienced a recurrence of the Blake–Cromek controversy between two critics and found in it the parallel relationship between Blake and Cromek: Dennis M. Read attributed the idea to paint an illustration of the Canterbury pilgrims to Cromek and argued that 'everything Blake did in his *Canterbury Pilgrims* project was an attempt to surpass corresponding parts of Cromek's project' (Read 1988: 171). Aileen Ward regarded Blake's version of the affair as 'a gradual reconfiguration of the events during his years of obscurity after 1810' and his relationship with Cromek as 'the most telling example of his loosening grip on reality during those years [between 1807 and 1812]' (Ward 1988–9: 87–8). We know how Bentley, in the spirit of Gilchrist, re-examined the relationship between Blake and Cromek by steering through incongruous evidences[15] to the fundamentally same conclusion reached by his predecessor with minor revisions.[16]

Just as Bentley points out that Gilchrist's *Life* gathered enthusiastic reviews and some reviewers carefully examining their words for years (*BB* 25), so Swinburne's *William Blake: a Critical Essay* developed out of a review published in 1868. While he paid the highest tributes to 'the high sincerity, the clear sagacity, the vigorous sense of truth and lucid power of proof' in Gilchrist and infinitely valued his *Life* as the first 'acceptable and endurable portrait of Blake' (Swinburne 1868: 80), its deficiency was also apparent to him, as he put it:

> If the 'Songs' be so good, are not those who praise them bound to examine and try what merit may be latent in the 'Prophecies'? – bound at least to explain as best they may how the one comes to be worth so much and the other worth nothing? On this side alone the biography appears to us emphatically deficient . . . But a biographer must be capable of expounding the evangel (or, if such a word could be, 'dysangel') of his hero, however far he may be from thinking it worth acceptance. And this, one must admit, the writers on Blake have upon the whole failed of doing. (Swinburne 1868: 116)

Swinburne's work, as he articulates (Swinburne 1868: ix), was intended as a supplement to Gilchrist's *Life* to redress its defects. Indeed, he was the first who firmly held the end of the golden string, and who, far from being repelled by the 'grotesque' exterior of Blake's prophetic works,[17] was able successfully to wind the string towards a profound understanding of Blake's heterodoxy. Although the further task of tracing Blake's genealogy was left to Yeats, Swinburne greatly contributed to establishing Blake's reputation as a poet, and directed people's serious attention to his writings rather than his commercial engravings: as Bentley indicates, by 1890 there were already facsimile reproductions of all of Blake's illuminated books except *The Book of Ahania* and *The Book of Los* (Blake 1893a: 3–4).

The great achievements of Gilchrist and Swinburne, which were respectively perceived by Yanagi as the classic of Blake biography (Y 740) and the best of Blake criticism (Y 742), certainly gave him an enormous incentive not only to write an essay on Blake as published in *Shirakaba* in Spring 1914 but also to develop it into a book which combines both of their achievements.[18] Indeed, Yanagi's *William Blake* can be best regarded as a critical or panegyrical biography of a rare kind for the first time presented to the Japanese public, the author of which fulfilled the task of what Swinburne felt requisite, 'expounding the evangel of the hero' now firmly embraced as truth. The work is almost reminiscent of the Gospels of the New Testament as the association between Jesus and Blake is also made in Yanagi. He says:

> If Jesus had ever begged his enemy pardon in a meek voice, there would never have been churches built for him on the earth. If Blake had not been in wrath, we could not have read the *Descriptive Catalogue* nor seen the design to the *Canterbury Pilgrims*. As Jesus was strong, Blake praised his life. As Blake was proud, I wrote this critical biography. (Y 343)

Although neither Bentley's *Blake Studies in Japan* (Bentley 1994: 128) nor his recent *The Stranger from Paradise* (Bentley 2001: 447–51) shows the recognition of Yanagi's work as such, the author clearly states that he fulfilled the task of the first biographer of Blake in Japan (Y xi). Yanagi's work, of course, is decidedly different from a biography of the ordinary kind: although he fully integrated

Blake's biographical facts as examined as truth, in order to illuminate his internal life Yanagi primarily regarded Blake's works as autobiographical as this perception was first expressed by John Sampson (Y 736; Blake 1905: xix). Yanagi read Blake's earliest to latest works as reliable evidence of his spiritual history. Also, in his work, as often recognized (Yura 1990: 700), Yanagi is so united in inspiration with Blake that the readers sometimes cannot tell whether he is expounding his own philosophy or Blake's. Yanagi turned to various editions of Blake to access the most reliable text and its interpretations. While he acknowledges his large debt to the British scholarship of Blake studies, he also confidently declares that he believes he made clear his own original understanding of Blake in his book (Y xiii–xiv). This is where the chief enduring value of his work lies, apart from the rare quality of the critical biography.

Among those who recognized almost incomparable genius in Blake and those who struggled to defend him, Yanagi was one of the very few who valued him highly because of his religious heterodoxy. Even Samuel Palmer, the most enthusiastic devotee, who made his pilgrimage to Blake's flat and 'kissed Blake's bell-handle before venturing to pull it' (*BR* 403), only accepted those of Blake's ideas that were congenial to his conventional beliefs: Bentley notes that just as Yeats said of Linnell's grown children, so Linnell and Palmer were equally 'no little troubled at the thought that maybe he [*Blake*] was heretical' (Bentley 2001: 409). Also noteworthy is how Frederick Tatham claimed that 'he [Blake] was in all essential points orthodox in his belief', discrediting many anecdotes of Blake's eccentric speeches (such as those recorded by Crabb Robinson) as 'a piece of sarcasm, upon the Enquirer' (*BR* 684–5).[19] Even Gilchrist was almost repelled by Blake's religious heterodoxy as either his own or derived from the early Gnostics and found him 'otherwise so erratic in his religious opinions as to shock orthodox Churchmen' (Gilchrist 1945: 326). Swinburne, who regarded Blake as 'neither Christian nor infidel' but as a 'heretic', said: 'Such men, according to the temper of the times, are burnt as demoniacs or pitied as lunatics' (Swinburne 1868: 210). In *The Sacred Wood*, Eliot, Yanagi's almost exact contemporary, although discerning genius in Blake, famously branded his prophecies an 'ingenious piece of home-made furniture', which sadly lacks 'a framework of accepted and traditional ideas' (Eliot 1928: 133–4). While, in the West, this misconception promoted critical excavation of a variety of possible genealogies – Neoplatonic, cabbalistic, artisan[20] – but remained a major stumbling block to Blake's reception, Yanagi was without any such inhibitions. To Yanagi, Blake's philosophy not only foreshadowed the thoughts of such modern philosophers as Nietzsche, Bergson and James[21] but also went far beyond them into the infinite future (Y 526–33). He confidently prophesied: 'There comes the day when Blake will emerge before the human beings as a profound revelation' (Y 519).

Now, our focus must be on Blake's religious heterodoxy that was embraced as the eternal truth by Yanagi. In the very centre of his perception of Blake exists Jesus as 'the Human Form Divine'. Jesus was by far the most remarkable figure to Blake as in him the unity of the human and the divine is most conspicuously attained. Blake's first comprehensive and most direct attempt to let each individual realize their own divinity and thereby reach the tree of life is made in *The Marriage of Heaven and Hell*. To attain this end what Blake attempted to redress was the dualistic perception of the human existence in which the body was separated from the soul and in which the former was moralistically devalued against the latter. However, his blessing of the improvement of sensual enjoyment (E 39) that derive from the body as well as his consecration of the Poetic Genius were taken as blasphemous even by his devotee: Samuel Palmer thought that 'the whole page [*from the MARRIAGE*] . . . would at once exclude the work from every drawing-room table in England' (Bentley 2001: 409). The dialectical mode of the work that added counterpoint to the Swedenborgian angelic wisdom was perceived by modern critics as 'a kind of holy satire' (see Blake 1993: 127). Here, however, as Harold Bloom diagnosed, a difficulty in reading the work in terms of marking the 'limits of its irony' and thereby knowing where Blake speaks straight would inevitably loom up (see Bloom 1971: 55). A genuine difficulty in becoming a fit audience of the *Marriage* seems to lie elsewhere – as David Fuller put it, 'It is impossible adequately to *hear* a great or noble thing unless the spirit is moved' (Fuller 2005: 142).[22] During Blake's early reception, Swinburne and Yanagi are those who never spared superlatives for the work. By quoting the entire work in his book, Swinburne first 'published' the *Marriage* in a typescript form.[23] Indeed, he paid the highest tribute to it as 'the greatest of all his books . . . and the greatest produced by the eighteenth century' (Swinburne 1868: 226–7). Also, it was the *Marriage* that gave Yanagi a crucial understanding of Blake's genius. As Yanagi esteemed it as 'the authoritative work which deserves the highest throne of the English literary history in light of its freedom of thought and depth of truth manifested' (Y 121), the unusual significance of the work was plain to him.

Its second 'Memorable Fancy', in which the poet dines with the prophets Isaiah and Ezekiel, was taken as 'indubitable evidence of Blake's insanity' by both contemporaries and later critics (see Keynes 1949, notes on plates 12–13) and described by modern critics as 'a naughty satirical banquet scene' which turned Isaiah and Ezekiel from the priesthood into poets after the manner of Sweden-borg's 'Memorable Relation' (Blake 1993: 213). It contained, however, 'higher tones of exposition' to Swinburne (Swinburne 1868: 237) and in it to Yanagi 'Blake's sublime thought of the Poetic Genius is most beautifully shining' (Y 137–8). The poet hears Isaiah endorse the idea that when unity is attained with the divine they are no longer two but one and the divine is not directly seen externalized, as he says: 'I saw no God. nor heard any, in a finite organical percep-tion' (E 38).[24] Here, the poet further lets him communicate what can be regarded as the very sign of this crucial unity: he says, 'but my senses discover'd the infinite in every thing' (E 38). In this most powerful moment of imagination or the Poetic Genius that is perceived as the first principle of human existence Blake also felt that 'every thing that lives is Holy' (E 45). Yanagi repeatedly noted down as the eternal poem the following lines which were conceived in such a moment:

> To see a World in a Grain of Sand
> And a Heaven in a Wild Flower
> Hold Infinity in the palm of your hand
> And Eternity in an hour
> ('Auguries of Innocence', 1–4; E 490)

The incommunicable vision of the world far beyond the highest point attainable by Cartesian or empiricist reasoning is also expressed by S. T. Coleridge as 'the one Life' ('The Eolian Harp', 26; 1970–2001 Vol. 16: 233), dearly remembered by Wordsworth as 'obstinate questionings / Of sense and outward things, / Fallings from us, vanishings' ('Ode' 142–4; 1952–63, 4: 283), and called by Daisetz Suzuki the Zen Buddhist 'the continuum' (Suzuki 1972: 48).[25] The poet who was immediately associated with Blake by Yanagi as well as Swinburne, however, was not one of the English Romantics but Walt Whitman (see Swinburne 1868: 334–7; Y 553–66). While Yanagi particularly marked Blake's heterodoxy as Oriental, what he found manifested in the poems of Blake and Whitman was 'Oriental pantheism' (Y 559): as Blake said in *There is No Natural Religion*, 'He who sees the Infinite in all things sees God' (E 3). It was Swinburne, however, who first recognized 'Oriental pantheism' in Blake as his comments on *Milton* indicate:

> . . . he [Satan] represents Monotheism with its stringent law and sacerdotal creed, Jewish or Christian, as opposed to Pantheism whereby man and God are one, and by culture and perfection of humanity man makes himself God. The point of difference here between Blake and many other western Pantheists is that in his creed self-abnegation (in the mystic sense, not the ascetic – the Oriental, not the Catholic) is the highest and only perfect form of self-culture. (Swinburne 1868: 292)

Swinburne's perception of Oriental 'self-abnegation' in Blake is also shared by Yanagi as he says:

> Self-Annihilation is not the self-denial but the absolute expansion of the self and the infinite expression of the individuality. It means the union between the self and the universe . . . It is no longer we but God who exists. (Y 424)

Yanagi's perception of Blake seems to be indebted to or at least has much in common with Swinburne's in most essential points. Here, however, there are reasons to believe that they similarly benefited from the knowledge of the homogeneous origin of Hindu thought. Although Yanagi's understanding of Blake has so far been explained in terms of his knowledge of Zen Buddhism, mostly due to his relationship with Daisetsz Suzuki (see Yura 1990: 31),[26] among his extensive readings it can be more securely attributed to his knowledge of the Upanishads, the concluding part of the Vedas. Swinburne also shows his knowledge of 'the fragments . . . of the Pantheistic poetry of the East' (Swinburne 1868: 335),[27] which are associated with the works of Blake and Whitman. Indeed, while the last chapter of Yanagi's book is entirely devoted to the analysis of Blake's direct or indirect genealogy or kinship with various mystics, philosophers, artists and poets from the ancient to the modern age (Y 517–66),[28] what is presented first and foremost, and what only explains Blake's Oriental heterodoxy among them, is the kinship he suggests between Blake and the ancient scriptures of Brahmanism. Indeed, the Upanishads preach the highest knowledge of self-realization through the union between Brahma (the incomprehensible and imperishable universal Self) and atman (the individual self). Yanagi also pinpoints the distinct characteristic of this ancient philosophy as 'the most radical pantheism' (Y 520). A few lines from the Upanishads will suffice to illustrate the point:

> He [Brahma] is the one God, hidden in all beings, all-pervading, the self within all beings, watching over all works, dwelling in all beings, the witness, the perceiver, the only one, free from qualities. (Svetâsvatara-upanishads 6.11; The Upanishads Vol. XV, 263–4)

The last lines of *Jerusalem* read:

All Human Forms identified even Tree Metal Earth & Stone. all
Human Forms identified, living going forth & returning wearied
Into the Planetary lives of Years Months Days & Hours reposing
And then Awaking into his Bosom in the Life of Immortality.
And I heard the Name of their Emanations they are named Jerusalem
(99.1–5; E 258–9)

What is unfolded here is the infinite vision that is the very sign of oneness attained between the self and the innermost divinity, who is perceived as both inside and outside, pervading all the universe. Yanagi affirms that 'in terms of the idea of imagination (expanded to the idea of God) and the idea of life, Blake's thought is essentially homogeneous to the most ancient Oriental philosophy' (Y 520). This is the crucial point addressed by Yanagi; just as Gilchrist worked on an entirely different point, by the dynamics of which, one who was cursed as insane is turned to sane and the one who was regarded as heterodox is turned to most orthodox – although Blake, who most gloriously conquered the natural man, is already in a sphere far beyond the reach of those dualistic qualities.

## Notes

This is a detailed version of a paper delivered to the International Blake Conference ('Blake in the Orient') at Kyoto University, 29 November 2003. I'm grateful to Steve Clark, David Fuller and Peter Malekin for their encouragement and invaluable comments.

  1  The first reference to Blake in Japanese was made in *Bankoku Jinmei Jisho* (*A Biographical Dictionary of the World*) (1893) published by Bimyo Yamada (whose given name is Taketaro); the first appearance of a Blake poem in Japanese was 'The Ecchoing Green' in *Obei Meika Shishu* (*Anthology of English and American Poetry*) (1894) translated by Takeki Owada (see Matsushima 2003: 245–7; Bentley, *Blake Studies in Japan* (1994), xv). For the list of the translators of Blake's lyrics and writers of some articles on Blake before Yanagi, see Bentley 1994: xviii–xxi. An article of 1911 by Tetsuro Watsuji (1899–1960) entitled 'Blake as a forerunner of symbolism' is identified by Kunihiko Nakajima as the translation of Chapter VIII (part II: 'Mad Naked Blake') of James Huneker's *Egoists: a Book of Supermen* (1909) with some introductory remarks by Watsuji (see Nakajima 1991: 94–6). For a notable difference between Watsuji's view on Blake and Yanagi's, see Nakami 2003: 55–8.
  2  One is 'Blake – The First English Mystic', *Interpretations of Literature*, ed. John Erskine, 2 vols (New York: Dodd, 1915), Vol. 1, 51–71; the other is 'William Blake', *Some Strange English Literary Figures of The Eighteenth and Nineteenth Centuries*, ed. Ryuji Tanabe (Tokyo: Hokuseido, 1927), 3–21.
  3  Hearn's extensive coverage of English literary history during his seven years' lectureship between 1896 and 1903 can also be known by his exhaustive notes for students, which were posthumously published as *A History of English Literature*, 2 vols (Tokyo: Hokuseido, 1927). Hearn's view of Blake apparently changed from 'insane' (Hearn 1927b: 7) to 'the greatest poet of the eighteenth century' in the best of Blake's work, and 'the first great English mystic' (Hearn 1927b: 115); each view of which, however, seems to be indebted to William Michael Rossetti (Rossetti 1885: lxxxviii–lxxxix), A. C. Swinburne (Swinburne 1868: 226–7) and W. B. Yeats (Blake 1893b: xxxi) respectively. Hearn's own voice seems to be more clearly heard in his comment: 'Blake blossoms like a wild-flower of unfamiliar colour and yet more unfamiliar perfume' (Hearn 1927b: 116). Hearn's behest to the students of the highest seat of learning was: 'Remember always that familiarity with a single great author is infinitely better than a superficial knowledge of

even a thousand second or third-class authors . . . the study must begin in every case from the solid parts – the greatest work – never from the work of small or curious writers' (Hearn 1927a, Vol. 2, preface).

4    *Shirakaba*'s monthly journal entitled *Shirakaba* greatly contributed to the promotion of art and literature in Japan between 1910 and 1923. Particularly noteworthy is the issue published in April 1914 where Blake's 18 monochrome photographic reproductions as well as Yanagi's article on Blake made their first appearance.

5    The exhibition of Blake's reproductions together with other artists' reproductions was first held in Tokyo in February 1915. Also, the exhibition entirely devoted to Blake's reproductions was first realized by Yanagi in Tokyo and Kyoto in November 1919 – the tenth anniversary of the publication of *Shirakaba* – to raise funds for the *Shirakaba* museum. This was eight years before the centenary Blake exhibition was held in Onshi Kyoto Museum in collaboration with Makoto Sangu and Bunsho Jugaku in December 1927.

6    As Keiko Aoyama notes (Aoyama 1995: 25–7), what cannot be entirely dismissed as peripheral is the local Blake exhibitions organized by Yanagi at seven local sites in Nagano (Shinshu) two months before the major ones were held in 1919. According to Nobuo Imai, Shinshu was then the outpost of the sympathizers of the *Shirakaba* school, where the mostly inspired elementary school teachers put into practice the idealisms advocated by it for the sake of each pupil's fulfilment of life (see Imai 1975: 2–3, 9). Their fervent response to the Blake exhibitions as well as Yanagi's lecture on Blake resulted in a large number of sales of Blake reproductions in spite of their costliness (see Imai 1975: 58–9). Yanagi not only took the trouble of importing them from Frederick Hollyer in London, but, for the highly discerning audience in Shinshu, ordered 80 copies of John Sampson's 1913 edition of *Blake's Poetical Works* (thirty more of which were ordered in addition) as the text for his four-day intensive lecture on Blake in January 1921 (see Imai 1975: 59–60). Due to Yanagi's grassroots' 'evangelism', a spirit of Blake was pulsating in the remote countryside of the Far East in 1919–21.

7    Yanagi did not specify which of the two brothers he meant by Rossetti, but both are probably referred to: although Yanagi valued the former's 'annotated catalogue of Blake's paintings and drawings' in the second volume of Gilchrist's *Life* while he wasn't so impressed by the latter's editing of Blake's lyrics in it, he, nevertheless, deeply appreciated their collaborative efforts which enabled the crucial work to be completed two years after the premature death of the author in 1861.

8    All quotations from Yanagi are taken from *William Blake: kare no shogai to seisaku oyobi sono shiso* [*his life, works and thought*] (Tokyo: Rakuyodo, 1914), cited as 'Y' followed by page number (quotations from this book are translated into English by myself). Although his work is reprinted in *Yanagi Muneyoshi Zenshu* [*The Complete Writings of Muneyoshi Yanagi*], Vol. 4, here the page reference is only to the original edition as some discrepancies exist between them: the latter failed to reproduce the exact copies of the designs which Yanagi expounded and thus weakened his 'academic exactitude'. For details, see Wada 2004: 17–36. Quotations from Yanagi's other writings are taken from *The Complete Writings* and cited as 'YC' followed by volume and page numbers.

9    It was the period during which a reliable complete edition of Blake was not yet available and the edition that mostly covered Blake's major works by E. J. Ellis (i.e. *The Poetical Works of William Blake*, 2 vols [London: Chatto & Windus, 1906]) was still full of the editor's emendations. Nevertheless, since the publication of the 1893 Ellis–Yeats edition, in which Yeats showed Blake as a symbolist of mysticism of mostly the hermetic tradition (Blake 1893a: Vol. 1, 235–45) and also in which the rewritings of Blake ascribed to Ellis culminated, a repulsion towards the emendations had already been induced: Maclagan and Russell's reverence for Blake as 'the greatest of English mystics' (Maclagan and Russell 1904: vii) motivated them to prepare a scrupulously faithful transcript of *Jerusalem* in 1904; John Sampson, who also questioned the competence of editors to improve the work of 'a man of singular and individual genius' (Blake 1905: v), prepared

the verbatim text of Blake's lyrics in 1905; the purpose of Sampson's 1913 edition was to include in one volume the main body of Blake's poetry although the major prophecies were still in fragments.

10  Smith's 'Biographical Sketch of Blake' in *Nollekens and his Times* is reprinted in Bentley's *Blake Records* (2004a), which is hereafter cited as *BR*.

11  Sir Walter Scott echoes Smith in calling Cromek 'a perfect Brain-sucker living upon the labours of others' (see Bentley 1991: 676).

12  Cunningham's choice was commented on in *The Edinburgh Review* as 'partiality' towards Blake (see Gilchrist's *Life*, quoted from Ruthven Todd's 1945 edition recommended as the best by Bentley (see *Blake Books*, 1977 [hereafter cited as *BB*]: 26: 815–16). Bentley notes that '. . . most of those who knew something of Blake appear to have learned of him through Cunningham' (*BB* 23).

13  Cunningham's 'Life of Blake' in *Lives of the Most Eminent British Painters, Sculptors and Architects* is also quoted from its reprint in *BR*.

14  Although Aileen Ward brought into question the reason why Blake remained silent about his work in progress when he saw Stothard's (Ward 1988–8: 81), whether Cunningham's testimony was entirely reliable ought to have been first questioned: according to Bentley, he was the contributor of *Remains of Nithsdale and Galloway Song* and collaborated in Cromek's 'modern forgeries' of antique border ballads (see Bentley 1991: 658–9). Bentley also points out 'many secondary and tertiary witnesses whose ignorance and bias distort the issues' (Bentley 1991: 671).

15  Noteworthy are the two seemingly identical but entirely different Prospectuses of Blair's *Grave* illustrations dated November 1805 (see *BR* 210–19; Bentley 1991: 662–9). Also crucial are Cromek's two letters of entirely different tones: one to James Montgomery of April 1807 and the other to Blake of May 1807 (see Bentley 1991: 672–3).

16  In *The Stranger from Paradise*, Bentley reached a slightly different conclusion concerning the origin of the designs by integrating some biographical details of Cromek and Stothard provided by their immediate relations, although some of their testimonies were previously turned down as 'worthless' (Bentley 1991: 679): i.e. when Cromek went to Blake, the former had a proposal of the illustration to the Canterbury Pilgrims, although he found the latter already embarking on the subject (see Bentley 2001: 299).

17  Swinburne's comment on *Jerusalem* is: 'The externals of this poem are too incredibly grotesque – the mythologic plan too incomparably tortuous' (Swinburne 1868: 314).

18  Yanagi apparently lacked the same level of incentive concerning Walt Whitman, on whom he equally wished to write a book, but only left, although highly respectable, an annotated bibliography.

19  Tatham's 'The Life of William Blake' (1832), originally published in *The Letters of William Blake*, ed. A. G. B. Russell (London: Methuen, 1906) is quoted from its reprint in *BR*.

20  Blake was defended in terms of Hermetic, alchemical as well as Neo-platonic tradition by S. F. Damon (*William Blake: His Philosophy and Symbols* 1924); Milton O. Percival (*William Blake's Circle of Destiny* 1938); George Mills Harper (*The Neoplatonism of William Blake* 1961); Kathleen Raine (*Blake and Tradition*, 2 vols 1968). Désirée Hirst located Blake in the cabbalistic tradition in *Hidden Riches* (1964). A. L. Morton traced Blake's genealogy to the antinomian tradition, specifying a kinship between Blake and the Ranters in *The Everlasting Gospel* (1958); E. P. Thompson related Blake to the Muggletonians in the same tradition in *Witness Against the Beast* (1993).

21  As Arthur Symons identified the kinship between Blake and Nietzsche (Symons 1907: 1–9), in Nietzsche's protest against Christian 'slave morality', Yanagi heard the distinct echo of the Devil's voice denouncing the passive restrained by Reason in the *Marriage* (Y 526–7). Yanagi also regarded Blake as the forerunner of Henri Bergson and William James in terms of their anti-intellectualism and spiritual empiricism (Y 529–33).

22  Bloom also marks a particular state of mind which only enables the reader to understand the work thus: 'The unity of the *Marriage* is in itself dialectical, and cannot be grasped

except by the mind in motion, moving between the Blakean contraries of discursive irony and mythical visualization' (Bloom 1971: 55).

23   Gilchrist may have excluded the work partly due to a foreseen opposition of Macmillan, who, as later known by Anne Gilchrist's letter to W. M. Rossetti, was 'far more inexorable against any shade of heterodoxy in morals than in religion' (see Bentley 2001: 409n).

24   All quotations from Blake are taken from *The Complete Poetry and Prose of William Blake*, ed. David V. Erdman, newly rev. ed. (New York: Anchor-Doubleday, 1988), cited as 'E'. Quotations are identified by plate (or page) and line number, followed by page number in Erdman.

25   Daisetsz Suzuki (1870–1966), who attained enlightenment at the age of 27 and was in the US for eleven years to spread the idea of Zen Buddhism to the Western world, became Yanagi's English teacher while in Gakushuin and knew him personally (see Tsurumi 1994: 52; Nakami 2003: 48).

26   Yanagi's letter (in English) dated 8 November 1915 to Leach (who had left Kobe for China on 8 November 1914) calls into doubt the speculation. It communicates the exact course of spiritual journey Yanagi took after the 'laborious and joyous' study of Blake was brought to fruition in 1914: his interest was first directed to the study of Christian Mysticism (probably influenced by Yeats); and while writing to Leach he was in a state of excitement due to his true encounter with Zen. Yanagi says, 'I began to study Zen systematically . . . I feel very sorry that you left Japan without knowing adequately what is Zen [Zen is]. . . . Though Zen originated in India, its renaissance was in China . . . Japanese Zen, I regard, is far better than anything here' (YC21[Vol. 1] 668–9). Nakami, who noted this letter (see Nakami 2003: 57), did not particularly regard Suzuki as the introducer of Zen to Yanagi but that of the ideas of Swedenborg: two years after accepting an invitation from the Swedenborg Society in 1908, Suzuki published Swedenborg's *Heaven and Hell* in Japanese (see Nakami 2003: 48).

27   Although Swinburne did not specify from where he obtained the 'Pantheistic poetry of the East', a possible source might be the *Bhagavad Gita*, which was translated by Charles Wilkins from Sanskrit into English and published in London in 1785.

28   They are respectively the Upanishads, Plotinus, Boehme, Swedenborg; Nietzsche, Bergson, James; Michelangelo, El Greco, Redon, Rodin, the Postimpressionists, Augustus John; Milton, Dante, Emily Brontë, Francis Thompson, Whitman.

# 13 Self-Annihilation in *Milton*

Hatsuko Nimii

Soetsu Yanagi's *William Blake*, published in Japan in 1914, was the earliest study of this poet and engraver to be written by a Japanese scholar. It is a comprehensive survey of Blake's achievements, and is remarkable for its insight into the nature of his genius, especially as Yanagi, who lived from 1889 to 1961, was writing at a time when Blake studies were still in their infancy, even in Britain and America. It is particularly to be valued for a chapter entitled 'Blake as a Thinker', in which Yanagi perceptively discusses the intense veneration for the imagination which is Blake's leading characteristic. He argues that 'the human imagination' means for Blake 'immediately the world of God or the fundamental realistic world of Nature' (Yanagi 1914b: 4: 305) and continues:

> The imagination is not an abstract world outside our Self. It is always our pure and concrete experience. It is our actual feeling of a harmonious creation. It enables our mind to enter the infinite spiritual world, our life to return to life and us to feel religious exaltation filled with glory. Everything that surrounds us begins to live in our mind and this small self gains infinite expansion. Things and I are in perfect conformity and subject embraces object. This is an experience of which Paul proclaimed 'yet not I, but Christ liveth in me.' In the imagination, we are unified to the grandeur of nature and drift in a state of self-oblivion . . . Self-annihilation does not mean the denial of self, but the perfect expansion of self, infinite expression and union with the universe. When the mind entrusts itself to the bosom of nature and becomes oblivious of self in the world of Love, we come face to face with the eternal God, and become alive. We are endowed with Cosmic Consciousness and Self is immersed in its own boundless expansion. We rid ourselves of all of our material forms and are integrated into the life of the great Nature itself. (Yanagi 1914b: 4: 305–6)[1]

It is clear that Yanagi believed that the imagination can make us intuitively aware of our union with the universe, as we attain a state of mind in which self and nature, I and thing, inside and outside are viewed in their state of suchness, subject embracing object. This non-dualist entirety, or liberation from all duality, is the state of self-annihilation; the Christian self-annihilation to which Yanagi compares it is defined by St Paul in Galatians 2.20. His statement 'yet not I, but Christ liveth in me' is an affirmation that in his experience, a new self is created in a Christian when he or she is unified with Christ by faith.

Yanagi was later to connect his view of the imagination with the Buddhist conception of self-emptiness or self-effacement; for instance, in *The Beauty of Crafts* (1927), he was to find this conception embodied in the work of unknown craftsmen (1927: 113). He called their work folk craft, or the 'art of the people' (*The Unknown Craftsman* 1972: 94), and detected in it the 'abandonment of ego-centricity' (1927: 112), arguing that 'in crafts, people enter the world of salvation. Is it not possible to say that the way of craftsmanship is that of salvation through the benevolence of Buddha in the religion of beauty?' (1927: 111). His close friend the potter Shoji Hamada affirms that Yanagi studied Buddhism closely: 'as a religious philosopher and as a disciple and friend of Dr Daisetsu Suzuki, he searched his way through the development of Buddhist thought – Zen first, for the lone seeker, followed by Jodo Shinshu and Jishu for the many, the two aspects called *jiriki* ("Self Power") and *tariki* ("Other Power") respectively' ('Yanagi and Leach', *Craftsman*: 10). It is not clear how much Yanagi owed to Suzuki when he wrote his book on Blake[2], but I would like to quote here the Buddhist scholar's explanation of the idea of nirvana in order to enforce Yanagi's explication of Blake's work in the light of Buddhist thought.[3] Suzuki defines nirvana (or 'the deliverance of one's soul') as follows in his study of Christian and Buddhist mysticism:

> It is Absolute Emptiness transcending all forms of mutual relationship, of subject and object, birth and death, God and the world, something and nothing, yes and no, affirmation and negation. In Buddhist Emptiness there is no time, no space, no becoming, no-thing-ness; it is what makes all these things possible; it is a zero full of infinite possibilities, it is a void of inexhaustible contents. (Suzuki 1957: 28)

Suzuki is saying that the state of Absolute Emptiness is that of Absolute Fullness. In his *Namuamidabutsu*, Yanagi was to define 'Absolute Emptiness' as entering 'Perfect Freedom', a state in which you cast off all deep attachments to the world, and the world is identified with yourself (Yanagi 1955; 1988: 190). The world of Absolute Emptiness, where the distinction of subject and object is extinct, he calls the world of 'suchness' or 'thusness'. He claims that Blake's most typical attribute is his understanding of this state of 'thusness'. He claims also that 'opposition' is 'the approval or compatibility of two opposites' (Yanagi 1914b: 4: 333).

Yanagi suggests that in *Milton*, 'the ultimate ideal is revealed, in which the ultimate glory to humankind of our being unified with God is achieved. In other words, it is the embodiment of the eternal life of the imagination, or the efface-ment of self, the expansion of individuality' (ibid: 4: 190). He is confident that 'What Blake means by self-effacement is self-fulfillment, that is, a complete expression of individuality' (ibid: 4: 474–5). Yanagi's biographer Hiroshi Mizuo notes that self-effacement is not the demise of individuality, but a striving after 'the higher state of self-enrichment and the expression of individuality' (Mizuo 1992: 52).

Inevitably, some of Yanagi's insights remained undeveloped, and this is true of his suggestion that self-annihilation (or self-effacement) is one of the most signifi-cant themes in *Milton*, a view which is now customary. But the value of Yanagi's interpretation of Blake lies in the opportunities it provides for readers to increase their understanding of the poet, by looking for parallels between Christian and Buddhist thought. I would like to analyse the last five plates of *Milton*, with reference to Yanagi's approach to Blake, for the actual meaning and function of self-annihilation in this poem seem to me to need further discussion.

## 1

Blake's Milton declares that he comes 'in Self-annihilation & the grandeur of Inspiration' to 'cast off Bacon, Locke & Newton from Albions covering' (*Milton* Plate 41 [48]: 5 E 142). In his *Essay Concerning Human Understanding* (1690), Locke defines self (or what might later have been termed ego) as follows:

> *Self* is that conscious thinking thing, (whatever Substance, made up of whether Spiritual, or Material, Simple, or Compounded, it matters not) which is sensible, or conscious of Pleasure and Pain, capable of Happiness or Misery, and so is concern'd for it *self*, as far as that consciousness extends. (Locke 1975: 341)

Locke believes that whenever we perceive external things, or think, or exert will, we are conscious of doing so. 'Thus it is always as to our present Sensations and Perceptions: And by this every one is to himself, that which he calls self' (Locke 1975: 335). He denies the Cartesian belief in innate ideas and advocates epistemological empiricism, asserting that all ideas are derived from experience; that is, from perception. What he calls an idea is the basis of knowledge, or all that is objectified by understanding. He observes and describes the mental process by which self, the subject of understanding, and the external world, its object, are perceived as separate ideas. The external world and other beings self-evidently exist and what Locke explores by experience and observation is the internal processes of the understanding. One of his consequent achievements was to establish the concept of an independent human being who understands and acts, relying upon no other authority than him or herself. This image of a free and independent being is the outcome of Locke's complete confidence in the autonomy of the human understanding: its sense perceptions, its perceptions based on reflection and its rational thinking, from which Blake is most consistently engaged in dissenting.

Robert N. Essick and Joseph Viscomi, the editors and annotators of the Tate Gallery edition of *Milton*, cite two books which may have influenced the formation of Blake's idea of self-annihilation: Jacob Boehme's *Signatura Rerum* and David Hartley's *Observations on Man* (Blake 1993: 139).[4] Blake engraved the frontispiece to Hartley's book, which he is almost certain to have read, in 1781 and his indebtedness is not confined to *Milton*, but can be traced back at least as far as the *The Marriage of Heaven and Hell*.

The German mystic Boehme (1575–1624) believed that he was called to penetrate the deepest mysteries concerning God, man and nature, and that the 'Godhead has two wills, one good and one evil, "love" and "wrath", which drive Him to create nature' (*The Oxford Dictionary of the Christian Church*: 183), while he insisted 'Recognition of one's hidden, free will is a recognition of God manifested in the world, so that human salvation completes God's act of self-revelation' (*The Cambridge Dictionary of Philosophy*: 91). In his view, God contains both the affirmative and the negative. He is not merely a pure and single being; he is not only the source of love and the creator of Heaven, but also the source of anger and the creator of Hell. In his *Signatura Rerum*, Boehme proclaims that 'self-hood' is 'eternal dying' and 'an enmity against God': 'viz. in a dominion full of contention and strife, it cannot either will or do anything that is good', but brings about falsehood and death. Therefore, 'All sins arise from self'. He suggests that to overcome these evils, it is necessary to resort to 'real resignation', that is, to give oneself together 'with mind and desire, senses and will' into God's mercy. The ultimate model for this self-annihilation is 'the dying of Jesus Christ' (Boehme 1730: 190, 198–9). He explains in more detail how this change is to be made:

> But if he departs out of his self-hood, and forsakes his own damnation, and continually casts himself only into God's mercy, viz. into the suffering and death of Christ, and into his resurrection and restoration, and wills nothing of himself, but what God wills in him, and by him, then the will is dead to the life and desire of God's anger; for it has no own life, but lies in the death of self-hood and the desire of the devil; and the anger of God cannot reach him; for he is as a nothing, yet is in God, and lives in the divine essence wholly, but not to himself, but to his first mother of eternity; (Boehme 1730;1969: 200–1)

In conclusion, Boehme suggests that the essential duty of the Christian believer is to annihilate selfhood in the human will. In order to be a true Christian, one must 'bring human self-hood in true resignation into divine obedience'. Boehme derives this conviction from his firm belief that 'all things are generated out of imagination' and that 'the eternity might be manifest in a time'. It is a mystic faith in Christ, as both example and intermediary:

> A true Christian has nothing to contend for, for he dies to his reason's desire; he desires only God's knowledge in his love and grace, and lets all go which contends and strives about the form, for Christ's spirit must make the form in himself; the outward form is only a guide: God must become man, or else man becomes not God. (Boehme 1730: 203, 204–5, 206)

His association of the Christian faith with the human imagination resembles Blake's version of Christianity, and this similarity will be discussed later.

In the third chapter of his *Observations on Man*, entitled 'Of the Rule of Life', Hartley argues that people seeking a solid foundation for their lives resort either to 'Self-interest' upon which 'a System of Morality can be erected' or to 'Self-annihilation' in which 'Man can rest'. But he attempts to reconcile the two attitudes and to describe 'what passes in our Progress from Self-interest to Self-annihilation'. Among the three kinds of Self-interest, Rational Self-interest begets in us 'the virtuous Dispositions of Benevolence, Piety, and the Moral Sense, and particularly that of the Love of God' and these dispositions 'check all the foregoing ones, and seem sufficient utterly to extinguish them at last', which 'would be perfect Self-annihilation, and Resting in God as our Centre' (Boehme 1730: 280–2). Hartley is known to have claimed that our moral sense is attributable to the association of ideas, and is not innate. He does not proceed here to make a psychological or epistemological enquiry into self-annihilation, but merely points to it as a means of attaining happiness and security. But it is noteworthy that he regards the idea of self-annihilation ultimately as a matter of faith and pure love of God, which is the highest moral stage attainable by means of the transcending of selfhood. This suggests that the empiricist tradition is capable of producing concepts analogous to self-annihilation.

**2**

In its most recent edition *Milton* consists of 46 plates divided into two parts. Opinions differ as to the fundamental theme of this lengthy and complex poem. Blake is undoubtedly telling the story of Milton's return to this world one hundred years after his death to atone for his errors by discarding reason, his Spectre, and redeeming Ololon, his Emanation. The story is interwoven, however, with Blake's personal mythology and prophetic visions, and characters familiar in these contexts have a part to play, especially Los (for a fuller summary see Blackstone 1949; 1966: 148). Some critics consider that Blake is primarily concerned with the role in society of the poet and prophet (for example Mitchell 1973: 282–3); others posit that Blake is endeavouring to set up an effective interaction between the author, the story and the reader (for example Behrendt 1992: 155–7). These widely divergent analyses are indicative of the difficulties which must be faced in any attempt to unravel the esoteric mythology of Blake's later prophetic works. I concur with those who believe that the poem is both apparently and essentially a story about the way in which human beings may reform their most common and most serious errors, and that it concentrates on the form these errors took in the life and work of Milton. I believe also that Blake intended to make manifest his personal vision of the way in which self-annihilation, which is the only possible remedy, may be achieved.

Plates 14–17 in Book I[5] reveal the purpose of Milton's descent to the earth. The reason why he descends to 'the earth of vegetation' is that he cannot participate in the Last Judgement as long as he is subjected to his selfhood. This is the world which Milton failed to explore in his work and in his life, and now needs to re-enter in order to live the limited life of 'A mournful form double; hermaphroditic; male and female / In one wonderful body' (Plate 14 [15] pl. 14: 37–8 E 108). In this world, sexual conflicts and discords between men and women have led to a dangerous state of confusion. The poet Blake accompanies the soul of Milton as it makes this pilgrimage as an allegory of a struggle both poets must undertake in order to ascertain the kind of mental state they must attain to write poetry. For them the preconditions are the kind of inspiration possessed by the Hebrew prophets, and an imagination which has passed through the hell fires of selfhood.

In a speech that he makes when he descends to Blake's cottage at Felpham, Milton reveals his understanding of what is meant by 'Self-annihilation':

> Mine [purpose] is to teach Men to despise death & to go on
> In fearless majesty annihilating Self, laughing to scorn
> Thy (Satan's) Laws and terrors, shaking down thy Synagogues as webs
> I come to discover before Heavn & Hell the Self-righteousness
> In all its Hypocritic turpitude, opening to every eye
> These wonders of Satans holiness shewing to the Earth
> The Idol Virtues of the Natural Heart, & Satans Seat
> Explore in all its Selfish Natural Virtue & put off
> In Self annihilation all that is not of God alone:
> To put off Self & all I have ever & ever Amen (Plate 38 [43]: 40–9 E 139)

Milton names and denounces the signs and effects of selfhood represented by Satan: its fear of death, its tyrannical laws, its bogus churches and its self-righteous and hypocritical exaltation of 'the Natural Heart' and 'Natural Virtues'. It is crucial for him to recognize these evils in himself before seeking to embrace their contraries: self-sacrifice for the good of others and 'Self annihilation' or the renunciation of 'all that is not of God alone'.

In *Milton*, one of the most conspicuous 'Contraries' is the conflict between the masculine and the feminine. The first is represented by Milton, the second by Ololon: they contrast with each other in will, perception and deeds. The male–female relationships are presented as sexual, and there are gendered polarities such as reason and faith, male initiative and female submission. Since Ololon is described as 'Sixfold', it has been supposed that she embodies Milton's three wives and three daughters (pl. 2: 19 E 96);[6] in any case she represents the 'female will', which is the object of his love and hate. Her initial relationship to Milton has often been regarded as secondary or submissive: when 'all images of a separated female will cease to mean anything', her virginity will sever itself from her (Frye 1947:354); at the third climax of the poem, Ololon, who is called a virgin, discards her 'false femininity' (Mitchell 1973: 305); 'Separate from Milton, she is a delusion' (Howard 1976: 253); 'Milton strips off everything opposed to the Blakean imagination and emerges from his rotten robes as an inspired man to whom Ololon "vows obedience" ' (Webster 1983: 270); her quest for infinity 'occurs as the *object* of thought rather than as its *subject*' (Bracher 1985: 226); 'Ololon is saved by Milton's heroic act of self-sacrifice, which Blake calls "self annihilation" ' and that when he 'comes to recognize the Satanic nature of his own errors and to repudiate them', she is redeemed (Werner 1986: 16); she is routinely designated a merely 'passive' power (Otto 1991: 91). Brought face to face with Milton, she [they] addresses him, asking 'Are those who contemn Religion & seek to annihilate it / Become in their Femin[in]e portions the causes & promoters / Of these Religions' (pl. 40 [46]: 9–10 E 141), reflecting the historical fact that many deists made use of Milton's work for the consolidation of their rationalistic arguments. After naming the five rational and skeptical philosophers who contributed to the propagation of natural religion, Ololon expresses her fear again that those who live in the true faith might be eliminated. Milton uncompromisingly replies:

> The Negation must be destroyed to redeem the Contraries
> The Negation is the Spectre; the Reasoning Power in Man
> This is a false Body: an Incrustation over my Immortal
> Spirit; a Selfhood, which must be put off & annihilated always
> To cleanse the Face of my Spirit by Self-examination. (pl. 40 [46]: 32–7 E 142)

Milton rejects Negations and regards the oppositions between them as Contraries. This constitutes his act of self-annihilation and makes it possible for him to bring about their unification. In the course of his pilgrimage, Milton has conversed with the Seven Angels of the Presence, who have instructed him that he himself is 'a State about to be Created / Called Eternal Annihilation' (pl. 32 [35]: 26–7 E 132). Introducing the ideas of 'Contraries' and 'Negation', he implies that both he and Ololon can and should be united as Contraries.[7]

In Plate 41 Milton makes his final speech. He is now a poet–prophet full of assurance and is able to identify his self-annihilation with poetic and imaginative creation:

> I come in Self-annihilation & the grandeur of Inspiration
> To cast off Rational Demonstration by Faith in the Saviour
> To cast off the rotten rags of Memory by Inspiration

> To cast off Bacon, Locke & Newton from Albions covering
> To take off his filthy garments, & clothe him with Imagination
> To cast aside from Poetry, all that is not Inspiration
> That it no longer shall dare to mock with the aspersion of Madness
> Cast on the Inspired, by the tame high finisher of paltry Blots,
> Indefinite, or paltry Rhymes; or paltry Harmonies.
>     . . .
> These are the Sexual Garments, the Abomination of Desolation
> Hiding the Human Lineaments as with an Ark & Curtains
> Which Jesus rent: & now shall wholly purge away with Fire
> Till Generation is swallowed up in Regeneration. (Plate 41)

In this speech, Milton refers appropriately to the state of the nation and the change he will make in its conception of knowledge of poetry and of faith. He does not treat these as separate issues but blends them in a single theme. It has been pointed out that the frequent use of clothing images in the poem shows that Milton knows he must discard, like clothes or veils, the rational demonstrations, memories and empirical knowledge that have encumbered his spirit, and that he must put on the garments of Christian faith and inspiration instead (Bloom 1963: 358; Vine 1993: 147–50). Generation is to give place to Regeneration, the human is to be 'swallowed up' by the sacred, or the Ulro by Eternity. But it would be truer to say that when the Ulro is assimilated into Eternity, the state filled with both is that of 'Self annihilation'.

Those critics who stress the ambivalence of the figure of Milton point out that although Milton declares his determination to annihilate selfhood, his act of annihilation is not fully developed (for example Butter 1978: 151). This is true, but what Blake seems to be demonstrating in this connection is the essential nature of self-annihilation, which is a dramatic conversion within the self: a process which is in effect a transition from nullity to fulfilment. In other words, the annihilation of self means the unification of various contraries within the self, which is in consequence liberated from those contraries. In the resulting state of fulfilment, all is affirmed without discrimination or limitation. The self is liberated as well as unified. This internal paradise is what Yanagi regards as 'Love' or the world of self-annihilation. He asserts that 'Love is the integration of subject and object, the unity of individualities, the joy of discovering oneself in the outside world, the sense of self-oblivion, the experience of oneself permeated and expanded in the whole nature' (Yanagi 1914b: 4: 196).

In Plate 3, the Bard refers to 'the Human Imagination / Which is the Divine Body of the Lord Jesus' (pl. 3: 3–4 E 96). The life, death and resurrection of 'Jesus, the image of the Invisible God' (pl. 2: 12 E 96) constitute the perfect model of self-annihilation. He showed perfect selflessness when he accepted death in order to redeem the sins of the human race. His incarnation and resurrection represent the unification of the Contraries such as God and man, heaven and earth, eternity and time, glory and humiliation. In the end the true self-annihilation in terms of creative activity is to imitate Jesus Christ. It follows that if art is to translate the invisible world into the visible form of painting and writing, the Being of Jesus is the greatest artistic creation.[8] Having progressed to this conception of art, Blake felt impelled to rewrite *Paradise Lost* in the form of *Milton*. In Plate 14, Milton condemns the fact that 'The Nations still / Follow after the detestable Gods of Priam' (pl. 14 [15]: 14–15 E 108), but he does not proclaim that inspiration originates from Christ's true humility and self-sacrifice which make salvation possible. What Blake actually suggests is that creative activity is one with belief in Christ. To have faith in Christ is to cast off selfhood. The imagination of those who have attained the unification of subject and object is holy and only to them is given the title of creator and the joy and glory of creation. Blake, owing much to Boehme, has shown this in Milton's journey of redemption.

On the title page of *Milton*, Blake inscribed, with the alteration of one word, the last line of the opening section of Book I of *Paradise Lost*, 'To Justify the Ways of God to Men'. There, Blake criticizes Homer, Ovid, Plato and Cicero and their followers (including the neoclassicists of his time) and insists on the supremacy of 'the Sublime of the Bible' and 'those Worlds of Eternity in which we shall live for ever; in Jesus our Lord' (Plate 1) (E 95). When Ololon faces Milton after her descent to Felpham's vale, she sees Jesus the Saviour who appears as 'the Starry Eight', joined by Milton now:

> . . . with one accord the Starry Eight became
> One Man Jesus the Saviour, wonderful! round his limbs
> The Clouds of Ololon folded as a Garment dipped in blood
> Written within & without in woven letters: & the Writing
> Is the Divine Revelation in the Litteral expression: (pl. 42 [49]: 10–14 E 143)

The passage has received a variety of sometimes less than pellucid glosses: 'To become one man is to submerge selfhood in the individual so that the true identity may unite with the true identity of all others. The place of unity is in the source of identity, that is, in the One Man, the essential great humanity divine, Jesus' (Howard 1976: 173); Ololon 'is the body of his prophetic Poetry' and that 'in the final consummation, when error has been burned away and all that remains is vision, Ololon takes the form of the apocalyptic scroll "Written within & without in woven letters" ' (Werner 1986: 54). It is at all events clear that Jesus, clothed in clouds 'as a Garment dipped in blood', appears not only as the epitome of self-annihilation but as the everlasting source of inspiration in whom the literal and the divine are united.

The unification of Contraries which must precede self-annihilation is typified in the final meeting of Milton and Ololon. Again the commentary is arguably more obscure than the poem itself (for example Bracher 1985: 272–3; Otto 1991: 94; Bloom 1963: 359). The final description of Ololon's clouds enfolding Jesus indicates her expected integration with Milton as she has come to possess the vision of Jesus both as saviour and victim, the model of self-annihilation as well as the source of inspiration. The confrontation of Milton and Ololon is not a mutual denial but an opportunity for them to achieve unification, if each of them can submit to self-annihilation, and this is made a more attainable outcome after her virginal self divides from her and flies 'as a Dove' (pl. 42 [49]: 6 E 143) into Milton's Shadow. From the perspective of Buddhist thought, their assimilation may be seen as representing allegorically Enlightenment or nirvana which Daisetsu Suzuki calls 'Absolute Emptiness', which 'in its ultimate signification' is 'an affirmation – an affirmation beyond opposites of all kinds' (Suzuki 1957: 56). This dynamic world of nothingness is paradoxically a magnetic field of creative activity, too. It is 'to see unity in multiplicity and to understand the opposition of the two ideas as not conditioning each other but as both issuing from a higher principle; and this is where perfect freedom abides' (ibid: 141).

Milton continues his 'Eternal Annihilation', but Albion is not fully awake yet. His salvation will take place in *Jerusalem* where self-annihilation is endowed with another meaning. In *Milton*, as I have already discussed, the salvation of the soul and the liberation of the artistic imagination are indivisible from the example of Christ, whose self-annihilation is the necessary precondition. This is what Yanagi suggests by claiming that 'the human imagination means for Blake immediately the world of God'. He further expresses the idea of the imagination as follows: 'In the world of the imagination, which is the world of God, every human being is equal and universal Being. The distinctions of subject and object cease to exist and born is the synthesized individual existence. Every one is united hand in hand by Love in this hall where the light of the imagination shines' (Yanagi; 1914b: 4: 195). To sum up, 'self annihilation' is incapable of discrimination by the negation or exclusion of others and is engaged in repeated acts of annihilation. That is a creative process in which the divisions between Milton and Ololon, and between Milton and Blake, are extinguished, or integrated into the world of suchness.

## Notes

1   All quotations from Yanagi's work except from *The Unknown Craftsman* are my own translations.

2   Daisetsu Suzuki (1870–1966) returned in 1909 from an eleven-year stay in the United States, where he had translated Buddhist and Taoist texts, while working for a publishing firm. In the same year, he became a teacher of English in the high school which Yanagi attended from 1907 to 1910. It is probable that Yanagi's lifelong interest in Buddhism was encouraged by his Buddhist teacher. See a relevant commentary by Hideo Shinoda on Suzuki's *Japanese Spirituality* (Tokyo: Iwanami Shoten, 2003; first published 1944): 271–2.

3   Yanagi does not refer to any Buddhist texts or sources when he speaks of self-annihilation in *Milton*, but in his note to this term, he says that the idea has been most profoundly investigated by Buddhist teachers with whom it originated (Yanagi 1914b: 4: 474–5). The way in which he refers to self-annihilation in his *William Blake* proves that he is drawing upon Buddhist teaching, if his account is compared with the generally accepted definition, for instance Suzuki's.

4   For the intellectual background of eighteenth-century notions of selfhood, with particular reference to Swedenborg and Boehme, see Howard 1976: 56–62.

5   All the quotations from Blake's work are from David Erdman's edition of *The Poetry and Prose of William Blake* (1988) except in parts of my discussion of *Milton*, where I make cross-references for the plate ordering to Essick and Viscomi's edition of *Milton* (1993).

6   See Frye 1947: 316, 336, and Blake 1983: 157.

7   Bloom's discussion (in *Blake's Apocalypse*, 1963: 356–60) on the relation of Milton and Ololon is particularly illuminating.

8   Thomas Dilworth discusses 'the self-annihilation which is essential to all true art' in his essay, 'The Hands of Milton: Blake's Multistable Image of Self-Annihilation'. *Mosaic*, 16 (1983): 24.

# 14 An Ideological Map of (Mis)reading: William Blake and Yanagi Muneyoshi in early-twentieth-century Japan

## Kazuyoshi Oishi

In 1952, Yanagi Muneyoshi (1889–1961), one of the earliest Japanese critics of William Blake, stopped briefly at New York on his way back from a research trip to Britain. His purpose was to visit his mentor Suzuki Daisetsu (1870–1966), who was then delivering lectures on the Zen philosophy to the American people. When Yanagi walked into Suzuki's flat, his attention was instantly drawn to a picture hanging on the wall, which displayed the wooden statue of Maitreya Bodhisattva at the Koryuji Temple, Kyoto (Figure 14.1). The serene, graceful Maitreya meditating on how to redeem fallen multitudes reconfirmed to him the spiritual profundity of the Oriental philosophy. The great Zen master then pointed out a striking contrast which the peacefulness of the statue would make with the masculine dynamism of Rodin's *Thinker* for *The Gate of Hell*. The latter, he said, 'manifests most zealously the agonies of the solemn, contemplative human mind, but conveys no internal peace: it thus indicates the destiny of the material-istic view of life in the Western society' (Yanagi 14: 474).[1] To this statement, Yanagi gave an immediate and ready assent. To him, who had learnt Buddhism as well as the English language from Suzuki, the physical and mental equability exhibited by the Koryuji Bodhisattva appeared to be symbolizing the ultimate state of the Zen mentality which alone could solve and transcend what he saw as the existential anxieties prevailing in the modern Western civilization.

This reproof, however, poses a serious question to the prevailing view of Yanagi as a legitimate Japanese interpreter of William Blake. First of all, there was no denying his enthusiasm for Rodin around 1910. He admired the corporeal energy and beauty of Rodin's sculptures as an 'art of destruction', an artistic embodiment of the new philosophy and religion which defied the established, therefore depraved, value-system of contemporary Europe (Yanagi 1: 480–5).[2] More sig-nificantly, Yanagi's enthralment with Blake took place in 1911, immediately after this rapport with Rodin.[3] Within Blake's engravings and poems, Yanagi dis-covered an equally dynamic form of art and religion and thus exalted him as Rodin's direct ancestor (4: 373). It is not surprising, then, that he coupled both artists as the greatest geniuses who had followed the footsteps of Michelangelo, exhibiting the 'power' and 'beauty' of the human body in a 'naked manner' (4: 342). Nor would it be entirely misleading to assume that his interest in such a 'pathos formula' in the works of Rodin and Blake opened his eyes to the artistic merits of Japanese folk crafts and artefacts, including the sculptures produced by the obscure monk-sculptor Mokujiki, and led him further to initiate the *Mingei*

**Figure 14.1** The Statue of Maitreya Bodhisattva, Koryuji Temple, Kyoto. Photo: Benrido, © Koryuji.

(folk craft) movement nationwide.[4] Among coarse, lowly handmade crafts, Yanagi identified the same artistic virtues that he had found in Blake and Rodin, such as 'unconventional', therefore 'free' and 'natural' forms impregnated with 'primitive passion', 'crude wildness' and 'animated vigour' (7: 581–5, 592–4; 4: 14, 34, 96). This appraisal of the animated and often Gothic glamour of common folk crafts would have been impossible if Yanagi had not encountered Blake's works which incorporate the evil in the good, the grotesque in the beautiful and Hell in Heaven in pursuit of spiritual liberty. A contradiction emerges in Yanagi's aesthetic and ideological principles, therefore, when he disapproves of Rodin in favour of the Maitreya Bodhisattva; it means not just a rejection of Blake and his work, but more significantly a renunciation of all his critical and political principles and his lifelong achievements made on their basis.

The purpose of this chapter is to examine the aesthetic and ideological contradictions in Yanagi's writings on Blake which were caused by a self-reflexive reading of the Romantic poet in the unique historical context of early-twentieth-century Japan. Several studies have been made from the perspectives of both Blake and of Yanagi regarding whether the latter's reception of Blake's philosophy might be compatible with Zen Buddhism.[5] No attention, however, has ever been paid to the ideological ambiguity latent in Yanagi's Blake–Buddhism equation. Despite his emphasis on the primary virtue of Blake's works being their capacity to subsume all contradictory or negative elements into the unified Zen world of 'Oneness' (Yanagi 2: 341–3), the association of Blake with Zen paradoxically, yet inevitably, runs the risk of wiping out physical vitality, masculine energy and spiritual enthusiasm from Yanagi's portrayal of Blake and thus ending up with transforming the Blakean 'pathos formula' into the tranquil, controlled elegance of the Maitreya Bodhisattva.

The reception of foreign literature always involves historical, ideological and cross-cultural 'misreading'. Yanagi's case is not exceptional. I should like to locate his reading of Blake in the historical and ideological circumstances produced when Japan underwent significant social and cultural changes, and then further to examine the aesthetic and political links between his Blake worship and his *Mingei* movement. By carefully analysing Yanagi's perceptive, but essentially self-serving interpretation of Blake, we should be able to explore the ideological ramifications through which Blake was received in Japan at the beginning of the twentieth century. The seeming symmetry between Blake and Yanagi belies curious ideological incongruities, the exploration of which will elucidate important political meanings of English Romantic literature as received in early-twentieth-century Japan.

Yanagi's enchantment with Blake had its roots not just in his own aesthetic taste, but also in the unique historical conditions during the late *Meiji* and the *Taishō* periods (*c*.1900–26). It was the period of angst, disorder, democracy and wars, very close to the so-called Romantic age in Britain. Blake had already been introduced to Japan in a fragmentary form, but, as Nakami Mari has shown, Yanagi's extraordinary, almost empathetic, devotion to Blake cannot be fully understood without explicating the turbulent ideological circumstances of the age (Nakami 2003: 35–99). Japan's victory over China in 1895 and Russia in 1905 established her international status as an advanced imperial power in the East. This was a triumphant outcome of the rapid modernization and industrialization promoted eagerly by the *Meiji* government for the few previous decades in order to catch up with the Western powers. And yet the achievement was made at the expense of the welfare of common people. Various economic and social problems, such as inflation, distress and destitution, supplied ample causes for public discontent and incessant social unrest. Disturbances erupted on a massive scale all over the country in the 1910s and 1920s, as recounted in detail by Michael Lewis in *Rioters and Citizens* (1990). A reform movement began to gather momentum in the urban areas, while the number of industrial strikes and peasants' revolts continued to rise at an alarming rate in the rural regions. The 'rice riots' which stormed across the Japanese mainland in 1918 testified to the increasingly active, and sometimes explosive, presence of famished and exasperated agricultural labourers (Kinpara 1967: 29–202; Hane 1982: 160, 196). They can be taken in part as a collective critique of the *Meiji* idea of imperialist nationalism, but more generally as violent protests against capitalism and the bourgeois ideology formulated and disseminated with the aid of the imported ideas, such as those of J. S. Mill and Herbert Spencer (Miyakawa and Hijikata 1977: 71–7; Tōyama 1991: 173–98).

To the Japanese public, the *Taishō* era began with a sense of crisis, with deep anxieties over political, economic and cultural instability both at home and abroad after the death of the *Meiji* Emperor in 1912. While the whole world was shaken by the Russian Revolution and the New-Democratic Revolution in China as well as by the First World War, people in Japan were harassed by the sense of the need for political and ideological reconstructions at all levels, individual, national and international (Giffard 1994: 45–64; Harootunian 1998a: 84). They had to seek for a new definition of 'individualism' and a way of mediation between the claims of individuals and those of the state.[6] This process of establishing new national and individual identities inevitably necessitated a thorough reassessment of Japan's political and intellectual relationship with the West.

The situation was particularly tense and often disconcerting for young intellectuals of a liberal bent. They remained anxious to fix their political stance in this complicated ideological context, but without much success or even certainty (Duus 1982: 412–33; Uchida and Shioda 1959: 237–82). While claiming intellectual independence from the nationalist government, they were compelled by the growing class conflicts and social upheavals to adopt the principles of democracy, socialism, communism or anarchism in the interests of the destitute and in defence of individual liberty (Mitani 1995: 44–60). Much to the horror of the government, revolutions in China and Russia in 1911–12 and 1917 galvanized many of them into communist, even anarchist, ideals. While making compromises with some groups of working-class radicals, the government set out to suppress and vanquish all influential anarchic intelligentsias. The so-called Treason Trial in 1910–11 provoked outcries both at home and abroad by dealing with the case secretly without much evidence and passing a death sentence on the anarchist Kōtoku Shusui and 23 others. Twelve of them were executed within a month. The incident inflicted a psychic trauma, in particular, upon the minds of young moderate reformers. The mixed anxieties over their awkward situation incessantly disturbed and unsettled their process of determining their position in the muddled ideological matrix of the *Taishō* age.[7] They resisted the government's repression and defied its narrow-minded principle of patriotism on account of their intellectual independence, but they could hardly escape from an anxiety of influence from the West either. Furthermore, despite their sympathy towards the poor, the repeated outbreaks of terrifying mass riots held them back from associating themselves openly and personally with socialist and communist activities.

In these circumstances, Yanagi and his friends in the *Shirakaba* (White Birch) circle sought eagerly to establish a new national identity through moral and political self-realization by way of transplanting Western art, literature and philosophy, such as Rodin, Blake, Maeterlinck and Tolstoy, into the native soil of Japanese and Oriental philosophy. Thanks to their wealthy, upper-class upbringing, the *Shirakaba* youngsters possessed more advantages than other intellectuals in having easy access to Western culture and literature and ample means to indulge their humanitarian ambition to ameliorate a deeply troubled society.[8] And yet their ideal was, in essence, a naive one conceived primarily to overcome the anxiety over their own ideological uncertainty, but also secretly to appease the guilty consciousness of their privileged background. The unsuccessful 1918 project by the leading member Mushakoji Saneatsu of building a pseudo-communist utopia – an equivalent of the Pantisocracy scheme of Southey and Coleridge – disclosed the characteristic naivety of their romantic, patronizing attitude towards the real world of hard labour and human egoism. It is true that concerns about social welfare made the *Shirakaba* members critical of contemporary decadent aesthetes, who took little interest in the deprived condition of industrial and agricultural labourers, but they never joined the camp of the realist, naturalist or proletarian literature either. Their contact with foreign and Japanese socialists and anarchists, such as Peter Kropotokin, Ōsugi Sakae and Kaneko Kiichi, never grew into prosperous alignments (Nakami 2003: 19–33); for they could not fully identify themselves either as socialists or as communists, much less as anarchists. Accordingly their activities were in principle confined to the polite, inactive sphere of individual moral enhancement in pursuit of gradual social improvement through art and literature, perhaps in a manner similar to what William Godwin envisaged in *Political Justice*. In his earliest essay 'Science and Life', Yanagi had already conceded that the best he could do was to dedicate the early half of his life to the cultivation of his intellect and character and then the latter half to exerting them for the improvement of social welfare (1: 137).

William Blake emerged in the eyes of Yanagi, as before other *Shirakaba* comrades, as a catalyst who appeared to overcome all this ideological insecurity; Blake provided a model of reconciling humanitarian ideals with uneasy historical circumstances. As one of his earliest essays entitled 'Self Interest and Altruism' (1905) reveals, Yanagi had been persistently harassed by the question of how to maintain a balance between the modern principle of individualism and the interests of society, and, as a solution, he had been exploring the possibility of unifying art, science, religion and philosophy as one entity, which he believed would restore moral welfare to the nation. It was in this context that Yanagi encountered Blake through the introduction of the *Shirakaba* members. Blake's engravings and poetry appeared to him not only as embodying the unification of art, science, religion and philosophy, but more crucially as demonstrating the 'Realisation of Life', the free, spontaneous 'Emanation' of divine energy in the individual human mind (4: 327). In his view, Blake was a philosopher who attained a self-fulfilment by embracing all human desires, good and evil at once, and therefore by extolling the primitive and dynamic energy of the human soul through art and literature.

Yanagi's ardent study of Blake's philosophical system culminated in *William Blake* (1914), the first-ever substantial monograph on Blake in Japan. As he admitted himself, Yanagi read Blake as a double of his own ideal self (Yanagi 4: 627); through the reading of Blake, Yanagi sought a way of liberating himself from the rigid ideological framework imposed by the religious and intellectual authorities of the age and then of attaining an enlightened vision of the eternal truth through what he calls 'imagination' (4: 596–9). Blake's art, he asserted, is 'perfect self-realization', 'total emancipation of self', an 'expression of solid intuitive experiences' (4: 204, 253, 256). For him, *Jerusalem* was a 'Song of Liberty' which would forgive and emancipate all sentient beings into the 'pantheistic' world of 'Love' where God and Nature are united (4: 222). His reading of *Milton* and *The Marriage of Heaven and Hell* anticipates modern Blake scholarship in hearing a 'rebellious' and 'prophetic' voice against the established regime of the British society, and in capturing a millenarian vision in which all distinctions between the mind and the body, between the subjective and the objective, between good and evil and between the beautiful and the grotesque, dissolve through the all-subsuming power of imagination (4: 93–4, 187–9). Apparently Yanagi was attracted by Blake all the more because his religious and philosophical system seemed to outstrip logical argument: 'He is a man of great temperament, not of logical thinking; his spiritual world is a profound atmosphere, not a system of logos' (4: 302).[9] All this interpretation is remarkably insightful, especially given the limited access to foreign Blake studies in *Taishō* Japan. Blake's antinomian and anti-rational system was perhaps easy to digest for Yanagi, who studied Swedenborg as well as Bergson under the influence of contemporary Japanese philosophers, such as Suzuki and Nishida Kitarō (1870–1945).[10]

What is most distinctive about Yanagi's reading of Blake is that he associated the Blakean world of imagination with the world of Zen mysticism. Certainly his definition of Blake's 'imagination' as the power to liberate the inner life and the inner truth in human nature and to create the world of an 'Immediate Communion between the Self and God' (4: 305) coincides with the idea of 'Romantic Imagination' as examined and fashioned by twentieth-century Romantic scholars. We have to remember, however, that Yanagi's concept of 'imagination' in essence originated in what he understood to be Zen philosophy. For him, the most advanced concept of 'imagination' was to be found in Buddhism (4: 474), and even in his later years, he continued to hold Blake to be the only artist that could represent the Oriental philosophy of 'imagination' (14: 73). The Blakean imagination is a 'Contradictory Way' through which dual or antithetical elements of the material world dissolve into a harmonious 'golden ring' leading towards the gate of Heaven, towards 'God', that is, the world of 'Oneness' (2: 47–52, 341–3, 370–1). This imagination is most powerful in extinguishing individual self-consciousness. In defining the mode of 'self-annihilation' which he found operating fervently in *Milton* and *Jerusalem*, he argued in a Japanese religious framework which conjoined pantheism and Zen philosophy:

> Self-annihilation is by no means self-negation; it means a perfect expansion of the Self, an unconstrained expression of individuality. It is a unification of the Self and the Universe. We just breathe in the blessed world of eternal God when we immerse our hearts into the depth of Nature and annihilate self-consciousness in the world of Love. We then attain 'Cosmic Consciousness' and the Self is experiencing a limitless expansion. (4: 306)

While aptly capturing the principal tenet of Blake's philosophy, the terms and phrases in this passage bear an obvious resemblance to those which he employed elsewhere in his argument on Zen. More interestingly, he even viewed Blake's self-annihilation and his concept of 'imagination' as compatible with all sorts of oriental spiritualism ranging from the Islamic religion to the Upanishad philosophy (2: 130–3; 14: 65).

This Blake–Zen association was at its base driven by Yanagi's earnest hope of reconstructing his own individual identity and that of his country through the reassessment of Oriental philosophy in relation to Western thought. Assimilating foreign ideas alone was not satisfactory for him. The invaluable model he had at hand was Kōri Torahiko (1890–1924), a fellow *Shirakaba* associate, who left Japan for Britain after a mesmerizing encounter with Blake's art and poetry and became an influential figure in the Modernist movement in Britain, introducing *Noh* plays to Yeats and adapting traditional Japanese plays for English theatres. Yanagi was the only colleague who appreciated the real significance of Kōri's literary achievements in the international domain of literature. In his eyes, Kōri embodied the ideal virtue which was gravely lacking, but vitally important for their contemporary critics, namely the virtue that could dissolve the boundary between the East and the West and between self and society through the harmonious unification of art, religion and philosophy. Blake, or rather the Blake envisaged by Kōri, prompted Yanagi's radical self-transformation from a juvenile essayist into an ardent religio-philosophical art critic with a cosmopolitan outlook.

But even this metamorphosis did not necessarily secure a clear and stable political identity for Yanagi. Indeed, he identified himself with Blake in opposing all sorts of repression of the moral liberty of individuals, and upon the emanation of divine energy from human bodies. We can also find his sympathy lying most conspicuously with Orc burning with flames of fury and fighting for liberty (4: 124, 127). Nakami Mari even suggests that what Yanagi saw as Blake's anti-dualism has a resonance with the communist idea of 'mutual aid' which he derived from the outspoken anarchist Peter Kropotokin (Nakami 2003: 81). Nevertheless, it is hard to deny that in the contemporary Japanese context, Yanagi's humanitarianism remained polite and its ideological stance uncertain and indeterminate. His self-centred reading moderated, even displaced some radical tenets in Blake by locating them emphatically in the mystifying framework of the polite version of Zen Buddhism. His eclectic religious view had little sympathy with the new, plebeian or millenarian kind of religions, such as Ōmoto-kyō founded by Deguchi Nao and Hommichi founded by Ōnishi Aijirō, not to mention with the nationalistic teachings of other modernized Buddhist sects.[11] Oddly enough, he often became evasive about his own political adherence by deliberately eliminating direct historical engagement in Blake's works. 'It is erroneous', he asserted, 'to view Blake as a political revolutionary engaged furiously with social issues' (4: 117): he was neither interested in changing society nor in attacking the government or the wealthy for oppressing the people, but he 'rebelled only against the established moral codes which dominated and controlled the freedom of people's minds' (4: 119). This Blake as a pseudo-Zen Buddhist and moderate moral reformer is Yanagi in disguise. Just as Yanagi himself took an ambiguous detachment from active political commitments in contemporary Japanese society, his Blake was kept cautiously dissociated from revolutionary politics in Britain.

Yanagi's ambivalent ideological liaison with Blake becomes even more problematic when we seek to clarify the political orientations of the *Mingei* movement which he initiated from the 1920s. Despite his repeated denial of the anti-oligarchic purport of the movement, a radical principle lay at the heart of his lifelong efforts to promote its manifesto and a few other related campaigns which had some distinctly political resonance.[12] *Mingei*, literally meaning 'people's art' in Japanese, was seen by Yanagi as a 'communal' and 'democratic' genre of art in direct contrast with the individual, sophisticated, 'aristocratic' kind of art as well as with the mechanical or industrial products prevailing in the contemporary age (8: 291). The remark echoes Blake's defence of 'Art' against 'the Contemptible Counter Arts' in *Public Address* (E 580) and his line 'The whole business of Man Is the Arts and All Things Common' in *The Laocoön* (E 273) – the statements against commercialism and capitalism promoted by imperialists and traders in early-nineteenth-century England (Eaves 1992: 158–68).[13] Yanagi's *Mingei* movement appears even 'Romantic' in corresponding to the ballad revival movement in contemporary Japan. He went as far as to redeem folk crafts in Korea and Okinawa from obscurity, and this action is to be taken as a critique of the imperial colonialism of the Japanese government in the early twentieth century. Furthermore, Yanagi's lectures on Blake and Oriental mysticism in the rural region of Nagano stimulated another *Shirakaba* movement (the *Shinshu Shirakaba* movement) in the surrounding area, where young schoolteachers tried to introduce a liberal teaching method in opposition to the government's nationalistic mode of education.

It was during his engagement with this regional movement that Yanagi found by accident the religious sculptures produced by the monk Mokujiki, whose Blakean Gothic beauty captured his connoisseur's eye. The Mokujiki sculptures, he argued, are 'unconventional', therefore 'original' in being free in style and ignoring the traditional aesthetic concept of religious art (7: 583–4). Though seemingly rough, even ugly at a glance, their 'coarseness', 'clumsiness' and 'deformed imperfection' incarnate the 'primitive passion', 'enthusiasm and simplicity' of 'faith' and 'sound spirit' prevailing among common people (7: 592–4). Their true beauty is constituted by 'crude wildness', masculine strength and 'animated vigour and proportion' (7: 596). This view corresponds exactly to what Yanagi saw as characteristic of Blake's engravings, including 'dynamic passion', 'energetic vitality' and 'active vigour' within their 'grotesque' and 'savage' appearance (4: 34, 96; 14: 63). In fact, the image of a Buddhist guardian god carved by Mokujiki (Figure 14.2) bears a curious resemblance in its design and manner to, for instance, Blake's representation of Urizen in Plate 8 of *The Book of Urizen*, or perhaps 'Howling Los' in Plate 6 of the same book. As he admitted himself, his earlier study of Blake clearly provided the aesthetic and ideological foundation upon which he could fully appreciate the uncouth, yet inspired artefacts as an embodiment of the vital energy of common human life and religious faith (7: 257). Yanagi even went as far as to view Mokujiki as a 'liberator' who, like Blake, had created a new age in history with his free and pure spirit of faith (7: 584). As Jon Mee examined with care and insight in *Dangerous Enthusiasm* (1992), the primitivism, barbarism and antiquarianism in Blake's work carried distinctively radical implications in late-eighteenth-century British politics. Similarly, the near-idolatry of Yanagi's exaltation of Mokujiki sculptures and his campaign for common folk crafts cannot be exempted from involvement, if only

**Figure 14.2** The Wood Carving of Acala, by Mokujiki. © The Japan Folk Crafts Museum.

an implicit one, with the turbulent political situations of early-twentieth-century Japan.

We have to pause here, however, to question whom the 'people' or 'folk' in the Japanese word *mingei* refers to. Yanagi was aware of a series of heated controversies raised in the contemporary period over the meanings of *minshu geijutu* ('people's art') (Okamura 1991: 11–38). In August 1916, Honma Hisao contributed an article to the *Waseda Bungaku*, expressing a condescending middle-class view that 'people's art' should cultivate the taste of the uneducated working-class people, enlighten their world-view and provide moments of recreation for them in the midst of poverty and hardship. The essay provoked a number of responses in various periodicals. The *Waseda Bungaku* hosted a debate by leading authors on the definition of 'people's art' in the February issue of the following year, but it could merely offer general, all-inclusive definitions: firstly 'people's art' can be either colloquial, popular or plebeian; secondly it should be placed against the *fin-de-siècle* principle of 'art for art's sake'; lastly it should represent the active energy and power of people in opposition to the corrupt culture of the aristocracy (Shimamura 1917: 42–9; Tomita 1917: 49–53; Nakamura 1917: 53–5). The class category of 'people' was left unspecified. The anarchist Ōsugi Sakae, dissatisfied with these mediocre arguments, took a bold step to champion the working class, attacking all middle-class intellectuals for their snobbery and patronising attitude. 'People's art', he claimed, must be 'art by proletarians, for proletarians, and of proletarians': it should function as the source of their daily 'energy' and 'vigour', as well as providing the source of their 'joy' and 'pleasure' and the basis of their moral and intellectual security (Ōsugi 1917: 241, 246–8; Stanley 1982: 121–3). Yanagi's campaign for lowly folk crafts appears to conform to Ōsugi's professed ideal, and yet, strangely enough, he deliberately kept his definition of *mingei* vague and unclear until a year before his death, when he finally, and rather awkwardly, observed that 'people' in the word *mingei* should refer to both middle and working classes. As a consequence, the ideological principle of Yanagi's *Mingei* movement remained incoherent, vague and sometimes abstract, just as the contemporary studies of native ethnology formulated by Yanagita Kunio (1875–1962) and by Orikuchi Shinobu (1887–1953) turned towards constructing an illusory, unsubstantial image (as Harootunian argues in 'Figuring the Folk' 1998b). The exact position of the *Mingei* movement is difficult to pin down on the political map of the age. The movement can be regarded as far more radical and practical than Yamamoto Kanae's unfeasible 'Art Movement for Agricultural Labourers', which tried in vain to introduce the skill of painting in the manner of Scandinavian rural pictures as part of daily routines among Japanese agricultural labourers,[14] but at the same time, Yanagi's ideal was too westernized and polite to extend its influence any further than to a small group of young intellectuals.[15]

Yanagi's misreading of Blake becomes most obvious in overlooking the importance which Blake attached to the physical exertion of artisans. As personified in the figure of Los, persistent labour is the essential basis for art, poetry and all other artistic creation in Blake's philosophy. Indeed, he was scornful of the 'Lifes Labour of Ignorant Journeymen' in the *Public Address*, but this was merely because he considered them to be hired hands and bodies, deprived of their real physical and intellectual capacity by the vulgar system of commerce (E 573–5; Eaves 1992: 168–74). He never ignored the hardship of labour itself; he knew its real value and importance in artistic creation from his own experience. In *The*

*Book of Urizen*, Los thus represents part of Blake's grave concern about the joyless and dehumanizing condition of labourers at the time of war, industrialization and rising imperialism (Erdman 1977: 243–63, 330). While incarnating the Creative Imagination in the human world, Los shows himself as a 'blacksmith' who, repressed by Urizen, howls, gnashes and groans, yet continues to cast the molten iron into new forms, construct Golgonooza and create Jerusalem where science, religion and art are all unified:

> Forgetfulness, dumbness, necessity!
> In chains of the mind locked up,
> Like fetters of ice shrinking together
> Disorganiz'd, rent from Eternity,
> Los beat on his fetters of iron;
> And heated his furnaces & pour'd
> Iron sodor and sodor of brass.
> (*The Book of Urizen*, Plate 10, ll. 24–30 E 75)

This appreciation of toil and sweat lay at the basis of Blake's continual opposition to the industrialism which began to develop the factory system in his age and thereby to replace human life governed by the natural rhythms of labour with a stale unfeeling life dominated by the sound of machinery (Blackstone 1949; 1966: 315–16). As he denounces in strong terms in *The Four Zoas*, the so-called Industrial Revolution condemned human hands under the heavy burden of wheels and made 'laborious workmanship' useless and valueless: the 'wisdom' of artisans and craftsmen was to be exhausted '[i]n sorrowful drudgery to obtain a scanty pittance of bread / In ignorance to view a small portion & think that All' (*The Four Zoas, Night the Seventh*, Plate 92, ll. 31–2 E 364).

This sympathetic view of labour is curiously absent in Yanagi's *Mingei* movement. Indeed, Yanagi absorbed Blake's fascination with 'All Things Common' and even Ruskin and Morris's antipathy towards manufacturing machines (10: 149–50). Nevertheless, their radical or socialist concern about the pain and suffering of labour was not given much significance in his discourse on *mingei*. He rather optimistically tended to take for granted the joy and happiness that could be derived from physical exertion. His appraisal of craftsmen's labour is simply due to the beauty created through their patient, day-by-day performance. Even if he saw God's hand operating in the handwork of nameless artisans, the trace of their physical exertion was curiously erased from his discursive sketches of the elegant quality of the products (13: 93). For instance, in admiring the skill of an aged woman who had been compelled by financial necessity to paint thousands of pots for as long as 60 years, his attention was directed not to her living or material conditions, but merely to the skilful ease with which she was painting pot after pot. What fascinated him was the fact that the labourer's self-consciousness as well as the sense of pain was numbed and obliterated in the timeless, impersonal surface of artwork: 'her handwork transcends her self-consciousness', with the endless drudgery not only alleviating the pain of labour, but also refining her skill up to the point of divine perfection (10: 99, 151–2). Blake's hardships in his later years also appeared to him as 'a blessed opportunity for disinterested, happy labour' (4: 260). The virtue of folk crafts, he argued, was the peacefulness and tranquillity created through nameless artisans' quiet obedience to dispassionate, routine chores.

In order to justify this eradication of individuality and painful labour, Yanagi recurrently employed the Zen concepts of religious virtue, such as *buji* (peacefulness) and *mushin* (non-mindedness) (10: 177).

> Labour itself casts a physical restraint upon the human body, but in a way it can also set the human mind free. Expertise enhances the human mind to the height of non-mindedness. Consequently it creates plenty of room for spiritual freedom in their creative performance . . . The beauty of folk crafts is in part a result of such freedom. (10: 99)

In short, labour, for Yanagi, was almost a pseudo-religious duty conducted to annihilate artisans' self-consciousness and replace every trace of their individual physicality and vital energy with the graceful quality created by the impersonal hand of 'non-mindedness' (3: 541; 9: 77). Even the Christian virtue of holy mendicancy, as exhibited in the life of St Francis, was extolled by Yanagi as leading towards the Zen state of 'nothingness' by way of the ungrudging practice of hard work in poverty: 'the divine power descends on all natural beings' and restores them back to the sphere of 'nothingness' when they want nothing (3: 535). The self-annihilation, a virtue which he found both in Blake and in Zen, now extinguished the emanation of the artisan's personality, labour and energy in the greater ideological order of the Zen tradition. Los as a labouring artisan is not given his role in this aesthetic and philosophical system. Nor would fiery Orc be born or reborn without the paternal presence of Los. In spite of the Blakean sympathy towards the base, the low and the grotesque, which formed the ideological backbone of Yanagi's art criticism and *Mingei* movement, Yanagi tended to neglect the real value and immediate physicality of labour itself in the work of common craftsmen.

Blake was certainly a departing point for Yanagi's philosophy which discovered and promoted the virtue of Japanese philosophy and the quality of ordinary folk crafts. His art and poetry relieved Yanagi's mixed anxieties over his adolescent ideological uncertainty up to some point by providing a model of self-realization through the exercise of the all-encompassing power of imagination which, like the Zen spirit, dissolves all antithetical aspects of human society and then liberates the self into the sphere of Nothingness. There is no doubt about the symmetry between Blake and Yanagi. But the symmetry is curious and indeterminate. Yanagi's value system oscillated between the Blakean dynamics and the un-Blakean, moderate politeness. This ideological ambivalence is a result of his strenuous attempt to read Blake as a pseudo-Zen mystic by moderating and depoliticizing dangerously radical implications in his work, and so containing the volatile, insurrectionary enthusiasm inherent in his religio-political message. In Yanagi's discourse on Blake and also on the *Mingei* movement, there lay a profound, ineradicable anxiety over violent radicals and riotous mobs, perhaps in a similar way to that in which English Rational Dissenters and polite reformers suffered from the anxiety of plebeian enthusiasm, as fully scrutinized by Jon Mee in *Romanticism, Enthusiasm and Regulation* (2003). Yanagi and his *Shirakaba* friends remained fundamentally 'polite', and yet such educated, privileged intellectuals alone could afford to assimilate and disseminate foreign philosophy and Romantic literature most ardently within the Japanese ideological framework in the age of wars and disturbances, in part for their own self-fulfilment and yet also with a view to social amelioration. Despite his initial fascination with Blake's work, Yanagi had to control and modify its political tenets in the process of recreating Blake as a means of propagandizing for a rather apolitical Buddhist philosophy. His aspiration towards two opposite poles, the Blakean masculine energy on the one hand, and the Zen tranquillity of Bodhisattva on the other, ended up by disciplining and restraining the wild, liberating power of the former. By eliminating the presence of afflicted labourers, Yanagi's seemingly Blakean campaign for the people's art unsettled its own ideological basis: just as he kept standing away from radical activists and working-class riots, it remained detached from the muddle of agonizing distress and turbulent politics. Blake was integrated into Yanagi's religio-philosophical system as a polite, politically indeterminate artist–philosopher. The picture of the graceful Maitreya Bodhisattva at the Koryuji temple continuously haunted Yanagi's writings as a ghostlike catalyst, if not a guardian angel, which moderated the Blakean radical and 'dynamic enthusiasm' into the tranquil and peaceful state of 'non-mindedness'.

## Notes

1  All quotations from Yanagi Muneyoshi are from *Yanagi Muneyoshi Zenshu*, 26 vols (Tokyo: Chikuma Shobō, 1980–92) with volume and page numbers in parentheses. All translations from the volumes are my own.

2  There is no evidence, however, that suggests Yanagi's awareness of Rodin's *Thinker* becoming a socialist symbol in Paris in 1906.

3  Yanagi must have read Blake's *Songs of Innocence* around 1906, but it was not until his reading of *The Marriage of Heaven and Hell* in 1911 that he discovered and was fascinated by the quality and power of Blake's work.

4  Janet Warner and Christopher Heppner both develop Aby Warburg's concept of a 'pathos formula' to characterize those figures in Blake's engravings which embody Dionysiac and primeval passions in an intense and heightened manner (Warner 1984; Heppner 1995: 22–55).

5  The most important and influential study of Yanagi's reception of Blake is Yura Kimiyoshi's 'Yanagi Shiso no Shihatsu Eki: *William Blake*', appended to *William Blake*, the fourth volume of *Yanagi Muneyoshi Zenshu* (4: 679–707). Other notable studies include Bunsho's *Blake*, Saito's 'Yanagi Muneyoshi no Taicho "William Blake" ', and Matsushima's 'Romanticism to sono Kenkyu'. See Bentley 1994.

6  The question of 'individualism' haunted intellectuals and authors in the late *Meiji* era, as Harootunian examines in the cases of Natsume Sōseki and Kitamura Tōkoku, and it grew to be a more serious and obsessive preoccupation in the literature of the *Taishō* era (Harootunian 1974: 110–38). Yanagi and his fellow members of the *Shirakaba* circle largely inherited the dilemma of Sōseki, whose lecture on the importance of individualism captured their hearts while at Gakushuin High School, their alma mater.

7  Despite the prevailing view that literature in the *Taishō* era is generally apolitical, the Treason Trial casts an 'ominous shadow' upon most of the literary and philosophical works during the *Taishō* age (Pollack 1992: 39–52; Sakimura 1965: 87–111). While most intellectuals made some sort of remarks on this trial, Yanagi and his friends, whom I am going to discuss below, kept a curious silence, which seems ironically to indicate the traumatic shock they must have felt at the incident.

8  They were wealthy enough to purchase foreign books and art works, while founding and distributing their own periodical *Shirakaba* at their own cost. Their adoration of Blake drove them to host exhibitions of his works in 1919 in Nagano, Kyoto and Tokyo.

9  For Yanagi's unique definition of 'temperament' and its importance in his philosophy, see Yanagi 1980–92: 2: 214–15, 221–2.

10  Nishida also taught at Gakushuhin from 1909 to 1910. See Nakami 2003: 51.

11  For the political implications of these new radical, therefore persecuted religions, see Murakami 1968: 548.

12  We cannot ignore the influence of the socialist guild movement of John Ruskin and William Morris upon Yanagi's *Mingei* movement (Yanagi 1980–92: 10: 43, 49, 149). In his article on the relationship between Morris and Yanagi, Kusamitsu discerns a clear parallel between Morris's idea of 'The Lesser Art' and Yanagi's concept of *Hetamono*, which means 'lowly or clumsy product' in Japanese (Kusamitsu 1995: 137–8).

13  There is no evidence that Yanagi read *The Laocoön* or *Public Address*, but it was most likely that he comprehended the tenor of Blake's views on art from other major works of his. At the same time, we must admit that this anti-commercial attitude should be carefully balanced against Blake's demand for a fair price for art.

14  For Yanagi's own apology for his *Mingei* movement in distinction from Yamamoto's movement, see Yanagi 1980–92: 10: 171–2; 9: 57–63.

15  Other contemporary institutions, such as Yuaikai and the University of Liberty, another establishment in Nagano, were clear in their socialist orientations and far more successful than Yanagi's *Shinshu Shirakaba* movement in providing educational opportunities to labourers and even to *geisha* girls.

# 15 The Female Voice in Blake Studies in Japan, 1910s–1930s

Yoko Ima-Izumi

This chapter will centre on the following question: how did early Blake scholars in Japan, in the 1910s through to the 1930s, interpret the female voices of such characters as Thel, Oothoon, Ahania, Enitharmon, Jerusalem and Vala? The first high point of Blake studies in Japan came around the 1910s and lasted two decades. It was the time when the emerging power of the so-called 'new women' was being acknowledged in Japan and the power relations between man and woman were changing. During that period, two prominent scholars, Muneyoshi Yanagi and Bunsho Jugaku, were actively engaged in introducing Blake to the Japanese people. They were well aware of the concept of 'new women' but, at the same time, demonstrated the difficulty of consistency even for proclaimed supporters of women's independence. I will analyse their comments on Blake's depictions of the female in their publications from the 1910s through the 1930s against a backdrop of the burgeoning feminist consciousness in early-twentieth-century Japan.

As G. E. Bentley, Jr.'s statistics in his *Blake Studies in Japan* shows, the year 1914 saw the first flowering of publications related to Blake, for there were 14 publications on the poet in that year, whereas in each of the preceding 21 years there were no more than three publications on him per year, and in some years none at all (Bentley 1994: xvii). This sudden surge of Blake studies in 1914 was the result of the activities of Yanagi and a group of artists engaged in the *Shirakaba* journal, to which he himself had been contributing. Yanagi sparked interest in Blake's works among the members of the group, and they were enthusiastically awaiting the completion of his book on Blake; and indeed were reporting his progress on the book in almost every monthly issue of *Shirakaba* in 1914. These progress reports, together with Yanagi's essays published in the journal, account for 13 out of 14 publications on Blake in 1914, the fourteenth being Yanagi's book itself.

Yanagi's *William Blake* (1914), a heavy tome nearly 800 pages long, was well received by *Shirakaba* members. We cannot be sure whether the book was widely read by lay people, for it contains numerous quotations from Blake's poems in their original language, but it was certainly read and reviewed by the intellectuals who were well versed in English. There was one reviewer, Takeshi Saito, who was sensitive to Yanagi's continual assertion of self and, grasping the subjective nature of the voluminous study, said partly in jest: 'We are not sure whether Yanagi is introducing Blake or Blake is introducing Yanagi' (Yanagi 1980–92: 4: 706). What is remarkable in the study of Blake is Yanagi's exultation at having discovered a kindred spirit in Blake. Yanagi was pleased with Saito's point and dedicated to him a short essay, 'About My Blake Study', in which he emphasized his subjective reading of Blake.

> As you [Saito] pointed out in your review of my book, I did not intend to write about Blake objectively (except for his biographical facts). I wrote about myself who wanted to live by Blake . . . My Blake is real to me. How could I write about someone else's Blake? . . . I was seeking the essence of Blake. My book must convey my delight at having found this essence. (ibid: 5: 627)

In a word, Yanagi tried to discover himself via Blake. He locates himself at the centre of his study of Blake, as the motto of the *Shirakaba* group was to turn inward on one's self and approve one's outpouring of emotion.

Art is, for Yanagi, a means of heightening awareness of self and improving the quality of inner self. He wanted to share the same motto with his lover, Kaneko Nakajima, three years his junior, whom he met in 1910. He repeatedly wrote love letters to her, in which he encouraged her to accept his value judgements and, specifically, to share his preference for post-impressionist painters such as Van Gogh, Cézanne and Gauguin. He explained why he regarded the post-impressionists as vitally significant: 'Most artists (as well as philosophers and people of religion) in today's Japan . . . lack individual spirituality. The art of Rodin and Van Gogh is terrifyingly spiritual. Artistic technique is subservient to this spirituality' (6 March 1913; Matsuhashi 1999: 61).[1] Yanagi wished to 'deepen [his] inner life' (4 March 1913; Matsuhashi 1991: 61) and made it clear that he 'wished the same [for his lover]' (6 March 1913; Matsuhashi 1999: 61). Kaneko absorbed the way of thinking behind what Yanagi spoke and wrote to her. Later in their married life, she was able to proofread all the pages of Yanagi's *William Blake*, such an achievement being a considerable intellectual feat in its own right.

With his sensitivity cultivated by his contact with the post-impressionists, Yanagi labelled Blake's poetical work as immensely profound and marked some lines as unforgettably impressive. The lines that Yanagi noted as being especially to his taste in *William Blake* are all spoken by the female characters. The first instance is the banquet scene of Los and Enitharmon on the second Night in *The Four Zoas*. Yanagi comments that 'The most beautiful lines of *The Four Zoas* are these words blessing the sexual union [of Los and Enitharmon]' (Yanagi 1980–92: 4: 154). Though Yanagi does not explain, their union is actually a struggle of one's winning over the other. The passage begins as the sexual attraction that Los and Enitharmon have to each other: 'And Los & Enitharmon were drawn down by their desires' (*FZ* 2 34:1; E 322).[2] Enitharmon does not easily yield herself to the arms of Los, and Los tries to 'grasp thy [Enitharmon's] vest in vain' and, calling himself 'the poor forsaken Los', complains that 'Therefore fade I [Los] thus dissolvd in raptur'd trance' (*FZ* 2 34:18, 34:21, 34:32; E 322–3). He finally concedes and tries to prove that 'repining Los / Still dies for Enitharmon' (*FZ* 2 34:35–36; E 323).

With Los's surrender to Enitharmon through his death, she begins to sing loudly while taking up a harp. This song by Enitharmon is what Yanagi calls 'the best part' (Yanagi 1980–92: 4: 154) of the banquet scene. The 'best part' of the 'most beautiful lines of *The Four Zoas*', by which Yanagi is deeply fascinated, represents nothing but Enitharmon's triumph over Los in their power struggle:

But thus she sang. I sieze the sphery harp I strike the strings

At the first Sound the Golden sun arises from the Deep
And shakes his awful hair
The Eccho wakes the moon to unbind her silver locks
The golden sun bears on my song
And nine bright spheres of harmony rise round the fiery King

The joy of woman is the Death of her most best beloved
Who dies for Love of her
In torments of fierce jealousy & pangs of adoration.
The Lovers night bears on my song
And the nine Spheres rejoice beneath my powerful controll

They sing unceasing to the notes of my immortal hand
The solemn silent moon
Reverberates the living harmony upon my limbs
The birds & beasts rejoice & play
And every one seeks for his mate to prove his inmost joy

Furious & terrible they sport & rend the nether deeps
The deep lifts up his rugged head
And lost in infinite hum[m]ing wings vanishes with a cry
The fading cry is ever dying
The living voice is ever living in its inmost joy

Arise you little glancing wings & sing your infant joy
Arise & drink your bliss
For every thing that lives is holy for the source of life
Descends to be a weeping babe
For the Earthworm renews the moisture of the sandy plain

Now my left hand I stretch to earth beneath
And strike the terrible string
I wake sweet joy in dens of sorrow & I plant a smile
In forests of affliction

(FZ 2 34:57–87; E 323–4)

The passage contains an unmistakable declaration of woman's triumph over man such as 'The joy of woman is the Death of her most best beloved / Who dies for Love of her'. That is expressive of a kind of *femme fatale* exuberance, and Enitharmon enjoys her unlimited sexual control over Los. We could take Los's death as the exhilaration of erotic infatuation as in the cliché of the sex/death equation. Eager to control not only her beloved Los but everything that lives, Enitharmon further talks about keeping all 'the nine Spheres . . . beneath my powerful control'. This is rephrased in sweet, mellifluous words: she sings and plays an instrument so that she may 'wake sweet joy in dens of sorrow & [I] plant a smile / In forests of affliction' as we have seen in the above-quoted passage. She propagates her power under the guise of 'sweet joy' and 'smile', arguing that every creature is entitled to happiness and holiness using this memorable phrase: 'every thing that lives is holy'. Yanagi is fascinated by these words and candidly declares: 'The passage of Enitharmon's song was so appealing that I could not refrain from quoting it' (Yanagi 1980–92: 4: 156). The question that I wish to raise here about his declaration is: did he really understand what the passage conveys; that is, Enitharmon's will to power and the sexual struggle between Los and Enitharmon? In order to give an appropriate answer, I will now turn to an examination of Yanagi's attitude to women, especially to his wife, at the time of the early feminist movement in Japan.

In the 1910s, new artistic movements flourished through Japan's encounter with western art and culture, and new journals were published to introduce and express new ideas about art. Two remarkable journals of the times were the *Shirakaba*, in which Yanagi was deeply involved as its core member, and the *Seito* or *Bluestocking* (the term 'bluestocking' is obviously borrowed from its British precursor). Both journals were inaugurated about the same time (the *Shirakaba* in 1910 and the *Seito* the following year), and both intended to liberate the individual from moral and institutional restrictions and characteristically glorified free love. They served as the landmark journals when individuality counted more than ever before. The contributors to the *Seito* were all women while those to the *Shirakaba* were all men (though Kaneko was officially included in the *Shirakaba* group when its website was created after her death). The members of the two journals felt a strong affinity for and trust in each other, and it is no coincidence that *Shirakaba* men and *Seito* women often married, as is evident from the following examples: Kotaro Takamura (sculptor, poet) and Chieko Naganuma (illustrator); Saneatsu Mushanokoji (novelist, poet, painter) and Fusako Takeo – divorced later; Yoshiro Nagayo (novelist) and Fusako's schoolmate named Shigeko Ichikawa; Sadao Tsubaki (painter) and a sister of Shigeko named Takako Ichikawa; and Kenkichi Tomimoto (craft potter) and Kazue Otake (painter).[3] The *Seito* was intended to advance women's literature and to enhance their status in society, and every issue was full of comments on the dignity of woman. Restoration of women's rights was vigorously presented by Raicho Hiratsuka (1886–1971) in the inaugural issue:

> In the beginning, woman was the sun, an authentic person. Today, she is the moon, a pale-faced sick moon, living through others, and reflecting the brilliance of others. (Hiratsuka 1971: 328)

Yanagi was familiar with these self-assertive words and was, as a *Shirakaba* man, supportive of the empowerment of woman (within rather strict limits, as I shall make clear shortly). His sensitivity to the words of the *Seito* women was of the same quality as his appreciation of Enitharmon's words to express her will to power. The members of the *Seito* were called 'new women' and endeavoured to defy the long-established convention of 'good wife and wise mother' who must reside in a highly cloistered society.

Yanagi proved himself an advocate of the kind of feminist movement promoted by the *Seito* group through his act of continually encouraging his lover Kaneko to become a professional singer, and not a mere housewife. Yanagi and Kaneko exchanged numerous love letters for four years before they got married. In his letters, he related to Kaneko his wish to share what he called 'ideal love', which would require equal labour and responsibility of both man and woman. This 'love', according to Yanagi's letter to Kaneko, would 'enable us to work hard together to attain something no one else could have ever done' (2 August 1913; Matsuhashi 1999: 64). He wanted Kaneko to be equal to him and, pointing out 'female weakness in the study of philosophy and religion', he asked her to over-come such failings (2 August 1913; Matsuhashi 1999: 64). Yanagi gave a clear picture of exactly what Kaneko should be like: 'If you could not become an excellent singer', he wrote to Kaneko, 'it would be as painful to me as if I were stabbed in the chest . . . If you ended up being a singer established only in Japan, I would have to question my fate of being your lover' (30 March 1913; Matsuhashi 1999: 61–2). Kaneko responded to his letter, confirming her desire to become a world-class singer as he wished: 'I will be an excellent artist by any cost, for I will be your wife' (1 April 1913; Matsuhashi 1999: 62).

When encouraging Kaneko to work hard to become a world-class singer, Yanagi understood the effect of social pressure on professional women. He pointed out in his letter to her on 22 December 1911:

> It is difficult for a woman to become an artist in Japan, as we witness that there are remarkably few women who have become professional after having graduated from a music school. Most women give up art and become house-wives. Any woman artist would be expected to remain single, and this is disagreeably unnatural. (Matsuhashi 1999: 34)

He assured her in the same letter that she 'was sent into this world to be a woman and, at the same time, an artist' (Matsuhashi 1999: 34). And he begged for a chance to reconcile for her the conventionally conflicting states – work and housework, or living as a professional singer and living as a wife. He confidently wrote to her: 'It is my mission to help you achieve your calling as an artist' (22 December 1911; Matsuhashi 1999: 34–5). He continued to appeal to Kaneko that he 'alone could help you use your talent to the full', and that their love would nourish her quest to attain the very essence of a musician (13 May 1912; Matsuhashi 1999: 41). He even encouraged her to go abroad to pursue her career as a singer: 'You should get opportunities to listen to a great number of the geniuses playing, and I believe you should go abroad as soon as possible' (12 September 1912; Matsuhashi 1999: 50).

Kaneko was persuaded that accomplishing her vocation as a singer would be the same as nurturing their love, and she promised Yanagi that she would make efforts to become a truly great artist 'for your sake' (12 September 1912; Matsuhashi 1999: 50). And that is exactly what she did. She was selected to sing at a concert held in commemoration of the retirement of a professor at Tokyo Music School where she was a student in the singing course and, as she told Yanagi, she would 'sing with heart and soul for [Yanagi] alone on a stage' (10 December 1912; Matsuhashi 1999: 56). She showed the first signs of becoming an international contralto who would eventually be received with admiration in Germany.

Being a radical thinker who was a member of the *Shirakaba* group, Yanagi accepted the idea of new independent women working to earn their own living. And he helped at least one woman to become a professional singer (whose earnings he was to spend on books and craftwork). It is not difficult to under-stand that this man, who was immersed in the flow of the 1910s feminist movement, showed himself sensitive to the joy of a glorious life praised by Blake's female characters.

The second instance of some of Yanagi's favourite lines from Blake is a passage spoken by Vala. Yanagi even called it the greatest in English literature: 'The lines that show Blake's grand love most clearly are the following lines that he sang towards the Sun. No lines have ever been equal to these lines in great depth in thought in the history of English Literature. I will never forget my affection for Blake as long as these lines exist' (Yanagi 1980–92: 4: 160). This passage is a part of the ninth Night in *The Four Zoas*, where Vala is first dejected at the thought of mortality. She weeps and blames the Sun for giving her the hope to flourish. When she weeps at the idea of passing away, as she says 'Hopeless if I am like the grass & so shall pass away' (*FZ* 9 127:23; E 396), she hears a voice that says: 'Yon Sun shall wax old & decay but thou shalt ever flourish' (*FZ* 9 127:25; E 396). She does not know that the voice is Luvah's, and wonders momentarily 'whence came that sweet & comforting voice' (*FZ* 9 127:28; E 396), but soon she exults and triumphantly tells the Sun that 'thou art nothing now to me' (*FZ* 9 127:29; E 396). She then feels a kind of alliance between herself and the Sun, and suggests that both of them should flourish together. The lines singled out by Yanagi, which come right after this suggestion of Vala's, run as follows:

> Rise up O Sun most glorious minister & light of day
> Flow on ye gentle airs & bear the voice of my rejoicing
> Wave freshly clear waters flowing around the tender grass
> And thou sweet smelling ground put forth thy life in fruits & flowers
> Follow me O my flocks & hear me sing my rapturous Song
> I will cause my voice to be heard on the clouds that glitter in the sun
> I will call & who shall answer me I will sing who shall reply
> For from my pleasant hills behold the living living springs
> Running among my green pastures delighting among my trees
> (*FZ* 9 128:4–12; E 397)

Vala creates a world around her, locating herself at the very centre. She commands the Sun to 'rise up' and airs to 'flow' and 'bear the voice of my rejoicing'. She commands waters to 'wave', and flocks to 'Follow me' and 'hear me sing my rapturous Song'. She intends to 'cause my voice to be heard' by virtually everybody and everything. She cares about herself, and others should follow her and respond to her. If she is happy, others should be happy too, as she makes clear: 'I sing & you reply to my Song I rejoice & you are glad' (*FZ* 9 128:15; E 397).

The assertiveness of the passage must have moved the *Shirakaba* group, as it did Yanagi. The impact of Vala's lines on Yanagi was so great that he repeated his admiration of the lines in a footnote. His sensitivity to the female's powerful and intense words, however, is limited. He did not realize Blake meant them to be disturbing (though the degree of irony is still a highly contentious issue). These lines about female glory and triumph are almost always expressive of the female domination over the male, but Yanagi was seemingly blind to the power struggle between the sexes, for he never quoted any lines spoken by females when they include such words as '[woman's] dominion', 'womans triumph', and 'This is Womans World':

> Who shall I call? Who shall I send?
> That Woman, lovely Woman! may have dominion?
> (*Europe* 5:2–3; E 62)

> And Rintrah hung with all his legions in the nether deep
> Enitharmon laugh'd in her sleep to see (O womans triumph)
> (*Europe* 12:24–5; E 64)

Can there be any secret joy on Earth greater than this?
Enitharmon answerd: This is Womans World, nor need she any
Spectre to defend her from Man. I will Create secret places
(*Jerusalem* 88:15–17; E 247)

It is not irrelevant to speculate that Yanagi deliberately left out of his favourite
lines any words that are explicitly indicative of female supremacy over the male.
Numerous episodes from his real life point in the same direction. It is dis-
couraging to discover that Yanagi, who was initially understanding and supportive
of his wife's right to pursue her professional life, turned out to be the principal
obstacle to her becoming a world-class singer. The domineering image of Yanagi
emerges from the letters that he and Kaneko exchanged around the time of her
trip to Germany in 1928. It was not easy for Kaneko to get permission from him
to make a trip to Germany. Yanagi, touring throughout Japan to collect folk crafts
for an exhibition, was quite displeased at her proposed trip abroad. He nibbled
away at the money Kaneko was saving for her trip to Germany, as she recollected
in 'My Music and Its History' (Matsuhashi 1999: 153). I wonder if this might have
delayed her departure for Germany. He not only spent Kaneko's money for
purchasing books and folk crafts but indignantly wrote to her when she brought
up the subject of her trip: 'I received your letter in Nagasaki. Being tired of
touring, I was feeling like going back home. But you depressed my spirit by
making an unreasonable demand on me. It always makes me sick to receive this
kind of letter while I am away from home' (16 January 1928; Matsuhashi 1999:
154).

Even after he reluctantly let Kaneko go to Germany, Yanagi seemed to have
kept reproaching her for going abroad. She later disclosed that several months
after her departure, she 'received a succession of letters from Yanagi ordering [her]
to return to Japan immediately' (Matsuhashi 1999: 174). These letters that
Kaneko received in Germany do not survive (except a postcard dated 2 August
1928), but we can easily surmise their content from her letters to him, which have
been kept in the Japan Folk Crafts Museum founded by Yanagi. Kaneko deplored
her fate in one of her letters:

> How many times did I think of giving up my music for you! But I have never
> thought of giving you up for my music . . . If it were better for me to give up
> music, I would do so right away. You may say, 'go ahead, then,' but please
> consider my particular set of circumstances [i.e. it was Yanagi who required
> her to show her love for him by becoming a world-class singer]. It is too
> much to call me self-centred . . . I thought you might be happy if I died.
> (6 July 1928; Matsuhashi 1999: 161)

She wrote to him again, two weeks later, in response to his letter: 'Your reproaching letter agonizes me.' She added that he 'must be thinking that all the misery
was created by Kaneko' (25 July 1928; Matsuhashi 1999: 163). He must have
harshly criticized her, taking her study abroad as expressive of her egoism. He
seems to have taken a spiteful attitude towards her from the very start of her life in
Germany, for she said 'the first letter you sent to me in this distant place was
saddening beyond expression' (25 July 1928; Matsuhashi 1999: 163). She had no
choice but to abandon the golden opportunity, giving up all the promised recitals
that were to have established her as a truly international singer.

Yanagi wanted Kaneko to be in Japan so much. Was he, then, understanding of the needs of his wife when she was in Japan? No. He got nervous at her coming home late because of her singing schedule, and made her give the first priority to housework as wife and mother and not to her professional work. In 1918 (ten years before Kaneko went to Germany), for example, Kaneko was on a concert tour in Kyushu, the southern part of Japan, where she received an impatient telegram from Yanagi – 'Return home immediately' – nine times in one day (Matsuhashi 1999: 88). It was Kaneko who was expected to dedicate herself to her husband's passionate pursuit of Blake and Japanese folk crafts. Kaneko recollected how she felt after four years of their married life: 'I was pretty amazed by the great gap between what Yanagi had said before our marriage and what he actually was in our marriage' (Matsuhashi 1999: 88). Kaneko seemed to believe that there was a difference between the image of Yanagi before and after their marriage, but the surviving love letters of Yanagi to Kaneko prove otherwise. Yanagi expected Kaneko to serve him as a subservient lover, and therefore became angry with her when, contrary to his expectations, he had not heard from her for two days: 'I was deprived of the peace of mind because you had not written me. I have been trying to concentrate on work in vain. Suffering from this unbearable agony, I will go on a trip. I do not know when I return. I will not write you for a while. Why don't you show concern and help me get much work done?' (5 August 1913; Matsuhashi 1999: 64). Kaneko had to plead for his forgiveness, though she had done nothing wrong: 'I reflected on what I did. I have no word for an excuse. I am responsible for your suffering, and I must accept the blame' (6 August 1913; Matsuhashi 1999: 65). This exchange of letters shows the nature of their relationship. It is not surprising therefore that Yanagi suddenly decided to go on a year-long trip to the United States without checking with his wife, who was actually left alone in Japan soon after she came back from Germany. Kaneko, a person of saintly patience, nevertheless complained about his selfishness: 'I gave up everything just before I was about to establish myself, and returned to you. And you, who used to say that you would hate going abroad, are leaving me alone' (16 July 1929; Matsuhashi 1999: 193). Kaneko was often conveniently turned invisible to Yanagi, who had an affair with a woman in the States and with others elsewhere. It is true that Yanagi spoke enthusiastically of her career as a singer, but he did so only in order to demonstrate his passion for art – i.e. as a means of enhancing his own stature.

Yanagi's blindness to the needs of his wife is reflected in his reading of the female characters in Blake's work. He heard the powerful speeches of Enitharmon, Vala and other females, but shifted attention away from what their words really mean by focusing upon the power of fiery rhetoric. He took the female voice as expressive of Blake's strong self. The female characters were thus made invisible to Yanagi. This tendency of his is seen in his appeal to the readers of the monthly journal *Blake and Whitman*, which he co-edited with Bunsho Jugaku. Encouraging his readers to become internationally recognized, Yanagi wished to make Japan or the East equal or even superior to the West in the field of English literary studies. He suggested that scholars should 'compare foreign [English] literature and theory with eastern thoughts' and 'examine Blake and Whitman from the perspective of eastern thoughts and paintings' (Yanagi 1931: 479). He thought in a framework of East versus West that a unique analysis of western literature could be made by Japanese scholars who were conversant with both western literature and eastern thoughts. But in his framework, the woman was not given any place, just as Kaneko was kept mainly invisible to Yanagi.

It is Jugaku who was truly concerned with the issue of women. He explained his view of women to the readers of *Blake and Whitman* when he wrote that it is 'optimistically blind' to think 'women were merely the means by which to please men, to bear children for men, and to take care of the household' (Jugaku 1931: 262). He rejected such a limited understanding of women as belonging to eighteenth-century England. He condemned the deprivation of women's personal and social rights and welcomed their independence and assertiveness. Giving a list of leading women such as Mary Wortley Montagu (1689–1762); Mrs Vesey or Delany Mary Granville (1700–67); Elizabeth Montagu (1720–1800); Mrs Thrale or Hester Lynch Piozzi (1741–1821); Hannah More (1745–1833); Fanny Burney (1752–1840); Hester Chapone (1727–60); Sarah Scott (1806–83); Catherine Talbot, Mrs Siddons or Sarah Siddons (1755–1831); and Mary Wollestonecraft (1759–1851), Jugaku noted that there were a few women in eighteenth-century England who tried to encourage their fellow creatures to raise their consciousness. He paid special attention to Elizabeth Montagu as one of the members of the Bluestocking Circle, elaborating on the way she made her salon successful. Such a portrayal of Montagu indicates his profound interest in the advent of such new intellectually active and socially concerned women as represented by the Bluestockings. Jugaku showed himself a man of enlightened views about women in his essays, and it will be my aim in the following pages to clarify how he interpreted Blake's representation of the female.

Jugaku regards women as the symbol of love in his interpretation of *The Book of Thel*. He introduced a gender-based reading of Thel's motto, with particular attention to the following lines: 'Can wisdom be put in a silver rod? / Or Love in a golden bowl?' (*The Book of Thel*, 'Thel's Motto'; E 3). He emphasized that what belonged to the male should not be put into the female sphere, and vice versa. Wisdom and love are not particularly gendered in Blake's lines, but Jugaku regarded 'wisdom' as 'typical of the male' (Jugaku 1934: 59) and 'love' as 'representative of the female' (Jugaku 1934: 60). Though he must have been well versed in Greek mythology, in which wisdom is personified by the female Sophia and love by the male Eros, he took it for granted that wisdom was connected to the male and love to the female.

The association of love and women was quite common in Jugaku's Japan, in which the changing social power of women was becoming gradually prominent. One of the fruits of this change was the formation of the *Seito* group and its 1911 manifesto presented by Hiratsuka, who I mentioned previously. The image of 'new women' was soon popularized, and the new coined word *mo-ga* was given to them as a term of endearment. 'Mo-ga' was the Japanized shortened form of 'modern girls', and it tended to be paired with 'mo-bo', which was the abbreviated form of 'modern boys'. The modern girls in Japan reached full bloom in the 1920s, being attired in western dress rather than the traditional Japanese kimono and working full-time to earn their own living. These independent women were regarded as aggressive in their relationship with men, and became the symbol of transgressors in love affairs. They were considered as a threat to established family values, and became synonymous with love, especially free love. We are rightly reminded here of Yanagi's praise for free love along with outpouring emotion.

It is quite right that Jugaku mentioned *Visions of the Daughters of Albion* to explain Blake's idea of free love. But Oothoon was curiously not analysed as a character or a performer of free love in his essays contributed to *Blake and Whitman* or his *William Blake* published a few years later. His sensitivity to the new women did not stand him in good stead when he interpreted *Visions of the Daughters of Albion* and other Blake poems. Enitharmon was not really analysed, either, except that she was always a supportive woman to her male counterpart without ever being a representative of the female will. Jugaku therefore affectionately called Blake and Catherine 'Los and Enitharmon' (Jugaku 1934: 23). He even listed Blake's relationship with Catherine as one of the five best things he liked about Blake.

It is striking how Jugaku repeatedly referred to Catherine Blake and made her quite visible in his criticism on Blake. He called Catherine 'a wonderful woman', and even said: 'Everyone should know that Blake owed his happy married life to Catherine's virtue' (Jugaku 1934: 27). Why Jugaku praised Catherine so much became clear when he explained that she was strongly determined to learn writing and painting from her husband and to help him complete his art. In other words, Catherine's virtue resides in her helpfulness to her husband. Jugaku further made his own wife, Shizu Jugaku, another Catherine Blake. Shizu helped her husband publish the handmade journal *Blake and Whitman*, in which Jugaku was passionately engaged. She bound each copy of the journal with needle and thread. As a kind of return for her incessant labour, she was allowed to write a brief history of the journal in the last issue, in place of her husband. However brief it may be, the writing by Shizu is significant; it was the only female voice that was heard in early Blake studies in Japan.

Shizu explained: 'I decided to help it [making the journal from editing to binding] as far as my strength would take me, because I understood the significance of such a work' (Jugaku 1932b: 567). Very few women could speak of the value of an academic journal (and that of a foreign literature journal) the way Shizu did in the early 1930s. She further deplored the shrinking number of subscribers, and indignantly gave a severe comment on the former readers who had deserted the journal. She defined them as people who were unable to 'be dedicated to one thing and pursue it', and posed a question: 'On what did they spend 50 sen [0.5 yen] that they used to pay for our journal?' (Jugaku 1932b: 567). At this time Japan, like the rest of the world, was suffering from the Great Depression, and 50 sen was a lot of money – enough to buy rice sufficient for as much as a month (8 kg).[4] But Shizu was so involved with *Blake and Whitman* that she sounded somewhat aloof from the affairs of the world. This is exactly the tendency that was shared by the members of the *Shirakaba* group including Jugaku and Yanagi. (We could say moreover that to be a member of *Shirakaba* implied privileges of class, education and wealth, which somewhat distanced its members from financial pressures.) She shared her husband's passion for literature and art and gave generously of her time and education to help him explore Blake's life and work. Jugaku could not have found a woman with a more accommodating view toward him than Shizu.

The wives of the editors of *Blake and Whitman*, Kaneko Yanagi and Shizu Jugaku, constitute an interesting example of gender politics in 1930s Japan, where, although women could be educated so as to attain the same level of accomplishment as their male counterparts, they were expected by society and their husbands to be subservient to the men. Blake was so much loved by Yanagi and Jugaku partly because the poet's wife was regarded as a wise and helpful woman. The parallelism of untiring female devotion to the male can be seen in the relationship between the hero and heroine of an American Hollywood film, *The Man I Killed* (later retitled *Broken Lullaby*), which Jugaku suddenly referred to in an essay in *Blake and Whitman*. Though he did not elaborate on its meaning, he left the readers with sufficient clues to understand his admiration. *The Man I Killed* was directed by Ernst Lubitsch in 1932 and was released in Japan the same year that Jugaku and Yanagi were publishing *Blake and Whitman*. This film was barely placed among the year's top ten foreign films by the Japanese cinema association called Kinema Jumpo,[5] but for Jugaku it was 'the best film that I have [he has] seen in years' (Jugaku 1932a: 191). When he mentioned the film, he was writing about human suffering and exploring human dignity by quoting Blake's repeated phrase 'every thing that lives is holy' (*The Marriage of Heaven and Hell* 27:45; E 45; *Visions of the Daughters of Albion* 8:10; E 51; *America a Prophecy* 8:13; E 54; *The Four Zoas* 2:34:80; E 324). Jugaku deplored the violation of human dignity at the time:

> It seems to me that human dignity is equally lightly violated today. Blake repeatedly wrote 'every thing that lives is holy.' We should become keenly aware that great mysterious power resides in the human soul when it grows, feels, and suffers. Every time I contemplate the misery of war, in my mind I hear the sad moaning of a dying soul. I also become overwhelmed by unspoken tragedies of the dead. In this sense, *The Man I Killed* directed by Lubitsch is the best film that I have seen in years. (Jugaku 1932a: 191)

The misery of war, the violation of human dignity, and all that is described by Jugaku here are what the protagonist of the film, Paul, is going through. Jugaku must have felt a strong affinity with him, especially when he had just witnessed the outbreak of the Manchurian Incident in 1931, which would develop into the Sino-Japanese War in 1937 and subsequently into World War II. Paul is a Frenchman who killed a young German named Walter during the war between France and Germany. Though the war is over, Paul is haunted by a sense of guilt and by his memory of Walter drawing his last breath. After three years of agony, he decides to go to Germany to ask forgiveness of Walter's family. He finds Walter's parents, is by mistake taken for a close friend of their son's, and is welcomed not only by Walter's parents but also by his ex-fiancée, Elsa. Paul unexpectedly falls in love with Elsa, who also comes to love him. But then he decides to confess the truth to Elsa.

The confession sequence and the succeeding violin sequence form the climax of the film, and Paul, or what Jugaku would call 'a dying soul', is finally saved from his intense agony by a means that is ideal for Jugaku; that is, through the help of a woman. The confession sequence begins with Paul sitting on a sofa and burying his head in his hand (Figure 15.1). Sitting next to Paul, Elsa lets him collapse in her lap and consoles him (Figure 15.2). She is determined to overcome adversity. Even when he confesses that he is the very man who killed her fiancé, Elsa (though shocked) instantly knows what to do. She forbids Paul both from committing suicide (which, she says, 'is easy') and from revealing the truth to Walter's aged parents, who have come to like him as if he were their own son. Paul can indeed become a replacement for their lost son, and can give them tranquillity

**Figure 15.1** *The Man I Killed* (aka *Broken Lullaby*). Paramount, 1932. Directed by Ernst Lubitsch. Confession Sequence 1.

**Figure 15.2** *The Man I Killed*, Confession Sequence 2.

and happiness once again after three years of misery and suffering, and for that purpose Elsa resolves that 'they must never know the truth'. She is determined to make Paul replace the family's dead son and firmly orders him: 'Run away or kill yourself – that's easy – and leave them behind with two sons to forget. Well, I won't let you. You are not going to kill Walter the second time. You are going to live for them.' She further announces to the parents: 'Paul is going to stay here.'

The aged father is so happy to hear the announcement that he calls Paul 'my son' and asks him to play the violin, which his real son used to play. Paul is perplexed at the idea of taking the place of the man whom he had killed, and keeps standing with his head down. It is Elsa who takes the violin out of the hands of the father and gives it to Paul (Figures 15.3 and 15.4). When he begins to play, she moves right next to him, giving him a warm supportive look (Figure 15.5). She gives him a gratified look (Figure 15.6), and he smiles back beatifically for the first time since his confession (Figure 15.7), probably feeling that he is accepted despite the dark deed he has perpetrated. The exchange of smiles between Paul and Elsa ensures a happy ending to the story, and the rest of the film actually proves it. Elsa begins to accompany him on the piano, which must have been untouched since the death of Elsa's fiancé (Figure 15.8). A delightful surprise overwhelms the old parents, who look at each other and then look at Paul and Elsa alternately, rejoicing at the happy sight of the young couple (Figures 15.9, 15.10 and 15.11).

**Figure 15.3** *The Man I Killed*, Violin Sequence 1.

**Figure 15.4** *The Man I Killed*, Violin Sequence 2.

**Figure 15.5** *The Man I Killed*, Violin Sequence 3.

The memorable happy ending of the film may have particularly appealed to Jugaku, for it presents a woman of Jugaku's type, another Catherine Blake who deeply impressed him by her supportive role to the poet. It is also not too difficult to see a similarity between the ending of Lubitsch's *The Man I Killed* and the final plate of Blake's *Jerusalem*. First of all, the two endings show a certain visual similarity. Elsa stands on our right and gazes at Paul while he is playing the violin (Figure 15.5). Enitharmon likewise stands on our right in the main part of the final plate of *Jerusalem*, and keeps an eye on Los, who is engaged in his work (Figure 15.12). The decision of Enitharmon to help Los, abandoning her attempt

**Figure 15.6**  *The Man I Killed*, Violin Sequence 4.

**Figure 15.7**  *The Man I Killed*, Violin Sequence 5.

**Figure 15.8**  *The Man I Killed*, Violin Sequence 6.

to be independent of and antagonistic to him, secures a bright prospect for their future. The fate of Los depends on female choice. In both works, the female character contributes significantly to regeneration in which the male protagonist is engaged – to his own salvation from the intense agony in *The Man I Killed* and to his grand task to build a holy city in England in *Jerusalem*.

Jugaku took up the issue of empowerment of women in his essays on Blake, but he ended in showing his fondness for the particular type of woman who is intellectually equal to or even superior to, but emotionally subservient to, her male partner. The juxtaposition of Blake and the newer medium of Hollywood cinema means that in the intellectual scene of 1930s Japan the impact of Blake was

**Figure 15.9** *The Man I Killed*, Violin Sequence 7.

**Figure 15.10** *The Man I Killed*, Violin Sequence 8.

**Figure 15.11** *The Man I Killed*, Violin Sequence 9.

**Figure 15.12** Blake's *Jerusalem*, Plate 100 (detail).

felt as part of the incorporation of western cultural products. But it also suggests that Blake may occasionally have been read in terms of the sentimental melodrama that had begun to be introduced by Hollywood cinema not long before the *Blake and Whitman* journal was issued. Jugaku was not yet ready to put into practice his notion of women's independence and equality, but Shizu would not complain about such limitations and faithfully supported him throughout her life. Both Yanagi and Jugaku were attracted to the female characters in Blake's works, but they did not explore the meanings of these characters or clarify the reason for their particular attachment to them. The feminist concerns were not yet fully developed in their interpretations of Blake's works, though they straightforwardly presented their strong favour for the female characters in the 1910s to 1930s.

## Notes

1  Keiko Matsuhashi, a friend of the late Kaneko Yanagi (nee Nakajima), collected most of the surviving letters between Kaneko and Muneyoshi Yanagi in *An Eternal Alto Singer: The Biography of Kaneko Yanagi* (Tokyo: Suiyo-Sha, 1999). This is the only resource for Yanagi's private life, which is not revealed in his official publications collected in *The Complete Writings of Muneyoshi Yanagi*, 22 vols (Tokyo: Japan Art Crafts, 1980–1992).
2  All references given in the text to Blake's works are to David V. Erdman, ed., *The Complete Poetry and Prose of William Blake, newly revised edition* (New York: Doubleday, 1982). They are given by work, plate or page number, and line number(s) where appropriate, followed by the page number in Erdman (abbreviated as E).

3   To this list of married couples, we could add the pairing of Yanagi and Kaneko, for Kaneko attended the First Open Lectures by the *Seito* women held in 1913, though she never became a member of the group. Matsuhashi refers to the headline of the scurrilous journals at the time: 'a woman of the *Seito* and a man of the *Shirakaba*'. See Matsuhashi 1999: 60.

4   It cost 5.73 sen for 1 kg of rice in those days: 50 sen must have bought as much rice as 8.72 kg. As to the change in rice prices in Japan from the seventeenth century to the end of the twentieth century, see http://home.e-catv.ne.jp/mibunoiitutae/cont09.html.

5   The best foreign film of the year 1932 was a French film, *A Nous La Liberté*, directed by René Clair. *The Man I Killed* was rated ninth. See the website 'Kinema Jumpo the Best Ten': http://www1.harenet.ne.jp/~sato2000/movie/cinema/cinemabest01.html.

# 16 Blake as Inspiration to Yanagi and Jugaku

## Shunsuke Tsurumi

The Russo–Japanese War (1904–5) meant to Japan the loss of 120 lives. Compared with Russia's loss of 115,000, Japan's loss seems hardly significant. To a nation whose population was less than ninety million, however, the loss was very great, unprecedented in the history of Japan. One side effect was the disclosure of cases of clairvoyance and psychokinesis in the psychology department of Tokyo University, ending up in the expulsion of an assistant professor of abnormal psychology.

Yanagi shared this national interest at the time. As a student in the high school of the Peers' School[1] and later at Tokyo University, he wrote on Sir Oliver Lodge, Lombroso and William James. His first book *Science and Life* (1911) touched upon psychical research and extra-sensory experience as revealed in ordinary life. A shift of interest was brought about by his becoming acquainted with William Blake's poetry. He was captivated by Blake's *Auguries of Innocence* when he was 17, still a student in high school. Yanagi published two books on William Blake and later, with the help of Jugaku, founded a quarterly, *Blake and Whitman* (1931–2),[2] devoted to providing an annotated bibliography of the two authors.

We will go back to the end of the Russo–Japanese War, for it played a part in fermenting individualism in the Peers' School, spreading its influence in the reading public in Japan.

In the Peers' School, from primary school up, there were sons of generals and admirals who had brought victory to Japan in the last war. They suddenly became important. That was not pleasant for their classmates who did not think them superior in any respect. It was one of the main catalysts for uniting literary circles in the Peers' School to a confederation that published a magazine called *Shirakaba* (*White Birch*), with contributions from a wide age range. At the time of its birth, the eldest contributor, Arishima Takeo, was 32 and the youngest, Kori Torahiko, was 20 years old. The next youngest, Yanagi Muneyoshi, was 21.

Yanagi was the son of an admiral, already deceased, but he came to be one of the magazine's major writers. When he was a pupil in the Peers' School he made a speech in the presence of the Headmaster General Nogi who had served as the commander bringing about the fall of Port Arthur in the Russo–Japanese War. He said that, according to his own definition, a brave man is a person who makes his design alone and fights his life alone and, according to his definition, the military are not brave.

Yanagi was on the verge of expulsion because of this speech. Indeed, he would have been thrown out of school but for loyal support from a young teacher of German on the faculty, Nishida Kitaro (1870–1945). Though fully aware of his debt, Yanagi did not join Nishida's philosophy, even though living in the same city of Kyoto. Yanagai wrote in plain words, far removed from the abstruse academic jargon employed by Nishida and his followers.

In his earlier years, Yanagi showed sympathy to psychic research. In later years he turned his attention to daily wares produced by unknown craftsmen and also to uneducated believers in the provinces. In the middle phase he published two books on William Blake.

An encounter with William Blake when he was 17 played a pivotal role in Yanagi's life, particularly the following two short poems:

*Auguries of Innocence*
To see a World in a Grain of Sand
And a Heaven in a Wild Flower,
Hold Infinity in the palm of your hand
And Eternity in an hour.

*Eternity*
He who binds to himself a joy
Does the winged life destroy;
But he who kisses the joy as it flies
Lives in eternity's sun rise.

These are akin to the short poems Yanagi used to write, in his last days, in the pattern of Buddhist verse ('*Gatha*' in Sanskrit). In those days, whether in writing or speech, Yanagi made no distinction between things and persons.

In summer 1940, I paid a brief visit to Yanagi. Before the visit, I had read several of his works and prepared a questionnaire. To the questions I put to him on his early works, drawing examples from Christian mysticism, Yanagi responded quoting from Buddhist texts. There was no evading the question. For those 20 years he had immersed himself in reading Buddhist literature. His transition from Christian mysticism to Buddhist mysticism was seamless. Here I find an echo of Blake's testimony, written in 1788, that 'All Religions are One' (E 1).

In 1928, a company of Japanese soldiers disguised as Chinese ruffians demolished a train transporting General Chan Tso-ling, a military leader in north-east China. That was the beginning of a long war between China and Japan, leading to what was known in Japan as the Great East-Asia War.

The postscript to *Blake and Whitman*, which continued under militarism, gave Yanagi a place to give vent to his view freely. There he wrote that he did not quite understand Soviet politics, adding that his sympathy was with Mahatma Gandhi in his resistance to Imperialism.

Yanagi did not choose open confrontation with the government. Even after Japan's annexation of Korea, however, he did not stop referring to Korea as another country. He published a major magazine (*Kaizo*) on a city gate (*Kokamon*) about to be demolished by the Japanese authorities. Finally the gate was preserved. The article encouraged Koreans. But Yanagi, for the first time in his life, was followed by the Japanese thought-police and put under surveillance for some time. Meanwhile he collected, with the assistance of his friend, Korean craftworks and took them to Korea, set up an exhibition, and let them remain there as a small museum. For this trip Mrs Yanagi, a well-known singer at the time, gave several recitals to cover travel expenses.

Another time when Yanagi came into conflict with the police was during his trip to Okinawa in 1940. Then he wrote in an Okinawan paper, criticizing the Japanese government's policy enforcing the standard language upon the people of Okinawa. He referred to Onna Nabe, who composed fearless poems in his native dialect. Dante, Yanagi then said, wrote *The Divine Comedy* in everyday Italian. World literature has a greater chance of birth in the vernacular rather than the state-designed standard language. The police deemed these opinions sufficient to warrant Yanagi's arrest.

From the beginning, Yanagi's interest was never confined to arts in Japan. The folk craft movement which made him known in Japan and elsewhere started with the works of Korean craftsmen. He then turned his eyes to works by Japanese craftsmen and launched the folk craft movement.

After World War II, Yanagi reopened the folk craft museum. He began a post-war programme focusing on Okinawan craftsmanship, inviting a native scholar to lecture on the history of Okinawa. Born in modern Japan, Yanagi with his internationalism did not look only to Europe and the United States. His folk craft movement, with his interest in Korea when he turned to the craftwork in Japan, paid homage to the cultural heritage outside the mainland of Japan, namely that of Okinawa and the Ainu. His cosmopolitanism preserved the international heritage of Japan.

In war-torn Japan, Yanagi delivered a speech entitled 'Beauty as a Gate of Law', pointing out that there was no separation between what is beautiful and what is ugly. In all things we feel an inclination to respond to beauty. This intuition came to Yanagi when he was reading a Buddhist sutra (*Daimuryojukyo*).

At that time in Japan, writers and scholars wrote that they had anticipated Japan's militarism would come to such an end. Against this background, Yanagi's speech was filled with sorrow, in a style which confirms him as a religious figure.

As a biographer of Yanagi, I have spoken mostly about him. Yanagi could not, however, have accomplished his work without the help of many craftsmen and scholars, especially not without the collaboration of Jugaku Bunsho and Jugaku Shizu, both in the folk craft movement and in the study of Blake. Jugaku Bunsho (1900–92) was born into a Buddhist priest's family. He married Shizu (1901–81), a novelist, and they had a daughter, Akiko, a scholar of Japanese language, and a son, a scientist. The four formed a small republic which was to endure the whole length of the fifteen years' war. Their writings were published as *The Works of Jugaku Bunsho and Jugaku Shizu* (1970), and included Blake studies and documents on handmade paper. They continued a correspondence with peace workers in prison; and when released from prison, the economist Kawakami Hajime confided in the couple so much as to allow them to read his journal in original manuscript form, which came to be published after the war.

An episode handed down in the neighbourhood unit tells how Mrs Jugaku punctually attended compulsory bayonet training. This testifies, in the light of history, to the compromises necessary for Mrs Jugaku to devote her energy to maintaining her anti-militarist republic within the military state.

## Notes

1   Gakushuin in Tokyo, an exclusive school for children of the elite Japanese classes.
2   A literary magazine published by Yanagi and Jugaku in Kyoto from 1932 to 1938.

# 17 Individuality and Expression: The *Shirakaba* Group's Reception of Blake's Visual Art in Japan

## Yumiko Goto

In the early decades of the twentieth century, many Japanese people were familiar with William Blake. Elementary school children recited his poems; magazines and book covers featured his artworks; and exhibitions of Blake reproductions were held throughout Japan. Japanese interest in Blake peaked during this period and laid much of the foundation for how he would be received in subsequent years. The fire that started this Blake boom was lit by *Shirakaba* (*White Birch*), a magazine that was extremely influential in both the literary and art worlds of that period. I will first discuss the great changes in the reception of Blake: from the late nineteenth century and the early twentieth century, when he was first introduced to Japan, and then a new stage during the 1910s and 1920s. Then, I will explore the way that *Shirakaba* featured Blake and its important role in popularizing Blake in Japan. Lastly, I will discuss what attracted people of the 1910s and 1920s by comparing the reception of Blake's works with those of the Post-Impressionists, which entered Japan in the same period and powerfully affected the direction of the reception of the earlier artist.

## 1

First, I will look at the way Blake was received through the first decade of the twentieth century. We know that Blake had already been introduced to Japan by the end of the nineteenth century when in 1893 the novelist and critic Bimyo Yamada (1868–1910) published the *Bankoku Jinmei Jisho*, a dictionary of famous names from around the world.[1] In 1895, Bin Ueda (1874–1916), a scholar of English literature, poet and critic famous for translating the symbolists and Parnassians in France, mentioned Blake in his writing,[2] and, around the turn of the century, Greek-born Irishman Lafcadio Hearn (1850–1904) gave three lectures about Blake at the Tokyo Imperial University.[3] Blake's name also appeared in some books, including collections of European and American poetry in translation and works of English literary history, but the most important introductions to Blake in this period were the translations by leading literary figures Ariake Kanbara (1876–1952) and Choko Ikuta (1882–1936).[4] In particular, Ikuta's translation of the poem 'The Sick Rose' had an influence on a younger poet, Rofu Miki (1889–1964), who was inspired to write 'Yameru Bara'[5] in 1908. This title also means 'the sick rose', but it was a strikingly original poem that gave new symbolic quality to the rose. This example is important because it shows that this poet not only knew of Blake, but had also thoroughly digested his work. At that time, Blake was mainly known for his poetry through translation, however, and his other role as a visual artist remained undiscovered.

In the 1910s, during the early *Taishō* period (1912–26), however, Blake came to be known for his visual works. In other words, interest in Blake in these decades mainly developed through images, rather than through translations as in the preceding *Meiji* period (1867–1912). The average Japanese, though, did not have an opportunity to view his actual works until the late 1920s. During this period, Western art was received mainly in the forms of books, magazine illustrations and reproductions.

In the nineteenth century, plate-making and printing had been mechanized in the West, making mass reproduction possible. Japan was a little behind, but in the first decades of the twentieth century, photographic printing methods including collotype, photoengraving and halftone relief printing were introduced. Four-colour halftone had been put into use around 1900 and offset printing and photogravure became practical in the 1910s. With the development of these kinds of reproduction techniques, literary magazines such as *Myojo* and *Subaru* began printing illustrations of artworks creating the foundation for the culture of art reproduction that would peak with *Shirakaba*. This magazine not only presented artworks in its pages, but also sponsored exhibitions of reproductions, establishing the practice of appreciation of western art through this medium in Japan. Before this, only the few people who had travelled abroad had been able to see Western art, but now many more had the opportunity to see examples of it in these reproduced forms. Of course, this became established as a new way of appreciating artworks in western countries also, but in Japan, the fact that it was almost impossible to see the originals made the Japanese even more enthusiastic about reproductions. By experiencing these works through a secondary medium, rather than the originals, there was more room for imagination, which allowed viewers to find new powers in the art. A famous writer of the *Taishō* period, Ryunosuke Akutagawa (1892–1927) was one such person who became familiar with Western art in his youth through illustrations in *Shirakaba*. He wrote, 'For me the appeal of the West always comes from the visual arts' (Akutagawa 1971: 161), which he believed could overcome the barriers of language to transmit the minds of their creators directly to viewers through their senses. Akutagawa was not alone in this belief. In the early part of the twentieth century, many people in Japan thought reproduced Western art represented Western culture itself, and therefore tried to understand the West through the images provided by visual art. How did this reception of the West by reproductions, by images preceding words, direct the initial reception of Blake?

## 2

The magazine that introduced Blake, *Shirakaba*, was founded in 1910 by a group of young literati, which included the novelists Saneatsu Mushanokoji (1885–1976), Naoya Shiga (1883–1971) and Takeo Arishima (1878–1923), the art critic, Kikuo Kojima (1887–1950) and the philosopher, Soetsu Yanagi (1889–1961). *Shirakaba* not only stimulated new ideas, advocating humanism over the naturalistic literature that had become the trend in the Japanese literary world, but also functioned as an art magazine that brought new movements of Western art into Japan. Jutaro Kuroda (1887–1970), an artist of Western-style paintings in Kyoto, once said, looking back over his past, that the mere sight of a copy of the magazine would draw art students in their twenties into a vortex of enthusiasm and excitement (Kuroda 1947: 206). *Shirakaba* had a large influence on young artists and fuelled their yearning for Europe. They admired and imitated the works of Auguste Rodin, Paul Cézanne and Vincent Van Gogh as they grew familiar with them through *Shirakaba* and tried to emulate these great masters not only in their artworks but also in their own lives.

From the beginning of the publication, the members made efforts to include articles about Western art, translations of art criticism from the West and colour and monochrome reproductions of artworks. During the 14 years from 1910 to 1923, *Shirakaba* published 160 issues and introduced over 70 Western artists. In Figure 17.1, the artists whose works were reproduced 30 or more times in *Shirakaba* are shown, with the number of illustrations in the bar graph. Blake was one of 12 such artists. From this graph, it is clear that *Shirakaba* put special emphasis on him.

The English potter, printmaker and poet Bernard Leach (1887–1979) first introduced Blake in *Shirakaba*. In his article on the English Impressionist painter, Augustus John (1878–1961) in Vol. 3, No. 3 of *Shirakaba* published in March 1912, Leach made the first reference to Blake in the magazine. Leach came to Japan in 1909 and taught *Shirakaba* members the technique of etching, which was the beginning of a lasting friendship with them. He also introduced Blake's fascinating works to Soetsu Yanagi, a member who would later write extensively on Blake. The next year, Leach was commissioned to design the cover of an issue

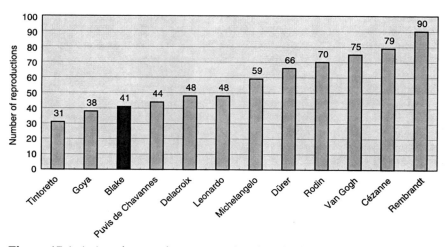

**Figure 17.1** Artists whose works were reproduced in *Shirakaba* over 30 times.

Note: The numbers include illustrations of front and back covers.

References: Exh. cat., *Shirakaba and the Art of the Taisho Period*, Tokyo Metropolitan Art Museum, 1977.

Exh. cat., *The Shirakaba School and Modern Art*, Chiba Prefectural Museum of Art, 1989.

**Figure 17.2**  *Shirakaba [White Birch]*, Vol. 4, No.1, January 1913. Tokyo: Rakuyo Do, The Japan Folk Crafts Museum. (Photo: The Japan Folk Crafts Museum.)

of *Shirakaba*. He borrowed a line from 'The Tyger' and designed the cover in the style of Blake (Figure 17.2). The appearance of this first Blakean image heralded the forthcoming introduction of Blake's visual art in the magazine. Yanagi contributed a brief note on this design in which he noted that Leach had captured part of the essence of the *Shirakaba* group with the design (Yanagi 1913b: 269–70). In fact, the design became a symbol of *Shirakaba* and was used also for the programme of the music concert organized by the group at the Tokyo Imperial Hotel in November 1913.

Then, Yanagi's well-known article on Blake appeared in the 5th Anniversary Commemorative Edition of *Shirakaba* published in April 1914 (Figure 17.3). 'William Blake 1757–1827' was the first time Blake's work as a visual artist was introduced in Japan. Sixteen black and white illustrations of Blake's paintings and prints were included along with the article, making this the first time that his works had been shown to a large Japanese audience. This article was rewritten and published as *William Blake: His Life, Works and Thought*[6] in December of that year with several additional chapters. Yanagi later became one of the major thinkers of modern Japan and is also known for promoting the Japanese folk craft movement, but at the time he wrote about Blake, he was a young and spirited critic who had just graduated from Tokyo Imperial University. Besides his own 137 page enthusiastic commentary on Blake, this issue also included an essay on Blake in English by Leach, 'Notes on William Blake'. Yanagi and Leach both found

**Figure 17.3** *Shirakaba*, Blake Issue, Vol. 5, April 1914. The Japan Folk Crafts Museum. (Photo: The Japan Folk Crafts Museum.)

common traits between Blake and the Post-Impressionists and Walt Whitman in their essays. From then on, Yanagi became a central figure in the promotion of Blake, and *Shirakaba* continued to feature Blake illustrations prominently.

As I mentioned before, the efforts of the *Shirakaba* group to promote the introduction of Western art did not stop with the publication of articles and illustrations in their magazine. For most Japanese, it was an era when contact with actual Western artworks was extremely difficult, but the efforts of the *Shirakaba* group, including holding art exhibitions of prints and large-sized reproductions from bookstores and print-shops abroad, contributed to the popularization of Western art. Around the turn of the century, there had been exhibitions of copies made by Japanese artists who had travelled or studied abroad, but the practice of exhibiting reproductions of Western art was new in the second decade of the twentieth century. Western-style painter, Ryusei Kishida (1891–1929) tells how these exhibitions gave a shock not only to the general audience but also to painters and other art specialists at the time and, as one of the young painters who were greatly influenced by *Shirakaba*, he himself later produced work clearly inspired by Blake.

> [. . .] a *Shirakaba* sponsored reproduction exhibition was held at Akasaka Sankaido [. . .] Seeing them for the first time, I was amazed by the high quality of the new Western art in the reproductions. Now reproductions have lost much of their novelty, but 10 years ago, they were precious and rare for us. [. . .] I felt much admiration for black and white reproductions in those days.[7] (Kishida 1919: 362)

The impossibility of obtaining original works of art made exhibiting reproductions the only option, but soon after *Shirakaba* invented this style of presenting Western art, many others began to imitate it. In the 1920s, as the Japanese economy grew, several private collectors of Western art appeared and held exhibitions, finally giving Japanese people the chance to see Western artworks in their original forms. Still, reproduction exhibitions continued to be held even into the post-war period. Blake was featured in *Shirakaba*-sponsored events along with other artists, but his were the only works to be given solo exhibitions.

Blake's works were first shown publicly in 1915 at the '*Shirakaba* 7th Art Exhibition of Western Paintings' in Tokyo and Kyoto (see Figure 17.4).[8] The exhibition was billed as the '7th Art Exhibition and Blake Exhibition'[9] in the promotional page of *Shirakaba* and this may be called the first substantial Blake exhibition in Japan. About 60 Blake reproductions were exhibited alongside reproductions of sketches and prints of Mantegna, Leonardo da Vinci, Michelangelo, Tintoretto, Rembrandt, Goya and Redon. In the pamphlet (Figure 17.5) introducing the artists, the article on Blake was written presumably by Yanagi, at that time preparing to publish his major study, and who also had a significant role in planning and selection, at first even calling this collective display, 'the Blake exhibition' (Yanagi 1914c: 5.11, 272; Yanagi 1914d: 5.12, 137).[10]

Frederick Hollyer (1837–1933) provided the Blake reproductions for the exhibition (Yanagi 1914c: 5.11, 272). Hollyer was a photographer who ran a London studio producing high-quality photographic reproductions of artworks. It is interesting to know that he was also famous for his association with William Morris and the Pre-Raphaelites, who had begun the revaluation of the art of Blake. Yanagi probably had no direct acquaintance with Hollyer, but by 1908 he

**Figure 17.4** View of the Kyoto Prefectural Library, the place where the '*Shirakaba* 7th Art Exhibition of Western Paintings' was held. The building was constructed in 1909 and designed in a Western style by Goichi Takeda, a representative of modern Japanese architecture.

had at least heard of the photographer as a publisher of art reproductions.[11] There are no documents with the details of the exhibited reproductions but 15 'quite elaborate colour reproductions' (*Shirakaba* 1914: 273) were exhibited. In addition, Kinyuki Sonoike (1886–1984), another *Shirakaba* member, wrote to Magane Koizumi (1886–1953) about four of the reproductions exhibited at Kyoto. Koizumi, who also belonged to the group, cites this letter in noting that four of the reproduced works were *Glad Day (Albion Rose)*, 'The Fall of Satan' from *The Book of Job*, *Ruth and Naomi* and 'The Soul Exploring the Recesses of the Grave' from Robert Blair's *The Grave, a Poem*. Some of the reproductions were on sale and Sonoike bought *Ruth and Naomi* (Koizumi 1915: 368).

As Yanagi himself claimed, the exhibition must have had a great impact in spite of the fact that all of the works were reproductions, for all the originals were outstanding pieces (Yanagi 1915a: 165). A large number of Blake's works were displayed in one place at sizes closer to those of the originals, in contrast to the necessarily small illustrations in the magazine. However, the even greater significance of this first Blake exhibition was that he was presented side by side with old masters, such as Leonardo, Michelangelo and Rembrandt, as a visual artist of the same canonical stature. Yanagi emphasized in his essay that Blake was an artist who should be ranked among the greatest modern painters even though specialists of that time did not recognize him as such and therefore he was not included in art history literature. In the study of art in the West at that time, only a few appreciated Blake (Yanagi 1914b: 491),[12] so this exhibition was pioneering in

**Figure 17.5**  Catalogue from the '*Shirakaba* 7ᵗʰ Art Exhibition of Western Paintings' (Taisei Bijutsu Tenrankai) organized by the *Shirakaba* group in 1915, deposited in Kanagawa Museum of Modern Literature. (Photo: Kanagawa Museum of Modern Literature.)

placing him as one of the representative artists of this tradition before he was recognized as such in his own culture.

Four years later, the 'Exhibition of Reproductions from the Works of William Blake: For the Establishment of the *Shirakaba* Art Museum' was held in Nagano (Figure 17.6), Tokyo (Figure 17.7) and Kyoto (Figure 17.8)[13]. This was both in name and in fact a solo Blake exhibition. For the Tokyo and Kyoto exhibitions, the London publisher Frederick Hollyer cooperated again, as he had for the 1915 exhibits, in providing 74 reproductions. There is no documentation of the details of the exhibition in Nagano, but it seems the works exhibited were almost the same as those shown in Tokyo and Kyoto. Soetsu Yanagi planned and chose the works for the exhibitions this time also and wrote all of the explanations for the catalogue (Figure 17.9). In his introduction, Yanagi introduces Blake as a poet and painter, and his occupation as 'engraver', praising him extravagantly as 'probably the only world-class painter that England has given birth to' ('Tame "*Shirakaba* Bijutsukan" ' 1919: ii). The 21 exhibited colour reproductions included *Albion Rose*, and the 53 in black and white included illustrations to Edward Young's *Night Thoughts* and *The Book of Job*. All the black and white reproductions on display seem to have been for sale. After the Blake exhibition, *Shirakaba* published articles for people who had bought reproductions of Blake, regarding the shipment from Hollyer (Yanagi 1920a: 126; Yanagi 1920b: 147).

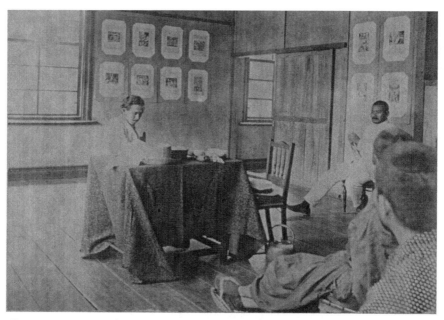

**Figure 17.6** View of Yanagi giving a lecture at the 'Exhibition of Reproductions from the Works of William Blake' at Omi Elementary School in Higashi Chikumi-gun, Nagano Prefecture, 1919. (Photo: The Japan Folk Crafts Museum.)

**Figure 17.7** View of the 'Exhibition of Reproductions from the Works of William Blake' at Ryuitsu So, Tokyo, 1919. (Photo: The Japan Folk Crafts Museum.)

**Figure 17.8** View of the YMCA Hall of Kyoto Imperial University (now Kyoto University), the place where the 'Exhibition of Reproductions from the Work of William Blake' was held. The building was constructed in 1913 and was designed by the architect W. M. Vories.

The article cited a letter from Hollyer to Yanagi, saying he was very surprised and glad to receive so many orders from Japan (Yanagi 1920a: 126).

Yanagi confidently wrote in his announcement about the 1919 Blake event that it would be impossible to have a better reproduction exhibition of his works (Yanagi 1919: 180). Close examination of the 74 exhibited works shows the items were carefully chosen and the content seems to have fully conveyed Blake's aspects as a visual artist. Works of the various media that Blake employed were included, with tempera and watercolour works of Blake the painter and relief etching, colour printing, engraving and etching works of Blake the printmaker. Furthermore, representative works from each of the media were selected. Compared to coverage of Blake in the post-war period, which tended to focus on his works as a poet, the *Shirakaba* introductions, which established the basis of his reception in the early days, actively and primarily presented Blake as a visual artist.

Furthermore, Blake was one of the artists that *Shirakaba* members planned to include in their collection. The subtitle for the 1919 Blake exhibition, 'For the Establishment of the *Shirakaba* Art Museum', shows that another goal was to raise funds to establish their own institution. From around 1917, *Shirakaba* members started to feel the need for a permanent art museum where Japanese people could encounter outstanding pieces of Western art. This plan to build a private art museum of its own in this period was one of the earliest examples of such a

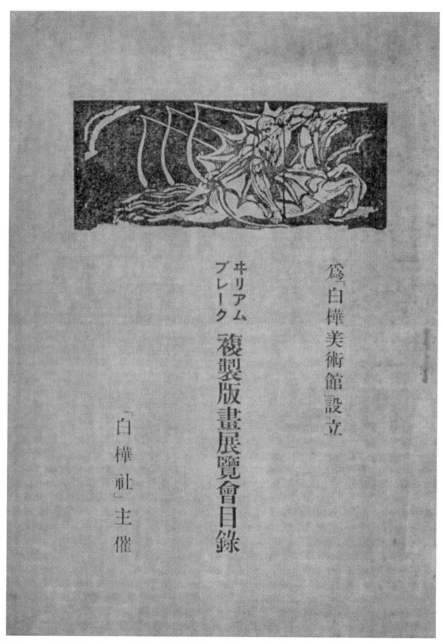

**Figure 17.9** Catalogue of the 'Exhibition of Reproductions from the Works of William Blake: For the Establishment of the *Shirakaba* Art Museum', 1919, The Japan Folk Crafts Museum. (Photo: The Japan Folk Crafts Museum.)

project in Japan, where not even one existed at the time. Blake's name appeared in relation to the museum in the article in *Shirakaba* explaining the building plan (*Shirakaba* Dojin 1917: 146). The article started with the complaint that it was difficult to see great works of Western artists in Japan, including Blake. In the same issue, Saneatsu Mushanokoji listed Blake among the names of artists whose works he wanted to buy for the museum (Mushanokoji 1917: 40). The funds collected were not enough to complete this project, but several artworks were purchased including pieces by Cézanne and Dürer. The museum was never built, but had it succeeded, and Blake's work been included in the collection, the history of his reception in Japan would have been significantly altered, with emphasis on the visual artist much more highly developed at an earlier time.

**3**

How exactly did the *Shirakaba* group members, who had so vigorously promoted Blake, view him as an artist? Where did they place Blake among the numerous artists introduced in the magazine? In this section, I will examine statements by the central figures of the *Shirakaba* group and illuminate the characteristics of their reception of Blake. First, the leading figure of the *Shirakaba* group, Saneatsu Mushanokoji, wrote about his feelings towards Blake as follows:

> I can easily tell you the English painter who I respect the most. / Blake. / He is the deepest, strongest and most creative. I believe that he is a person that we should truly respect. He is one of a kind [. . .] Blake will always be my favourite and I believe that he is the most admirable artist and person. (Mushanokoji 1927: 4–5)

In an anecdote, Yoshiro Nagayo (1888–1961) expresses that he wanted to write his undergraduate thesis on Blake, but was stopped by his teacher of English Literature from England (Nagayo 1960: 103), and tells us how few people appreciated Blake in those days:

> What about Blake, Van Gogh, and Millet, for example? It goes without saying that I respect them [. . .] Blake's mystical beauty is special. He apparently did not use oils, but the depth of his paintings is limitless. He was a genius who should be ranked among the greatest of people for the unusual beauty and depth born from his very remarkable character. He shines like a comet in Hades. When I see his work, my soul is taken to a world of stars. (Nagayo 1918: 1–2)

The poet Motomaro Senge (1888–1948), who frequently used Blake works on the covers of magazines that he edited,[14] wrote about him:

> In the modern age, among artists who are open, strong and moving, including Puvis de Chavannes, Cézanne, Daumier, Van Gogh [. . .] and Millet, Blake's heavenly, mysterious, religious painting and the lyric spirit of his poetry is overwhelmingly inspirational [. . .] For me, Blake was a painter of the flame of the spirit, who will forever be deeply revered as a genius who grasped the key to the mysteries of the divine beauty of heaven and earth. The height of his humanistic expressive art is like a star that will be an eternal guiding hand for us, Eastern poets. (Senge 1927: 5)

What is striking is that all three[15] choose to refer to Blake as a painter and list him alongside other artists rather than writers. In his thesis about Blake, Soetsu Yanagi himself presented many paintings, but also quoted frequently from Blake's poems, and wrote, 'Readers could think of this book as a collection of the most outstanding selections of Blake's poetry' (Yanagi 1914b: 12). In short, Yanagi presented Blake as both a poet and a painter. However, the magazine *Shirakaba* and the *Shirakaba* group as a whole seem to have had the tendency to introduce Blake primarily as a painter. This is indicated by the fact that Blake's illustrations appeared in many issues of their magazine, but surprisingly few of his poems,[16] which had been well known in previous decades.

If we look at the writings of the group members again, it is interesting that not only do they praise Blake's works, but they also hold his human qualities in high regard. Mushanokoji expresses this by saying he believes that Blake 'is a person that we should truly respect'. Motomaro Senge wrote that Blake achieved 'great humanistic expression in his art'. The *Shirakaba* group's interest in artists' person-alities is also shown by the self-portraits and photographs often printed in the magazine. Blake was no exception, and a 'life mask' by phrenologist J. S. Deville appeared in the magazine, and other publications about Blake by the members, many times (Figure 17.10).[17]

This interest appears in Soetsu Yanagi's thesis about Blake, which expounded on his appearance and personality, even entitling a chapter 'Blake as a Person'.

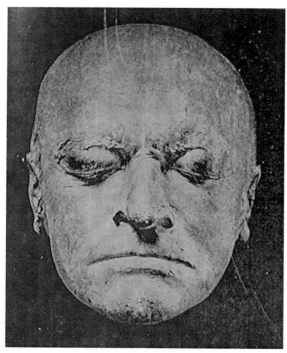

**Figure 17.10** Frontispiece of Soetsu Yanagi, 'William Blake (1757–1827)', *Shirakaba*, Vol. 5, No. 4, April 1914. (Rpt. By Rinsen Shoten, 1969–72.)

At the beginning of the chapter, Yanagi wrote, 'every aspect of his character is expressed by his appearance [. . .] Appearance is the clearest indicator of individuality' (Yanagi 1914b: 281). He goes on to describes Deville's life mask of Blake using terms such as 'endless', 'eternal', 'great' and 'joyous' (Yanagi 1914b: 282), the same words he uses when describing Blake's artworks. Yanagi was interested in Blake's appearance because he thought that it visually revealed the artist's inner nature, and he maintained this viewpoint when looking at Blake's art as well. Here we could interpret the coincidence of this idealistic idea of uniting inner and outer qualities of human beings through Johann Caspar Lavater's physiognomy as coming from Blake, who had a strong interest in people's faces, but it would be hasty to reach the conclusion that Yanagi was necessarily indebted to Blake for this concept. We should rather associate it with the *Shirakaba* perspective on art, which unites not only the appearance of the artist, but also the work itself with the artist's inner qualities.

This strong concern with artists' appearances and characters underlies the *Shirakaba* group's orientation in their understanding of art. Yanagi himself was instrumental in forming this *Shirakaba* perspective on art. His article, 'Revolutionary Painters (Kakumei no Gaka)', which appeared in the January 1912 issue of *Shirakaba*, marks the beginning of its development. This thesis discusses the Post-Impressionists, contemporaries of the *Shirakaba* group, and was the most epoch-making introduction of Western art in the magazine. This exposure to the Post-Impressionists oriented the *Shirakaba* view of art from then on and became pivotal to the direction of art in Japan at that time. This thesis introduces a well-known exhibition organized by Roger Fry (1866–1934), held two years earlier, 'Manet and the Post-Impressionists',[18] in which the word 'Post-Impressionist' first appeared. The artists Yanagi called 'Post-Impressionists' were the artists introduced at that event, including Van Gogh, Paul Cézanne, Paul Gauguin and Henri Matisse.[19] What is important is that Yanagi called them 'expressive artists' (Yanagi 1912: 5), and defined their art as reflections of 'character' and articulations of 'individuality' or 'life' (Yanagi 1912: 4). Then he placed 'self-expression' rather than 'beauty' as the ultimate purpose of art (Yanagi 1912: 4). In other words, this view regarded art not as being made by shapes, colours and techniques, but by 'individuality' that indicates the way of life of a unique human being. In short, the art reveals the 'character' of the artist. This view which connects art and life[20] foretells the course the *Shirakaba* group would take in the future. For Saneatsu Mushanokoji, the way to give the most energy to individuality was to live like great artists, who were people that lived fully to express their own individualities, and therefore should be taken as models for the lives of their admirers. Mushanokoji wrote about the sculptor Auguste Rodin, one of the artists that he valued most highly, that he had been able to 'pour his self into his works and give birth to genius' (Mushanokoji 1910: 74). His stance was that artists should be evaluated by their characters and ways of living that became apparent in their works of art, rather than by the works of art themselves.

The first lines of Yanagi's thesis – 'This writing is not a commentary on Blake. It is an appraisal of humanity itself' (Yanagi 1914b: 9) – indicate that in his understanding of Blake, there is an undercurrent of the *Shirakaba* group perspective that emphasizes the artists themselves over their art. 'The goal of understanding Blake is to touch the character of the man himself. Apart from his nature, there is no other idea of him. The substance of Blake's works always returns to the substance of his individuality' (Yanagi 1914b: 303). In this and other remarks, Yanagi tried to connect Blake's art with his individuality and character. His essay is also filled with remarks praising Blake's humanity: 'In the eyes of the viewer, the immense limitless human depth of his character is apparent. In him, we can discover the complete expression of humanity. His immense character should receive the reverence and adoration of the human race' (Yanagi 1914b: 19).

If we return to the question of the 'painter Blake' as conceived by the *Shirakaba* group, modern painters who were active from the second half of the nineteenth century to the twentieth century had a role in the process of creating this image of Blake. With the exceptions of Walt Whitman and Beethoven, Blake was listed mainly alongside painters such as Puvis de Chavannes, Cézanne, Daumier, Van Gogh and Millet. Among those artists, Blake was most often compared to the Post-Impressionists, whom Yanagi had discussed in his 'Revolutionary Painters', such as Van Gogh, Cézanne and Gauguin, as supporting the ideal of the awakening of the individual in the *Shirakaba* group. The inclusion of Blake along with those modern painters as one of their ideal artists shows that they considered him to be one of the painters who embodied their perspective on art. To the *Shirakaba* group, Van Gogh was a man who had sacrificed his life for art. Yanagi particularly emphasized the link between Van Gogh and Blake because of their common use of motifs of the sun. It goes without saying that Blake's poem 'Ah! Sunflower' was in Yanagi's mind, but he also thought that Blake, 'like Van Gogh, paints the shining sun with the endless adoration of a starving man' (Yanagi 1914b: 343), and that in the work of both artists, the sunflower was seen as a symbol of 'life' (Yanagi 1914b: 343). For Yanagi, life was the starting point for 'the expression of the fulfilment of individuality' (Yanagi 1914b: 376), 'individuality' was an axis of Blake's thought (Yanagi 1914b: 328) and Post-Impressionists required 'individuality' unceasingly (Yanagi 1912: 7). In the last chapter of his thesis, entitled 'Before and After Blake', Yanagi discusses the historical lineage of Blake's ideas. Beginning with ancient Indian Brahmanism, he finds connections with philosophers, including Jacob Boehme, Swedenborg, Nietzsche and Bergson, and artists, including Michelangelo, Redon and Rodin, and, at the end of the chapter, even places Blake as a forerunner of the Post-Impressionists (Yanagi 1914b: 376).

Yanagi showed that Blake shared the common themes of 'expression' and 'individuality' with the Post-Impressionists, the modern painters of the era, and the *Shirakaba* group ranked him among their ideal artists. The means used to receive and introduce Blake's visual art – reproductions – may have caused them to promote the presentation of his work as a painter more than as a poet. Furthermore, the interpretation of Blake as a forerunner of the Post-Impressionists, that is, connecting him with artists who have little in common in their visual style, can be thought to be, at least in part, the result of the rapid development of reproduction technologies, which allowed for equal, nearly simultaneous exposure to both old and new art, and resulted in bringing both Blake and the Post-Impressionists to Japan around the same time. In addition, the flat, homogeneous media of reproductions, lacking the materiality of the actual works of art, may have also reduced the differences between them. On the one hand, the oil paintings of the Post-Impressionists have visible brush marks and simplified forms that reveal the flatness and materiality of their paintings. On the other hand, the media of Blake's works were watercolours, tempera and copper-plate prints, media that de-emphasize the materiality of the works themselves compared to oil painting. In printed reproductions, however, the gap between the two is sharply diminished.

Moreover, the *Shirakaba* group discovered not only Blake and the Post-Impressionists, but also various Western artists from the Renaissance to the twentieth century, and diffused awareness of their works to younger generations in a very short time. The reason the *Shirakaba* group was open to the reception of art from many entirely different cultures and eras was that they shared a strong belief, as stated by Mushanokoji, that in the works of 'humanist' artists 'the fundamental aspects can be grasped' without knowing anything about the history of their countries or the conditions of their times (Mushanokoji 1913: 144). At the foundation of the *Shirakaba* group's perspective on art was a belief in the universality of geniuses and the timelessness of their art. For them, artworks were representations of individual genius, and through those artworks they thought they could discover not only artists' identities but also the essence of the West itself. As Akutagawa's claim reveals, in those days, at a time when Japan was trying to model itself on the West, art was placed as a pre-eminent means of access to previously unknown traditions, and Blake, still frequently regarded as a marginal figure in his own culture, was one of the artists who provided a way for Japanese people at the time to experience the West.

With this in mind, the *Shirakaba* group's interest in Blake's visual works was not so much in the meaning of the works themselves, but rather in his conspicuous individuality. Their vigorous introduction of Blake's art may have just been their way of endorsing Blake's life as an artist. On the other hand, we must not forget that the *Shirakaba* group found significance in another side of Post-Impressionism. They recognized that these painters followed their passion to cause a revolution in art and by expressing their unique personalities succeeded in creating a new role for individuality in future art. The now clichéd idea that art is an expression of individuality above all else was established by the young men of *Shirakaba*. Until the late nineteenth century, realism had driven the development of Japanese painting, so this stance can be seen to have been motivated both as a criticism of this practice and a declaration of departure from it. Furthermore, Soetsu Yanagi, who sought to discover the expression of 'individuality' in Blake's art, found that reading his poetry and other writings helped to deepen his perspective of art and at the same time overcome the subjectivism of the *Shirakaba* group.

When Yanagi found Blake's art to be the result of the merging of self, God and nature, his perception of art was probably both reinforced and transformed. In the poem 'The Divine Image', Blake's ideas of God and humanity overlap, Yanagi concluded. 'For him [Blake], humanity was divinity. We adore God because God is within us' (Yanagi 1914b: 68). In his interpretation, Blake placed importance on human individuality because God dwells in each person and the will of God appears in the individuality of each person. Yanagi, who had formerly seen artworks simply as an 'exclamation of the existence of the self' (Yanagi 1912: 4), through encountering Blake's art, now perceived that 'individuality' was endowed with 'God', and that art exceeded the consciousness of individual artists, giving it a new dimension as the 'manifestation of God'. Later, the word 'God', which here indicated 'something with absolute power existing behind [individuals]' (Yanagi 1914b: 256), had the meaning, for Yanagi, of traditions or ages that connect people. This idea would be the basis for Yanagi's life work of promoting *Mingei*, or 'folk craft' made for everyday life developed by ordinary people. His purpose in promoting this movement was to develop the contemporary 'culture of fine art' that emphasized individuality into a 'culture of craft' that was aware of a power that exceeds individuality. According to Yanagi, the possibility of finding the real individual is in the craft itself.

> The beauty of craft is the beauty of tradition [. . .] All the beauty we see in it is the result of accumulated traditions [. . .] Tradition rather than individuality shows more wonders that are free from everything. We are to believe that there is something greater than the individual. And to believe that leads you to find the real self. (Yanagi 1984)

### Notes

1  Bimyo Yamada (Taketaro Yamada), author and editor, *Bankoku Jinmei Jisho* (Dictionary of Famous Names around the World) (Tokyo: Hakubunkan, 1893). Umejiro Kinugasa first cited this work in 'Early Literary References to Blake', *Shomotsu Tenbo* (Book Survey) 6.12 (1936).

2  Bin Ueda (anonymous when the article was released), 'The Posthumous Writings of Walter Pater', *Teikoku Bungaku* (Imperial Literature) 1.5 (1895).

3  In 1899, Lafcadio Hearn gave his third lecture on Blake at Tokyo Imperial University (now Tokyo University), and it seems that he had given two previous lectures after 1897, though their dates are unknown.

4  Ariake Kanbara's first translation of Blake, which was 'Ah Higurumaya (Ah! Sunflower)' appeared in the June 1902 issue of the literary magazine *Daini Myojo* (The Second Venus), and his translation of 'Aobae (The Fly)' appeared in the February 1906 issue of *Myojo*. Choko Ikuta also produced his translation of 'The Sick Rose (Yameru Bara)' in the *Meiji* period (1867–1912), though the date and the name of the publication are unknown.

5  The poem appeared in the literary magazine *Shumi* (Taste) in May 1908. The poem was republished in *Haien* (A Deserted Garden) (1909) and *Rofu Shu* (Collected Works of Rofu) (1913). A musical setting to the poem composed by Kosaku Yamada (1886–1965) further increased its popularity.

6  Yanagi 1914b.

7  The exhibition Kishida refers to here was the first exhibition of reproductions by *Shirakaba*, 'Taisei Hanga Tenrankai (Exhibition of Western Prints)', held in October 1911 in Akasaka, Tokyo.

8  The exhibition was held in Tokyo, 20–28 February, at the Hibiya Museum of Arts and in Kyoto, 5–14 March, at the Kyoto Prefectural Library (Figure 17.4).

9  *Shirakaba*, 6.2 (1915): no page number.

10  See the letter to Bernard Leach of 3 August 1914 (Yanagi 1980–92: Vol. 21–1: 179–80) and the letter to Leach of 11 September 1914 (ibid., Vol. 21–1: 181–2). In the earlier letter, Yanagi tells Leach that he is planning a Blake exhibition in the autumn of that year and has started negotiating with the reproduction publisher, Frederick Hollyer. In the latter letter, he says he has finished writing his Blake book and is sending it to the printer in anticipation of its publication in early November. It seems that he was going to publish his book to coincide exactly with the exhibition. In fact, Yanagi's book was published that December and the exhibition was postponed until the next year because of the delay of the arrival of the reproductions.

11  In a letter to Naoya Shiga on the 24th of an unspecified month in 1908 (Yanagi 1980–92: Vol. 21–1: 9–10), Yanagi gives Shiga the name and address of Hollyer's studio as a place to buy a reproduction of a George Frederick Watts (1817–1904) work.

12  Yanagi himself points out that one of the representative books of modern art

history, Julius Meier-Graefe's *Entwicklungsgeschichte der Modernen Kunst* (Stuttgart: Julius Hoffmann, 1904), did not even refer to Blake.

13  In Nagano, a Blake exhibition was held at seven elementary schools, 3–10 September 1919. Yanagi gave lectures on 'Religion in Blake's Art' at every school. In Tokyo, the exhibition was held at Ryuitsu So, 7–11 November 1919 and in Kyoto at Teidai Kirisutokyo Seinen Kaikan (the YMCA Hall of Kyoto Imperial University), 18–22 November 1919.

14  Examples of magazines edited by Motomaro Senge that used Blake's artworks on the cover page are *Seimei no Kawa* (River of Life) and *Jun Bungei Zasshi: Geijutsu* (Pure Literary Magazine: Arts).

15  In *Shirakaba*, different Western artists were covered by other members of the group. Yanagi was the one who was responsible for Blake, so there are not so many references to Blake by other *Shirakaba* members. The quotations here are therefore picked from other magazines that were edited by *Shirakaba* members, including magazines issued after *Shirakaba* had ceased publication.

16  The poetry of Blake was included in only three articles in *Shirakaba*. Soetsu Yanagi (anonymous when the article was released) explains the Blake-like cover design by Bernard Leach and quotes from 'The Tyger' in 'Concerning the Cover Design', *Shirakaba*, 3.4 (1913); Yanagi also quotes from Blake's poetry extensively in his 'William Blake 1757–1827', *Shirakaba*, 5.4 (1914); finally, there was 'Five Poems of Blake', translated by Kantaro Yahata, *Shirakaba*, 13.11 (1922).

17  Blake's life mask appears in the following articles: as a frontispiece of Soetsu Yanagi, 'William Blake 1757–1827', *Shirakaba*, 5.4 (1914) as shown in Figure 17.10; on the back cover of the '*Shirakaba* 7th Art Exhibition of Western Paintings' catalogue of 1915; as the frontispiece of Soetsu Yanagi, *William Blake: Kare no Shogai to Seisaku Oyobi Sono Shiso* (1914a); as illustrations for Soetsu Yanagi, *Bureiku no Kotoba* (Aphoristic Words from Blake) (Tokyo: Sobun Kaku, 1921); as the frontispiece of the catalogue of the 'Hyakunenki Kinen Bureiku Sakuhin Tenrankai (William Blake Sakuhin Bunken Ten) (Exhibition of Blake's Works Commemorating the 100th Anniversary of His Death (Exhibition of the Bibliography of Blake's Works))' of 1927, which Yanagi helped plan; and as the cover design of the Blake issue of *Taiyoka* 10 (1927), a magazine edited by the former *Shirakaba* members.

18  The exhibition was held at the Grafton Galleries, London from 8 November 1910 to 15 January 1911.

19  In recent years, Matisse's works from this period have come to be regarded as Fauvism rather than Post-Impressionism.

20  There are many critical writings that discuss the *Shirakaba* group's connecting of art and the artist's life, but the representative ones are Shugo Honda, *Shirakaba ha no Bungaku* (Literature on *Shirakaba*) (Tokyo: Shinchosha, 1960) and Shuji Takashina, *Nihon Kindai no Bi Ishiki* (The Aesthetic Sense of Modern Japan) (Tokyo: Seidosha, 1993).

# PART III

## Blake in the Orient:
## Later Responses

# 18 Blake's Night: Tanizaki's Shadows

Jeremy Tambling

> In the mansion called literature I would have the eaves deep and the walls
> dark, I would push back into the shadows the things that come forward too
> clearly.
>
> (Tanizaki, *In Praise of Shadows* (1984), 42)

This chapter attempts to rethink how to compare texts written within a completely western tradition – virtually all of William Blake's poetry was written
in London, where he lived for nearly all his life – with writing from a Japanese
context, well aware of the West, however, and wanting to critique it. In this case,
the Japanese text is Tanizaki's *In Praise of Shadows*. And since Tanizaki writes on
shadows, the corresponding European subject must be the night, with all its
evocations of dream and nightmare, and the gothic; and the approach to the night
will be through recent French commentary. In contrast to Tanizaki's darkness,
which withdraws into further shadow, Blake's 'Tyger' burns 'in the forests of
the night' (E 24). Its being is nocturnal, and its character is brought out most fully
in the night, when in contrast to its brightness 'the stars threw down their
spears', which implies loss of light (E 172). His 'sick rose' experiences the love
of the 'invisible worm' that 'flies in the night' (E 23): the 'night', perhaps,
increases the sickness. In 'A Poison Tree', the speaker describes the wrath he has
nurtured:

> And it grew both day and night
> Till it bore an apple bright
> And my foe beheld it shine
> And he knew that it was mine
>
> And into my garden stole
> When the night had veild the pole . . . (E 28)

'Day and night' sounds like the repetition of a children's rhyme, which it is, but
the lines are not only that. The apple's brightness, which also makes a person
'sick', as poison does, and which is not 'burning', a word whose energy suggests a
contestatory power, working against the night, is brought out because it shines in
the night. It is an alternative and meretricious form of light, unlike Andrew
Marvell's oranges, remembering, that in 'Bermudas', God 'hangs / In shades the
Orange bright, / Like golden Lamps in a green night' (13). Hence the attraction
of the 'apple' to the 'foe'. Night does not cancel sight, but it induces another form

of looking, including another way of reading colours; for example, in the way that the 'worm' in 'The Sick Rose' has found out the rose's 'bed / Of crimson joy' whose 'crimson' still means something in the night. In *Songs of Experience*, the nocturnal disorganizes or imprisons – 'Can delight / Chained in night' (E 18–19), yet night-images are calling out, fascinating, even alluring towards death – as in 'A Poison Tree'.

Throughout Blake, this attraction returns, as with the haunting inscription for emblem No. 14 in *For the Sexes: The Gates of Paradise* (*c.* 1818): 'The Traveller hasteth in the evening' (E 266). Here is what Morton Paley calls 'a pilgrim-like walker wearing a broad-brimmed hat and tailed coat, striding purposefully forward with the aid of a stick as the shadows lengthen', and he compares it with No. 9 of the woodcut illustrations to Thornton's Virgil (1821), full of nocturnal suggestiveness, which takes place at the last moment of sunset: 'there is a sliver of setting sun behind the hills, and its light strikes and illuminates a church steeple in the background'. In the foreground, there is a traveller who is a shepherd that has passed a wayside cross. He has also passed a milestone, inscribed 'LXII miles London', perhaps Blake's then age, perhaps the distance from Felpham to London (Paley 2004: 16, 41–2). Paley's suggestive title, *The Traveller in the Evening*, makes the reader wish that he had pursued more the resonance of its central terms. The moment of closing – 'I haste away / To close the Labours of my day' – is reversed in 'The Door of Death I open found / And the Worm Weaving in the Ground' (E 269). As in 'Ah! Sunflower!' the sun's travel aims after 'that sweet golden clime / Where the travellers journey is done' (E 25). The traveller's fatigue is of the day in contrast to 'The Son of Morn in weary Nights decline', from the Epilogue to *For the Sexes: The Gates of Paradise*. His dream, 'under the hill' – another decline – is of the accusatory power of the 'God of this world', who in Blake's illustration flies away from the traveller's sleeping body (E 269 and Erdman 1974: 279).

Some sentences from the French theorist and writer Maurice Blanchot, from an essay 'The Outside, the Night', in *The Space of Literature* (1982), indicate the investment that modern western thinking has made in the concept of night:

> But when everything has disappeared in the night, 'everything has disappeared' appears. This is the *other* night. Night is this apparition: 'everything has disappeared.' It is what we sense when dreams replace sleep, when the dead pass into the deep of the night, when night's deep appears in those who have disappeared. Apparitions, phantoms and dreams are an allusion to this empty night. It is the night of Young, where the dark does not seem dark enough, or death ever dead enough. (Blanchot 1982: 163)

Blanchot alludes in the last sentence to Edward Young: to *The Complaint, Or, Night Thoughts, on Life, Death and Immortality*, written between 1742 and 1746, and illustrated by Blake in 1797, the same year of Novalis's *Hymnen an die Nacht* (*Hymns to the Night*). These contrast day, associated with Enlightenment thought, and night, linked with the erotic, the Dionysiac and, through the grave, with death. Blanchot considers the night in two ways: first, as giving values the complement or opposite of the day, and here his example is Novalis. The other is as neutralizing concepts, abolishing meaning before it can be established: Young's *Night Thoughts* are linked with that other night. This writing 'desires the night, the first or pure night of Novalis's hymns, but discovers only the *impossibility* of the night' (Critchley 1997: 63 and also 31–83 generally). Hence wakefulness, vigilance, the state of the opening of Proust, where what happens is a waking in the night after having fallen asleep early, but where there is nothing to wake for. It is the moment of the opening of *Night Thoughts*:

> Tir'd nature's sweet Restorer, balmy *Sleep!*
> He, like the World, his ready visit pays,
> Where Fortune smiles; the wretched he forsakes;
> Swift on his downy pinion flies from Woe,
> And lights on lids unsully'd with a Tear.
> From short, (as usual) and disturb'd Repose,
> I wake: How happy they who wake no more!
> Yet that were vain, if dreams infest the Grave.
> I wake, emerging from a sea of Dreams
> Tumultuous; where my wreck'd, desponding Thought
> From wave to wave of *fancy'd* Misery,
> At random drove, her helm of Reason lost;
> Tho' now restor'd, 'tis only Change of pain,
> A bitter change; severer for severe:
> The *Day* too short for my Distress! and *Night*
> Even in the *Zenith* of her dark Domain
> Is Sun-shine, to the colour of my Fate.
> (Young 1989: 1: 1–17)

The speaker's rhetoric fuses Macbeth on sleep (*Macbeth* 2. 2. 38–40) and Hamlet on dreams (*Hamlet* 3. 1. 66), where dreams, for Young, have been equated with Hamlet's 'sea of troubles'. Hamlet and Macbeth have been aligned, in the sense that they do not know what lies behind and beyond their personal existence. But Young's first lines also undercut Shakespeare in that they make sleep an aspect of the social world and of the day, allied with Fortune; human, deceptive, even treacherous. Having 'night thoughts' separates the self from the social world. In this, the speaker differs from Macbeth, who idealizes sleep in the moment when he has lost its power because it keeps him back from awareness of the existence – what Levinas and Blanchot refer to as the *il y a* – the 'there is' – that underlies his being as an 'existent'. In the same way, the Ghost in *Hamlet* speaks of the 'fat weed / That roots itself in ease on Lethe wharf' (*Hamlet* 1. 5. 32–3) – because the Ghost, whose personal failure of vigilance in the day is what he must now mourn, considers sleep as that which confers oblivion. Dreams, in Young, as in *Macbeth* and *Hamlet* alike, are reminders that the night is never dark enough. The repeated 'I wake' leaves the speaker to face the darkness alone, to know the night as real, and as an indicator of something beyond. That is an aspect of Blake, too, who is not solely the poet of 'glad day', but of the night.

In *The Writing of the Disaster* (1986), where 'the disaster' is exactly that which has no conceptual limits, Blanchot takes night as 'the extreme shuddering of no thoughts' (Blanchot 1986: 49). By this he means it is the time of the abolition of what can be conceptualized, what can be laid out in 'Newton's sleep' (E 722). Blanchot begins with a sense of 'white, sleepless night – such is the disaster: the night lacking darkness, but brightened by no light' (Blanchot 1986: 2). In the first night, it is possible to think of inspiration, and of the subject of writing. In the second night, which is marked by absence of work (*désouvrement*) and by that state called 'the neuter', the subject has been taken away by death (Blanchot 1986: 66).

The strangeness within *Night Thoughts*, perhaps more strange than could be known, consciously, by Young – who was of the social world – is of Blanchot's 'other night'. According to Levinas, the nature of the *il y a* is an 'ambiguity' in which 'the menace of pure and simple presence, takes form. Before this obscure invasion it is impossible to take shelter in oneself, to withdraw into one's shell. One is exposed. The whole is open upon us. Instead of serving as our means of access to being, nocturnal space delivers us over to being' (Levinas 1978: 59).

How can this sense of night be related to Japanese writing? A first comparison may be taken from *waka* poetry, from the *Shin Kokin Waka Shu*, completed in 1205: the first (No. 369) of many possible examples, a translation of a text by Fujiwarano Nagayoshi:

> Dreary indeed the dusk
> in which cicadas cry,
> and thus am I
> ever forlorn.

the second (No. 486) by Fujiwarano Michinobu:

> When I see the moon at midnight
> toward the end of autumn,
> I can not but weep
> wetting the sleeves with tears.
> *(Shin Kokinshu* 1970: 103, 133)

The melancholic associations of autumn and the moon and dusk, with the sense that the coming of night marks the period of having waited too long, are reminiscent of western pastoral but do not include a fascination with the night as the formless, the neuter. The void, in Buddhist thought, may be too positive, too absolute, and the investment in muted quietness differs from the sense of night as violent to thought because deranging it. It has been said that traditional Japanese culture has 'continuously shown a marked lack of interest in the computation of time, and, generally speaking, in astronomy: they seem preoccupied only by the astrological use of calendars' (Caillet 1998: 15). Here the importance falls on spring and autumn; for example, on the first full moon in autumn (*bon*), which as a Buddhist festival has prayers for the spirits of the dead, and the viewing of the full moon in the middle of autumn. 'The annual course of time appears like a cobweb bringing together all the annual rites' and these rites give meaning to time in-between (Caillet 1998: 26). This absence of abstraction suggests a difference from darkness in Young or Blake, and a return to the poet who dominates both: Milton, poet of 'the void profound / Of unessential night . . . / Wide gaping' and threatening 'with utter loss of being' whoever is 'plunged in that abortive gulf' (*Paradise Lost* 2: 438–41). Milton offers an example of a modern Western imagination, the more fascinated because blind, searching out night as formless (OED cites Milton as the first to use the word 'void' in the sense of 'the empty expanse of space'). Belial has already referred to 'the wide womb of uncreated Night' in line 150 of the same book: Alastair Fowler, Milton's editor puts the two uses of 'abortive' and 'uncreated' together, and so imagines 'a miscarrying womb, which renders a traveller' through the realm 'Of Chaos and eternal Night' (3: 18) 'as if unborn' (Milton 1998: 131). Night is 'old' (2: 1002); while another term used for it, which appears just after 'th' unreal, vast, unbounded deep' (10: 471), is 'unoriginal Night' (10: 477). This means 'uncreated' (according to OED, which gives this passage as a unique citation). Night has neither origin nor reality nor form. Just as OED gives Milton first usage of 'space' in its modern astronomical sense, so the place to find 'chaos' is in:

> The secrets of the hoary deep, a dark
> Illimitable Ocean without bound,
> Without dimension; where length, breadth and highth,
> And time and place are lost; where eldest Night
> And Chaos, ancestors of Nature, hold
> Eternal anarchy . . .
>
> *(Paradise Lost* 2: 891–6)

Satan moves across this 'wild abyss' (2: 910), that which, because it has no bottom, remains formless, the sphere of Chaos, where 'Chance governs all' (2: 910), the place which is 'the womb of Nature and perhaps her grave' (2: 911). The line comes out of *The Faerie Queene*:

> For in the wide wombe of the world there lyes,
> In hateful darknes and in deep horrore,
> A huge eternal Chaos, which supplyes
> The substaunce of natures fruitfull progenyes.
>
> (Spenser 2001: 347)

The lines translate Lucretius, '*ominparens eadem rerum commune sepulcrum*' (*De Rerum Natura* 5: 259) – 'both universal parent and common grave of things' – though this phrase speaks of the earth, not of Chaos. This may be compared with the 'vast abyss' of 1: 21, which was made pregnant by the Spirit as the Dove, but here it seems as though Chaos and the 'abyss' remain, still non-fertile. In the quotation, the sexual sense of 'secrets' (like Hamlet (2. 2. 235) speaking of 'the secret parts of Fortune') may be noted: this quasi-pudenda threatens with the loss of sexual difference, and of the meaning, which, in psychoanalytic terms, is established through the existence of phallic authority. Chance and Chaos hold a close relationship to each other. Here, in the nethermost abyss, Satan meets Chaos, and 'sable-vested Night, eldest of things' (2: 961–2), his consort. Yet it would also seem that Night is the mother of Chaos. It is older: 'eldest Night' (3: 18 and Leonard 2000: 198–217). The prevalence of Chaos and the pre-existence of Night threaten the formed existence of creation: Night precedes Light, and it is a question whether Milton's sense of order can survive such a disorganizing force intact. It is reminiscent of the Lacanian 'Real', that which is outside signification, which can neither become part of language (the symbolic), nor can be part of that which sustains the narcissism of the subject (Lacan 1979: 53–64).

It is time to contrast the abyssal western night of Milton, Young, Blake, Blanchot and Levinas with its representation within Japanese culture, and a fascinating access to thinking about darkness and shadow, including the night within it, comes from the essay *In Praise of Shadows* (*In'ei raisan*) by Jun'ichiro Tanizaki (1886–1965). Tanizaki was born in Tokyo, and his student days were influenced by the *poètes maudites*, European writers such as Poe, Baudelaire and Wilde, and by Western tastes. After the earthquake of 1923, he moved to the Kansai area, which began the period when he was most recognized as a novelist, and when he articulated a desire for the older Japan, not represented in either the modern Tokyo, or Yokohama, where he had also lived prior to 1923. The 1930s was to be the period, too, when he began work on his translations (three in all) of *Genji monogatari* (*The Tale of Genji*), the text which most wonderfully embodies the power of the feminine, both because it is by a woman (Murasaki Shikibu) and because it praises the power of femininity. Tanizaki's commitment to this text is part of a refusal of Japanese masculinity, significant in the decade leading to the novel which praises the feminine at the expense of the masculine, *The Makioka Sisters* (1943–8), a novel which Seidensticker points out has no hero at all, not even – as elsewhere – a masochistic one (Tanizaki 1984: 258).[1]

In 1933, *In Praise of Shadows* (*In'ei raisan*) was published, offering what the text calls 'the empty dreams of a novelist' (Tanizaki 1984: 8). The phrase may mean that the essay (*zuihitsu*) is actually another form of novel, and of course means that it is not to be presumed as the voice of the 'author'.[2] It also suggests what Tanizaki notes about Western modernity as being that to which Japanese civilization has had to surrender – its fascination with light, its dislike of shadows and the dark – and which cannot be turned back. Shadows are positive; not the 'shadow of horror' that rises in Eternity in *The [First] Book of Urizen* (E 70) and that implies the presence of brooding self-consciousness, but a realm that enriches. Yet only a novelist who works intensely with an enriched sensory perception of the power of night could spend time on such illusions, and give a reading of Japan as a culture of shadows. And the novelist in Tanizaki is complemented by something else: by a fascination with the medium of film (expressed in the essay, 'The Present and Past of the Moving Pictures' (1917)). Film is produced by the power of shadows, dissolving the distinction between reality and fantasy, and so offering another reality which is neither that of the everyday nor of the convention-bound theatre: in his novel *Flesh* (*Nikkai*, 1923) appears Tanizaki's comparison of 'the entire universe – all the phenomena of the world round us' to a film, so that it may be that 'we are all nothing but shadows that disappear quickly and without a trace while our reality lives on in the film of the universe' (quoted in Bernardi 1997: 298).

*In Praise of Shadows* is, like other works of the 1930s by Tanizaki, gender-orientated in its liking for darkness and shadow as feminine. It seems to polarize Western light and traditional Japan, and faults Japan for having given way to a Western obsession with light, expressed in its technology. Tanizaki finds darkness significant for aesthetic, not metaphysical reasons. He is fascinated by the point that even in the times before Europeans used either electricity or gas – the appearance of gas-lighting happened in London within Blake's Lifetime – 'the West has never been disposed to delight in shadows'. Punning on ghosts as shadows he says that even Western ghosts are 'as clear as glass'. In contrast to that, the 'night' theme emerges when it is stated that 'pitch darkness has always occupied our fantasies'; the Japanese sensibility prefers 'colours compounded of darkness' (Tanizaki 1984: 30).

As Blake's 'night' poetry in the *Songs of Experience* brings together the woman and the erotic, so, to different effect, does *In Praise of Shadows*, which draws on Tanizaki's sense of the erotic and sensual value of colours, for example: white (Orsi 1998: 1–14). Darkness and shadows in Japanese architecture seem to him a form of innocence. His prose seeks to give added 'depth to shadows', as he says that a hanging scroll does in the alcove of a Japanese room (Tanizaki 1984: 19). He notes in the Chinese love for jade an analogous interest in 'muddy light' . . . 'melting dimly, dully back, deeper and deeper' as also, in the taste for crystal, a preference for the impure varieties, those 'with opaque veins crossing their depths' (Tanizaki 1984: 10–11). He passes to darkness as an indispensable part of the beauty of lacquerware, where 'florid patterns recede into the darkness, conjuring in their stead an inexpressible aura of depth and mystery' (Tanizaki 1984: 13–14). The absence of the visual calls up other senses. Whereas the Gothic, for Western thinking, may imply gloom, or Milton's 'dim religious light' (*Il Penseroso*, line 160), here it implies the wish to place the pinnacle as high in the heavens as possible, whereas Japanese traditional architecture magnifies darkness (Tanizaki 1984: 17). The Western desire for a hard clarity, which is the art of Enlightenment, because 'the progressive Westerner is determined always to better his lot', is linked to attitudes to colour which became manifest in the American Civil War (Tanizaki 1984: 31–2). The analysis here touches on the ambiguity of 'whiteness' within modern Western thought, as not just a source of Enlightenment value, and the colour of the hegemonic settlers in America, but also as a power of horror, because it is the absence of colour, the power of death: a theme that Melville's *Moby Dick* pursues particularly when, in Chapter 42, Ishmael meditates on the 'Whiteness of the Whale'.

This leads into a discussion of space and of Japanese rooms which allow for the darkness of alcoves, while he says that the dress of the nineteenth-century Japanese woman is 'in effect, no more than a part of the darkness, the transition between darkness and face' (Tanizaki 1984: 28). At that moment, the associations of the darkness with the woman whom the darkness idealizes, and therefore the mother, become apparent. For 'our ancestors cut off the brightness on the land from above and created a world of shadows, and far in the depths of it they placed woman, marking her the whitest of beings' (Tanizaki 1984: 33). The shadows, then, are a frame for the feminine and the erotic, a point further articulated when he praises Noh drama above Kabuki, on the basis that in the darkness of Noh, male actors playing women could be both beautiful and feminine. 'If actors of old had had to appear on the bright stage of today, they would doubtless have stood out with a certain masculine harshness, which in the past was discreetly veiled by darkness' (Tanizaki 1984: 27).

Whiteness in Tanizaki is not the binary opposite of darkness, but something within it, an affinity: not a deep contrast, as in 'there is in God (some say) / A deep, but dazzling darkness' (Vaughan, 1976: 'The Night', 290) where the darkness is a form of excess of light, but a sense that white is another form of shadow. The whiteness is 'other-worldly' (Tanizaki 1984: 34): it may not actually exist, it may be part of a novelist's invention, but it is also something to be created, a way of thinking which is different from Japan as it has been modernized – as he concludes – to a much greater extent than a European city such as Paris. He calls what was before in Japanese houses 'a visible darkness' (Tanizaki 1984: 35) and the phrase, which he presents as a quotation, recalls what Milton's Satan finds in Hell, 'darkness visible' (*Paradise Lost* 1: 63).

The 'praise of shadows' is part of a metaphysics which does not try to bring out what is of the night into the light; 'we Orientals tend to seek our satisfaction in whatever surroundings we happen to find ourselves, to content ourselves with things as they are; and so darkness causes us no discontent, we resign ourselves to it as inevitable' (Tanizaki 1984: 31). In contrast, Milton suggests that the reason for such an impulse is a fear of the night, and of Chaos, as the absorbing, consuming, annihilating feminine. Yet if that note is not sounded in Tanizaki, it does not mean it could not be there, for immediately after the allusion to 'darkness visible' he continues that within Japanese darkness:

> Always something seemed to be flickering and shimmering, a darkness that on occasion held greater terrors than darkness out-of-doors. This was the darkness in which ghosts and monsters were active and indeed was not the woman who lived in it, behind thick curtains, behind layer after layer of screens and doors – was she not of a kind with them? The darkness wrapped her round tenfold, twentyfold, it filled the collar, the sleeves of her kimono, the folds of her skirt, wherever a hollow invited. Further yet: might it not have been the reverse, might not the darkness have emerged from her mouth and those black teeth, from the black of her hair, from the great earth spider? (Tanizaki 1984: 35)

The images of hollows, of the mouth, of gaps within dark spaces, the final reference to the 'great earth spider' – all these invoke the castration fears at the heart of Milton's Western night. Dreams of emptiness are anything but vacant. This quotation comes back, via Milton, to something of a concession to the Western modern and masculine conception: the darkness attracts because it contains powers of horror which have been gendered as having qualities of the woman – their teeth purposefully blackened in the practice of 'ohaguro' (Tanizaki 1984: 28) – from whom darkness emerges. The dark is both the place of the erotic woman, and of the terrifyingly monstrous one. Perhaps what is invoked here is the spirit of the Rokujo lady in *Genji monogatori*, the woman who, as a malign spirit, possesses Aoi, Genji's wife, when she is about to give birth, just as she has already come to Genji in a dream when he was with another woman: the episodes comprise parts of *Genji* Chapter 4, 'Evening Faces' and of Chapter 9, 'Heartvine' (Shikibu 1981: 71–2, 167–8 and see also Bargen 1997). These night-moments in *The Tale of Genji*, which interweave jealousy with love, and link the night with dreams which take over and possess the dreamer, are what *In Praise of Shadows* moves towards, but not in any spirit that wishes to distance itself from such powers, but rather in one that is full of the power of its possibilities.

*Europe* (Plate 5: 1–10) evokes 'the night of Enitharmon's joy!' in which she sends out messengers whose effect will be that 'Woman. lovely Woman! may have dominion':

> Go! tell the Human race that Womans love is Sin! . . .
> Forbid all Joy, & from her childhood shall the little female
> Spread nets in every secret path.
>
> My weary eyelids draw towards the evening, my bliss is yet but new.
> (pl. 5: 5, 8–10 E 62)

Enitharmon's eyes are weary of the day; her 'bliss', yet to come, is associated with the night which is identified with two things: the woman herself, and the period when she holds 'dominion'. Her interdiction of all 'Joy' returns, by contrast, to the plaint within 'Earth's Answer', which both sees the night as negative, and attributes that to patriarchal power.

> Prison'd on watry shore
> Starry jealousy does keep my den
> Cold and hoar

Weeping o'er
I hear the Father of the ancient men

Selfish father of men
Cruel jealous selfish fear
Can delight
Chain'd in night
The virgins of youth and morning bear. (6–15 E 18–19)

Jealousy seems masculine, 'starry', associated with water and with tears, as stars are in 'The Tyger'. The sphere of the night-heavens is saturated with water (if 'the starry floor' and 'the watry shore' are the same) and, as 'cold and hoar', it gives the possessive aspects of jealousy. Earth's speech repeats the words 'jealous' and 'selfish', and balances the 'ancient men' with the 'selfish father'. Both she associates with night and both she opposes to 'the virgins of youth and morning' as she opposes the 'hoar' to 'youth'. In what follows, 'bear' means both to give birth, and 'to tolerate, to bear with' or 'support' as with the woman bearing the incubus squatting on her body. Can the 'virgins . . . bear' the 'night'? Can 'delight' endure that 'delight' should be 'Chain'd in night'? Light itself seems confined in the 'night', the period which de-lights (where the de- may be a privative, giving the sense 'takes away light'). The antithesis between night and light could not be stronger. But in the previous poem, the 'Introduction':

Night is worn
And the morn
Rises from the slumberous mass. (13–15 E 18)

Perhaps night is 'worn' because it is weary, weary of bearing, unable to give birth and unable to tolerate other existences. The 'morn' – placed by metonomy for the sun – is said to rise out of that 'slumberous mass' associated with the night, and is therefore not so differentiated from it in terms of origin, even if 'Mass' implies unformed, undifferentiated matter. Light is 'fallen, fallen' – which recalls Lucifer, Son of the Morning (Isaiah 14.12) – yet the morn 'Rises'. Is this 'The Son of Morn in weary Nights decline' (E 269)? But the possible affirmation also carries the negative which it bears in the 'Epilogue': that 'decline' is all there is. The Night in Blake is deeply ambiguous, male and female together, cold, different from the day yet perhaps bearing it. But with all its ambiguity, and setting the tone for *Songs of Experience*, it is, while the source of fascination, much less to be affirmed than Tanizaki and his tradition, by comparison, allow.

## Notes

1   For Tanizaki's 'return to Japan' and relationship to Japanese tradition, both embracing and rejecting its 'commodification' in the twentieth century, see Golley 1995: 365–404.

2   For a biographical sense of Tanizaki, see Gessel 1993: 68–132.

# 19 Ōe Kenzaburo's Reading of Blake: an Anglophonic Perspective

Barnard Turner

> Jerusalem coverd the Atlantic Mountains & the Erythrean,
> From bright Japan & China to Hesperia France & England.
> (*Jersualem* 24: 46–7; E 170)

As a cardinal, if indefinite, point in Blake's work, 'bright Japan' serves as a limit of expansion, both, geographically, of the Euro–Asian landmass, and, historically, of those relations, be they metonymies, synecdoches or metaphors ('Asia' as the 'East', the 'Orient'), through which Blake opens up the geomorphology, through which he then shapes his world. That both England and Japan have been and in some ways still are insular (in both senses) makes them at once both part of and removed from the main. John of Gaunt and Engelbert Kaempfer make surprisingly similar points about the happiness of seclusion with regard to the respective nations, the latter making the comparison explicitly and claiming, near the end of his 1712 *Amoenitates exoticae*, partly translated into English in 1727,[1] that Japan 'was never in a happier condition than it now is, governed by an arbitrary Monarch, shut up, and kept from all Commerce and Communication with foreign nations' (Kaempfer 1728: Vol. 2, Appendix VI: 75). And yet the report got out, perhaps to influence Swift's *Gulliver's Travels*, also of 1727, and even Blake in his apprenticeship years through Jacob Bryant's *New System*.[2] Bryant calls Kaempfer 'a writer of great credit' (Bryant 1774: Vol. 3: 571) and quotes from him extensively in the following pages. In the associative mythopoeia, the dearth of precise details, the range of interpretative possibilities, and the fanciful etymologizing, there is much here for an apprentice to belabour: the greater the geopolitical seclusion the more the speculation.

A report and more so a critical response from Japan to England therefore refract the positions of both cultures, particularly if the representation is fresh enough not to have been long buried under critical sedimentation, and this most of all in a strong, creative reading which acknowledges not only the import but also the local indigenous traditions; the global and the local perhaps. Kaempfer describes the Chinese and the Japanese by a series of vague propositions which relate where they purport to differentiate: the former are 'peaceable, modest, great lovers of a sedate, speculative and philosophical way of life, but withal much given to fraud and usury'; while 'the Japanese on the contrary are war-like, inclin'd to rebellions and a dissolute life, mistrustful, ambitious, and always bent on high designs' (Kaempfer 1728: 86). 'Fraud' is however surely a sign of the 'dissolute', and 'speculation' and 'philosophy' are surely 'high designs'. The combination then of the egregious and the conflicting in each categorization may still bemuse through the juxtaposition of the detailed and the generic. For present-day readers, at a time when 'bright Japan' has materialized more distinctly geopolitically and culturally, in a 'mutual[ity]', a 'Vision of [capitalist] Regeneration' very far from that envisioned in *Jerusalem* (24: 47; E 170), one might reflect upon the ways in which many discourses are still entrenched in comparable rhetoric. Following, even if because of one's minimal Japanese, the parabola back to England from this other island establishes negotiations between cultures, as in the particularity of Blake's resonance in Ōe Kenzaburo.

Ōe provides a significant contemporary response to Blake, both in Japan and internationally perhaps, but he is not unique in either respect. Reading Sato Haruo, for example, we come across two passages pertinent to my discussion of the Nobel Prize-winning author. 'After sensing the infinitely vast, a person will see the thing nearby as infinitely small . . . You may say [this] is the awakening of the soul', Satō writes in the 1924 essay '*Fūryū*' (*Elegance*) (quoted in Rimer 1993: 11). At the end of his novella, *Gloom in the Country* (originally called *The Sick Rose*, 1918), the protagonist examines some flowers his wife has picked, only to find that they have been infested with insects. Suddenly, Blake's line 'O Rose thou art sick' springs into his mind, like the 'voice of another', and, as a refrain which is also a commentary on both his well-being and his relationship with his wife, it gets louder as it is accompanied by the barking of dogs. The novella ends: 'Where did the voice come from? Was it a revelation from heaven? Was it a prophecy? Whatever, the words kept hounding him. Endlessly, endlessly . . .' (Sato 1993: 97). In these two quotations, from very different contexts, expansion and limitation mutually configure the nominal, as an abstract – the word 'Rose' which the protagonist loves *as a word* even more perhaps for its name than for its physical being – comes together with the personal, and these resonate, jarringly perhaps, inexplicably, but 'endlessly'. Earlier, he had thought that a word once created, that could be used, will give immortality, whether or not the person who invented it is known. If nothing then, once created, can pass away, and if there is both a historical groundedness – an ideological formation in question – and an abiding aesthetic and extrasensory presence here, this is beginning to resonate with the numinal in Blake. A word – in this case, 'rose', but it could be any word – is source, target and boundary of the connotative and is replete with 'infinite particulars', which belong to the narrator as he realizes them, knowing – and here to paraphrase Blake's letter of 16 August 1799 to the Reverend Dr Trusler – 'they are not [his]' (E 701) as they come from somewhere else: Satō's 'infinitely vast'; Blake's reference to Milton's Urania who visits him 'when' – appropriately enough for the present, Japanese context – 'Morn / Purples the East' (*Paradise Lost* VII: 29–30). As material things, one can see through words, just as – at the end of the 'Vision of the Last Judgement' – Blake compares his 'Corporeal or Vegetative Eye' to 'a Window': 'I look thro it & not with it' (E 566).

The introspective dimension characteristic of Satō here is counterbalanced by the Blake of Yanagi Sōetsu (1889–1961), in his emphasis on 'The unknown craftsman' and Japanese folk craft, *minshu-teki kogei* (people's craft), or *mingei*. Since Yanagi in 1914 wrote one of the earliest extensive readings of Blake, and later (1929–30), while lecturing at Harvard, edited the Japanese journal *Blake and Whitman*, it is not surprising that the points of comparison and contrast are many, and one cannot read Yanagi's 'The Way of Craftsmanship' (1927) or 'Responsibility of the Craftsman' (1952) (both in Yanagi 1972b; 1989) without thinking of Blake. 'A Machine is not a Man nor a Work of Art it is Destructive of Humanity & of Art', writes Blake in the *Canterbury Pilgrims Public Address* (E 575); Yanagi similarly comments: 'Machines are not bad in themselves, but a completely mechanized age would be a disaster . . . if machinery is master and man the slave, the effect is disastrous . . . Man is most free when his tools are proportionate to his needs' (Yanagi 1989: 206). 'Simple workmanship' has – as Blake writes in *Jerusalem* – been replaced by 'intricate wheels' designed to 'perplex youth' 'kept ignorant of [their] use' (65: 17–27; E 216). One must, that is, 'striv[e] with Systems to deliver Individuals from these Systems' (*Jerusalem* 11: 5; E 154).

In the *Public Address*, Blake cries: 'Englishmen rouze yourselves from the fatal Slumber into which Booksellers & Trading Dealers have thrown you' (E 576). In 'The Way', it is argued that the capitalist system 'impoverishes' the folk crafts 'in a whirlpool of competition' so that the artists are 'forced to use sensational means to attract buyers. The immediate reflection of this is to be seen in bad colours and poor shapes. This bad influence unconsciously affects man's very heart'; under capitalism, 'quality, beauty and health of an object are all secondary considerations' (Yanagi 1989: 205). The resistance to the garish, spectacular and momentary is also of course an important feature of Blake's aesthetic pronouncements. 'The Rich Men of England form themselves into a Society, to Sell and Not to Buy Pictures' he writes in his Reynolds annotations (E 642) and 'fine tints are loathsome', in the *Public Address*, a view which – fortuitously – appears also at the end of Tanizaki's *In Praise of Shadows*, with its foundation in distinctly Japanese aesthetics: 'I would push back into the shadows the things that come forward too clearly, I would strip away the useless decoration' (Tanizaki 1984: 42).

Thus in the perspectives granted by Satō and Yanagi here, and which serve as preface to Ōe, are detectable, ironically and perhaps rather generically, two opposing forces which appear as restatements of the mystical and the historical readings of Blake which have characterized Anglo-American criticism. The ideological and the utopian, as in the work of Marcuse and Bloch perhaps, are not to be separated in Yanagi's practice, any more than they are in Blake's. These strands however must be carefully nuanced in any study of cross-cultural appropriation, as their intersection and division may not be so inflected in target as in source culture or text.

In working through related issues, Ōe carefully foregrounds particular nuances of compatibility and divergence in his engagement with European ideology, whether this be Scandinavian, French, English or Irish, and fashions his sources along writerly productive, rather than explanatory, generic lines. While he alludes to Blake in several novels – in *An Echo of Heaven* (first published in 1989) for example, Marie Kuraki mentions the narrator's acquaintance with 'The Mental Traveller' – his interest peaks in *A Personal Matter* (*kojinteki na taiken*, 1964) and '*Rouse Up O Young Men of the New Age!*' (*atarashii hito yo mezameyo*, 1983); there are also some Blakean nuances (at least as gathered in Yeats) apparent also in the 1994 Nobel Prize speech and addresses collected in the *Japan, the Ambiguous and Myself* volume (1995). One way of reading the title of the 1983 volume, of course – and as it has been translated back into English – is as an adaptation of a sentence from the Preface to Blake's *Milton*, a passage Ōe quotes in the final paragraph of this novel when he finally refers to his son by his own name, Hikari (light), rather than the juvenile 'Eeyore' used to that point. The novel represents almost both a self-critique of and dialogue with the novelist's former use of Blake, including, again towards the end, the passage from *Matter* (1964) I shall discuss, and a reassessment – a primary Blakean trait in his own work – of his own established positions, as these have been criticized by more radical younger intellectuals. The book is written in the form of a 'chronicle of William Blake superimposed on [his] life with [his] son' (Ōe 1964; 1969: 210); in a sense as a *substitute* for a book of definitions (*orizdein?*) he had planned on writing for the mentally disabled (Ōe 1964; 1969: 21); and as an expression of the parent's hopes and fears for his child.

As with any appropriation of a major writer by another, Ōe is selective, but the implications of his borrowings are extensive for his own creativity. In *Rouse Up* (1983), he quotes widely from Blake; chapter titles come from the works, including the 'Let the inchained soul' passage from *America* (E 53) in his book's most political chapter (with references to the end of the Second World War and the perception of his apolitical status with younger readers), but without noting how much of this passage, Plate 6, is reproduced at the end of *The Four Zoas* (E 403–6). A comment here would have added a nuance, perhaps, as such repetition provides much in Blake. In Ōe's own work also, there is a certain thematic and structural cyclicity within and between his chapters, as in his references to the ninth Night in particular. Such palimpsestic features have been emphasized in William Hamilton Reid (McCalman 1994: 35), or in a more general concept of *bricolage* applied to Blake's own work (Mee 1992: 4ff.) This might of course be applied to most literary texts in some form, and in Ōe's own work Asian traditions conglobe with French existentialism, and then specific writers like Blake, Yeats and Neruda; the patterning of his own return to Blake is significant, particularly, as I shall discuss later, when Ōe presents it as serendipitous and fortuitous.

Ōe shows a detailed first-hand knowledge of much of Blake's work, and mentions seminal critics like David Erdman (both *Prophet against Empire* and the *Concordance* [161]), Sir Geoffrey Keynes, Kathleen Raine and Mona Wilson as having contributed to his understanding. Ōe notes however that 'the mood of Blake's age has nothing in common with our own' (Ōe 1983; 2002: 162), and at issue today, far beyond the canonicity of these critics, are the ways in which Ōe's reception negotiates, consciously or not, with Blake's modulations of the textual; how, for example, he relates to the disruptions of narrative time, the literal and cognitive *unheimlich*, a floating, homeless mythopoeia in which the details *are* the myth. 'Given the nature of Blake's epic poetry, it might be said that anything less attentive than poring over the details is not reading it at all', he claims (Ōe 1983; 2002: 27). Yet how, in a transcultural reception, to instantiate these? J. Thomas Rimer has written that Satō and other *Taishō* figures (including Yanagi perhaps) were able to take 'advantage of any literary congruence' (Rimer 1993: 2) and it is this 'taking advantage', this creative interaction, which is worth foregrounding in Ōe also. While such syncretism may have been already formulated in Blake's own culture, sometimes it can be the wilful product of the vision of the fortuitous and coincidental. One might for example see in Garnet Terry's 'Hieroglyphic Print of Daniel's Great Image' (Plate 3 in Mee 1992) resemblances to a Buddha figure, but these are presumably accidental, West (Babylon) rather than East Asian. In a similar vein, David Weir speculates about correspondences between details in Blake's work and illustrations in the works of writers on Hindu antiquities, such as Thomas Maurice and Edward Moor, leaving some intriguing possibilities but establishing what he admits are at best but 'tenuous link[s]' (Weir 2003: 59, 74).

Ōe states the reasons for his interest in Blake in one succinct paragraph:

> What attracts me to Blake so powerfully is that he not only formulates his own uniquely mythological world based on a tradition that extends from Christianity to esoteric mysticism, he also empowers this mythology to develop on its own by infusing it with energy from his life and times. And the motion he achieves in this way allows him to drive his mythological world through and beyond his motifs of contemporary politics and international relations to a place beyond time. (Ōe 1983; 2002: 166)

For Ōe, then, 'infusion' of the historical and the living is the key; Blake absorbs, refocuses and projects, and while the last words in the quotation may betoken the mere abstract, the dialectical force of the reception is clear. The dialectic, then, acts as a caution against the tendency, in Los's raging words from Chapter 2 of *Jerusalem*, to 'Generaliz[e] Art & Science till Art & Science is lost' (38: 54; E 185), or – to quote from Chapter 4 – to 'accumulate Particulars' only to 'take the aggregate' (91: 26–7; E 251). Acts of juxtaposition such as Ōe's here imply a shared process and ground, a common 'Poetic Genius', which is expressed through a particular ideology and predisposition, a focusing of cultural mediation in 'Each Nations different reception of the Poetic Genius' ('All Religions are One' [E 1]) through which 'Ideas cannot be Given but in their minutely Appropriate Words' (*Public Address* [E 576]).

Ōe then positions his reception in an implied negotiation with patterns of reception in his own context, as above prefigured in Satō and Yanagi, and more widely in a Buddhist context, pertinent here as a point of his contention with and differentiation from Blake. Comparable negotiations are inherent in Blake's own problematic generic relation to his own sources, particularly in regard to what Ōe perceives in the Nobel Prize speech as 'ambiguous' cultural and geopolitical placement (Ōe 1995: 117), in which the taking and examining a position are somewhat akin to what Harold Bloom might term 'revisionary ratios', which express key relations between Blake and the Japanese writers here considered (Bloom 1973: 14–16). While these 'ratios' are implicit in a critical assessment of the strength of Ōe's reading, their rationalist assumptions, even if involuntary, have of course negative connotations, not least of course in Blake (e.g. in *Jerusalem* 74: 11; E 229 and *Milton* 32: 35 E 132).

Chapter 5 of *Rouse Up* is entitled 'The Soul Descends as a Falling Star, to the Bone at My Heel', and is thus borrowed from *Milton*, Plate 15 (E 110) when the poet enters Blake's left foot, and which is itself an intimation of that later incident in the poem when Los 'enter[s] into [Blake's] soul' (22: 13; E 117). Here, from within Blake, we might regard the manner of Ōe's approach to the poet within his own cultural contexts. Blake sublates his own perception, and in the later incident becomes 'posses'd' of Los' terrors, arising 'in fury & strength' and causing what we might now call a rift in space–time, an awe-ful kind of channelling (22: 14; E 117). Such a moment of sublation, in Bloom's term, is both precursor to and attendant with creative work, an expansion of the receiver through submission to a tradition of power and significance, which is cardinal in Asian aesthetics, and certain specific nuances in which Ōe's reception is prefigured in Yanagi's practice. In the 'Way of Craftsmanship' piece, it is declared that 'even in one single piece of good work, one finds expounded in material form the commandment to refrain from attaching oneself to the ego' (Yanagi 1989: 215); Yanagi goes on to talk of Zen 'no-thought', but could also perhaps have mentioned Zhuang Zhi's 'butterfly dreamer' and of course Blake here. 'One finally feels real self-affirmation in the abandonment of self', he writes in the 'Responsibility of the Craftsman', to which the epigraph comes from Section 18 of the *Tao-te-Ching*, a passage which (and especially Section 19) in turn might also well be from somewhere in Blake:

> When the Great Reason [the 'Way': *da dao*] is obliterated,
> We have benevolence and justice. (Yanagi 1989: 223, 216)

(I am tempted to put quotation marks around the two, justifiably termed 'abstract', nouns in the second line, or to add 'a pretence of', as in the 'pretence of Liberty / To destroy Liberty' [*Jerusalem* pl. 38 [43]: 35–36 E 185]).

Yet of course sublation is only part of a wider strategy of creation, the second tactic being that of creative discontinuity, Bloom's *kenosis* or emptying, or Blake's 'true Style of Art . . . Art of Invention not of Imitation' (*Public Address*; E 580). In the first sentence of *Rouse Up*, Ōe suggests that he takes books he has been reading with him on journeys to provide 'presence and emotional balance' (Ōe 1983; 2002: 1), that is to incorporate their vision into his own. He then continues the novel with the 'swerve' to Blake from reading Malcolm Lowry, especially the posthumous novella *Forest Path to the Spring* (ibid: 3). It would not of course be difficult to trace Blakean analogies to Lowry, although these are not forthcoming in Ōe. The prefatory 'To the Public' in *Jerusalem* (E 145–6) is an intimately comparable, if not directly source, text and the lines Ōe does quote, beginning 'I, being full of sin, cannot escape false concepts' are almost an – again albeit unwitting – paraphrase of Blake's 'I am perhaps the most sinful of men! . . . We who dwell on Earth can do nothing of ourselves' there (E 145). That these are both partly conventional statements, traditional in these contexts, should not detract from Ōe's negotiation with them here, particularly since Lowry was – as one should perhaps expect – at least generally familiar with Blake's work.[3]

While, early on in *Rouse Up*, Ōe makes a rather disingenuous claim that he has 'made a practice of finding [his] way along the stepping stones of what [he is] able to understand unaided' (Ōe 1983; 2002: 29), and in one paragraph later on he can assert that in the 'forest' of Blake's symbolism he has 'only [an] amateur, self-taught understanding as a guide' (Dantean echoes here might be pertinent), he can also later assert that 'Blake may enable [him] to construct a model for living [his] own life' (ibid: 124). The difficulties of constructing a model of that of which one has only a limited understanding are here of course inherent, but are inevitable.

Here Ōe fashions the antimonies both within Blake criticism and between Blake and himself in familiar, yet specific, terms. In *Rouse Up*, the narrator claims that 'It is extraordinary how the grotesquely odd and the familiar can reside together in Blake's invention' (ibid: 121). Such sentiments, of course, are not new in Blake reception: Thomas Frognall Dibdin reported in 1816 that 'the sublime and the grotesque seemed, somehow or the other, to be for ever amalgamated in [Blake's] imagination' (Bentley 2004a: 326–7). And yet while Dibdin gives an early – and unfortunately adhesive – labelling of the intractable otherness in Blake, his departure from the diurnal and commonplace, Ōe takes up this label's critical other and complement, his relation to the personal and the familial; and this WRIT LARGE. Kiyoshi Ando notes that Ōe once mentioned that he had written *Rouse Up* with 'an edition of Blake at one side of him, and his own life with his handicapped son' at the other (Ando 1991: 19). The passage about Milton entering Blake's foot is placed as a preface to a discussion of Eeyore's 'unreasoning love for, or at least extraordinary interest in, his father's feet' (Ōe 1983; 2002: 122). He sees such an interest as a point of mediation to help his afflicted son engage more with his world, but cannot be certain that Eeyore's intentions conform to his explanations of them, as he self-consciously points out; thus, as with all mediation or 'channelling' (the word the narrator uses for this relation [ibid: 123]), both the purposes of the participants, and the contrastive but interdependent relations of periphery and centre, of target and source, are to be gauged patiently and minutely.

Both *A Personal Matter* and *Rouse Up* involve the redemption of the lost father confronted with an intellectually disabled first-born child, and are based on the experiences with him of the novelist who, in *Matter*, is masked as 'Bird', using the *kanji* for the *CHO/tori* creature, but with a *furigana* (*katakana*) pronunciation to make it sound like the English 'Bard' (*bādo*). Both texts revolve around the power of the imagination to transfigure reality: in *Rouse Up*, the son is at one point thought to suffer additionally from epileptic seizures; one might recall how for example Dostoevsky had conceived of his own condition as an enabling device, and how he had woven it into his own writing. Faced by such an event, Bird considers letting the child die; in *Rouse Up*, the narrator records how Professor W[atanabe], his mentor, condoned such a view. Immediately, thematic correspondences to Blake's work surface, and indeed Bird's lover Himiko, who has written a thesis on Blake, utters a phrase perhaps famous enough to be inevitable in this context: 'Sooner murder an infant in its cradle than nurse unacted desires'; since the sentence is in the original English in the novel, one must turn the page to accommodate the direction of the printing (Ōe 1964; 1969: 68), an act which of course has its significance to the whole enterprise of quoting Blake to justify one's own conduct: one sees it awry. It would be tempting then – not least sometimes by the novelist himself – to view Ōe's relation to Blake here on the thematic or analogical level, that is to relate passages like these to such short lyrics as 'Infant Joy' and 'On Another's Sorrow' on the one hand (the latter partly quoted in 1983; 2002: 26), and 'Infant Sorrow' (quoted in 1983; 2002: 40) and 'To Tirzah' on the other, since what is of course in question is what in nature is a 'spiritual body'. Reading the passage about the narrator's 'mystical reverie' (Ōe 1983; 2002: 49), which revolves around the issues of how the experiences which the father had fortunately but narrowly escaped could be visited on the child (the father's head wound not leading to serious physical consequences which then appear in the son's congenital problem), one might think of a visual correspondence, for example with the frontispiece to *Experience*. There is in fact a photograph in the *Ōe Kenzaburo Album* which has Ōe and Hikari in this pose, also used for the frontispiece to Ōe's novel of 1995 (*Ōi naru hi ni; On the Great Day*), the third part of the *moeagaru midori no ki* (*Green Tree in Flames*) trilogy.

Yet all these connections, whether verbal or visual, would be but generalizing correspondences, synthetic levellings, the reduction of the unknown to the known by surface thematic analogy. 'As none by travelling over known lands can find out the unknown. So from already acquired knowledge Man could not acquire more', to quote the Fourth Principle of *All Religions are One* (E 1). A creative translation, or a repositioning such as Ōe's, then, both recomposes and works in defiance of those tendencies through which 'Men are hired to Run down Men of Genius under the Mask of Translators' as Blake writes in his annotations to Henry Boyd's *Historical Notes* on Dante (E 634). Ōe restates this case in a 1986 speech at Duke University when he claims that mere 'transplanting and translating new Western concepts into Japanese' is often mistakenly itself taken as a sign of intellectual effort (Ōe 1995: 87). In the act of 'transplanting' Blake's works into Japanese, it might not be inappropriate to claim the 'prophetic books' as symbolic narratives, with analogies if not specific conceptual foundation in many an East Asian extended novel (*Genji, The Red Chamber, Journey to the West*). A fourfold, exegetical or at least layered reading is however necessary to position the prophetic, a technique not exclusive to scriptural texts and, of course, in its own way culture-specific. Not only the availability of texts, linguistic ability but also specific procedures of adaptation and use serve to differentiate one plausible spiritual reading from another, or a spiritual from a secular.

The possibilities for such intercultural nuance prompt consideration of not only contraries in Blake, but also on other contexts where his appropriation of Welsh or kabbalistic writings is considered (Taylor 2004: 83–5). Equivalences of attribute, place and figure are often illusory, as for example with regard to those of self and fate implied in Japanese *shizen* (nature, literally perhaps 'self-concord'): their intersections with the historical, and not only the topographic, make each distinctive. Transformation, as a main theme in Blake's work from the geomorphological and toponymical to the cognitive and spiritual, has many resonances in Asian aesthetic and traditions literary, historical and spiritual. Such congruences – as for example between West Asian mysticism or East Asian Zen – yield productive areas for comparative approaches. One might consider certain resonances in Blake's prophetic books, for example, with passages in the *Nihon shoki/Nihongi* which describe the reed-shoot that becomes a God that gives rise to an eternal land-substance (*Kuni-toko-tachi no Mikoto* [Ashton 1896: 3]) or with the story of the island-children of the chthonic siblings/parents Izanagi and Izanami (Ashton 1896: 12). Both these mythic materials and Blake's own practices are able to accommodate various versions, even of course in Blake's case with the incorporation of the same passages in different works. Yet one is not here of course claiming influence; each is formed by and requires its own act of attention, and something similar could be said to delimit the speculation surrounding Blake's indebtedness to Welsh or kabbalistic works, as antecedence (of reading to production) alone does not prove influence, as acts of attention are implicit here also.

'The Mental Traveller' gives an insight into these reconfigurations, as it is not only a symbolic narrative of the transmission and regeneration of the mythic across cultures and times (as Raine notes with specific reference to lines 53–6 [Raine 1969; 2002: 316]), of reincarnation more generally, but also – if seen in the light of Blake's concern to find a purchaser for *The Four Zoas* (Magno and Erdman 1987: 13); his relations with Johnson, Hayley and so on – a presentation of persistent issues in Blake's own life. Yet this poem takes on an added, if merely analogical, significance here for it almost precisely describes the condition with which Ōe as father figure is confronted in the two novels. The closing stanzas about 'the frowning Babe' give a context not only for the violent Eeyore at the opening of *Rouse Up* (Ōe 1983; 2002: 6) but also, in the image of the 'Woman Old', for the narrator's mother who claims that *chi kara*, 'through the blood' (the family history), of Eeyore's mother the child will be helped where contemporary therapeutic methods alone may not. Ōe quotes extensively also from *The Four Zoas*, specifically from Nights the Fifth, Eighth and Ninth; the confidence expressed by the narrator's mother in an intersection of tradition and science, in the face of anguish, fear and grief, intimates the closing of Blake's long work, where 'ancient strength' 'form[s] the golden armour of science' and 'intellectual War' displaces 'the war of swords' and 'sweet Science' dispels 'dark Religions' (pl. 39: 8–10 E 407).

The limitation of an abstracted concept of the human body is a Blakean theme which Ōe addresses throughout his writings on the handicapped and those who must care for them. In an incident early on in *A Personal Matter*, for example, Bird has a fortuitous Blake encounter in which he describes a reproduction in Himiko's room: 'bizarre' (Ōe 1964; 1969: 43) he calls it ('*kimyō*' [ibid: 68]). The reproduction is of the watercolour 'Pestilence: Death of the First Born' (Butlin 1981: 193) of around 1805, and now in the Museum of Fine Arts, Boston. The narrator describes it thus: 'The creature's eyes and mouth were virulently grotesque. Grief, fear, astonishment, fatigue, loneliness – even a hint of laughter boiled limitlessly from its coal-black eyes and salamander mouth' (Ōe 1964; 1969: 43). Bird is especially acute in delineating possible traits of the plague figure here as he seems to have internalized the qualities of Blake's personification such that the adjectives used could easily respond to his own predicament. He is not, however, so forthcoming in 'rising up' to the occasion, although after claiming that he doesn't know the Bible well he does reveal enough knowledge to guess that the scene is from Exodus (ibid: 52); he is not however capable of that change of vision which would make of the afflicted sons the new (redeemed?) babies of Israel as is implied at the opening of the following chapter of Exodus. The plague is sent in order – as Exodus 12.31 has it – for the children of Israel to 'Rise up' and 'serve the Lord'. Bird remains in the fallen state, suppressing any affinity which actions like that of 'cradling infants' – an aspect of the picture which he himself describes – or references like Himiko's to 'oldest sons' might suggest. He is therefore unable to act on that which has been given him accidentally, as the watercolour, placed back into its Biblical context, depicts not only omen but hope. Himiko goes on to tell Bird how, as a child, she could have died, and relates this to what might be seen as a Nolan vision of parallel universes (Ōe 1964; 1969: 45). Engrossed however in her own self-promotion, Himiko here – perhaps too 'wrapd up / In [her] own [unexpressed] sorrow' (*The Four Zoas*: 70; E 347) – expresses too much the mystical and thus abstract for her response to penetrate the reality of Bird's own situation; it is too 'Spectral' as a consequence of 'the Reasoning Power / An Abstract objecting power, that Negatives every thing' (*Jerusalem*: 10: 13–15; E 153).

Yet a similar adjustment is necessary in order for Bird to see the infinite potential in any child, including his own. Bird here however represses such a vision only for it to surface later, as he dreams of a similar scaly man (Ōe 1964; 1969: 52), an intimation of his mind working on and over the significance of the reproduction. In Chapter 4 of *Rouse Up*, the narrator talks of a contrastive but thus related dream 'rooted in [his] memory' of 'Blake's painting, Glad Day', with its 'gorgeous young man' which he, creatively, 'call[s] Orc' (Ōe 1983; 2002: 93), then qualifying this with reference to the later 'Albion' description; all this is put into the context of his conversation with the graduate student Martha Crowley, including a reference to her petite, delicate stature and lengthy passages about one 'M' (presumably Mishima), whose image – albeit that, as the narrator says, he is short 'even for a Japanese' (ibid: 79–80) – is that of an equally 'gorgeous young man'. This in turn is superimposed onto a similarly imposing dream-image of his son. Again, the constructive swerve – Bloom's *clinamen* or 'poetic misprision' (Bloom 1973: 42) – is the basis for Ōe's transmission of Blake, as a Blakean figure or figuration is given to the varying aspects of Bird's speculations about the spiritual and the corporeal.

In a comparable manner, each chapter of *Rouse Up* oscillates around a Blake quotation, at times along seemingly serendipitous connections, at others more through synchronicity; the significance of the encounter, then, hangs in the balance. The time has to be right for the influence to work, both for Ōe's narrator and for our reading of his response. When the exposure to Blake is fortuitous, its effects are assessed only afterwards, as when he recalls his story 'The Day He Himself Shall Wipe My Tears Away', and realizes that the term '*ano hito*' (that man), translated as 'a certain party', referring to the father, and with significant Gothic boldface type to suggest '*Man* with a capital *M*', was a sign that he 'had been influenced by Blake's language' (Ōe 1983; 2002: 112). Of particular significance here was that passage in *The Four Zoas: Night the Eighth*, just after the 'Man should labour and sorrow' lines to which he refers throughout the text (around which he constructs a chapter, and which, he claims, he came across accidentally), which talks of how 'The Eternal Man is seen is heard is felt' (110: 27; E 385), as this refracts on his own more optimistic observations of the human.

Yet in Ōe's attention to the typeface (the bold in the quotation used in my previous paragraph) it is the visual, and particularly the calligraphy, which resonate with meaning, and this even if Ōe's Blake is from the Keynes Oxford edition rather than from illuminated editions. Similarly, *Rouse Up* comments on Blake in its very choice of title alone. I have said earlier that this title is borrowed from the famous lines in the Preface to *Milton*: 'Rouze up O Young Men of the New Age! set your foreheads against the ignorant Hirelings! . . . We do not want either Greek or Roman Models if we are but just and true to our own Imaginations' (E 95). Yet this is not altogether so, since the title to which I refer is of course a back translation from the Japanese: *atarashii hito yo mezameyo*. Literally, this would mean 'new man, arouse [yourself]', with the implication that the 'man' is a reference to the narrator's son, who does in fact come into puberty during the course of the novel; a time when self-assertion has particular implications for the handicapped. The narrator says that the son has 'arrived at that age' when his pet-name Eeyore is to be replaced by his given name, Hikari, and this – since this is in fact the name of Ōe's own son – breaks down the divisions of fiction and actuality. Indeed, the informal, even brusque, command form '*mezameyo*' ('arouse [yourself]') would be appropriate for a father addressing a child, and thus the back translation into the *Milton* line does not address the issues of making such an address in the two statements, with Blake's admonition more that of an elder campaigner than of a paternal figure, as is Ōe's. The father's perception is determinant, not least visually in the choice of *okurigana* and *kanji* Ōe uses here in *mezameyo*, which include not only the radical for *eye* (*me*) but also the non-general use character for *stop* which Henshall describes as originating in the form for an eye on twisted legs, indicating 'a person turning around and staring' (Ōe 1983; 2002: 77). While some of Henshall's reconstructions are perhaps etymologically fanciful, the source and target of memory, their interpretative qualities are of the essence here, as what we *make* of the signs is the issue. Ōe does not use the two *kanji* which are more usual for the verb *mezameru*, that is *me* itself and then *za* which includes an original designation of 'hands which see' (*learning* and *KAN/mi* to see).

An opportunity should however not be lost here to thicken the description by contrasting Ōe's construction of his title with the premises of the key 'Man should Labour & sorrow & learn & forget & return' passage. The construction implies perception; Blake's passage action. While the original 'rouze up' line therefore combines new awakening sight with vigorous action, with the accent on the latter (and here the Exodus 'rising' is worth recalling), the Japanese specifies more the former, and therefore is set against words like *okiru/okosu*, related in meaning but with their accent on physical movement (the *ashi* [leg] *kanji*). Again, Ōe has creatively adapted the source to fit his context, grafting and supplanting root meanings, and thus transforming productively the discrimination of linguistic origins and their contemporary use. In his translation of 'innocence', similarly (e.g. Ōe 1983; 2002: 37), Ōe uses the non-*jōyō kanji* for *muku* ('not dirty'), but with the *furigana* reading *inosensu* (innocence) which would, through the use of *katakana*, signal the foreignness of the word in its wavering placement literally between two texts. Thus in both cases he creatively adapts his translations to work in the margins of the Japanese, not only giving Blake's term his own nuance (that is, choosing not to translate connotations of candour, frankness, etc.) but also embracing a shared intellectual horizon with his audience.

In assessing the context, then, the specific articulation is foregrounded, both in Ōe's reading of Blake and (I hope) my own discussion of it; the importance of such *specifics* is the *general* point to be made in this chapter. Ōe mentions reading Kathleen Raine's *Blake and Tradition* and *Blake and the New Age*, and there is one passage in particular from the former book which should be incorporated here: 'The most enduring and universal symbols have evolved and have survived by reason of their natural fitness' (Raine 1969; 2002: I: 5); she then goes on to criticize 'pseudo-symbolism' in Swedenborg and Blake. Such natural selection is significant in a transcultural context as well, so long as – to quote 'The Mental Traveller' again – 'some other take [it] in' (E 485). While Ōe *thinks* that his reception of Blake is fortuitous, one suspects that his memory was enhanced by a text, in one case Mona Wilson's biography, which he mentions reading (Ōe 1983; 2002: 108); this indeed quotes from and discusses – as might well be expected – at some length the 'Man should Labour & sorrow' passage (Wilson 1927; 1971: 139) which later is of such moment for Ōe. Just as Satō's narrator had been attracted by the *name* rose (as for Coleridge, names become things), Ōe here notes that Wilson's was 'a name [he] had been hearing for some time'. Yet how one sees the rose as an individual is an issue, just as is the particular manner of appropriating the critical material into one's own understanding of a text.

One such appropriation can be noted in how Ōe, if much later, reflects on both his own position and that of his country, in relation both to its own imperialist legacy with regard to Korea and the Pacific, and to the ways in which, in a humorous passage from the 1986 Duke University talk to which I have alluded earlier, young Japanese scholars fall to the fashions of theory (Ōe 1995: 86), passing over one before it has been assimilated (Blake and Milton/Los). Here, as with Blake, 'contraries are positives' (reversed writing 'argument' in the illuminated part of the first plate of Book the Second of *Milton* [E 129]). If 'the present nation of Japan and its people cannot but be ambivalent', as Ōe claims in his Nobel Prize speech on the country's 'ambiguity' (Ōe 1995: 118), this is productive, as artists relate to and grapple with its complexities and creatively adapt the legacies of imperialism abruptly curtailed, of hyperdrive modernization from the 1930s to the 1990s, and then the – some would say, inevitable – stagflation at the end of this period. Towards the end of this speech, Ōe claims that he not only distances himself from the characteristically Japanese forms of metropolitan consumerism but also wants to reach out as a figure from an Asia seen not as 'a new economic power' but as 'marked by everlasting poverty and a tumultuous fertility', and this in 'positive, concrete terms' (Ōe 1995: 125). To see dearth and abundance, to be positive about the one and negative about the other, is to think dialectically about one's position, that is to think in terms of contraries.

In his seminal 1830 appraisal of Blake, Allan Cunningham claims that 'It would, perhaps, have been better for his fame had he connected . . . more with the superstitious beliefs of his country' as 'their popular character would perhaps have kept him within the bounds of traditionary [*sic*] belief, and the sea of his imagination would have had a shore' (from Bentley's selection of 'Early Essays'; 1969: 489). While this view is of course exaggerated (Essick's estimation that Blake had produced 'more than 135' 'pictorial responses to the most important text in his cultural heritage' (that is, of course, the Bible) militating against it [Essick 1989: 6]), the incorporation of *what has been taken for* pseudo-symbolism and abstractionism, against which Blake himself fulminates (and which Raine restates), give credit to Cunningham's argument, and a reception such as Ōe's, at the other end of the Eurasian landmass, on another island that is often a mirror, a refraction of, or – at least for Blake (but guided of course by geophysical reality) – a limit, in relation to Blake's own, would demonstrate that his work – and particularly *The Four Zoas* – continues to shake against the boundaries of its reception. Ōe gives a restrained, at times even self-conscious, introspective and probing response to Blake, a personal – that is, a non-academic – one, which makes use of the popular ecstatic Blake as in the iconography of almost half a century ago. In its implications for his perception of his son, and thus of all marginalized individuals, he probes once more the implications for the 'Divine Humanity', and does so at a time when, in some senses, this Blake has been displaced and again marginalized by readers who – to quote from Blake's letter of *c.* late June 1806 to the Editor of the *Monthly Magazine* – have been 'connoisseured out [of their] senses' (E 768): while searching for the appropriate, timely and focused (*to kairon*), we inhibit the integral prolific.

Given not only the interest shown in Blake by the post-war generation of anglophonic youth and by the *Taishō* artists and writers in Japan itself, but also the affinities (but the differences are more compelling) between some of Blake's work and Buddhist texts including the *Hwa Yen/Kegonkyo* (*Avatamsaka*) *Sutra* or *Flower Ornament Scripture* (which includes of course the dust-motes/world image which is easily related to the first line of 'Auguries of Innocence' [*Flower Ornament Scripture*: 1993: 891–904]), it is not surprising then that a young Japanese writer, coming of age in the 1950s, with an interest beginning in and expanding out of nineteenth-century Europe (French Symbolism in particular), would eventually encounter Blake, and would incorporate personal meanings into his own work, more impressionistic than critical, but nonetheless insightful in their new context. In the William Blake Trust/Princeton University Press *Milton*, the editors write that 'almost all criticism of *Milton* [and one might add, of the longer prophetic books also] has been written by scholars for scholars' (Blake 1983: 9); there was a time – many of us will remember it well – of intimations of a much wider readership, as Essick notes elsewhere (Essick 1989: 224), and Mark Lussier in 'Resisting Critical Erasure, or Blake Beyond Postmodernity',[4] has demonstrated that Blake is well entrenched still at the beginning of the new millennium in popular iconography and advertising; 'no real Style of Colouring ever appears / But advertising in the News Papers' indeed (E 511).

While such uses arise in the domain of sheer semiotic arbitrariness,[5] their range implies at least a possibility that Blake's signs are rooted enough to emanate so prolifically, and therefore what Essick calls 'the pursuit of the motivated sign' (Essick 1989: 28 ff.) is in itself meaningful, even if it might yield few results. Ōe places one of Blake's engravings, perhaps his most used in the last half-century – *Albion Rose/Glad Day* – on both the cover of *Rouse Up* and on the inside cover of the novel *Ōi naru hi ni (On the Great Day)*, although one suspects mostly for the positive associations rather than those implied by the reference to 'the dance of Eternal Death' on the inscription (this too of course has its positive side, its contrary, as in Jesus's words to Albion [*Jerusalem* 96: 23–8; E 256]). The repositioning, creative appropriation continues, the response to that which is fundamental in Blake, however we explicate this (through our own appropriations of Marx, Jung, Campbell, ontology, wisdom literature, etc.). And, then, in Japan too.

## Notes

1   The title page however gives 1728; the *imprimatur* is 1727.

2   Blake almost certainly helped contribute some plates for Bryant's *New System, or An Analysis of Ancient Mythology* (1774; 2nd edn 1775–6), and of course much has been written about the influence and the debt. Blake refers to Bryant explicitly in the 1809 *Descriptive Catalogue* (E 543) and perhaps also implicitly there when he claims to have been 'taken in vision into the ancient republics, monarchies, and patriarchates of Asia' and many other places and times (E 531); many of the places named could come from Bryant. While Blake could have encountered Kaempfer in Bryant (for example, Plate 2 in the second volume), another early European commentator (more a collator) on Japan, Bernhardus Varenius, might have given a different nuance to the point about Asian 'ancient republics': 'Only in Europe,' contends Varenius, 'are political systems other than monarchy to be found'; 'in Asia', the systems 'can be called only monarchies' (*Descriptio Regni Iaponiae* [1649]: 28 [my translation from a 1974 German edition]). The nature and significance of Blake's reception of Bryant are discussed, among others, by Keynes (1949; 1971: 27–30), Mee (1992: 121; 132–3), Matthews (1998) and Essick (1989: 23–4).

3   In a 1946 letter, for example, he parodies 'The Little Vagabond': 'In Canada . . . / The churches and the taverns are both cold' (Lowry 1995: 625; here Thompson's discussion of antinomian meetings [1993: 57ff.] might be recalled, and particularly the William Hurd quotation there about pub meetings [ibid: 58]).

4   I am grateful for the helpful comments on the initial draft of this chapter by Masashi Suzuki and Steve Clark, who informed me that there is a revised version of Lussier's essay

in a forthcoming book; Steve Clark and Jason Whittaker (eds), *Blake, Modernity and Popular Culture* (Basingstoke: Palgrave Macmillan, 2006/7).

5   In his annual 'Checklists' for 2003 and 2004, Bentley habitually notes in passing the many emanations of a contemporary interest in Blake, ranging from 'audio books' to 'T-shirts, tattoos' and e-mail, thus both recording the pleonastic plethora of such *materia disjecta* and intimating his own disdain (Bentley 2004b: 4; 2005: 8–9).

# 20 Nebuchadnezzar's Sublime Torments: William Blake, Arthur Boyd and the East

Peter Otto

The historical Nebuchadnezzar ruled Babylonia for 43 years, from 605 to 562 BC. For those at the centre of Nebuchadnezzar's empire, this was a period of unprecedented power and prosperity, exemplified by the creation of Babylon's Hanging Gardens, judged one of the seven wonders of the ancient world, and by the transformation of Babylon itself into a city more splendid, according to Herodotus, than any other in the known world.[1] Illustrating Bacon's view that 'whatsoever is somewhere gotten is somewhere lost',[2] for those on the margins of that empire this was a time of catastrophe, marked for the Jewish people by the destruction of Jerusalem and Judea, the ruin of the Temple of Solomon, and the Babylonian exile.

In the biblical account, Nebuchadnezzar's pre-eminence was broken by seven years of mental illness, of lycanthropy, which relegated him to the margins of his empire. According to the prophet Daniel, when Nebuchadnezzar was at the height of his power, and it seemed that Babylon had been built 'by the might of [his] power, and for the honour of [his] majesty' alone, he heard 'a voice from heaven' warning that he would be compelled to dwell 'with the beasts of the field . . . The same hour', Daniel continues, Nebuchadnezzar 'was driven from men, and did eat grass as oxen, and his body was wet with the dew of heaven, till his hairs were grown like eagle's feathers, and his nails like birds' claws' (Dan. 4.29–33).

Nebuchadnezzar's madness was not in itself a common subject of medieval or renaissance art, perhaps because Christian tradition gave it no 'precise typological meaning'.[3] Attention focused instead on Nebuchadnezzar as regal oppressor, a prime example of those who deserve punishment by God. Similarly, in eighteenth-century England, before George III's bout of 'actual madness in 1788–9, allusions to Nebuchadnezzar stress his actions as a tyrant and his appropriateness as an object of divine retribution'.[4] George's illness, however, suggested a much closer, more causal link between despotism and madness, while making more commonplace the link between George and Nebuchadnezzar, the aristocracy and disorderly 'oriental' cultures.

For radical writers George was, like Nebuchadnezzar, a tyrant whose despotism and idleness, being inimical to the rule of enlightened reason, had driven him mad. This association was strengthened, as Mee notes, by 'the Richard Brothers controversy of 1794–5', which provided 'an interpretation of biblical prophecy that identified Babylon with London and George III with the King of Babylon'.[5] Inverting radical rhetoric, conservatives argued it was the body politic that had fallen prey to an eastern disease, to the point where its head was threatened. The anonymous author of *A Word of Admonition to the Right Hon. William Pitt*, for example, wrote of acts that would 'let loose horror in our streets, when an army of *Brotherites*, like Mahometans of old', would rise up to crown their prophet. He prayed earnestly that 'the People of Great Britain' would be saved from

> the innumerable herd of villains, the MARATS, the ROBESPIERRES, and the MAHOMETS, who would spill their blood, drain their treasures, and subject them to the most gross slavery, that of the mind, beneath the debasing yoke of Fraud and Superstition.[6]

It is now French revolutionaries, in league with the founder of Islam, who enslave the body and the body politic, threaten legitimate authority and so portend a descent into madness. Despite these differences, radicals and conservatives imagine the East as a realm of bodies disordered by the ravages of illegitimate power and, as such, the other against which the ordered bodies of the West must defend themselves.

These controversies and this rhetoric provide the backdrop for Blake's representations of Nebuchadnezzar, which develop over the course of nearly ten years from the rough drawings on Pages 44 and 48 of his Notebook to the more elaborate designs of Plate b11 of *There is no Natural Religion* (1789), Plate 24 of *The Marriage of Heaven and Hell* (1789), the colour print of Nebuchadnezzar (1795), and Page 299 of Blake's watercolour illustrations to Young's *Night Thoughts* (1795–97). In these designs, Nebuchadnezzar is used to critique conservative <u>and</u> radical attempts to transcend the dangerous, purportedly Eastern, realm of the body. Further complicating Blake's representations of Nebuchadnezzar, in a letter written in 1804 Blake's comparison of himself with the Assyrian king recalls the traditional yet nevertheless surprising identification of Nebuchadnezzar as a prophet.[7]

Blake's multifaceted treatment of Nebuchadnezzar is the iconographic starting-point for more than 70 Nebuchadnezzar designs produced between 1966 and 1972 by Arthur Boyd (1920–99), one of the greatest Australian painters of the twentieth century. Blake's work exerts a strong influence on Boyd's *oeuvre* as a whole, no doubt in part owing to his early exposure to the remarkable Blake collection in the National Gallery of Victoria. Boyd notes, however, that his interest in Blake's representations of Nebuchadnezzar was fuelled by politics, more specifically the use of self-immolation as a protest against the Vietnam War.[8] It is at first surprising, therefore, that Nebuchadnezzar provides the template for later designs by Boyd that explore the plight of the artist, possessed by a fantasy that draws him apart from, and yet ensures he is tormented by, the material forces of the world and physical desires of the body.

In the pages that follow, I will focus my remarks on Blake's earliest representations of Nebuchadnezzar, and on designs drawn from *Nebuchadnezzar*, a volume published in 1972 by Boyd and T. S. R. Boase. I will argue that, for Blake and Boyd, Nebuchadnezzar's sublime torments mark the collapse of the division between body and mind that in Western, colonial discourses is often used to divide East from West. I conclude by suggesting that, albeit with somewhat different inflections and in radically different contexts, for Blake and Boyd this collapse opens the possibility of an art that would undo the opposition between mind and body, Europe and what it tropes as its other.

## 1 Blake's Nebuchadnezzar

On Page 44 of Blake's Notebook, Nebuchadnezzar is contained by a roughly-drawn rectangular frame that seems to float on a page empty apart from three lines of prose (Figure 20.1). The Assyrian king is depicted crawling towards the right of the page, with unkempt hair, and a beard so long it trails on the ground beneath him. His body is framed by what might be the leaning trunks of two huge, oddly featureless trees that form an upside-down 'V' or, alternatively, two large triangles, the smaller contained by the larger. The apex of the smaller triangle can be seen immediately above Nebuchadnezzar; the apex of the larger, the drawing implies, lies unseen above the upper border of the design. The triangles recall the shape of the ziggurats built by Nebuchadnezzar and the hierarchical structure of both his own kingdom and the one to which he is now subjected. They anticipate Blake's claim that 'The gods of Greece & Egypt were Mathematical Diagrams' (E 274). The king who believed he was at the apex of his empire now finds himself at its base, subject to a power able to shape him and his empire as it pleases.

Rather than suggesting only that Nebuchadnezzar is a prime example of those who deserve punishment by God, the design develops a striking set of relations between the triangular forms that enclose Nebuchadnezzar and his own debased human form. For example, lines defining Nebuchadnezzar's right foot also outline the base and complete the sides of the trunk that leans to the right of the page. The horizontal line that connects the toes of Nebuchadnezzar's right foot, his knees, and the palms of his hands, defines the base of the larger triangle. The base and lower half of the smaller triangle are also defined by Nebuchadnezzar's body. At the same time, his torso divides the smaller triangle into two, creating the impression both that he carries a third triangle on his back and that his torso, legs and arms form the base that supports the upper portion of the triangle. (This element is echoed by the design on Page 48 of the Notebook, in which Nebuchadnezzar, wearing a crown of leaves, appears to be carrying on his back a triangle that towers above him.) Nebuchadnezzar's body, whether considered as the body politic or his own body of flesh, provides the base that supports the structures of empire.

Nebuchadnezzar's body is able to play this role only to the extent that his human form becomes congruent with what it supports. Evidently, this process is well advanced: his corporeal body has been reduced almost to a loose assemblage of horizontal, vertical and diagonal lines that define a panoply of triangles: the upper and lower portions of his right and of his left leg, his torso and arms, torso and legs, torso and beard, his two arms, and so on, all form triangles which seem to float in an atemporal world, beyond the fleshly existence that nevertheless defines and so supports them.

We can therefore say that, on Page 44 of the Notebook, the bestial emerges as the body assumes the abstract forms demanded by empire. Just as importantly, the design suggests that the order of empire and the disorder of the subjugated body are parts of a single system: the latter provides the matrix which supports and within which one is able to see the purportedly unchanging contours of the

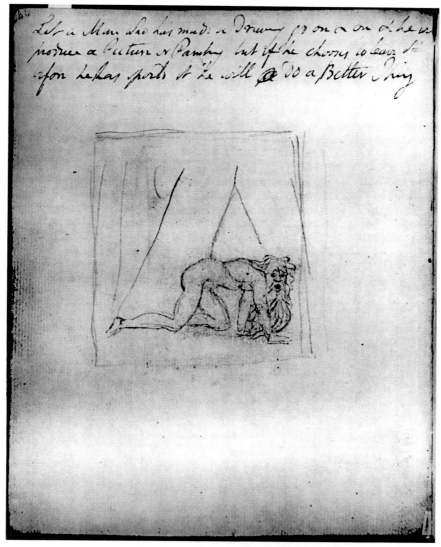

**Figure 20.1** William Blake, *The Notebook of William Blake* (the Rossetti Manuscript) (*c.* 1787–1818), p. 44. (Reproduced by permission of the British Library.)

former. In this system, order produces and itself depends on disorder. It is, therefore, inherently unstable. As order increases, so too does disorder, until the body, unable to support what rests upon it, threatens the whole, and in so doing is thrust from the background to the foreground. This is the moment depicted in Blake's design, when Nebuchadnezzar's kingdom is engulfed by the material, fleshly world that supports it.

These exchanges between the ordered forms of empire and the disordered bodies on which it rests might seem at first to have little to do with the world of enlightened reason, yet on Plate b11 of *There is no Natural Religion* reason itself appears as Nebuchadnezzar (Figure 20.2). In this design, Nebuchadnezzar is contained by a small, egg-shaped space defined by the trunk and outstretched lower branch of a large tree, and by lines drawn behind and in front of him. Resting on his knees, and holding his upper body parallel to the ground, Nebuchadnezzar looks intently at a triangle he has discovered in, or drawn on, the dust. His right hand holds a second triangle which shares a base with and mirrors the first, creating the impression that the former is being drawn up or folded out from the latter.

Nebuchadnezzar is here Locke's reason, closed within the 'Closet' of the mind (Locke 1975: 163), while the triangle is one of the simple ideas (inscribed by the senses on the blank slate of the mind) that in Locke's system provide the primary building blocks of knowledge. Arguably, the same figure can also be seen as Newton, depicted in the colour print from 1795 as engaged in an analogous extraction of discrete, disembodied form from the undivided flux of existence. In both cases, rational knowledge is founded on a radical reduction of existence.

One might hope that the abstract could be redeemed if it were returned to the world of the flesh but, as I have argued, in Blake's Nebuchadnezzar designs these

**Figure 20.2** William Blake, *There is no Natural Religion*, Copy L, Plate 10. (Reproduced by permission of the Pierpont Morgan Library.)

realms are bound to the same system (there is no 'innocent' body to which one might return). In the design we are considering, Nebuchadnezzar's body has been reduced almost to a two-dimensional grid, formed by the vertical lines of his left arm and upper right leg and the horizontal lines of his torso and lower right leg. His two arms, head and right arm, torso and right arm, and so on, all form triangles, ghostly doubles of the figure he grasps with his right hand. Nebuchadnezzar is here Narcissus, seen in the process of becoming the image he desires.

In the famous Question 30 of the *Opticks*, Newton suggests that even 'gross Bodies and Light' are 'convertible into one another', and 'Bodies receive much of their Activity from the Particles of Light which enter their Composition'. Such exchanges and transformations, he continues, are 'very conformable to the Course of Nature, which seems delighted with Transmutations'.[9] Clearly, Nebuchadnezzar hopes to transmute heavy bodies of flesh into light, not the reverse. Plate b11 suggests, however, that these opposites are part of a single system: the transformation of flesh into spirit brings the body to the edge of dissolution, and so leads inevitably to the collapse of lighter forms back into the body that they briefly seemed to have risen above. Alone in a wilderness, shrouded by an overhanging tree, Nebuchadnezzar's lower limbs have already been engulfed by the dark, chaotic world he had hoped to transcend. However, as Blake suggests in his major prophecies, the collapse this portends is likely to spark only a still more intense attempt to transcend the disorder of the flesh: sublimation and desublimation are locked in an eternal cycle.[10]

## 2  Boyd's Nebuchadnezzar

In *Nebuchadnezzar*, reproductions of 34 paintings and 18 drawings by Boyd are arranged in a visual narrative that begins with Nebuchadnezzar's fall from the sublime apex of his power into a chaotic world. The world (and mental state) he enters is explored in remarkable detail, including, as the sequence nears its conclusion, the possibility it contains of escaping the destructive oscillation between transcendence and fall, sublimation and desublimation.

In the first phase of this visual narrative, Nebuchadnezzar attempts to turn the temporal into the eternal, to make his kingdom independent of the gross bodies that sustain it. In the third design, for example, 'Nebuchadnezzar's dream of the tree', Nebuchadnezzar lies on his back amidst an arid landscape (Figure 20.3). The lines formed by his recumbent body and by the horizon above him divide the canvas into three rectangular planes. The empty, brown earth below Nebuchadnezzar's body finds its mirror opposite in the equally empty, mauve sky above the horizon.

These very different realms are joined by a large tree that reaches up from the king's belly and loins to touch, with its highest branches, the line dividing the sky from the earth. The tree is, of course, a reference to the one seen in Nebuchadnezzar's dream, interpreted by Daniel as an allegory of Nebuchadnezzar's kingdom, which stood 'in the midst of the earth' and reached 'unto heaven'. The trunk of the tree recalls the pyramidal shapes of Nebuchadnezzar's ziggurats, while the tree recalls his hanging gardens, held aloft by stepped banks of earth. The tree, of course, also suggests Nebuchadnezzar's phallus, an organ whose

**Figure 20.3** Arthur Boyd, 'Nebuchadnezzar's dream of the tree' (1969). Oil on canvas. (The Arthur Boyd Gift. National Gallery of Australia, Canberra. Arthur Boyd's work reproduced with the permission of the Bundanon Trust.)

periodic rise above the body makes it, for Blake and Boyd, an apt symbol of a religion of transcendence.[11]

At the same time, however, it is important to note that Nebuchadnezzar is white and that his dreaming takes place in a distinctly Australian landscape. He is a colonial pioneer, dreaming the dream common in much early Australian literature, namely that the disorderly body of that continent might be transformed into a Garden of Eden, returning European civilization to its innocent roots. The tree that rises from Nebuchadnezzar's body is therefore also a symbol of this transformation. It is the Tree of Life, standing at the centre of the Garden of Eden, offering eternal life to those who eat of its fruit.

In each of these registers, the tree effects the transformation of gross bodies into much lighter ones. In so doing, it translates flesh into forms more consonant with the divine. This in turn produces a radical realignment of relations between sensible and supersensible worlds. Towards the right-hand margin of the design, the horizon has been breached and, reversing the tree's upward movement, some of the sky's mauve substance has moved downwards. It now flows from the right-hand margin towards the centre of the page where, mixing with now insubstantial earth, it swirls and eddies around the tree.

As in Blake's designs, the rise of Nebuchadnezzar's kingdom is sustained by and occurs at the expense of the flesh. The broad base of the tree rests on Nebuchadnezzar's body, pinning him to the ground. At the same time, the tree draws on Nebuchadnezzar's substance – his flesh, blood and semen – to sustain its growth. On the one hand, therefore, Nebuchadnezzar seems at the point of translation into a higher order of being; on the other hand, his body is at the point of collapse. At several points his flesh has already dissolved, revealing the brown earth that lies beneath him. His dark, unseeing eyes are attached to a mask-like, almost bestial face; his hair seems on the point of metamorphosis into ram's horns. The dissolution of Nebuchadnezzar's body, like the dissolution of the earth, takes his kingdom to the brink of the collapse depicted in the following designs and culminating in 'Nebuchadnezzar eating grass in a hilly landscape' (Figure 20.4).

Like 'Nebuchadnezzar's dream of the tree', this design is also divided into three planes, by the line of softly curved hills on the horizon, which divide earth from

**Figure 20.4** Arthur Boyd, 'Nebuchadnezzar eating grass in a hilly landscape' (1968–69). Oil on canvas. (The Arthur Boyd Gift. National Gallery of Australia, Canberra. Arthur Boyd's work reproduced with the permission of the Bundanon Trust.)

sky, and by the straight line of Nebuchadnezzar's back, which divides a featureless expanse of earth and grass. In contrast to the earlier design, Nebuchadnezzar looks down rather than up, confined to the lower third of the design. With ram's horns crowning his head, an animal mouth stuffed with grass, a bovine underbelly, and twin testicles glowing red (but without evident phallus), Nebuchadnezzar seems driven by the most elementary and discordant passions.

In Blake's Notebook design, Nebuchadnezzar's body formed the base, and his back held aloft the upper part of a triangle, reminiscent of the forms of his empire. In 'Nebuchadnezzar's dream of the tree', the tree bridged the gap between the sensible and the supersensible. Here the space between body and horizon is empty and, although the design strongly recalls Blake's Nebuchadnezzar, no triangle is held aloft save for that suggested by the white body of a strange animal, half dog and half stoat, that sits on Nebuchadnezzar's back. Although the snout of the animal points upwards, and its body forms at least two triangles, its one visible eye looks out towards the reader, not up to heaven.

As in Blake's designs, Nebuchadnezzar's attempt to transcend the body produces the disorder into which he is precipitated. Whether read as a critique of American imperial or British colonial attempts to shape, respectively, an eastern or antipodean empire, for Boyd, like Blake, such attempts paradoxically produce the disorder that they must then struggle again and again to master. Rather than bringing East and West or northern and southern hemispheres into relation, Nebuchadnezzar produces the disordered, heavy forms in which other cultures are misrecognized and the material determinants of his own desire for power and transcendence are forgotten.

## 3  Nebuchadnezzar as artist

Nebuchadezzar's plight seems at first sight far removed from Blake's and Boyd's work as artists. Yet, in a letter to Mr Butts dated 11 September 1801, Blake complains of his 'Abstract folly' and of a 'Spirit of Abstraction & Improvidence' that 'hurries me often away while I am at work, carrying me over Mountains & Valleys which are not Real'. Even when he attempts to chain his 'feet to the world of Duty & Reality', reality proves insubstantial and 'far from being bound down', Blake claims that he takes 'the world with me in my flights & often it seems lighter than a ball of wool rolled by the wind' (E 716).

It is tempting to read this 'Spirit of Abstraction' as being akin to the 'spectrous Fiend' identified by Blake in a letter dated 23 October 1804 as 'the ruin of my labours for the last passed twenty years of my life' (E 756). Given that both letters were written in Felpham and that the second is addressed to William Hayley, it is likely that the 'spectrous Fiend', like 'the Spirit of Abstraction', entices Blake away from reality with an unreal vision of worldly success. Nevertheless, whatever the content of their visions, 'Fiend' and 'Spirit' treat the actual, material world as so much dross, to be displaced by or reshaped into the ideal forms they conjure.

The Fiend is therefore, in Blake's words, 'the Jupiter of the Greeks, an iron-hearted tyrant, the ruiner of ancient Greece'; and to the extent that Blake comes under his power, he is cast in the role of Nebuchadnezzar, confined to a body and a material world that resists its transmutation into the ideal. Blake writes:

I speak with perfect confidence and certainty of the fact which has passed upon me. Nebuchadnezzar had seven times passed over him; I have had twenty; thank God I was not altogether a beast as he was; but I was a slave bound in a mill among beasts and devils. (E 756)

Boyd draws a still more explicit set of associations between Nebuchadnezzar and the artist in a remarkable series of works produced in the early 1970s. The most disturbing is 'Chained Figure and Bent Tree' (Figure 20.5), a painting which

**Figure 20.5** Arthur Boyd, 'Chained Figure and Bent Tree' (1973). Oil on canvas. (The Arthur Boyd Gift. National Gallery of Australia, Canberra. Arthur Boyd's work reproduced with the permission of the Bundanon Trust.)

recalls Plate b11 of Blake's *There is no Natural Religion*. In Blake's design, the tree that shrouds Nebuchadnezzar mimes in a different register the king's labours: the gross body of the tree's trunk, branches and leaves are transmuted into the lighter bodies of Blake's text, and the still lighter bodies of the meaning it signifies. In Boyd's painting, the tree performs an analogous role. Its trunk grows upwards, joining earth and sky until, just above the horizon, it bends to the right. This upper portion of the trunk provides a horizontal plane from which spring a forest of branches. Seen against the blue of the sky, they seem to be a hanging garden, suspended in the air.

In a barren landscape, chained to this tree, and with his head enclosed in a wire cage, the artist is depicted in the midst of an attempt to repeat this transmutation of matter. The upper left-hand corner of the design he is painting seems to have lifted itself from the canvas, forming an ideal, three-dimensional world of water, rocks and blooming flowers that disturbs the otherwise flat, arid landscape within which he is chained. The brush he holds in his right hand divides his painting into two large triangles. The brushes he holds in his left hand point from the upper left-hand corner of his painting towards two animals copulating in the distance. One stands passively on all fours while the second, sporting large ram-like horns, rises above his partner, placing his front legs on her back so he can enter her. The artist's attempt to turn material into visionary form is, it seems, no more than the lifting of one material form above another and the subsequent insemination of the lower by the higher. The painter's visionary ideal has turned the landscape into a wasteland and reduced the painter's body to that of a beast.

For both Blake and Boyd, escape from the cycle that enslaves Nebuchadnezzar and that holds the West in agonistic struggle with its imagined others involves embrace rather than division, exodus rather than transcendence. The letter from Blake to Hayley quoted above continues:

> I was a slave bound in a mill among beasts and devils; these beasts and these devils are now, together with myself, become children of light and liberty, and my feet and my wife's feet are free from fetters (E 756).

In this context, to be a child 'of light and liberty' is to be shaped by both spiritual and material realms, to claim a freedom of thought <u>and</u> the body. This is achieved by releasing the body from, rather than yoking it to, a transcendent goal; and this in turn proves the foundation not of empire but of a republic composed of radically disparate elements.

In Boyd's *Nebuchadnezzar*, the beginning of an analogous movement can be seen in the remarkable 'Nebuchadnezzar blind on a starry night with lion's head'. While Nebuchadnezzar's weight is carried by his upright left leg, the bulk of his body (his head, torso and right leg) form a diagonal running from the lower right-hand to the upper left-hand corner of the page. His left foot rests on and his right foot is raised above the ground. The garden that sprouts from his back forms large wings that lift his body not to a transcendent world but to the space that lies between the stars above and the roaring lion below. The regal tyrant is now blind and vulnerable, as he reaches down towards the lion and turns his head towards stars that he cannot see. Without sight he is unable to shape the world into forms consonant with his vision and, as a result, human, transcendent and material worlds move into dangerous proximity to each other. This equivocal rapprochement anticipates a still more radical intimacy, seen in designs such as

'Seated Nebuchadnezzar and crying lion', where it is the lion's sympathy for Nebuchadnezzar that partially restores his humanity.

Arguably the radical visual and verbal strategies of Blake's major prophecies, and the iconoclastic visual structures of Boyd's later work, are attempts to work through the implications of the closely related points that, I have argued, are explored through their representations of Nebuchadnezzar: first, that conservative and radical cultures are alike to the extent that they pit mind against body, the organized bodies of the West against the disorganized bodies of the East. And second, that these oppositions form part of a single system that closes Europe in upon itself, rather than opening it to the worlds, discourses and traditions that lie beyond it. But to substantiate the claim that the mature works of Boyd and Blake are informed by their attempt to think outside the logic of transcendence, whether of enlightened reason, of empire or of certain kinds of artistic vision would demand a much longer argument.

## Notes

1 Sack 1991: 72. See also Wiseman 1985: 43.
2 Bacon 1798: 69.
3 Boyd 1972: 39.
4 Carretta 1990: 162. See also Mee 1998: 108–11.
5 Mee 2002: 194.
6 Anonymous 1795: 16, 19. Quoted in Rocher 1983: 164.
7 T. S. R. Boase in Boyd 1972: 38. According to Swedenborg 1975: Para. 788, Nebuchadnezzar's dream recounted in Daniel Ch. 2, foretold that the Swedenborgian 'New Church is the crown of all the Churches which have hitherto been on the earth' and that it would 'endure for ever'.
8 Hoff 1986: 59. See also Pearce 1993: 26.
9 Newton 1730; 1952: 374.
10 See Otto 2000.
11 See Otto 2001: 4–22.

# 21 William Blake in Taiwan

## Ching-erh Chang

William Blake (1757–1827), an early English[1] Romantic poet, artist, engraver, publisher and visionary mystic,[2] has never been popular with the reading public in Taiwan. Even to students of English literature, their knowledge about him has rarely gone beyond the few short lyrics chosen in anthologies of British authors.[3] Statistics also show that over the 50 years (from 1946 to 2000), there were in total only 33 translations, newspaper articles, critical essays, MA theses and scholarly research papers in Taiwan devoted to his works. Such records rank Blake at number 139 among 2,784 creative writers in Western literature as a whole. Even among the 517 British writers in Taiwan, he ranks only 37th (Chang 2004: I: 700–3).[4]

## 1 Romanticism: Vision and Visionary Poetry

Taiwanese critics, like their counterparts in the West, have almost always noticed the 'vision' in Blake's life and works, in particular the influence of Swedenborg for suing the 'Holy Bible as witness' to 're-establish Man's union with God' (Liang 1985: II: 1,105).[5] At the age of 4, Blake was surprised to see the face of God pressed against the window. When he was about 8, he once beheld a tree starred with angels on one of his walks. Another time he saw the prophet Ezekiel walking in a field, and talked with Gabriel, the Virgin Mary and many historical figures. By the time he was 14, he often embarked on his favourite ramble at dusk, sauntering along the sounding shore by himself to hold visionary conversations with Moses, the Prophets, Dante and many other majestic shadows from the past. He also reported how, while wandering alone in his garden, he had seen a fairy's funeral. Sometime in his thirties (1787), he nursed his youngest and most beloved brother Robert (1767–87) continuously for a fortnight, day and night, till the last moment came when he saw the released spirit ascending heavenward joyfully clapping its hands; and henceforth learned from him in a vision the secret of relief etching. He was 32 when he revealed that he had had a vision of 'devils, nightmares, sea-pythons, the Gorgons and giant carcass-eating fish' (Yü 1960: 15). The door into the visionary world, through which he had strayed from time to time since his childhood, seemed to have constantly opened wide for him.

What then is a 'vision'? A 'vision', Ch'ung-hsüan Tung argues, 'is a particular experience in which a personage, thing or event appears vividly or credibly to the mind, although not actually present, under the influence of a divine or other agency' (Tung 1997: 2). Almost all the Romantic writers had visions of one kind or another. To Blake, a 'vision' is prophetic or apocalyptic. It is an unchangeable image that remains in one's imaginative mind eternally, and that leads to an understanding of eternal beauty, a revelation of the Paradise of Jerusalem and an elevation of one's soul to the Golden Age of Paradise (Liu 1993: 177–214). Meanwhile, Kuang-chung Yü interprets 'vision' as something equal to 'hallucination', or 'fantasy' on the one hand, and considers Blake a 'daydreamer' (Yü 1960: 15) on the other. Both 'hallucination' and 'fantasy' are terms in psychology, denoting sensory impression or intellectual activity. 'An hallucination', according to William James, 'is a strictly sensational form of consciousness, as good and true a sensation as if there were a real object there' (Yü 1960: 759); a fantasy refers to the creation of a situation in one's mind's eye or 'a situation that has never occurred' (Kalish 1973: 110); and a daydreamer indicates one who has a dreamlike thought, as of a future or desired event, situation, etc. Daydreaming and fantasy mean approximately the same thing, 'although fantasy may be more extreme' (Harlow, McGaugh and Thompson 1971: 372). A vision, 'though in need of fantasy', is 'not fantasy', which is a creation either helpful in achieving self-actualization or harmful when confused with reality, but 'the manifestation of vision often presents a refreshing real world' (Chu 1975: 116).

In actual fact, a vision is 'a special kind of imagination', 'a constant image kept in the imaginative mind for good', a faculty 'not different from imagination' (Tung 1997: 195). The defence of poetry against the claims of scientism and neoclassicism had been feeling its way during the eighteenth century towards the formation of some kind of poetic autonomy (Li 1973: 35–9; Feng 2002: 33–4). Blake's lifelong aspiration was to propagate the spirit of Romanticism against the restriction and domination of Rationalism. To him, imagination 'transcended time and space' (Lan 2000: 88). While Rationalism placed its major emphasis on 'decorum and regulation', by which it moulded and formed human nature through education so as to help it reach moral perfection, Romanticism insisted on one's intuition and imagination to discern the invisible. 'The evil of the world is nothing worse than that imagination became obscure', and man's potentiality undermined by doctrines (Kao 1999: 303–27; Ch'iu 2002). Rationalism, which followed Christian doctrines, insisted on a clear-cut demarcation of good and evil, and persistently forced man towards virtue. Yet Blake thought that such an insistence inevitably weakened man's creative 'energy'. The two forces, interestingly compared by Yüan-hwang Ts'ai, are something like the two principles of *yin* and *yang* on the Ultimate Design of Chinese philosophy (Ts'ai 1996: 53–7)

It is only natural that Blake's vision found its way into his art theories and practices. The 'Introduction' of *Songs of Innocence* tells of the poet encouraged by a child 'on a cloud' to pipe his 'happy songs'. This, to Yüan-hwang Ts'ai, is exactly the 'vision', or a sort of 'extrasensory harmony', that leads the Romantic to compose his 'visionary poetry' (Ts'ai 1996: 52–9).

Blake's notion of vision, as Ch'ung-hsüan Tung has further pointed out, is a dialectical one, though somewhat different from Hegel's. While Hegel's opposites seem to disappear in a higher synthesis, Blake's contraries always remain there as a momentum of progression. Even if the contraries constitute cyclical phases, they coexist at the same time in all phases. The ever-changing binary opposition reflects Blake's typical Romantic idea, which has mastered him in such a way that in his works all concepts involving the number three or four can always be reduced to two fundamental dialectical concepts.

## 2 Humanitarianism: Protest against Social Injustice

Social justice is an eternal, universal value. Writing in the tradition of prophecy, Blake spoke the truth under the command of God and stood on the humanitarian side to attack 'oppression' prevailing in all kinds of social injustice. 'The Little Black Boy' in *Songs of Innocence* points to the prejudice of racial discrimination; 'The Chimney Sweeper', too, in pitying the overworked child, directs its anger against the slavery and exploitation of the poor. In much the same token, 'Holy Thursday' in *Songs of Experience* is a complaint about the hidden hypocrisy in the hospital; 'The Chimney Sweeper' attacks the corruption of the Church for its indifference to the fate of a child worker; 'The Garden of Love' expresses a strong protest against the restraint of love given by religion (Chen 1997). In these poems, Blake's concerns for equality, liberty, compassion, friendship and true love strongly contrast with the profit-seeking society of eighteenth-century London (Chen 1997: 23–34).

Here 'London', Blake's most frequently commented on, discussed and analysed poem by Taiwanese critics, will be chosen for a demonstration of his social consciousness (for a critical summary, see Weng 1979: 78). 'With the adroitness of its symbolic technique and complicated references', as Tien-en Kao has pointed out, 'the poem launches a severe attack on the inhuman oppression of contemporary British society, politics, economy, religion and sexual morality' (Kao 1990: 151). Shih-ch'iu Liang gives a general comment on the poem as a whole before he proceeds to investigate the poem stanza by stanza, saying that it is one that 'Blake uses to protest against the corruption of London society. It describes the ugliness of the city to criticize London life. Such an antisocial poem can be compared in a way with Johnson's "London" ' (Liang 1985: II: 1111). Through such descriptions of the ugly aspects behind the superficial prosperity of London, the reader is extremely 'shocked' (Yen and Zhang 1996: 116). C. T. Hsia, who has studied the historical background of the poem, states that Blake means to voice his objection to the institutions that keep society in order – the Government, Church and Marriage – an objection in which he speaks for 'every Man', 'every infant', 'Chimney-sweepers', 'hapless soldiers' and 'youthful harlots', and articulates his strong 'social consciousness and revolutionary spirit' (Hsia 1993: 11). While expressing his admiration for the poem as an excellent example of the fusion of 'social satire' and 'humanitarian compassion', Peng-hsiang Chen has also carefully discerned the bitterness of tone, and the gloomy vision of human life. With 'realistic' images, he holds that the poem 'dramatically' depicts 'the various sufferings created by the regimental, exploiting society' (Chen 1997: 32–3). Chen further clearly states in his paper that the poems he has studied, including 'The Little Black Boy', 'London', 'The Chimney Sweeper' and 'Holy Thursday', all satirize 'the community in which the poet lived' (Chen 1997: 23; Li 1973; Chou 1974).

## 3  Comparative Literature: Mutual Illumination of Poetry and Painting

However, to Taiwanese comparatists, the mutual relationship of Blake's poetry and illustrations deserves special critical attention, and essays on the relationships of Chinese–Western poetry and painting have not ignored his achievements (Liu 1993: 88). Noticeable here is the fact that the translations rendered for 'Introduction' (Yü 1960: 13), *Selected Translations of Blake's Poetry* (Zhou 1966) and some stanzas taken from *Poetical Sketches* (Liang 1985: II: 1107–8) consist of words only, and that the stanzas selected from 'God Creating Adam' (Zhong 1988), 'Love Song' (Zhang 1980) and 'The Lamb' (Zhang 1982) are translated with the juxtaposition of lines and illustrations. The translations without illustrations miss something significant, indeed. However the juxtaposition of poems and illustrations does not necessarily guarantee a proper understanding of the intention and significance therein. To read a Blakean poem in a printed text without any illustration placed beside it is to see only an abstraction from an integral and mutually enlightening combination of words and designs. For this reason, Blake's poems and illustrations are from time to time used to exemplify the dialectical relationship of the sister arts.

In addition to his 'London', Taiwanese scholars have also been attracted by 'A Poison Tree', a poem in *Songs of Experience*. It was written during the early period of the French Revolution when the British government took some offensive measures, to which Blake expressed his strong objection. Through it, Blake proclaims the idea that the line of demarcation to differentiate friends and enemy must be clearly and definitely drawn (Yen and Zhang 1996: 118). It 'dramatizes the repressed anger which is deliberately allowed to fester and grow into a force destructive to others as well as to oneself. The central image of the poem is that of a tree, which grows and bears fruit, reminiscent of the Tree of Knowledge in the Book of Genesis' (Liu 1993: 202). To Zhifan Chen, a perusal of or a visit to an exhibition of Blake's poems and illustrations almost always gave him a sense of 'surprise', which in turn evoked 'deep thought' and 'mystery'. He once accidentally found in the library of Taiwan National University a volume of handouts of English literature edited by Lafcadio Hearn (1850–1904) for the Imperial University of Tokyo, in which 'A Poison Tree' was carefully interpreted to illustrate Blake's style. Having read it, he felt strongly 'shocked', 'horror-stricken' and 'fear lingering'. Henceforth while a glance at Blake's illustrations would make him feel more and more 'excited and puzzled', a reading of Blake's poems would also give him a sense of 'mystery and gloom' (Chen 1994: 37).

The third poem which has interested Taiwanese critics is 'The Tyger', one of the most popular poems in *Songs of Experience*. As *Songs of Innocence* and *Songs of Experience* together mean to 'Show the Two Contrary States of Human Souls', the 'tyger' represents the fierce strength of human souls, the 'lamb' stands for the state of innocence, and the dark 'forest' implies 'ignorance, repression and superstition'; the juxtaposed opposition eventually restores harmony (Wang 1985: 2). As Shih-ch'iu Liang has pointed out, the poem,

which is the most famous one in *Songs of Experience*, is contrasted to 'The Lamb'. Though the words used in the poem are simple, what it implies is profound and evocative. Such is the way critics have come to see it. The whole poem consists of a series of 14 questions. The one who is questioning is not Blake himself, but the reader. The answer need not be provided since we are able to feel it. The target of the poem is not the tyger, but God the Creator. The word, 'can', in the first stanza, which becomes 'dares' in the last stanza, is most significant. Almighty is God, who dares to create the tyger after He has created the lamb. (Liang 1985: II: 1111)

Han-liang Chang, however, contends that if this 'beautiful' and 'fearful' tiger described in words materializes the 'miracle and sublimity of the Creator', why is it turned into a 'mild and ridiculous sick cat' in the illustration? Is it because Blake does not know how to draw a fearful tiger? (Chang 1981: 308–9) Finally Ping-hui Liao simply wonders at the description of the 'tyger' as 'fearful', and 'burning bright' with 'dread hand', 'dread feet', and eyes like 'fire' in the forest of the 'night', which turns out as mild as a 'cat' against the background of 'dawn' on the plate (Liao 1988: 78–9). Regrettably, the three critics have irresponsibly come to a unanimous agreement that the 'answer need not be provided'. (For further discussion of indeterminacy, see Liao 1988: 82.)

## 4 Miscellaneous Descriptions of Blake's Poems

The interest of Taiwanese scholars in Blake has been immensely diversified. Introductory information is helpfully presented in the *Anthology of English Literature* by Shih-ch'iu Liang (1985: II: 112–25). I shall here concentrate on recent MA theses. A graduate student in the MA programme in Taiwan, having completed required credits and passed required exams, is still required to submit a thesis in English to the institute concerned in partial fulfilment for the degree of the MA. The thesis usually consists of 100 pages, which amounts to around 30,000 words. It is too short to be published in book form, and too long to be accepted by a scholarly journal. Such a requirement, however, is considered 'a necessary evil', since it provides an opportunity for practice, a practice which will enable a graduate student to handle the problems of how to collect, arrange, classify and interpret materials before he is officially admitted to the academic world.

There have been only eight MA theses on Blake's works produced in Taiwan over the last 60 years (1946–2005). Four of them have dwelt on the different aspects of *Songs of Innocence* and *Songs of Experience*. As the theses of Ch'ing-hsüan Li (1973) and Ch'ung-hsing Chou (1977) are not available, we must leave them alone. The aim of Yün-shan Leu's thesis is in a way self-evident in its topic, 'Goodness and Evil: Human Nature in Blake's and Wordsworth's Poetry through the Relationship of Innocence and Experience' (1992). The thesis, 'A Study of Social Criticism in William Blake's *Songs of Innocence and of Experience* and Its Application to English Teaching' (1997) by Pei-chün Chen, investigates the protest of the poet against racial discrimination, poverty and religion on the one hand, and discusses the poem 'London' for the pedagogical purpose on the other. Beatrice H. C. Hsü, who entitles her thesis 'William Blake Revisited: A Kabbalistic Reading' (1993), enquires into the religious thoughts of Blake by way of a Kabbalistic reading of his poetry, a reading which refers to a theory of creativity advanced by the Jewish mystic Isaac Luria (1534–72). Jin-li Xie revolves her topic, 'Chastity and the Feminine in William Blake's Poetry' (1994), around the images of women, Mary, the fallen Eve and the renewed Eve, in an attempt to examine the poet's mental process of mystical devotion. Yü-wen Ch'iu, in her thesis, 'The Romantic Poetics of the Unconscious' (2002), discusses Blake and his fellow Romantic poets, considering visions, dreams and insights as unconscious experience.

Here, we will use the most recently finished thesis, 'Re-visioning Milton: William Blake and the Poetics of Appropriation' (2003) by Jerry Chia-je Weng, as an example for a more detailed illustration. The thesis is, besides its introduction and epilogue, divided into three chapters. It intends to see 'how Blake consciously *used* and appropriated Milton to his own ends' (Weng 2003: 3–4). Chapter 1 investigates, through biographies, editions and criticism, the reputation of Milton in the eighteenth century, who was then hailed as 'an exemplar of moral virtue, a forerunner of constitutional monarch', 'England's "classical" epic poet', and 'a national and cultural icon' (Weng 2003: 41). Chapter 2 gives a mythic account of Milton's determination to return to the world after roaming in Heaven for a hundred years, when he has suddenly discovered himself 'that Satan', and 'that Evil One'. Though such an action 'brings to the world an immediate apocalypse', Blake, taking advantage of this, actively distorts and appropriates the cultural icon for his own purpose (Weng 2003: 42). He tries to 'debunk the Milton myth' (Weng 2003: 39) in the title page of *Milton*, the portraiture and the poem itself, aiming at a total deconstruction of Milton's deified image, and thereby giving the literary giant humanity and compassion.

Chapter 3 revolves around Blake's attempt to re-establish the tradition of the prophet originating from the Old Testament, proceeding through Milton, and eventually being handed down to Blake himself. To him, as long as he speaks truth, he is considered 'a specially elected prophet' (Weng 2003: 74), whose moral duty is to transmit God's message. The thesis has given rise to quite a few problems. First, it might be expected that the author should define 'poetics of appropriation' at the beginning of the thesis. Secondly, of the 92 critics or commentators cited or consulted in the thesis, the author has come to consider the following as particularly 'important': Harold Bloom's 'modern conception of poetic influence'; Joseph Antony Witteich's insight into 'the reception of a poet within a culture'; and Northrop Frye's 'influential interpretation of Blake's symbolism' (Weng 2003: 7, 10, 6). Regrettably, the author fails to have taken advantage of the 'important' views or theories proposed in his introduction to support his later arguments.

## 5  Tentative Conclusion

In general, Taiwanese understanding of Blake still remains at a very preliminary stage. We do have some scholars urging our people to broaden their world outlook by following the advice Blake has suggested, and by bearing in mind the ultimate concerns of Blake's creative activity regarding 'the formation of the world, the fall and redemption of mankind, the promise of a return to the Garden of Eden and the coming of a New Jerusalem' (Kao 1990: 148–54). We do see our critics try to understand Energy and Reason through an apt comparison to the *yin* and *yang* in Chinese philosophy. By and large, however, most of the essays and scholarly products are not unique enough. What we know of Blake's life story is almost always faithfully taken from some short introductions to his works, or from the biographies written by Gilchrist, Wilson and the like. Few insights are discernible in the scholarly products, as their views are for the most part influenced by their British and American counterparts.

After all, Blake has never been a popular writer in Taiwan. Taiwanese scholars have neither been as attentive as their Euro-American counterpart nor as enthusiastic as the Japanese (Suzuki and Clark 2003: 5–53). There are, however, quite a few translations, newspaper articles and critical essays devoted to his works, specifically to *Songs of Innocence* and *Songs of Experience*. All this proves at least that we do have some understanding critics here in Taiwan to appreciate the beauty and mystery of his poetry. At present, through the efforts of Euro-American scholars, most of the difficulties and ambiguities in Blake's works have been cleared away. This, to Taiwanese translators and scholars, is indeed a good tiding. Under such favourable circumstances, Blake's works, such as *Songs of Innocence* and *Songs of Experience* can be much more easily translated into Chinese. If the complete works of William Blake cannot be rendered into Chinese in the near future, the first priority of translation can be placed on *Songs of Innocence* and *Songs of Experience*. The second priority will then fall on the feasibility of the translation of *Milton* and other longer poems. Meanwhile, scholarly attention must also be paid to some of the long poems by Blake, specifically the relationships of Blake's poetry and illustrations, whose true value is still waiting for the people of Taiwan to explore. And it is hoped that we will soon find more attention paid to him and his works, as they deserve.

## Notes

1   Kuang-chung Yü, having adopted the view advanced in the Ellis–Yeats edition of Blake's complete works in 1893, affirms that Blake was from Ireland (Yü 1960: 15). This theory, however, has already been refuted as 'one of the most idiosyncratic and poorly put-together among literary critiques' (Dorfman 1969: 192).

2   Yangmu questions the appropriateness of the description of Blake as a mystic poet by Zhifan Chen. Actually, however, Kuang-chung Yü considers 'mysticism' as one of the characteristics of Blake's works (Yü 1960: 14), Tien-en Kao calls him 'a mystic' (Kao 1990: 149) and Alexander Gilchrist names him straightforwardly 'a mystic poet' (Gilchrist 1998a: 4).

3   See, for example, the variant editions of *The Norton Anthology of English Literature* (Abrams 1962, 1986, 2000).

4   The *Research Bibliography of Western Literature in Taiwan* is a comprehensive guide to Western literature in Taiwan, and includes 65 national literatures, 2,784 creative writers and 28,223 entries. The first 20 writers whose works are translated and/or studied in Taiwan are headed by Shakespeare with 1,218 entries down to Samuel Beckett with 150.

5   It must be noted that Blake once criticized Swedenborg's dualism of good and evil in *The Marriage of Heaven and Hell* (Chen 1977: 24). It must also be noted that Blake annotated Swedenborg's writings such as 'Heaven and Hell', 'Divine Love and Divine Wisdom', 'Divine Providence', etc.

# 22 'Walking thro' Eternity': Blake's Psychogeography and other Pedestrian Practices

Jason Whittaker

> It is tempting for the stalker striking south towards Roman Road to block out the civic tidiness of Victoria Park by invoking the spirit of William Blake, the godfather of all psychogeographers[.]
> (Iain Sinclair, *Lights Out for the Territory*, 1997: 214)

> And all this Vegetable World appeard on my left Foot,
> As a bright sandal formd immortal of precious stones & gold:
> I stooped down & bound it on to walk forward thro' Eternity.
> (*Milton* 21:12–14; E 115)

In his essay 'Secret City: Psychogeography and the End of London', Phil Baker points out some of the eccentricities of psychogeographic practice as it transferred away from its Parisian routes and situationism into London during the 1970s. Indeed, with particular regard to Iain Sinclair, who is the doorway into this unravelling of Blake's golden thread through the Jerusalem–Babylon of London, Baker observes that Sinclair's roots are not really with the situationists at all, but rather the 'Earth Mysteries' school that experienced a resurgence during the emerging Age of Aquarius (more commonly known as the 1960s), emphasizing as it did 'the land's apparently ancient lore and sacred geometry' as espoused in the theory of ley lines proposed by Alfred Watkins in the 1920s (Baker 2003: 326). Blake, whose own strange geometries of Albion half-intelligibly anathematize the British Isles by enfolding them within the consecrated history of the chosen people of Israel, is an obvious starting point for this peculiarly English variant of mapping Orient and Occident, although Sinclair has also made it clear that if Blake was the godfather, then De Quincey quickly adopted the child. Identifying Blake as a source of English psychogeography is an obvious move on the part of Sinclair: as has frequently been observed, 'Blake was an astute recorder of what he saw and heard in London's streets' (Miner 2002: 281), and it is the specificity of Blake's records involved in what may be termed part of the practice of everyday life that makes potential connections between him and situationism so potentially fruitful.

Part of the intention of this chapter is to offer one theoretical perspective on Blake's map-making through some of the viewpoints offered by Sinclair, thus commenting on his activities as a sacro-geometer and psycho-geomancer who created ludic and liminal spaces whereby new orders emerge out of games of disorder (Nudelman 2003: 33–5). I have written rather tersely of Sinclair's appropriation of Blake elsewhere (Dent and Whittaker 2002: 60–4), and to be honest my own opinion of *Lud Heat* (1975) and *Suicide Bridge* (1979), the works most directly indebted to Blakean obfuscations, remains fairly low: their anti-quarianism is not worn lightly, so that the experience of reading them can be pedantic and tedious. Even *Downriver* (1991), apparently marking a transition into a wittier, more 'postmodern' metropolis after the macabre atrocities of *White Chappell, Scarlet Tracings* (1987) is far too brittle with its own cleverness, stylistic and otherwise. And yet by the end of the nineties, with the publication of *Lights Out for the Territory* (1997) and especially *London Orbital: A Walk around the M25* (2002), Sinclair's vision of the Great Wen seemed to have undergone some alchemical transformation, as though repetition of rather dry and dismal themes had sublimated an alchemical white eagle from the dung. *Lights Out* demonstrated Sinclair's real humour, self-deprecatory and even tender in contrast to the grim announcements of his earlier supposedly comic moments. Yet it is *London Orbital* that perhaps offers a real key to unlocking the door onto Blake's own process of orientation. First of all, there is the sheer fun of the whole enterprise that brings the reader along: the deliberate and rather delightful perversion of walking around the most notorious motorway in Britain. More than this, however, *London Orbital* is a clear indication of the progress that Sinclair has made away from the desiccated delights of mere antiquarianism. Instead of wearing every obscure piece of learning on his sleeve to impress the reader, Sinclair's perambulations uncover the villages, woods, abandoned asylums and chemical dumps buried beneath the bitumen and asphalt, new housing estates and fields of oilseed rape lining the M25. Near Waltham Abbey, for example, Sinclair interviews Beth Pedder, a local activist who, investigating why so many people suffered illness from an asbestos-like smoke, discovered that the land that the Fairview estate had been built on in 1996 was formerly owned by the Ministry of Defence, under whose tenure it had become contaminated by arsenic, zinc and the by-products of other petrochemical industries (Sinclair 2002: 59–62). Immediately one can see the value of such knowledge: ignorance of one's immediate place in the universe can, quite literally, be deadly.

Sinclair compares himself to Los entering the Door of Death, a successor to Blake's spiritual hoplite in *Jerusalem* searching 'the interiors of Albions / Bosom' (45: 3–4; E 194): Sinclair wishes to achieve something similar by walking around the M25, reaching into the interior of Albion's bosom by tracing its arterial periphery, the ring where public spaces, buildings, commons are sold off for private housing estates, golf courses, landfill. To go all Winstanley-ish for a moment, the significance of *London Orbital* is its account of how our birthright is being sold from beneath us, the common land privatized as part of a neocon-servative, New Labour legacy. For me, the reason why Sinclair's psychogeography becomes effective is because it reconnects with, and further develops, some of the key tenets of situationism: English mysticism is never entirely abolished – and this is why, ultimately, it is Blake rather than Debord who is godfather for Sinclair – but by ditching much of the New Age mumbo-jumbo of his earlier works Sinclair ironically moves much closer to the spirit of Blake by investing his texts with a little more hard-headed, Parisian political scepticism.

Although more immediately influenced by Foucault and Bourdieu, Michel de Certeau's *The Practice of Everyday Life* is in many respects the mature (or, perhaps, recuperated and compromised) academic application of situationist principles, and includes an operational and discursive account of walking the city that also provides one of the most evocative descriptions of the practice of psychogeography:

> [At the top of a skyscraper] one's body is no longer clasped by the streets that turn and return it according to an anonymous law; nor is it possessed, whether as player or as played, by the rumble of so many differences and by the nervousness of New York traffic. When one goes up there, he leaves behind the mass that carries off and mixes up in itself any identity of authors or spectators. An Icarus flying above these waters, he can ignore the devices of Daedalus in mobile and endless labyrinths far below . . . The ordinary practitioners of the city live 'down below', below the thresholds at which visibility begins. They walk – an elementary form of this experience of the city; they are walkers, *Wandersmänner*, whose bodies follow the thicks and thins of an urban 'text' they write without being able to read it. These practitioners make use of spaces that cannot be seen; their knowledge of them is as blind as that of lovers in each other's arms . . . The networks of these moving, intersecting writings compose a manifold story that has neither author nor spectator, shaped out of fragments of trajectories and alterations of spaces: in relation to representations, it remains daily and indefinitely other. (de Certeau 1984: 92–3)

De Certeau's erotics of the urban text captures more the joyous play of Constant's New Babylon and Raoul Vaneigem's *The Revolution of Everyday Life* (1967), rather than Debord's austere censure of the spectacle. If the moment of bliss in the above quotation appears to be the preserve of the eagle-eyed planner, as some sort of deistic architect of the urban environment he calls into existence merely through his monologic, spectral vision, for de Certeau embodied *jouissance* is experienced in the rifts and sutures of pedestrian experience, the operations of the streetwalker whose peripheral vision is always provisional: 'Escaping the imaginary totalizations produced by the eye, the everyday has a certain strangeness that does not surface, or whose surface is only its upper limit, outlining itself against the visible' (de Certeau 1984: 93). The urban practitioner, then, encounters throughout his or her drifting ambiences, or to use Paul Virilio's term, vectors, that are more limited than the manifestations of the architect, but also limitless because never defined by a single-fold visualization. And, as in 1789 or 1968, the edges of such vectors may always fold into unpredictable action.

As I mentioned at the beginning of this chapter, the origins of Sinclair's own psychogeography stem more from English earth mysteries rather than French situationism, something that is particularly clear from his mythographical grimoires, *Lud Heat* and *Suicide Bridge*, that begin as meditations on the occult significance of Hawksmoor's London churches. *Lights Out for the Territory* (1997) leaves behind much of the portentousness that disfigures Sinclair's earlier work, exploring London less via the opaque secrets of an English telluric version of psychogeography and more through the playful unitary urbanism and *dérive* of the situationists. Avoiding the clever but restrictive format adopted by Peter Ackroyd in *London: The Biography* (2000), which did offer a fresh approach at the time of publication but which has now been so often imitated that already it is a dull cliché, *Lights Out for the Territory* is instead an assemblage of documents on the often nomadic construction site that is London. As Sinclair remarks in what could be taken as a classic description of the art of drifting:

> Walking is the best way to explore and exploit the city; the changes, shifts, breaks in the cloud helmet, movement of light on water. Drifting purpose- fully is the recommended mode, tramping asphalted earth in alert reverie, allowing the fiction of an underlying patter to reveal itself. To the no-bullshit materialist this sounds suspiciously like *fin-de-siècle* decadence, a poetic of entropy − but the born-again *flâneur* is a stubborn creature, less interested in texture and fabric, eavesdropping on philosophical, conversation pieces, than in noticing *everything*. Alignments of telephone kiosks, maps made from moss on the slopes of Victorian sepulchres, collections of prostitutes' cards, torn and defaced promotional bills for events at York Hall . . . Walking, moving across a retreating townscape, stitches it all together: the illicit cocktail of bodily exhaustion and a raging carbon monoxide high. (Sinclair 1997: 4)

There is much here that is familiar from Constant's evocation of the New Babylon, both drawing on the experience of the *flâneur* to discover a playful ambience within this assault on the senses (although, as Sinclair perceptively remarks in *London Orbital*, he finds 'the term *fugueur* more attractive than the now overworked *flâneur*' [Sinclair 2002: 120]). Yet if London is the Babylon of the situationists, it is also haunted by another genius loci:

> It is tempting for the stalker striking south towards Roman Road to block out the civic tidiness of Victoria Park by invoking the spirit of William Blake, the godfather of all psychogeographers: 'thro' Hackney . . . towards London/ Till he came to old Stratford, & thence to Stepney & the Isle/Of Leutha's Dogs . . . and saw every minute particular: the jewels of Albion running down/The kennels of the streets & lanes as if they were abhorr'd.' (Sinclair 1997: 214)

This particular route is a favourite of Sinclair's (he uses the same path in *Down- river*). As part of this English psychogeography, Blake serves as psychopomp, but Sinclair also makes use of David Jones's *The Anathemata* (1955) and Aidan Andrew Dun's *Vale Royal* (1995) for further psychogeographic alignments, seeking to revive a spiritual centre, the mythus that Jones had identified as lost in the West: 'there is, in the principle that informs the poetic art, a something which cannot be disengaged from the mythus, deposits, *matière*, ethos, whole *res* of which the poet is himself a poet' (Sinclair 1997: 20). Behind them all lies Blake's *Jerusalem*.

*Lights Out for the Territory* is full of examples of Sinclair's psychogeography (what, elsewhere, he also refers to as 'schizogeography', the art of following 'bent ley lines that exist only to assert some deranged territorial piracy' [Sinclair 1997: 212–3]). Discussing the rediscovery of the Temple of Mithras in the City of London, Sinclair engages in a hieratic, occult geometry familiar ever since *Lud Heat*: 'the knowledge of *precisely* where the original Temple of Mithras stood is crucial − if we are to fumble our way back, if we want to uncover the subterranean mechanisms by which the contemporary City functions' (ibid: 116). One may very well ask why such knowledge is at all crucial, and if Sinclair is evoking practices familiar from *Lud Heat* he is also being tempted once again by the melodrama of his earlier works. Nonetheless, his explanation does offer an interesting interpretation of the mood of the city:

> If the present Temple [Temple Court, Legal and General HQ] stands for anything, it is a symbol of how the City has lost it; corrupted the integrity of

its founding greed, its pattern of ritual and sacrifice, decent human vices, by yielding entirely to secrecy, cynicism, surveillance . . . A policy of deliberate misalignment (the Temple of Mithras, London Stone, the surviving effigies from Ludgate) has violated the integrity of the City's sacred geometry; leaving, in the place of well-ordered chaos, regimented anonymity – a climate in which corruption thrives. (Sinclair 1997: 117)

Effigies of Ludgate, Mithraic cultists that may have walked these urban streets in ancient times, followers of a sect that vied with the Christian mythos – so far, so traditional and also very obviously Blakean. But Sinclair's coda on the movement of the Temple stands in a closer, critical relationship to the situationist that offers, I believe, a more pertinent interpretation of Blake because it returns attention to the fact that the Romantic's antiquarian interest in the city was also a political one. Thus, the violation that Sinclair speaks of is not some erudite and ultimately uninteresting religio-magical act, but the activity of the spectacle that, as a manifestation of late capitalism, has cloaked itself in the slick anonymity of advertising and corporate style. Sinclair's appraisal of the significance of money and greed is not entirely the same as the – rather innocent – radicalism of Debord and others in the 1960s (or, indeed, Blake), but his use of the particulars of the urban environment to criticize commercial corruption is closer to the situationists than hippy ley lines.

*London Orbital: A Walk Around the M25* (Sinclair 2002) further extends the potential link between an English psychogeography centred on spirituality and mystery, and a French practice more concerned with artistic and political activity: thus Sinclair's own procedure is described as 'Chorography, not topography', the hunger for place as (citing Paul Devereux) 'a trigger to memory, imagination, and mythic presence' (Sinclair 2002: 100). Likewise, invoking Ford Madox Ford at one point, Sinclair observes the importance of roads – 'the chief feature of a city's life' – but roads that are also to be walked as well as driven. 'The wellbeing of the man and the wellbeing of the city were linked, freedom of movement, walks were the key to the good life' (ibid: 169). The reference to Devereux indicates that Sinclair has not abandoned his earth mystery roots, but again and again in the text, and this is key to his particular psychogeography, specificity is key: imagination is not transcendent but immanent in a *particular* chorography, and one of the most startling examples of this is Shoreham.

> It comes as a shock to find Shoreham where it is, so close to London. I suppose, with confused notions of Blake's Felpham (a suburb of Bognor Regis), I had always assumed that Palmer's Shoreham was hidden among the South Downs: that Shoreham was in fact the Sussex Shoreham, Shoreham-by-Sea. Domesticated, after the Bloomsbury style, with a touch of Eric Gill's community at Ditchling. A morning's drive away. Shoreham was an exportable fable, an idyll; suspect, fraudulent, magical. Fixed at the equinox.
>
> Nothing of the sort. Shoreham rubs shoulders with the Swanley interchange, with Brands Hatch, Orpington. Shoreham is just a wheel-spin off the M25. Staying on the road, you don't notice it. It doesn't register. No theme park, no shopping mall, no imprisoned animals. (Sinclair 2002: 343)

Palmer, influenced by Blake, provided a clearer perception: for him Shoreham was 'the Gate into the World of Vision'. This is a classic example of *détournement* – returning the ordinary to the basis of its extraordinary, revolutionary potential.

It is in this ordinary, however, this particularity, that we find the visionary: 'Blake's visions were anchored in the ordinary. They happened. Angel trees. Voices. Visitations from the mythic dead. They dropped in, his gods, when it was convenient for the Lambeth artisan to receive them, when the day's work was done. Glistening fleas with bowls of blood. If they made a nuisance of themselves, they could be dismissed' (Sinclair 2002: 346).

The 'Valley of Vision' (*Jerusalem* 22: 9 E 167) is one minute particular of the landscape made anonymous by road building projects and the selling off of the common lands of Britain under Thatcherism and its continuation by other means, under New Labour, creating what the book refers to as a 'prostituted landscape'. While *London Orbital* sees an authentic political realization emerge in Sinclair's work, tempered by a humane and gently cynical understanding of what radicalism can achieve – or, more accurately, not achieve – in the New Britain of the twenty-first century (evident, for example, in the melancholy mockery of his own nostalgic desire to indulge Billy Bragg's invocation of Winstanley and the Diggers), the book differs significantly from the psychogeographical projects of the situationists. Especially significant, and a surprising change compared to most of Sinclair's own work, is the fact that it is remarkably rural, connected to the landscape outside the immediate urban environment and so connects its politics to English earth mysteries in an unpredictably attractive fashion. The differences between Sinclair and the Situationist International (SI) also draws attention to the fact that there is more than a degree of violence in yoking Blake to the Parisian-based harness outlined previously, most obviously when we consider one of the principal urban models celebrated by the SI to have been the New Babylon rather than the New Jerusalem, and by no means do I intend to claim that Blake was a situationist (or even a psychogeographer, in the mode of either Sinclair or Debord). Nonetheless, the connection proposed by Sinclair in *Lud Heat* and *Suicide Bridge*, and continued through *Lights Out for the Territory* and *London Orbital* is worthwhile, I repeat, because it is one strategy that draws attention to the political implications of Blake's often bizarrely antiquarian strategy of mapping out the city.

First of all, Blake's principal characters and chroniclers, Los in particular, are exemplary instances of de Certeau's pedestrian practitioner: indeed, the anonymous narrator of 'London' appears to be engaging in one of the first important examples of the urban *dérive* (and with a judgement more scathing than anything found in Debord), wandering chartered streets and encountering on each corner the vectors of insurrectionary action, while the narrator of *The Marriage of Heaven and Hell* constantly chances upon infernal situations as he drifts through the revolutionary precincts of hell: in such encounters, Blake's narrator constantly works against abstraction, so that 'the unreal or void spaces of the dissociative angelic imagination are transformed into habitable places by the devil's literally embodied reading of them' (Wardi 2003: 258). Nor should we forget Milton's great expedition from heaven into Ulro, which inspires Blake in turn to travel through Albion and walk into eternity itself, drawing on Israelite customs of ownership, alienation and redemption of land rights symbolized by transfers of a sandal or shoe (Suzuki 2001: 40–56). It is in *Jerusalem*, however, that the motif of walking is most evident. Blake's more immediate models in this text, of course, are the prophets and Jesus, either striding through the Holy Land purposefully or simply itinerant around Galilee and Jerusalem (how surprisingly vagrant

Christ appears in the gospels, loitering with publicans, prostitutes and the sick, or manufacturing wine for wedding parties), and it is in the light of such models that Los must be viewed as the great foot soldier of *Jerusalem*. It has been argued that 'we must distinguish two types of walking in the poem', the wanderings of Jerusalem herself and that of Los himself, but that both are 'expressions of a creative longing for union' (Michael 2002: 214). It is the journey of Los that concerns me here, but I would also warn about rushing towards a simple union as an outcome of such perambulation: whatever Blake's intentions, it is precisely because the journeys of Los are so frightening and strange, fragmented and terrible, that they have an effect on the reader. The frontispiece shows Los, on foot as ever, entering through Death's Door, ready to explore the interior of Albion to save him from his own tyranny, while much of the action of the first book is taken up with Los travelling back and forth through Albion, or marking out routes and locations in London. These activities of fixing and marking, as when 'Los fixd down the Fifty-two Counties of England and Wales' (16: 28; E 160) or delineates the place of Albion's death from Hampstead across to Muswell Hill (15: 30–16: 2; E 159), appear to run counter to the nomadic, deterritoralizing drifting of Sinclair and the situationists, as indeed they are to some degree. Yet it is worth bearing in mind that what Los is engaged in is a very particular – even peculiar – visionary reterritorialization that bears little in common with the architectural spectacles of a deistic planner. Los's hammering at the anvil is also a metaphor for his pounding the streets, mapping out and remapping Albion so that the byways of London bisect those of Jerusalem, and the counties of Albion are contoured alongside the hills and rivers of the Holy Land. When Los walks through the chartered streets, his own cartography is so radically bizarre compared to that of the successors of Wren that one cannot mistake his visions for the totalizing – and totalitarian – plans of urban authority. Los provides us with *his* London: a specific, particular and even anarchic (because defying central authority) territory. By contrast, the idealized, spectacular vision of the metropolitan engineer is, for Blake, that of Albion's Spectre.

What, then, of the particular journey of Los in Plate 45 of *Jerusalem* that is so specifically significant to Sinclair?

Fearing that Albion should turn his back against the Divine Vision
Los took his globe of fire to search the interiors of Albions
Bosom, in all the terrors of friendship, entering the caves
Of despair & death, to search the tempters out, walking among
Albions rocks & precipices! caves of solitude & dark despair,
And saw every Minute Particular of Albion degraded & murderd
But saw not by whom; they were hidden within the minute particulars
Of which they had possessd themselves; and there they take up
The articulation of a mans soul, and laughing throw it down
Into the frame, then knock it out upon the plank, & souls are bak'd
In bricks to build the pyramids of Heber & Terah. But Los
Searchd in vain: closd from the mintia he walkd, difficult.
He came down from Highgate thro Hackney & Holloway towards London
Till he came to old Stratford & thence to Stepney & the Isle
Of Leuthas Dogs, thence thro the narrows of the Rivers side
And saw every minute particular, the jewels of Albion, running down
The kennels of the streets & lanes as if they were abhorrd.

Every Universal Form, was become barren mountains of Moral
Virtue: and every Minute Particular hardend into grains of sand:
And all the tendernesses of the soul cast forth as filth & mire,
Among the winding places of deep contemplation intricate
To where the Tower of London frownd dreadful over Jerusalem
A building of Luvah builded in Jerusalems easter gate to
His secluded Court: thence to Bethlehem where was builded
Dens of despair in the house of bread: enquiring in vain
Of stones and rocks he took his way, for human form was none[.]

(45: 2–27; E 194)

This passage represents one of the heroic wanderings of Los, his task clear: it is not exactly to save the Minute Particulars, each man, woman and child degraded by the society of Albion, but to witness those degradations so that such errors may be denounced and those particulars eventually saved. The purposefulness of Los's task at first appears to make it the very opposite of the aimless drifting of the situationists, and indeed there is an urgency to this text that is more powerful than anything found in Constant or Debord. Yet there is an important similarity. Los is, initially, lost: he has no plan to find what he is looking for because he is a foot soldier and streetwalker, denied the maps of the generals of the war or the architects of the city. Hence his journey in a line, or rather a curve, from Highgate to the Thames, which is even more complex in the continuing section of the poem (39–44) as Los arcs around to Westminster and back to London Stone.[1] This journey is a substantial walk – the first part fairly brutal with the traffic of today's London, but once you move down from Holloway, past Hackney, the final stages comprise a surprisingly pleasant walk to the City (made even more pleasant by the recent introduction of congestion charges). As G. E. Bentley remarks, Blake was a great walker around London in his earlier days, although starting the journey at Highgate may have marked the northern limit of Blake's typical explorations: as he commented in a letter to Linnell shortly before his death, 'When I was young Hampstead Highgate Hornsea Muswell Hill & Even Islington & all places North of London always laid me up the day after & some-times two or three days' (cited in Bentley 2004a: 319). The hills of Highgate and Hampstead effectively marked the 'peripheral vision' of much of London during the eighteenth century, with formal incursions onto the heath only beginning to take place during Blake's day (McKellar 1999: 46–7). As a former occupant of north London, the walk down from those highlands was considerably easier for me than Blake striking out in the opposite direction, although what we must imagine for Los's expedition is the difficult descent from England's green and pleasant land on the periphery of the capital to the misery of the borders of the East End and the arrogance and power of the City.

   Like the anonymous narrator of 'London', Los is grimly marking the despair-ing ambience of the streets he traverses, and where they lead him to is the Tower of London and Bedlam. Although the Bethlehem Hospital had moved across the Thames to Lambeth by the time Blake wrote these lines, part of the process of the city authorities moving their difficult subjects south of the river, Blake's current route was probably fixed on the great building at Moorfields constructed at the end of the seventeenth century, and which by 1799 was described by a commission as 'dreary, low and melancholy' (Ackroyd 2000: 620–2).[2] The threat of Bedlam in particular was a recurring one during Blake's life, for example in the

1785 review of his painting of Gray's Bard in the *Daily Universal Register*, which remarked that Blake 'appears like some lunatic, just escaped from the incurable cell of Bedlam' (cited in Bentley 2004a: 40). These are the spots where 'all the tendernesses of the soul are cast forth as filth & mire', replacing human kindnesses with Moral Virtue and the Law. Interestingly, when Los looks for the minute particulars of individual men and women, the 'jewels of Albion', what he also finds are abstract terrors that hunt them down, a spectacle of the society that pretends to articulate men's souls while degrading their very desires. As Saree Makdisi remarks, the London that Blake evokes is a mechanized Dis of disciplined labour, where 'the existence of poverty itself could be exploited and maintained as a perpetual source of the raw material' for such factory systems (Makdisi 2003a: 103). For the deistic architect, planning the economy and environment of the cosmopolitan universe as a transcendental ideal, the unitary image of the city, the Minute Particulars of men and women are precisely that, raw material. It does not take situationism or psychogeography to recognize that something filthy is taking place in such rationalizations, but it becomes easier to see why Blake's imaginative perception of the city fixed in the meticulous recording of a precise location can be so influential on the radical *détournements* of later writers and artists.

## Notes

1   Morton Paley, following W. H. Stevenson, points out that 'unless Hackney and Holloway are reversed, Los's journey is not a straight route. If we assume that they were unintentionally reversed by Blake to begin with, Los goes eastward from Highgate to Holloway to Hackney to Stratford, then turns south to Stepney and the Isle of Dogs, west to the Tower, further west and south across the river to Lambeth, north to the Isle of Dogs, west to the Tower, further west and south across the river to Lambeth, north across the river again to Westminster, northwest to Marylebone, southeast to the Temple and east to the London Stone (the ancient central point)' (Paley 2004: 180). If we assume that Blake is referring to the previous site of Bedlam at Moorfields, then Los's journey is not quite as complex because it never crosses the Thames.

2   My thanks to David Fuller for pointing out that Blake was probably considering the earlier site of Bedlam in these lines.

# 23 Blake's Question (from the Orient)

## John Phillips

> Lost! Lost! Lost! Are my emanations
>
> (William Blake, *The Four Zoas*; E 301)[1]
>
> By the little that satisfies the spirit one can measure the extent of its loss
>
> (G. W. F. Hegel)[2]

'Blake in the Orient': what can this mean? To eighteenth-century Europe the Orient began immediately to the east of the Mediterranean, or it was still defined according to an old cartography of empire, as east of Rome. Blake had been to Asia, of course, in visions at least.[3] Since that time, he has been published, translated, taught, and no doubt is responsible in ways that are barely calculable for influences and exchanges in letters, in philosophical discourses, in political struggles and cultural revolutions all over what is now understood by the Orient, that is, the modern nations of East Asia. In a less formalist, historicist or empiricist mode, Blake in the Orient might designate that which in the Orient is constituted, predicated or qualified by Blake: Blake of the Orient (as one might speak of spices or fruits of the Orient) would be a particular quality, *Blake*, which like other ethnic, cultural or anthropological qualities, could be regarded as constituting part of the character of the Orient. Or there might be contenders for the role of the Blake of the Orient, an Oriental figure for whom one might claim by analogy a status and force comparable to Blake's, in the manner of Edogawa Rampo, the self-styled Edgar Allan Poe of Japan,[4] or Nāgārjuna, the second-century philosopher of the middle way, whom people have referred to (stretching credulity) as the Indian Derrida.[5] In any case the Orient might also be seen as returning the favour, touching Blake (the poet, artist and engraver of London) and also his works with a certain oriental flavour. This, anyway, had already happened, for Blake might plausibly be regarded as a leading light of the so-called Oriental Renaissance.[6] Blake is therefore perhaps less in the Orient (whatever it may be) than the Orient is in Blake.

A further question, which will be the focus of this chapter, concerns the events of production and reception that might be accommodated to the phrase 'Blake in the Orient', but which are yet to come and so belong in some indeterminate sense to a destiny that Blake still lies in wait to meet. There will always have been something of Blake that, reserving itself outside the normal duration of time-consciousness, has in this way sped on ahead like an accelerated angel of history and now lies in wait for the Orient to catch up. If anything, this enigma of a Blake to come is growing all the more seductive with the emergence of what is generally regarded as a powerful new world order.[7] In the search for alternatives the potential movement of history here becomes positively, paradoxically, Hegelian. But if the quest is for a quasi-Christian prophecy of a world to come we might also hear something of Blake and something, perhaps, of the Orient too.[8]

We are less likely to recognize Blake, though, in any call for what would add up to an unabashedly utopian alternative.[9] In this sense, contemporary thought envisaging such a future might be grasped as only the most recent in a series of songs to the dawn whose provenance is ancient.[1] Hegel, Blake's approximate contemporary, had also noted, in his preface to the *Phenomenology*, that a new world was in the process of birth: 'It is surely not difficult to see', he declares of his time, a period marked by bloody revolutions and desperate struggles against diverse tyrannies, 'that our time is a time of birth and transition to a new period'.[11] But while the process of reconstruction is slow, taking place unseen during the metaphorical night, 'dissolving one particle of the edifice of its previous world after another', the revelation will be sudden and unmistakable: 'this gradual crumbling which did not alter the physiognomy of the whole is interrupted by the break of day that, like lightning, all at once reveals the edifice of the new world'. If the motif of daybreak turns up as part of the rhetoric of a new world then this would always have been in disavowal of dawn's dark underside. Turning now to Blake, we'll find something of that darkness harnessed and directed against the bland yet forceful utopias of post-enlightenment rhetoric.

## 1 Aubade

Blake himself, in *Visions of the Daughters of Albion*, a work produced ten years before Hegel's, had included a version of the song-at-dawn that mobilizes a quite different attitude to daybreak, an attitude that belongs no less to a great tradition but one tinged with darkness and a despair that touches on the archaic experience of death.[12] The dawn breaks for Oothoon in terms that echo authentically the vocabulary of the classical aubade, the voice of the nightingale replaced by that of the lark and with all eyes on the East (towards Eos, the pagan goddess of Easter and the cycles of Estrogen):

> I cry arise O Theotormon for the village dog
> Barks at the breaking day. the nightingale has done lamenting.
> The lark does rustle in the ripe corn, and the Eagle returns
> From nightly prey, and lifts his golden beak to the pure east;
> Shaking the dust from his immortal pinions to awake
> The sun that sleeps too long. (pl. 2: 23–8 E 47)

The echo of Shakespeare is unmistakable too. *Romeo and Juliet*'s dramatized aubade (3. 5. 1–36), which culminates in a couplet linking the day with death ('*Juliet*: O, now begone! More light and light it grows / *Romeo*: More light and light, more dark and dark our woes!'), can be connected with the earlier epic *Lucrece*, which devotes several stanzas and a masterclass in classical rhetoric to warding off the breaking of day. The strategy would utilize the force behind the criminal violence of the night (Tarquin's rape of Lucrece) to prevent day's emergence and thus obscure the inevitable light of its revelation:

> O hateful, vaporous and foggy night,
> Since though art guilty of my cureless crime,
> Muster thy mists to meet the eastern light,
> Make war against proportion'd course of time:
> Or if though wilt permit the sun to climb
>     His wonted height, yet ere he go to bed,
>     Knit poisonous clouds about his golden head.[13]

Bromion's rape of Oothoon has brought on her not only the degradation of the crime but also the same incurable and externally determined status that Lucrece knows will certainly descend with the rising sun. Oothoon, unlike Lucrece, hopes her love for Theotormon, in the ideal scenario promised by a new dawn (and Theotormon's reciprocation), might help eradicate the crime. The day brings for Oothoon not respite but the same effects that Lucrece's rhetoric (which ironically *mobilizes* those effects) had tried to ward off:

> Instead of morn arises a bright shadow, like an eye
> In the eastern cloud: instead of night a sickly charnel house;
> That Theotormon hears me not! To him the night and morn
> Are both alike: a night of sighs, a morning of fresh tears; (pl. 2: 35–9 E 47)

The rhetoric of a revolution that changes nothing, a new world that repeats in a different way the old one, the planetary eye from the East depicted in the frontispiece to *Visions* that looks back as if it was still night, still dark: the spirit of the New World (the American Religion) is no more enlightened, then, than that of the old.

Both in the figure of Oothoon and in the responses of the chorus-like daughters, Blake presents the hints, not of an alternative ontology, but of a form of questioning which *declares* the limits of what we can know, how we ought to live and what we may hope for.[14] In the midst of her disillusion with the dawn, Oothoon observes:

> They told me that the night & day were all I could see;
> They told me that I had five senses to inclose me up.
> And they inclos'd my infinite brain in a narrow circle. (pl. 2: 30–4 E 47)

The worldliness of an empiricism, which allows no more than what the senses provide, here turns up as the measure also of what is lost. Hegel accounts for the overemphasis on the senses in the eighteenth century according to a dialectic that required this phase before moving on to a more advanced one. From the 'Preface' to the *Phenomenology* again, he writes: 'Now the opposite need meets the eye: sense [*sinn*] seems to be so firmly rooted in what is worldly that it takes an equal force to raise it higher. The spirit appears so poor that, like a wanderer in the desert who languishes for a simple drink of water, it seems to crave for its refreshment merely the bare feeling of the divine in general. By that which suffices the spirit one can measure the extent of its loss.'[15] The finitude of the senses suggest their contrary, the infinite, opposed by Blake, on the one hand, to the modern mind closed in the name of enlightenment and, on the other, to crimes against freedom in the name of freedom itself.

A long set of questions follow in *Visions*, which in their different ways achieve a statement of considerable force. Oothoon voices a series of laments, or more precisely, questions that activate several of the various senses of *erotima*, the rhetorical question, whose function is to affirm or deny a point strongly by asking it as a question. In this classical figure of persuasion the form of a question serves as the implicature of a statement. At its most basic it serves the ironic, even sarcastic, purpose of drawing attention to the obvious. It is often given in reply to a question, which in that case would serve to rhetoricize the question being replied to – stressing its irrelevance as a question.[16] The rhetorical question, conventionally, does not require an answer but, when one is given, the effect is to intensify the sarcasm. *Erotima*, nonetheless, tends to include an emotional dimension that can have subtle ethical ramifications. Here Oothoon's questions are voiced in the hope that Theotormon will hear them and respond, but in the knowledge that only Bromion will hear. In this way they express a combination of wonder, indignation, sarcasm and dismay.

> With what sense is it that the chicken shuns the ravenous hawk?
> With what sense does the tame pigeon measure out the expanse?
> With what sense does the bee form cells? have not the mouse & frog
> Eyes and ears and sense of touch? yet are their habitations.
> And their pursuits, as different as their forms and as their joys:
> Ask the wild ass why he refuses burdens: and the meek camel
> Why he loves man: is it because of eye ear mouth or skin
> Or breathing nostrils? No. for these the wolf and tyger have.
> Ask the blind worm the secrets of the grave, and why her spires
> Love to curl round the bones of death; and ask the rav'nous snake
> Where she gets poison: & the wing'd eagle why he loves the sun
> And then tell me the thoughts of man, that have been hid of old.
>                                                    (pl. 3: 2–13 E 47)

The rhetorical questions, apparently affirming a radical disjunction of beings in the differences they have from each other, double up too as a kind of natural scientific inquiry, an Aristotelianism of the expanding world environment. The questions are in this way both statements refuting received wisdom and questions about an enigmatic natural world to which one of the beasts, 'man' (the one who asks the questions), also belongs. A little further on, the daughters of Albion themselves first overhear and then become almost the official auditors of Oothoon's cries, her emotive reception. Now Oothoon's lament is addressed to the figure named, for the first time in Blake's *oeuvre*, Urizen ('Creator of men! mistaken Demon of heaven'). The field of possible reception is expanding and so is the range of questioning:

> Does not the great mouth laugh at a gift? and the narrow eyelids mock
> At the labour that is above payment? and wilt thou take the ape
> For thy councellor? or the dog, for a schoolmaster to thy children?
> Does he who contemns poverty, and he who turns with abhorrence
> From usury: feel the same passion, or are they moved alike?
> How can the giver of gifts experience the delights of the merchant?
> How the industrious citizen the pains of the husbandman.
> How different far the fat fed hireling with hollow drum;
> Who buys whole corn fields into wastes, and sings upon the heath:
> How different their eye and ear! how different the world to them!
>                                                    (pl. 5: 6–16 E 48–9)

The subjects (or topics) in question are now not only the beasts but also the political and social relations of the beast called man. In question particularly, within the economic rationality of exchange and ownership, is the non-rational excess that alone defines love and desire (in analogy with the incompatibility of habitations, pursuits, forms and joys of mouse and frog respectively, despite their supposedly sharing the five common senses). Oothoon thus represents the anti-thetical position implied by the crude empiricism of 'Mans perceptions are not bounded by organs of perception' (E 2). And echoing both Plato (the allegory of the cave) and Descartes (the analogy of the window), the mocking fairy in the opening lines of *Europe*: 'Five windows light the cavern'd Man' (pl. iii: 1 E 60). In the 'Preludium' of the same prophecy, the questions asked are again not simply rhetorical:

> And who shall bind the infinite with an eternal band?
> To compass it with swaddling bands? And who shall cherish it
> With milk and honey? (pl. 1: 13–15 E 61)

This time, the question seems addressed as if there may, from some unheard of time, come an answer. In the same way, Oothoon's rhetorical questions imply – not merely on her part but at the enunciative, emotive, level of Blake's text itself, in the address between text and as yet undetermined reader – a deeper question, unvoiced, unheard.

## 2  The Question of Three Kinds

The question emerges as a real or imagined relation, on the emotional axis, that is woven of enigma and desire: questions asked, questions provoked, questions begged and questions posed. There are at least two distinct kinds of question, which can be formalized as follows: questions that can be answered (Q1) and questions without answer (Q2). From the point of view of Q1 all questions imply an ultimate answer (even if this means waiting for eternity). This point of view would not accept the possibility of the existence of Q2 and would thus perhaps be an impossible or ideal perspective; it implies that there may be answers before the question has even been posed. A question is posed that masquerades either as a declaration or provides in a rhetorical and often emotive register the excuse or at least the cue for the provision of an answer.[17]

The aphoristic style of texts like *The Marriage of Heaven and Hell* implies questioning or at least the demand for a response. In certain cases, where answers can be found or suggested, they help to produce new readings inexhaustibly; yet in others, where answers cannot be found or where they fail, where a textual concern remains questionable, readings can nonetheless seem even more suggest-ive and fecund. Here we shade over into the perspective of Q2, from which it can be acknowledged that certain kinds of question are beyond even speculation and pose a problem so paradoxical that no definitive answer could be or even ought to be hoped for. Q2 secretly or silently scandalizes those who would adopt the perspective of Q1. The existence, if it was allowed, of this kind of question would raise the question of a question of a third kind.

To consider what I here refer to now as Q3, in relation to a possible reading of Blake, would require a responsive condition that, in some way, is always yet to be decided. Because the answers to questions of the third kind (Q3) occur at the level of modality of enunciation, no such question could have been posed in advance of the event of reception or response for it devolves upon the addressee to explicate it. The rhetorical question is transformed into the question of rhetoric, the question of the exchange, which implies – in this *relation between* – a temporal sundering, which at once keeps the potential of events to come safe yet at the same time estranges the moment of utterance from all possible moments of response. The question (Q3) would thus be situated in the future of the address, which is in principle illimitable.

Blake's texts include explicit and implicit statements on their modality of enunciation, for which no question existed in advance (see de Luca 1991: 42–3). The question of Blake's addressee tends towards the second kind, whether considered in terms of the small particular gatherings that account for his contemporary audience, or instead if we acknowledge the intended future activation of his texts and designs, dismissive of any actual readers or viewers of this basically prophetic idiom, though here Q3 can perhaps be at least anticipated. By virtue of their indeterminate future, the texts can now be read and commented upon as they variously concern the Orient: its ideological significance, its economic and geographical boundaries, or in terms of the complexity of global culture. Blake's texts include material that undoubtedly justifies the recent critical attention to issues of race and slavery and the ways in which his mythical topographies resonate with European global imperialism. Blake's own involvement in the production and exchange of both commodities and ideas and his mobilization of already existing global networks remains suggestive. But a consideration of Q3 as distinct from Qs 1 and 2 would anticipate an answer in Blake to questions posed *from* the Orient; such an answer would inevitably offer a further implicit question posed *to* it.[18] Here the Orient becomes the responsive, responsible, site of significant production and decision, against the classic model of Western projection, of orientalist construction, the Western self constructing its identity through the imposition of its ideas of 'the other'. With Q3 a productive dialogue is enjoined.[19]

## 3 Questions Posed

Questions in Blake can take deceptively simple rhetorical forms, like Thel's motto:

> Does the Eagle know what is in the pit?
> Or wilt though go ask the Mole:
> Can wisdom be put in a silver rod?
> Or Love in a golden bowl?[20] (E 3)

These are not quite the simple rhetorical statements they might seem to be. The residue of questioning infects and animates these lines, as a critical history of contradictory attempts to decipher them attests.[21] The question about who or what one poses the question *to* puts the question itself into focus as perhaps the topic of the motto. The 'Proverbs of Hell' includes a statement concerning questions that are never asked:

> The weak in courage is strong in cunning.
> The apple tree never asks the beech how he shall grow, nor the lion. the horse; how he shall take his prey.
> The thankful reciever bears a plentiful harvest. (E 37)

In the 'Proverbs' the phrases that stand for the fires and energies of perpetual revolution, which in political terms Blake is supposedly committed to espousing, seem to have been undermined by a transfer of their force to a 'cunning', which is associated elsewhere in this text to reason, and to questioning, the implication being that by doubting the plenitude of one's 'harvest' one somehow depletes it. These questions about how to live according to one's nature, when asked of something predicated of quite a different nature, would thus lead to 'cunning' as opposed to the courage needed to live as one desires. Jean-Jacques Rousseau's second discourse, 'On the Origins and Foundations of Inequality Among Men', from 1782, had considered man from the metaphysical and moral point of view, by contrasting him with animals: 'In any animal I see nothing but an ingenious machine to which nature has given senses in order for it to renew its strength and to protect itself, to a certain point, from all that tends to destroy or disturb it.'[22] The difference, he goes on to argue, between animals and the 'human machine' is that while nature contributes everything in the operations of an animal, man contributes as a free agent to his own operations. The question *as such* thus emerges as an excess.

Thel's motto echoes rather subtly the traditions of the proverbial utterance. The fact that the 'motto' appears in the form of a series of enigmatic questions draws attention to its questionable questioning.[23] The questions imply that the motto concerns questioning itself, and not just whatever we might decipher as being its proper topic from the text (say, moving from the body of the text to its protagonist's motto and back in a questioning way) or its possible contexts, given Blake's familiarity with numerous traditions of words, proverbs or songs of wisdom that both precede the biblical texts and are found in geographically wider domains (and which include the epic forms of the *Iliad* as well as the *Mahabharata*). However, the traces of Ecclesiastes 12 in the motto do yield some significant connections. The interpretation of the silver rod and the golden bowl as the backbone and skull respectively of much popular biblical hermeneutics can be set against the alternative treatment that regards the passage from Ecclesiastes as adopting the ancient metaphor of the Oriental storm.[24] In either case (or even in both cases, which in certain ways come to more or less the same thing) the question concerns the relationship between (from Swedenborg, of course) wisdom and love, on one side, and the finite material vessels on the other. It would thus be a question concerning the relative endurance, the survival beyond corruption, of those qualities excessive to life and death. Survival beyond corruption implies a boundary between mortal finite existence and an unbounded, or at least unlimited, realm that would lie beyond this boundary, beyond the limited senses.

## 4  Questions Answered

The celebrated analogy of the senses in Alexander Pope's *An Essay on Man* also provides a sense of the relation between limits and the unlimited that returns in similar ways in Blake. The analogy exploits the parallelism that pervades the eighteenth century between sense as feeling and sense as meaning.

> The Bliss of Man (could Pride that blessing find)
> Is not to act or think beyond mankind;

No powers of body or of soul to share,
But what his nature and his state can bear.
Why has not man a microscopic eye?
For this plain reason, man is not a fly.
Say what the use were finer optics given,
To inspect a mite, not comprehend the heaven?
Or touch, if tremblingly alive all o'er,
To smart and agonize at every pore?
Or quick effluvia darting through the brain,
Die of a rose in aromatic pain?
If nature thundered in his opening ears,
And stunned him with the music of the spheres,
How would he wish that heav'n had left him still
The whispering Zephyr, and the purling rill?
Who finds not Providence all good and wise,
Alike in what it gives and what denies? (1, 189–286)[25]

In the *Essay* Pope apparently puts to work a range of arguments, systems and philosophical conceits familiar from contemporary debates about theology, science, metaphysics and ethics, the latter still a really quite new topic in the field of increasingly autonomous intellectual domains. Exhausted philosophical systems jostle uneasily with speculatively modern arguments – concerning the nature of matter, the being of God, providence, fortune, fate and chance, the state of Man, what Man can know, what he ought to do and, yes, what he can hope for. Pope's essay aroused considerable interest – from praise to condemnation – in the continental intellectual scene as presenting some kind of systematic account of metaphysical, or onto-theological law. It is fair to say, however, that many commentators then and now have also criticized the philosophy in it as variously unorthodox, jumbled, derivative, contradictory, radical, conservative and commonplace.

With these considerations in mind we can return to the quotation on the 'Bliss of Man'. The senses of the word 'bliss' in this period of its etymological development remain affected by a long-term influence from the word 'blessed' (which for centuries has been confused with it) and so bliss can mean joy or happiness as well as perfection and grace.[26] Man here would be no more than the mere limit of his own bliss (perfection, joy), which in the analogy stands also for knowledge. The classical dialectic between soul and body (also the Cartesian distinction between mind and body) emerges as an aporia of limitation when informed by the notion of sensible limits beyond which only danger, pain and death await. Providence in this passage *saves* man from the evils of infinite sensitivity, from 'microscopic eye', infinite tenderness to the tactile world, etc. In other words, the five senses, as powerful defences against a terrifying material universe, stand for sense, in the sense of reason, order, harmony, a necessary limit to the dullness of an infinitely regressing and transgressing wit. Yet Man just is this limit, beyond which one cannot act, think or feel. So if the analogy of the senses provides the nature of the limit then the analogy itself most clearly and empirically embodies the condition it evokes. Man's condition, blindness to the future, is both the finitude of limited mortality and the infinite beyond of its futural repetition, which imposes on him the same conditions as those imposed by the future of the poem, which must be thought of as a condition of the 'whatever is', that is, of the being of the poem itself, and thus of the being of Man. Chance is not *opposed* to necessity; rather the necessary law is that there be chance.

The virginal Thel, in some ways, can be read as dramatizing Pope's failure of the will and the questions in Section IV of *Thel*, posed by a kind of spectral future beyond the grave from which she flees with a shriek, seem also to have adopted the scheme if not the attitude of Pope's mode of questioning:

> Why cannot the Ear be closed to its own destruction?
> Or the glistening Eye to the poison of a smile!
> Why are Eyelids stored with arrows ready drawn,
> Where a thousand fighting men in ambush lie?
> Or an Eye of gifts & graces, show'ring fruits and coined gold!
> Why a tongue impress'd with honey from every wind?
> Why an Ear, a whirlpool fierce to draw creations in?
> Why a Nostril wide inhaling terror trembling & affright.
> Why a tender curb upon the youthful burning boy!
> Why a little curtain of flesh on the bed of our desire?
>
> (pl. 6: 11–20 E 6)

Both passages in their structure confirm a relation between the limited and the unlimited. Perhaps Blake's questions serve to rhetoricize Pope's ironically, as if the possibility of sensual suffering, which is Pope's key analogical device, required more acknowledgement as a source of the powers *in* question. But Blake shares with Pope another assumption about the species-specific limitations of the senses. In *The Marriage of Heaven and Hell* the speaker recounts 'a memorable fancy':

> When I came home; on the abyss of the five senses, where a flat sided steep frowns over the present world. I saw a mighty Devil folded in black clouds, hovering on the sides of the rock, with corroding fires he wrote the following sentence now perceived by the minds of men, & read by them on earth.

> How do you know but ev'ry Bird that cuts the airy way,
> Is an immense world of delight, clos'd by your senses five? (E 35)

Now, Pope's questions (voiced by the reasoning intellect albeit carried on the wings of Pegasus) imply that the failure of the senses to perceive everything that, in principle, ought to be perceivable by them is a gift of providence, which thus filters out or depresses the more damaging sensible forces of the material world. And they imply that as this is the case for the senses, it is also the case for desire. The relationship between sensation and desire would be analogical; the supposedly obvious answers to the questions about sense become in the analogy pedagogic sentences about the judicious limitation of desire. Blake's questions (voiced as they are variously by devils, fairies or spectres) also imply a continuity between what can be perceived and what lies beyond sensation; but there's no safety in analogy – the questions asked in Blake's texts concern matters of sensation that go beyond sensation, as if desire was expressed fundamentally on the dangerous borders of what can be endured by Mankind's limiting senses. The sentence written by a Devil in 'corroding fires' and perceived by whoever reads it, once printed from Blake's corroded copper, operates as an analogue for what it is itself, as if it is the sentence that 'cuts its airy way'. In this precise sense the written text alone provides the most forceful critical alternative to empiricism.

## 5 Answers Unquestioned

In Blake's texts, on the contrary, sensation designates at once a partially determined realm of signals through which creatures interpret or even project their
natures and a kind of veil that keeps them from their natures. In *Visions of the
Daughters of Albion*, Oothoon's lament, a kind of rhetorical questioning, leads in
an implicit allusion to Pope to auratic imploring:

> Take thy bliss O Man!
> And sweet shall be thy taste & sweet thy infant joys renew! (pl. 6: 2–3 E 49)

The questions asked in this long and complex lament for thwarted possibility
shade already into questions of the third kind. The division between the abyss
of the senses and what lies beyond is structured in the form of a repetition,
where what cannot be perceived is repeated in a form that can be. A sentence –
which in each case takes the form of a question – concerns an impossible perception. But if a sentence is nothing more than the split-off, engraved repetition
of an earlier thought or perception, then the sentence already takes something
like that earlier form, which as a sense perception is already divided in itself.

This paradoxical division takes the form of a perception (e.g. the engraved
sentence) that repeats nothing that was ever present for perception, and leads to
a new kind of question. Pope's analogical narrative satire of man seeking the
infinite material of sensation from within his finite senses has intensified in Blake
to become a parody of modern reason. The questioning emerges most clearly in
the interminably worked and reworked *Vala* or *The Four Zoas*. Urizen's question is
presented as a form of seeking – a quest as distinct from a simple question – and,
again, in the tradition of the quest narrative, a quest without a goal outside the
quest itself. As is conventional with the epic form – here in a parody of Milton –
this apparently thwarted attempt at an epic or mythic treatment of world history
begins after fall and in division. 'Night the Ninth' – itself an impressive adaptation
of Revelation – has Urizen coming to realization of the self-destructive role his
quest has played in bringing about the apocalypse:

> I alone in misery supreme
> Ungratified give all my joy unto this Luvah & Vala
> Then Go O dark futurity I will cast thee forth from these
> Heavens of my brain nor will I look upon futurity more
> I cast futurity away & turn my back upon that void
> Which I have made for lo futurity is in this moment (pl. 21: 17–22 E 390)

Urizen's realization, then, is that the future is not something to be sought
but something that provokes seeking without end. This realization provokes a
further question – also without answer – that clearly engages with the paradoxical
condition of division and repetition:

> Where shall we take our stand to view the infinite & unbounded
> Or where are human feet for Lo our eyes are in the heavens
> (pl. 22: 24–25 E 391)[27]

There is yet a further echo (or it could be a repetition, simulation or appropriation) of Pope here, who in the *Essay on Man* invokes an absolute and infinitely
unknowable beyond:

> Heav'n from all creatures hides the book of fate,
> All but the page prescribed, their present state [. . .]
> The lamb thy riot dooms to bleed to-day
> Had he thy reason, would he skip and play?
> Pleas'd to the last, he crops the flow'ry food,
> And licks the hand just rais'd to shed his blood.
> Oh blindness to the future! kindly giv'n,
> That each may fill the circle marked by heav'n;[28]

This short passage, opened and closed by a circular 'heav'n', gives us what we cannot know, inscribes within the enclosure of our possible knowledge what is outside the 'circle', but it also prefigures the circles that Urizen inscribes by trying to escape them.

The main premise for this chapter derives from an attempt to think how a response to the rubric 'Blake in the Orient' could avoid *begging* a question. There are many ways to achieve this, of course, for instance by looking for signs of the Orient or orientalism *in* Blake (for which there are plenty of opportunities) or by documenting the various ways in which Blake is studied, adapted, translated or otherwise incorporated into regions of the world regarded as oriental. A third possibility, however, emerges when one considers the Orient as the possible source of questions about Blake that Blake's texts themselves fail to ask. In this way the future of Blake is assured (yet no salvation, no sacrifice and no tragic revelation could be guaranteed). As I have already observed, Blake's question from the Orient would put him opposite Hegel: two visions of world history, each with a place for the Orient and each with a quasi-systematic attempt to dissolve division and bring world history to an end. Blake would only ever have actually been *in* the Orient in visions, searching there amongst 'those wonderful originals called in the Scriptures the Cherubim' for signs with which to build his walls and cities. So the emanations – the writings, engravings and drawings – of his mortal and fallen state would in some sense ensure an unredeemed futurity. The Orient – as 'Night the Ninth' confirms – was always Blake's future.

## Notes

1 Quotations of Blake's Poetry and Prose are from the Newly Revised Edition of *The Complete Poetry and Prose of William Blake*, ed. David V. Erdman (New York: Anchor Doubleday, 1988) and are cited parenthetically in the text with the letter 'E'.

2 Hegel 1970: 17.

3 'The artist having been taken in vision into the ancient republics, monarchies, and patriarchates of Asia [. . .]' (E 531).

4 Rampo's name, a verbal translation of the Japanese pronunciation of Edgar Allan Poe, is probably more well known in Japanese mystery circles than Poe's. Rampo's first story was published in 1923 in the mystery magazine *Shin Seinen*, which up until that time had specialized in publishing translations of western mystery writers like Poe, Doyle and Chesterton. An edition of some of Rampo's stories exists in translation: *Japanese Tales of Mystery and Imagination*, trans. James B. Harris (Boston: Tuttle, 1956).

5 Nāgārjuna is possibly the most studied philosopher of Mahāyāna Buddism and the founder of the Mādhyamika, or Middle Way, school. Graham Priest has compared Nāgārjuna to Derrida in *Beyond the Limits of Thought*. A useful translation of Nāgārjuna's *Mūlamadhyamakakārikā* exists with commentary by Jay Garfield: *The Fundamental Wisdom of the Middle Way: Nagarjuna's Mulamadhyamakakarika*.

6 See Weir 2003.
7 See Michael Hardt and Antonio Negri on the 'enormous potential of subjectivity . . . constructed and consolidated in terms of a prophecy of a world to come, a chiliastic project': Hardt and Negri 2000: 21.
8 For an application of Hardt and Negri's 'deterritorialized' concept of Empire to contemporary China, see Callaghan 2004.
9 Hardt and Negri's second book, *Multitude* (2004), further pursues the hypothetical, or imaginary, alternative to empire in what they assert would be the realization of true global democracy, 'the rule of everyone by everyone, a democracy without qualifiers'.
10 For further discussion, see Arthur Hatto's huge and indispensable survey and anthology, *Eos: An Enquiry into the Theme of Lover's Meetings and Partings at Dawn in Poetry* (1965).
11 Hegel, *Phänomenoloie des Geistes* 18–19. Translation here modified from Walter Kaufmann, trans and ed., *Hegel: Texts and Commentary* (Indiana: University of Notre Dame, 1965): 20.
12 Blake returns to the classical aubade in the second book of *Milton* (pl. 31 [34]: 28–63 E 130–1).
13 Shakespeare, *Lucrece, The Poems*, ed. F. T. Prince (1960) lines 771–6.
14 These take the declarative form of the famous questions asked by Immanuel Kant and to which his three critiques were advertised as answers. He connected the three questions to a fourth that silently organizes the critiques too: 'What is Man?' in Kant 1800; 1974: 29.
15 Kaufmann's translation (Hegel 1965: 16).
16 Examples by their nature quickly become clichés: 'Is Rock Hudson gay?' 'Is the Pope Catholic?' 'Do horses eat hay?'
17 For further explication, see Jacques Derrida on 'The sign is that ill-named thing, the only one, that escapes the instituting question of philosophy: "what is . . . ?" ' (Derrida 1976: 18.
18 As an alternative to the notion of 'Empire', the concept of 'the empirial' is introduced in Kennedy and Balshaw 1998: 175–95, and developed further in Bishop, Phillips and Yeo 2003: 1–34.
19 See Wang 2000: 114.
20 Richard Dover's website 1995 commentary offers this apparently confused gloss: 'An enigmatic quatrain, and one that opens more questions than it answers' (www.newi.ac.uk/rdover/blake/thelnote.htm).
21 Den Otter (1999: 633–55) focuses on questioning as if that was the very *theme* of the text, which he sees as putting into dramatic form principles of education similar to those found in Rousseau's *Emile*.
22 Rousseau 1987: 44.
23 Den Otter, again, correctly points out that ' "Thel's Motto" implies not only that Thel lacks knowledge about the pit, but also that she does not know whom to ask for information' (Den Otter 1999: 637).
24 De Luca has also written suggestively on Blake's relation to the eighteenth-century tradition of reading scripture in terms of an oriental sublime (De Luca 1991: 84–7).
25 Alexander Pope, *Essay on Man*, in Pope 1966: 239–82 (line numbers in the text).
26 The *OED* notes that at a very early date the popular etymological consciousness began to associate the meaning of the noun bliss ('benignity, blitheness, joy, happiness') with that of the verb bless and that the two words have mutually influenced each other since this early period: 'confusion of spelling is frequent from the time of Wyclif to the 17th c. Hence the gradual tendency to withdraw bliss from earthly "blitheness" to the beatitude of the blessed in heaven, or that which is likened to it'. By the seventeenth century, bliss as blitheness, gladness, joy, delight, enjoyment, in the physical, social, mundane senses had already passed into the senses of: 'mental, ethereal, spiritual: perfect joy or felicity,

supreme delight; blessedness'. Already by 1650 the two words are found together in relation but also in distinction.
27  On this infinitely recessive questioning, see Freeman 1997: 43.
28  Pope 1966: I: 77–87.

# 24 Afterword

Elinor Shaffer

In tracing the reception in Europe of any group of British authors there needs to be a recognition of the requirement to consider the history and culture of Europe as a whole, rather than as isolated national histories each with a narrow national perspective. The perspectives of other nations greatly add to our understanding of individual contributors to that history. Often these responses provide quite unexpected and enriching insights into our own history, politics and culture. Sometimes a major thinker or poet elsewhere creates other works on the spur of our familiar domestic products which are striking, even shocking and inconceivably new. As the literary history of any one country has too often been confined to its own reception of its authors, it is necessary to challenge the practice of defining the 'afterlife' of a writer as referring to reception only within his own country (or at most language). In time it may become possible to achieve a complex set of understandings of world literature, from many starting points.

Neither the delay in his recognition at home nor the fascinating acclimatization of Blake in the varieties of European Symbolism fully prepares one for his astonishingly fresh and focused impact on early-twentieth-century Japan. I was completely taken by surprise by the extraordinary ways in which the Japanese reception of Blake bore out his singularity. The conference at Kyoto was an immensely stimulating and exhilarating experience, which provided a seasoned comparatist with the primordial experience of encounter with the author, the text and the image in a wholly new guise that was quite beyond any of the available cultural parameters.

The first form of the encounter came through the impact of the exhibition at the University of Kyoto which displayed the many little magazines and periodicals that introduced foreign writers and artists to Japan. The use of fine printing as known to Blake and his later followers as a mode of conveying new cultural materials is very familiar in Europe; yet I had never before seen a Japanese example. I was also greatly struck by the small examples of the painting of Murakami Kagaku, especially the preparatory drawing for the 'Death of Buddha' representing a lost painting, and the papers stressing the influence of Blake on Japanese artists attempting to find a new way of expressing Buddhist religious experiences, or finding a 'third way' in Blake's spiritual drawing between Eastern and Western styles.

I have not yet made my way back to the original book by Soetsu Yanagi that introduced Blake to Japan in 1914; but the tributes in this volume prove this to be the work of an individual mind, a Buddhist thinker and critic working finely in his own terms on the ground of Blake. A more recent encounter is represented by Kenzaburo Ōe's astonishing novel *Rouse Up O Young Men of the New Age!* (1983). This sets out from his own chance encounter in an open book at a neighbouring seat at the library with Blake's words –

> That Man should Labour & sorrow & learn & forget & return
> To the dark valley whence he came to begin his labours anew –
> (pl. 110: 19–20 E 385)

as prophetic for his own life, and working up into a series of chapters each of which is a literary-critical tour de force on a different text of Blake presenting a terrifying and original reading in the context of his experiences of his own abnormal child. Each chapter contains an interpretation of lines, sometimes whole poems of Blake, not only those that are represented in the title of the novel itself and individual chapters, sometimes events out of Blake's life, and interwoven in a variety of ways with his son's learning experiences and his own. This is work of the highest order; and expressive of a tragic genius that magnifies himself and his mentor Blake, so distant in time and space, but so compellingly near in a blinding power of insight. Little by little, his founding experience of the prophetic quality of a single line from Blake is built up into a coherent response to the entire *oeuvre*, a process combined with an increasingly intense bonding with his son, dramatized with a sombre depth and a reconciling beauty.

In such manifestations of Blake's originality in the workings of other minds in other times, other words and other images one finds the best of justifications for the whole enterprise of 'reception studies' – not just in 'anti-Imperialist' Blake, nor in 'archetypal Blake', nor 'international Blake', nor even 'world' Blake, but in the fresh demonstration of how individual minds may root themselves in others equally individual. Both this volume and the Kyoto Conference on Blake in the Orient, out of which it emerged, offer an exemplary record of such encounters, and may serve as a permanent reminder of the unpredictable fertility of a major writer, at home and abroad.

# Bibliography

Abrams, M. H. (ed.) (1962), *The Norton Anthology of English Literature*. (2 vols) New York: W. W. Norton.
—— (1986), *The Norton Anthology of English Literature*. 6th edn (2 vols) New York: W. W. Norton.
—— (2000), *The Norton Anthology of English Literature*. 7th edn (2 vols) New York: W. W. Norton.
Ackroyd, Peter (2000), *London: The Biography*. London: Chatto and Windus.
Adlard, John (1964), 'Blake and the "Geeta" '. *English Studies*, 45, 460–2.
Akutagawa, Ryunosuke (1971), 'Bungeiteki na, Amarini Bungeiteki na' ['Literary, Much too Literary], in *Akutagawa Ryunosuke Zenshu* [The Complete Works of Ryunosuke Akutagawa]. Tokyo: Chikuma Shobo (9 vols), pp.161–2.
Allen, Grahame (2003), *Inflation: the value of the pound 1750–2002*. Research paper, March 1982. London: House of Commons Library.
Allentuck, Marcia (1967), 'Fuseli and Lavater: Physiognomical Theory and the Enlightenment'. *Studies on Voltaire and the Eighteenth Century*, 55, 89–112.
Altick, Richard D. (1978), *The Shows of London*. Cambridge, MA: Harvard University Press.
Ando, Kiyoshi (1991), 'Reception of Blake in Japan'. *Tokai Ei-bei Bungaku*, 3, 1–22.
Anonymous *An Account of the Colony of Sierra Leone, From Its First Establishment in 1793* (1795a), London James Philips.
Anonymous (1757), *A Political and Satirical History of the Years 1756 and 1757. In a series of seventy-five humorous and entertaining prints, containing all the most remarkable transactions, characters and caricatures of those two memorable Years. To which is annexed, an explanatory account or key to every print, which renders the whole full and significant*. London: E. Morris, near St. Paul's.
Anonymous (1790), *Ode for the Summer Anniversary of the Royal Arch Constitutional Sols; held at Brother Willoughby's Highbury Place, on Monday, 30th August, 1790. With an emblematic and historical view of the rise, progress, and constitution of the order. By the poet laureate at the lodge* [London].
Anonymous (1795b), *A Word of Admonition to the Right Hon. William Pitt, in an Epistle to that Gentleman, Occasioned by the Prophecies of Brothers, Fellows, &c. and the Notable Expositions of the Scriptures Prophecies by Brassy Halhed, M.P.* London: Printed for Cullen.

Anonymous (1868), 'Mr Swinburne on Mr Blake'. *Argus* [Melbourne] 2 June 1868, 5–6.

Antiquités Etrusques, Grecques et Romaines (1766–7), *Tirées du cabinet de M. Hamilton, Collection of Etruscan, Greek and Roman antiquities from the Cabinet of the Honble. Wm. Hamilton*. Naples: [Francesco Morelli].

Aoyama, Keiko (1995), 'Nihon ni okeru William Blake juyo no ichidanmen (2) – Shirakabaha to Yanagi Muneyoshi ni yoru Blake juyo no arikata' ['A phase in the reception of William Blake in Japan (2) – the way the school of *Shirakaba* and Muneyoshi Yanagi received Blake']. *Gakushuin Joshi Tankidaigaku Kiyo* [Bulletin of Gakushuin Women's Junior College], 33, 1–32.

Archer, Mildred (1980), *Early Views of India: The Picturesque Journeys of Thomas and William Daniell 1786–1794*. London: Thames and Hudson.

Ashton, W. G. (trans.) (1896), *Nihongi: Chronicles of Japan from the Earliest Times to A.D. 697*. London: Allen & Unwin, 1956.

Audebert, J. B. (1800–2), *Les oiseaux dorées ou à reflets métalliques*. Paris.

Audi, Robert (gen. ed.) *Cambridge Dictionary of Philosophy, The* (2001). 2$^{nd}$ edn. Cambridge: Cambridge University Press.

Bacon, Francis (1798), *Essays Moral, Economical, and Political*. London: Printed by T. Bensley for J. Edwards and T. Payne.

Baine, Rodney M. (1986; 1956), *The scattered portions: William Blake's Biological Symbolism*. Athens, GA: Agee Publishers.

Baker, Phil (2003), 'Secret City: Psychogeography and the End of London', in Joe Kerr and Andrew Gibson (eds), *London: From Punk to Blair*. London: Reaktion Books, pp. 323–34.

Baker, T. F. T (ed.) (1976), *The history of the county of Middlesex*. Vol. 5, Victoria History of the Counties of England. London: Oxford University Press for the Institute of Historical Research.

Bargen, Doris G. (1997), *A Woman's Weapon: Spirit Possession in The Tale of Genji*. Honolulu: University of Hawaii Press.

Barrell, John (1986), *The Political Theory of Painting from Reynolds to Hazlitt: 'The body of the public'*. New Haven and London: Yale University Press.

Barry, Edward (1788), *A Sermon Preached at Lambeth Church, Before the Royal Grand Modern Order of Jerusalem Sols, On their Anniversary, Thursday, 17$^{th}$ July, 1788*. [London].

Bayly, C. A. (1988), *Indian Society and the Making of the British Empire*. The New Cambridge History of India. Cambridge: Cambridge University Press.

—— (1989), *Imperial Meridian: The British Empire and the World 1780–1830*. London: Longman.

Beer, John (1969), *Blake's Visionary Universe*. Manchester: Manchester University Press.

—— (1970), *Coleridge the Visionary*. London: Chatto and Windus.

—— (1993), *Romantic Influences*. Basingstoke: Macmillan.

Behrendt, Stephen C. (1992), *Reading William Blake*. Basingstoke and London: Macmillan.

Bellin, Harvey F. and Ruhl, Darrell (eds) (1985), *Blake and Swedenborg: Opposition is True Friendship, An Anthology*. New York: Swedenborg Foundation.

[Beloe, William] (1817), *The Sexagenarian, or, The Recollections of a Literary Life*. (2 vols) London: printed for F. C. & J. Rivington.

Bentley, G. E. (1977), *Blake Books. Annotated Catalogues of William Blake's Writings.* Oxford: Clarendon Press.

—— (1988), 'Richard Edwards, Publisher of Church-and-King Pamphlets and of William Blake'. *Studies in Bibliography*, 41, 302.

—— (1991), ' "They take great liberty's": Blake Reconfigured by Cromek and Modern Critics – The Arguments from Silence'. *Studies in Romanticism*, 30, 657–84.

—— (1994), *Blake Studies in Japan: a Bibliography of Works of William Blake published in Japan 1893–1993.* Assisted by Keiko Aoyama. Tokyo: Japan Association of English Romanticism.

—— (1995), *Blake Books Supplement: a Bibliography of Publications and Discoveries about William Blake 1971–1992, being a Continuation of Blake Books (1977).* Oxford: Clarendon Press.

—— (1996), 'The journeyman and the genius: James Parker and his partner William Blake with a list of Parker's engravings'. *Studies in Bibliography*, 49, 208–31.

—— (2001), *The Stranger from Paradise: A Biography of William Blake.* New Haven: Yale University Press.

—— (2004a), *Blake Records.* 2nd edn New Haven: Yale University Press.

—— (2004b), 'William Blake and His Circle: A Checklist of Publications and Discoveries in 2003'. *Blake: An Illustrated Quarterly*, 38.1, 4–37.

—— (2005), 'William Blake and His Circle: A Checklist of Publications and Discoveries in 2004'. *Blake: An Illustrated Quarterly*, 39.1, 4–37.

Berch, Victor and Maxted, Ian (2001), *The London book trades of the later 18th century* (Exeter Working Papers in British Book Trade History 10). Exeter: Devon Library Services.

Berington, Simon (1763), *The Adventures of Sig. Gaudentio di Lucca . . . Giving an Account of An Unknown Country in the Midst of the Deserts of Africa.* [London].

—— (1786), 'The Adventures of Signor Gaudentio di Lucca'. *Novelist's Magazine* XXI. London: for Harrison.

Bernardi, Joanne R. (1997), 'Tanizaki Jun'ichirô's "The Present and Future of the Moving Pictures" ', in Amy Vladeck Heinrich (ed.), *Currents in Japanese Culture: Translations and Transformations.* New York: Columbia University Press, pp. 291–308.

Bertholf, Robert J. and Levitt, Annette S. (eds) (1982), *Blake and the Moderns.* Albany: State University of New York Press.

Bewick, Thomas (1790), *A General History of Quadrupeds.* Newcastle-upon-Tyne: S. Hodgson, R. Beilby and T. Bewick.

*Bhagvat-Geeta, or Dialogues of Kreeshna and Arjoon in Eighteen Lectures; with Notes* (1785;1959), Charles Wilkins (trans.). London: C. Nourse. Facsimile edn George Hendrick. Gainesville, Florida: Scholars' Facsimiles and Reprints.

*Bibliotheca Lindesiana, Handlist of Oriental Manuscripts, Arabic, Persian, Turkish* (1898). Privately printed.

*Bibliotheca Splendidissima. A Catalogue of a Select Portion of the Library of Mrs. Bliss, Deceased, Removed from her Residence at Kensington . . . (Which will be Sold by Auction, by Saunders & Hodgson . . . on Wednesday, April 26th, 1826, and Three Following Days)* (1826). London: Saunders & Hodgson.

Bindman, David (1977), *Blake as an Artist.* Oxford: Phaidon Press.

—— (ed.) (1978), *The Complete Graphic Works of William Blake*. [London]: Thames and Hudson.

—— (1987), *William Blake's Illustrations of the Book of Job*. London: William Blake Trust.

—— (1997), 'Blake's Vision of Slavery Revisited', in *William Blake: Images and Texts, Essays presented at a symposium held on October 29, 1994 in honor of the Huntington Library's seventy-fifth anniversary* [also published as *Huntington Library Quarterly* 58, 3&4]. San Marino, California: Huntington Library, pp. 97–106.

—— (2002), *Ape to Apollo: Aesthetics and the Idea of Race in the 18th Century*. London: Reaktion Books.

Bishop, Morchard (1951), *Blake's Hayley: The Life, Works, and Friendships of William Hayley*. London: Victor Gollancz.

Bishop, Ryan, Phillips, John and Yeo, Wei-Wei (2003), 'Perpetuating Cities: Excepting Globalization and the Southeast Asian Supplement', in *Postcolonial Urbanism*. New York: Routledge, pp. 1–34.

Bishop, Ryan and Phillips, John, *Unhinging the Senses* (forthcoming).

Black, Susan Easton (1990), *Bunhill Fields: the Great Dissenters' Burial Ground*. Provo: Religious Studies Center, Brigham Young University.

Blackstone, Bernard (1949; 1966), *English Blake*. Cambridge: Cambridge University Press; Connecticut: Archon Books.

BL Add MS 3694, Smeathman to Cumberland, 31 August 1783, 10 October 1783, cited in Stephen J. Braidwood (1994).

Blake, William (1893a; 1973), *The Works of William Blake, Poetic, Symbolic, and Critical*. Edwin John Ellis and William Butler Yeats (eds). (3 vols) London: Quaritch; with introduction by G. E. Bentley. New York: AMS.

—— (1893b), *Poems of William Blake*. William Butler Yeats (ed.), The Muses' Library. London: Laurence and Bullen.

—— (1905), *The Poetical Works of William Blake: a New and Verbatim Text from the Manuscript Engraved and Letterpress Originals*. John Sampson (ed.). Oxford: Clarendon Press.

—— (1937), *The Illustrations of William Blake for Thornton's Virgil with the First Eclogue and the Imitation by Ambrose Philips*. Geoffrey Keynes et al. (eds). London: Nonesuch Press.

—— (1965; 1998), *The Complete Poetry and Prose of William Blake*. David V. Erdman (ed.). Newly revised edn. New York: Anchor-Doubleday.

—— (1966), *The Complete Writings of William Blake, with Variant Readings*. Geoffrey Keynes (ed.). Oxford: Oxford University Press.

—— (1975), *The Marriage of Heaven and Hell*. Geoffrey Keynes (ed.). Oxford: Oxford University Press.

—— (1980), *The letters of William Blake: with related documents*. 3rd edn Geoffrey Keynes (ed.). Oxford: Clarendon Press.

—— (1991a), *Jerusalem*. Vol. 1. William Blake's Illuminated Books. Morton D. Paley (ed.). London: Tate Gallery.

—— (1991b), *The Songs of Innocence and of Experience*. Vol. 2. William Blake's Illuminated Books. Andrew Lincoln (ed.). London: Tate Gallery.

—— (1993a), *The Early Illuminated Books*. Vol. 3. William Blake's Illuminated Books. Morris Eaves, Robert N. Essick and Joseph Viscomi (eds). London: Tate Gallery.

—— (1993b), *Milton a Poem and the Final Illuminated Works: The Ghost of Abel, On Homers Poetry [and] On Virgil, Laocoön*. Vol. 5. William Blake's Illuminated Books. Robert N. Essick and Joseph Viscomi (eds). London: Tate Gallery.

—— (1995a), *The Continental Prophecies*. Vol. 4. William Blake's Illuminated Books. D. W. Dorbecker (ed.). London: Tate Gallery.

—— (1995b), *The Urizen Books*. Vol. 6. William Blake's Illuminated Books. David Worrall (ed.). London: Tate Gallery.

Blake/Hu, Yunfen (ed.) (2001), *Yuzhou zaichuangzaozhe* (The Re-Creator of the Universe). *Yishu tashi shiji hualang* (Century Arts Gallery of Great Masters) 49. Taipei: Kelin guoji tushu gongsi (Greenland International Books).

Blanchot, Maurice (1982), 'The Outside, the Night'. *The Space of Literature*, trans. Ann Smock. Lincoln: University of Nebraska Press.

—— (1980; 1986), *The Writing of the Disaster*, trans. Ann Smock. Lincoln: University of Nebraska Press.

Bloom, Harold (1963), *Blake's Apocalypse*. London: Victor Gollancz.

—— (1971), 'Dialectic in *The Marriage of Heaven and Hell'*. *The Ringers in the Tower: Studies in Romantic Tradition*. Chicago: University of Chicago Press, pp. 55–62.

—— (1973; 1997), *The Anxiety of Influence: A Theory of Poetry*. 2$^{nd}$ edn New York: Oxford University Press.

—— (1975), *A Map of Misreading*. New York: Oxford University Press.

Blumenbach, J. F. (1775), *De Generis Humani Varietate Nativa*. Goettingae.

—— (1790; 1828), *Collectionis Suae Craniorum Diverarum Gentium Illustratae Decades*. Goettingae.

Blunt, Anthony (1959), *The Art of William Blake*. New York: Columbia University Press.

Boehme, Jacob (1730: 1969), *Signatura Rerum: The Signature of All Things*. With an Introduction by Clifford Bax. Cambridge: James Clarke.

Bonehill, John (2004), ' "This hapless adventurer": Hodges and the London art world', in Geoff Quilley and John Bonehill (eds), *William Hodges 1744–1797: the Art of Exploration*. London: National Maritime Museum, pp. 9–14.

Boulanger, Nicolas A. (1764), *Origins and Progress of Despotism in the Oriental, and other Empires, of Africa, Europe and America*, trans. John Wilkes. Amsterdam.

Boyd, Arthur (1972), *Nebuchadnezzar*. Text by T.S.R. Boase. London: Thames and Hudson.

Bracher, Mark (1985), *Being Form'd: Thinking Through Blake's Milton*. New York: Clinamen Studies.

Braidwood, Stephen J. (1994), *Black Poor and White Philanthropists: London's Blacks and the Foundation of the Sierra Leone Settlement 1786–1791*. Liverpool: Liverpool University Press.

Brockington, J. L. (1989), 'Warren Hastings and Orientalism', in Geoffrey Carnall and Colin Nicholson (eds), *The Impeachment of Warren Hastings: Papers from a Bicentenary Commemoration*. Edinburgh: Edinburgh University Press, pp. 91–108.

Bruce, James (1790), *Travels to Discover the Source of the Nile, in the Years 1768, 1769, 1770, 1771, 1772, and 1773, in five volumes*. Edinburgh: printed for J. Ruthven, for G. G. J. and J. Robinson, Paternoster Row, London.

Bruder, Helen (1994), 'The Sins of the Fathers: Patriarchal Criticism and *The Book of Thel*', in Steve Clark and David Worrall (eds), *Historicizing Blake.* Basingtoke: Macmillan, pp. 147–58.

—— (1997), *William Blake and the Daughters of Albion.* Basingstoke: Macmillan.

Bryant, Barbara (1987), 'The Job Designs: A Documentary and Bibliographical Record', in David Bindman (ed), *William Blake's Illustrations of the Book of Job.* London: William Blake Trust.

Bryant, Jacob (1774;1979), *A New System, or An Analysis of Ancient Mythology.* 2nd edn (3 vols) New York: Garland.

Buchheim, G. (1979), 'A bibliographical account of Icones plantarum sponte nascentium in regnis Daniae et Norvegiae, better known as *Flora Danica*'. *Huntia*, 3, 161–78.

Buffon, George Louis Leclerc, Comte de (1791), *The System of Natural History Written by the Celebrated Buffon.* Perth: Morison.

Bullock, Charles F. (1901), *Life of George Baxter, Engraver Artist and Colour Printer, Together with a Priced List of his Works.* Birmingham: W. J. Cosey.

Burke, Joseph (1973), 'The eidetic and the borrowed image', in Robert N. Essick (ed.), *The Visionary Hand: Essays for the Study of William Blake's Art and Aesthetics.* Los Angeles: Hennessey and Ingalls, pp. 253–302.

Butler, Albert Foster (1969), *Robert Browning's Father: His Way with a Book – An Account of Annotations Made by Browning's Father in his Copy of John Landseer's Lectures on the Art of Engraving Delivered at the Royal Institution of Great Britain.* Michigan: Edwards Brothers.

Butler, Marilyn (1981), *Romantics, Rebels & Reactionaries.* Oxford: Oxford University Press.

Butlin, Martin (1969), 'The Evolution of Blake's Large Color Prints of 1795', in Alvin H. Rosenfeld (ed.), *William Blake: Essays for S. Foster Damon.* Providence: Brown University Press, pp. 109–16.

—— (1981), *The Paintings and Drawings of William Blake.* (2 vols) New Haven: Yale University Press.

—— (1989), 'The Physicality of William Blake: The Large Color Prints of "1795" '. *Huntington Library Quarterly*, 52.1, 1–17.

Butter, Peter (1978), 'Milton: The Final Plates', in Michael Phillips (ed.), *Interpreting Blake.* Cambridge: Cambridge University Press, pp. 145–63.

Byron, George Gordon (1970), *Byron Poetical Works.* Frederick Page (ed.). Oxford: Oxford University Press.

—— (1973–83), *Byron's Letters and Journals.* Leslie Marchand (ed.). (12 vols) Cambridge, MA: Harvard University Press.

Caillet, Laurence (1998), 'Time in the Japanese Ritual Year', in Joy Hendry (ed.), *Interpreting Japanese Society.* London: Routledge, pp. 15–30.

Callaghan, William A. (2004), 'Remembering the Future – Utopia, Empire, and Harmony in 21st-Century International Theory'. *European Journal of International Relations*, 10.4, 569–60.

Camper, Petrus (1794), *Works of the late Professor Camper on The Connexion between the Science of Anatomy and The Arts of Drawing, Painting, Statuary, &c. &c*, trans. T. Cogan, M.D. London.

Carr, Robert (1987), 'Divine Construct and the Individual Will: Swedenborgian Theology in *The Book of Thel*', *Colby Library Quarterly*, 23, 77–88.

Carretta, Vincent (1990), *George III and the Satirists from Hogarth to Byron*. Athens and London: University of Georgia Press.

*Catalogue of the greater part of the valuable library of the Rev. S. R. Maitland, D.D., in which will be found . . . bibliographical works, and books in general literature, a volume of indian drawings . . . etc. etc. (Which will be sold by auction, by Messrs. Puttick and Simpson . . . on Monday, April 29th, 1850)* (1850). [London].

Centro Di (1979), *The Poetical Circle: Fuseli and the British: Henry Fuseli and James Barry, William Blake, John Brown, John Flaxman, James Jefferys, John Hamilton Mortimer, George Romney, Alexander Runciman: Australia, New Zealand, April–November*. Florence: Centro Di.

Chand, Tara (1965), *The History of The Freedom Movement in India*. (4 vols) Delhi.

Chang, Ching-erh (1988), 'Shi lun wenxue yu qita yishu jian de guanxi' [On the Mutual Illumination of Literature and Other Arts]. *Chung-wai Literary Monthly*, 16.12, 87–105.

—— (2004), *Research Bibliography of Western Literature in Taiwan 1946–2000*. (2 vols) Taipei: National Science Council.

Chang, Han-liang (1981), 'Blake de shi zhong hua yu hua zhong shi' [Blake's Painting in Poetry and Poetry in Painting], *Zhongguo shibao (China Times)*, 9 April, 8 (*Literary Supplement*); later collected in Chang (1986), *Bijiao wenxue lilun yu shijian* [Theory and Practice of Comparative Literature]. Taipei: Dongda tushu gongsi, pp. 305–10.

Chen, Pei-chün (1997), 'A Study of Social Criticism in William Blake's Songs of Innocence and of Experience and Its Application to English Teaching'. Unpublished MA thesis. National Chang-hua Normal University.

Chen, Peng-hsiang (1977), 'Social Satire and Humanitarianism in William Blake's Poetry'. *Studies in English Literature & Linguistics*, 2, 23–34.

Chen, Zhifan (1994), 'Shi kong zhi hai – chenggong hu bian sanji zhi san' ('The Sea of Time and Space – A Third Essay Written on the Side of Chenggong Lake'). *Lianhe bao (United Daily News)*, 8 January, 37 (*Literary Supplement*).

'Chinoiserie and Gothic' (1984), in Michael Snodin (ed.) *et al.*, *Rococo: Art and Design in Hogarth's England*. London: V & A, Trefoil Books.

Ch'iu, Yü-wen (2002), 'The Romantic Poetics of the Unconscious'. Unpublished MA thesis. National Ching-hua University.

Chou, Chung-hsing (1977), 'Twin-poems in William Blake's Songs of Innocence and Songs of Experience'. Unpublished MA thesis. Chinese Culture University.

Chou, Man-wen (1974), 'A Study of William Blake's *Songs of Innocence and Songs of Experience* Reflecting the Two Contrary States of the Human Soul'. *Taipei shangyie zuanke xuebao (Journal of National Taipei Junior College of Business)*, 3, 223–53.

Chu, Yen (1975), 'Ou Mei wenxue chuangzuo zhong de lingxiang' ('The Vision in Euro-American Literary Creation'). *Chung-wai Literary Monthly*, 4.1, 116–27.

Clark, Steve and Worrall, David (eds) (1994), *Historicizing Blake*. London: Macmillan.

—— (2003), *Blake in the Nineties*. Basingstoke: Macmillan.

—— (2005), *Blake, Nation and Empire*. Basingstoke: Palgrave Macmillan

Clarke, G. H. (1919), *Baxter Colour Prints*. London: Maggs Bros.

Clarkson, Thomas (1786), *An Essay on the Slavery and Commerce of the Human*

*Species, particularly the African*, translated from a Latin dissertation. London: T. Cadell, J. Phillips.

Clunas, Craig (1984), *Chinese Export Watercolours. Far Eastern Series.* London: Victoria & Albert Museum.

Coleman, Deidre (2005), *Romantic Colonization and British Anti-Slavery.* Cambridge: Cambridge University Press.

Coleridge, Samuel Taylor (1970–2001), *The Collected Works of Samuel Taylor Coleridge.* Kathleen Coburn (ed.). (16 vols) Princeton: Princeton University Press.

Colley, Linda (1992), *Britons.* New Haven: Yale University Press.

Connolly, Tristanne (2002), *William Blake and the Body.* Basingstoke: Palgrave Macmillan.

Copeland, Robert (1982; 2000), *Blue and White Transfer-printed Pottery.* Princes Risborough: Shire Publications.

Cordingley, James (1948–9), *Early Colour Printing and George Baxter (1804–1867): A Monograph.* London: The North-Western Polytechnic, Prince of Wales Road.

Cox, Philip (1994), 'Blake, Hayley and Milton: a reassessment', *English Studies*, 75, 430–41.

Critchley, Simon (1997), *Very Little . . . Almost Nothing: Death, Philosophy, Literature.* London: Routledge.

Cross, David A. (2000), *A Striking Likeness: The Life of George Romney.* Aldershot: Ashgate.

Cross, F. L. and Livingstone, E. A. (eds) (1978), *The Oxford Dictionary of the Christian Church.* 2nd edn Oxford: Oxford University Press.

Cugoano, Quobna Ottabah (1999), *Thoughts and Sentiments on the Evil of Slavery.* Vincent Carretta (ed.). Harmondsworth: Penguin.

Cumberland, George (1798; 1991), *The Captive of the Castle of Senaar.* G. E. Bentley (ed.). Montreal & Kingston, London: McGill-Queen's University Press.

Curtin, Philip D. (1965), *The Image of Africa: British Ideas and Action, 1780–1850.* London: Macmillan.

Damon, S. Foster (1924: 1958), *William Blake: His Philosophy and Symbols.* Gloucester, MA: Peter Smith.

—— (1971), *A Blake Dictionary: The Ideas and Symbols of William Blake.* New York: E. P. Dutton.

—— (1965: 1988), *A Blake Dictionary: The Ideas and Symbols of William Blake.* Revised edn with a new Foreword and annotated Bibliography by Morris Eaves. Providence, Rhode Island: Brown University Press.

Daniell, Thomas (1795–1807), *Oriental scenery: . . . views in Hindoostan drawn and engr. by T. Daniell.* (6 parts in 3 vols) London: T. Daniell.

Darwin, Erasmus (1791), *The Botanic Garden.* (2 vols) London: J. Johnson.

—— (1806; 1997), *The Poetical Works of Erasmus Darwin.* (3 vols) Rpt. Tokyo, Japan: Hon-No-Tomosha.

—— (1991), *The Loves of the Plants 1789.* Oxford and New York: Woodstock Books.

Davies, J.G. (1948), *The Theology of William Blake.* Oxford: Clarendon Press.

Davies, Keri (1999), 'Mrs Bliss: a Blake Collector of 1794', in Steve Clark and David Worrall (eds), *Blake in the Nineties.* Basingstoke: Macmillan, pp. 212–30.

—— (2003), *William Blake in Contexts: Family, Friendships, and Some Intellectual Microcultures of Eighteenth- and Nineteenth-Century England.* Unpublished PhD thesis. St Mary's College, University of Surrey.

Debord, Guy (1967; 1987), *Society of the Spectacle.* Exeter: Rebel Press.

—— (2002), 'Report on the Construction of Situations and on the Terms of Organization and Action of the International Situationist Tendency', in Tom McDonough (ed.), *Guy Debord and the Situationist International: Text and Documents.* Cambridge, MA: MIT Press, pp. 29–50.

De Certeau, Michel (1974; 1984), *The Practice of Everyday Life,* trans. Steven Rendall. Berkeley: University of California Press.

De Luca, Vincent A. (1991), *Words of Eternity: Blake and the Poetics of the Sublime.* Princeton: Princeton University Press.

De Man, Paul (1986), *Resistance to Theory.* Minneapolis: University of Minnesota Press.

Denize, Joseph (2000), 'La nature naturante: Blake et la Bhagavad-Gita'. *Rivista di Letterature moderne e comparate,* 53.4, 381–407.

Den Otter, A. G. (1999), 'The question and *The Book of Thel'. Studies in Romanticism,* 30, 633–55.

Dent, Shirley and Whittaker, Jason (2002), *Radical Blake: Influence and Afterlife from 1827.* Basingstoke: Palgrave.

De Ricci, Seymour (1930). *English Collectors of Books and Manuscripts (1530–1930) and their Marks of Ownership.* Sandars Lectures, 1929–30. Cambridge: Cambridge University Press.

Derrida, Jacques (1976), *Of Grammatology,* trans. Gayatri Chakravorty Spivak. Baltimore: Johns Hopkins.

Descartes, Rene (1984), 'Meditations on First Philosophy'. *The Philosophical Writings of Descartes.* Vol. II, trans. John Cottingham, Robert Stroothoff and Dugald Murdoch. Cambridge: Cambridge University Press.

Dibdin, Thomas Frognall (1814–15), *Bibliotheca Spenceriana: or, A Descriptive Catalogue of the Books Printed in the Fifteenth Century and of Many Valuable First Editions in the Library of George John Earl Spencer.* (4 vols) London: Printed for the author by W. Bulmer, Shakespeare Press, and published by Longman, Hurst, Rees [etc.].

—— (1817), *The Bibliographical Decameron, or, Ten Days Pleasant Discourse upon Illuminated Manuscripts, and Subjects Connected with Early Engraving, Typography, and Bibliography.* (3 vols) London: Printed for the author by W. Bulmer, Shakespeare Press.

Diderot, Denis and d'Alembert, Jean le Rond (1772), *Encyclopédie ou Dictionnaire Universel des Arts et des Sciences.* (17 vols) Geneva.

Doi Kochi (1977), *Doi Kochi Chosaku Shu* [Selected Works of Kochi Doi]. (5 vols) Tokyo: Iwanamishhoten.

Donoghue, Emma (1993), *Passions Between Women: British Lesbian Culture 1668–1801.* London: Scarlet Press.

Dorfman, Deborah (1969), *Blake in the Nineteenth Century: His Reputation as a Poet from Gilchrist to Yeats.* New Haven: Yale University Press.

Dörrbecker, D. W. (1994), 'Innovative Reproduction: Painters and Engravers at the Royal Academy of Arts', in Clark & Worrall (eds), *Historicizing Blake.* London: Macmillan, pp. 125–46.

Douglas, Bronwen (1999), 'Art as Ethno-historical Text: Science, Representation and Indigenous Presence in Eighteenth and Nineteenth Century Oceanic Voyage Histories in the Pacific', in Nicholas Thomas and Diane Losche (eds), *Double Vision: Art Histories and Colonial Histories in the Pacific.* Cambridge: Cambridge University Press, pp. 65–99.

Dover, Richard (1995), 'An enigmatic quatrain, and one that opens more questions than it answers'. www.newi.ac.uk/rdover/blake/thelnote.htm.

Drakard, David (1992), *Printed English Pottery: History and Humour in the reign of George III 1760–1820.* London: Jonathan Horne.

Drakard, David and Holdway, Paul (1983; 2002), *Spode Printed Ware.* London: Longman; Woodbridge: Antique Collectors' Club.

Duberman, Martin, et al (1991), *Hidden From History: Reclaiming the Gay and Lesbian Past.* Harmondsworth: Penguin.

Duus, Peter (1982), 'Liberal Intellectuals and Social Conflict in Taishō Japan', in Tesuo Nagita and J. Victor Koschmann (eds), *Conflict in Modern Japanese History: The Neglected Tradition.* Princeton: Princeton University Press, pp. 412–33.

Easton, Will (2005), 'William Blake and the Culture of Slavery in the late 1780s and 1790s'. *Blake Journal,* 9, 38–60.

Eaves, Morris (1982), *William Blake's Theory of Art.* Princeton: Princeton University Press.

—— (1992), *The Counter-Arts Conspiracy: Art and Industry in the Age of Blake.* Ithaca: Cornell University Press.

—— (1996), 'On Blakes We Want and Blakes We Don't'. *Huntington Library Quarterly,* 58.3–4, 413–39.

Egerton, Judy (1990), *Wright of Derby.* London: Tate Gallery.

*Ehon mushi erami. Illustrated by Utamaro with text by Yadoya no Meshimari* (1788), Ishikawa Masamochi (ed.). Edo: Tsuruya Shigesaburo.

Eliot, T. S. (1920: 1928), *The Sacred Wood: Essays on Poetry and Criticism.* 2nd edn London: Methuen.

Equiano, Olaudah (1789: 1995), *The Interesting Narrative and other writings.* Vincent Carretta (ed.). Harmondsworth: Penguin.

Erdman, David V. (1954; 1977), *Blake: Prophet Against Empire. A Poet's Interpretation of the History of his own Times.* 3rd edn Princeton: Princeton University Press.

—— (1974), *The Illuminated Blake.* New York: Dover Publications.

Essick, Robert N. (1980), *William Blake, Printmaker.* Princeton: Princeton University Press.

—— (1983), *The Separate Plates of William Blake: A Catalogue.* Princeton: Princeton University Press.

—— (1983–4), 'A Supplement to The Separate Plates of William Blake: A Catalogue'. *Blake: An Illustrated Quarterly,* 17, 139.

—— (1989), *William Blake and the Language of Adam.* Oxford: Clarendon Press.

—— (1991), *William Blake's Commercial Book Illustrations: A Catalogue and Study of the Plates Engraved by Blake after Designs by Other Artists.* Oxford: Clarendon Press.

Essick, Robert N. and Viscomi, Joseph (2002), 'An Inquiry into William Blake's Method of Color Printing'. *Blake: An Illustrated Quarterly,* 35, 2002a, 74–103.

Everest, Kelvin D. (1987), 'Thel's Dilemma'. *Essays in Criticism,* 37, 193–208.

Faderman, Lillian (1981; 1982; 1985), *Surpassing the Love of Men: Romantic Friendship and Love between Women from the Renaissance to the Present*. New York: Morrow; London: Junction; rpt. London: Women's Press.

Falconbridge, Alexander (1788), *An Account of the Slave Trade on the Coast of Africa*. London: J. Phillips.

Falconbridge, Anna Maria (1794; 2000), *Narrative of Two Voyages to the River Sierra Leone, During the Years 1791–2–3, Performed by A. M. Falconbridge. With Succinct Account of the Distresses and proceedings of that Settlement; a description of the Manners, Diversions, Arts, Commerce, Cultivation, Custom, Punishments, &c. And Every interesting Particular Relating to the Sierra Leone Company. Also The present State of the Slave Trade in the West Indies, and the improbability of its total Abolition*, ed. Christopher Fyfe. [London]; Liverpool: Liverpool University Press.

Fang, Shanghan (2003), *Shiti yu jidian – ershi shiji xieshixing shuicai de cailiao zhigan biaoxian zhi yenjiu* [Substance and Sediment: A Study of the Representation of Material in Twentieth-Century Realistic Watercolor Painting]. Unpublished MA thesis. National Taiwan Normal University.

Feldman, Burton and Richardson, Robert D. (1972), *The Rise of Modern Mythology 1680–1860*. Bloomington: Indiana University Press.

Feng, Pinjia (2002), 'Yingguo langmanzhuyi zaochi shizen: Huazihuasi yu Kelizhi' ('Early English Romantic Poets: Wordsworth and Coleridge'). *Youth Literature and Arts*, 579, 33–6.

Ferguson, Adam (1767), *An Essay on the History of Civil Society*. Edinburgh: A. Kincaird and J. Bell; London: A. Millar and T. Cadell.

Ferguson, Moira (1992), *Subject to Others: British Women Writers and Colonial Slavery, 1670–1834*. New York: Routledge.

Fischer, Rotraut and Strumpp, Gabriele (1989), 'Die Allegorisierung des Individuums in der Physiognomik Johann Caspar Lavaters und Carl Gustav Carus', in Rotraut Fischer, Gerd Schrader and Gabrielle Strumpp (eds), *Nature nach Mass: Physiognomik zwischen Wissenschaft und sthetik*. Marburg: Soznat, pp. 11–58.

Fisher, Peter F. (1961), *The Valley of Vision: Blake as Prophet and Revolutionary*. Toronto: University of Toronto Press.

Flaxman, John (1829), *Lectures on sculpture . . . As delivered by him before the president and members of the Royal Academy. With a brief memoir of the author*. London: J. Murray.

*[Flora Danica] Icones plantarum sponte nascentium in regnis Daniae et Norvegiae* (1761–1883). Copenhagen: Typis Nicolai Mölleri.

*Flower Ornament Scripture, The* (1993), A Translation of The Avatamsaka Sutra, trans. Thomas Cleary. Boston: Shambala.

Forster, John Reinhold (1778), *Observations Made During A Voyage Round the World, on Physical Geography, Natural History, and Ethic Philosophy*. London.

Frankau, Julia (1900), *Eighteenth Century Colour Prints: An Essay on Certain Stipple Engravers & Their Work in Colour*. London: Macmillan.

Freeman, Kathryn S. (1997), *Blake's Nostos: Fragmentation and Nondualism in The Four Zoas*. Albany: State University of New York Press.

Freud, Sigmund (1946), 'Die Verdrängung'. *Gesammelte Werke* X. Frankfurt: Fischer Taschenbuch Verlag.

Friedman, Joan M. (1978), *Color Printing in England 1486–1870*. New Haven: Yale Center of British Art.

Frye, Northrop (1947), *Fearful Symmetry*. Princeton: Princeton University Press.

—— (1957), 'Notes for a Commentary on *Milton*', in Vivian de Sola Pinto (ed.), *The Divine Vision: Studies in the Poetry and Art of William Blake*. London: Victor Gollancz, pp. 97–137.

Fulford, Tim and Kitson, Peter J. (1998), *Romanticism and Colonialism: Writing and Empire, 1780–1830*. Cambridge: Cambridge University Press.

Fulford, Tim (2001), 'Theorizing Golgotha: Coleridge, Race Theory and the Skull Beneath the Skin', in Nicolas Roe (ed.), *Samuel Taylor Coleridge and the Sciences of Life*. Oxford: Oxford University Press, pp. 117–33.

Fulford, Tim, Lee, Debbie and Kitson, Peter J. (2004), *Literature, Science and Exploration in the Romantic Era*. Cambridge: Cambridge University Press.

Fuller, David (2005), 'Mad as a refuge from unbelief': Blake and the Sanity of Dissidence' in Corinne Saunders and Jane MacNaughton (eds), *Madness and Creativity in Literature and Culture*. Basingstoke and New York: Palgrave Macmillan, pp. 121–43.

Fuseli, Henry (1768), *Remarks on the Writings and Conduct of J.J. Rousseau*. London: T. Cadell; J. Johnson and B. Davenport; and J. Payne.

—— (1831), *The Life and Writings of Henry Fuseli*. John Knowles (ed.) (2 vols) London: Henry Colburn and Richard Bentley.

—— (1975), *Henry Fuseli 1741–1825*. London: Tate Gallery.

Fyfe, Christopher (1962), *A History of Sierra Leone*. Oxford: Oxford University Press.

Garnier, Richard (1998), 'Arno's Grove, Southgate'. *The Georgian Group Journal*, 8, 122–34.

Gessel, Van C. (1993), *Three Modern Novelists: Sôseki, Tanizaki, Kawabata*. Tokyo: Kodansha International.

Giffard, Sydney (1994), *Japan among the Powers 1890–1990*. New Haven: Yale University Press.

Gilchrist, Alexander (1863; 1880), *Life of William Blake, 'Pictor Ignotus' With Selections from his Poems and Other Writings*. (2 vols) A new and enlarged edn London: Macmillan.

—— (1945), *The Life of William Blake*. Ruthven Todd (ed.). Rev. ed; London: J. M. Dent.

—— (1998a), *The Life of William Blake*. W. Graham Robertson (ed.). New York: Dover Publications

—— (1998b), *Life of William Blake with Selections from his poems and other writings*. (2 vols) Bristol and Tokyo: Thoemmes and Kinokuniya.

Goldsmith, Oliver (1774), *An History of the Earth, and Animated Nature*. (8 vols) London: J. Nourse.

—— (1795), *An History of the Earth, and Animated Nature*. (4 vols) Philadelphia: Mathew Carey.

Golley, Gregory L. (1995), 'Tanizaki Junichiro: The Art of Subversion and the Subversion of Art'. *Journal of Japanese Studies*, 21, 365–404.

Gourlay, Alexander S. (2002), ' "Idolatry or Politics": Blake's Chaucer, the Gods of Priam, and the Powers of 1809', in Alexander S. Gourlay (ed.), *Prophetic Character: Essays on William Blake in Honor of John E. Grant*. West Cornwall, CT: Locust Hill Press, pp. 97–147.

Graham, John (1979), *Lavater's Essays on Physiognomy: A Study in the History of Ideas*. Berne, Frankfurt am Main, Las Vegas: Peter Lang.

Grant, John E. (1999), 'On First Encountering Blake's Good Samaritans'. *Blake: An Illustrated Quarterly*, 33, 68–95.

Grégoire, H. (1810), *An Enquiry Concerning the Intellectual and Moral Faculties, and Literature of Negroes*. Brooklyn, NY.

Guest, Harriet (1992), 'Curiously Marked: Tattooing and Gender Difference in Eighteenth-century British Perceptions of the South Pacific', in John Barrell (ed.), *Paintings and the Politics of Culture: New Essays on British Art 1700–1850*. Oxford: Oxford University Press, pp. 101–34.

Haase, C. (1965), 'Georg Christian von Oeders Oldenburger Zeit'. *Oldenburger Jahrbuch*, 64.2, 1–58.

Hagstrum, Jean H. (1964), *William Blake, Poet and Painter: an Introduction to the Illuminated Verse*. Chicago: University of Chicago Press.

Hall, Carol Louise (1985), *Blake and Fuseli: A Study in the Transmission of Ideas*. New York: Garland.

Hall, Manly P. (1937; 1965), *Freemasonry of the Ancient Egyptians*. 4th edn Los Angeles: Philosophical Research Society.

Halmi, Nicholas (2004), 'Introduction', in Nicholas Halmi (ed.), *Collected Works of Northrop Frye*, Vol. 14. Toronto: University of Toronto Press, pp. xxiii–l.

Hamlyn, Robin & Phillips, Michael (2000), *William Blake. Exhibition Catalogue*. London: Tate Trustees.

Hane, Mikiso (1982), *Peasants, Rebels and Outcastes: The Underside of Modern Japan*. New York: Pantheon Books.

Hardt, Michael and Negri, Antonio (2000), *Empire*. Cambridge, MA: Harvard University Press.

—— (2004), *Multitude*. Cambridge, MA: Harvard University Press.

Harlow, Harry F., McGaugh, James L. and Thompson, Richard F. (1971), *Psychology*. San Francisco: Albion Publishing.

Harootunian, H. D. (1974), 'Between Politics and Culture: Authority and the Ambiguities of Intellectual Choice in Imperial Japan', in Bernard S. Silberman and H. D. Harootunian (eds), *Japan in Crisis: Essays on Taishō Democracy*. Princeton: Princeton University Press, pp. 110–38.

—— (1998a), 'A Sense of an Ending and the Problem of Taishō', in Peter Kornicki (ed.), *Meiji Japan: Political, Economic and Social History 1868–1912: Volume IV: The End of Meiji and Early Taishō*. London: Routledge.

—— (1998b), 'Figuring the Folk: History, Poetics, and Representation', in Stephen Vlastos (ed.), *Mirror of Modernity: Invented Traditions of Modern Japan*. Berkeley: University of California Press.

Hartley, David (1976), *Observations on Man*. With an Introduction by Theodore L. Huguelet. New York: Scholars' Facsimiles and Reprints.

Haskell, Francis (1987), 'The Baron d'Hancarville: an Adventurer and Art Historian in Eighteenth Century Europe', in *Past and Present in Art and Taste: Selected Essays*. New Haven: Yale University Press, pp. 30–45.

Hatto, Arthur (ed.) (1965), *Eros: An Enquiry into the Theme of Lovers' Meetings and Partings at Dawn in Poetry*. The Hague: Moulton and Co.

Hayley, William (1778; 1781), *An Essay on Painting*. 2nd edn Dublin: Pat Byrne.

—— (1785), *A Philosophical, Historical, and Moral Essay on Old Maids by a Friend to the Sisterhood*. (3 vols) London: T. Cadell.

—— (1802), *Designs to a Series of Ballads, written by William Hayley, Esq., and founded on anecdotes relating to animals, drawn, engraved, and published, by William Blake. With the ballads annexed*. Chichester: J. Seagrave; Felpham: W. Blake.

—— (1805), *Ballads Founded on anecdotes relating to animals, with prints, designed and engraved by William Blake*. London: Richard Phillips.

—— (1809), *The Life of George Romney, Esq*. London: T. Payne.

—— (1823), *Memoirs of the Life and Writings of William Hayley, Esq. The Friend and biographer of Cowper, written by himself. With extracts from his private correspondence and unpublished poetry. And memoirs of his son Thomas Alphonso Hayley, the young sculptor*. John Johnson (ed.). (2 vols) London: Henry Colburn and Simpkin and Marshall.

Hazlitt, William (1930), *The Complete Works of William Hazlitt*. P. P. Howe (ed.). (21 vols) London and Toronto: J. M. Dent.

Hearn, Lafcadio (1927a), *A History of English Literature: in a Series of Lectures by Lafcadio Hearn*. (2 vols) Tokyo: Hokuseido.

—— (1927b), *Some Strange English Literary Figures of The Eighteenth and Nineteenth Centuries: in a Series of Lectures by Lafcadio Hearn*. Ryuji Tanabe (ed.). Tokyo: Hokuseido.

Hegel, G. W. F. (1965), *Phänomenologie des Geistes*. Walter Kaufmann (trans. and ed.). Indiana: University of Notre Dame.

Henry, Lauren (1998), ' "Sunshine and Shady Groves": what Blake's "Little Black Boy" learned from African writers', in Tim Fulford and Peter J. Kitson (eds), *Romanticism and Colonialism: Writing and Empire, 1780–1830*. Cambridge: Cambridge University Press, pp. 67–86.

—— (1970), *Phänomenologie des Geistes*. Suhrkamp: Frankfurt.

Henshall, Kenneth G. (1988), *A Guide to Remembering Japanese Characters*. Rutland, VT and Tokyo: Tuttle.

Henty, G. A. (1896), *The Tiger of Mysore: A Story of War with Tippoo Saib*. London and Glasgow: Blackie and Son.

Heppner, Christopher (1977), ' "A Desire of Being": Identity and The Book of Thel'. *Colby Library Quarterly*, 13, 79–98.

—— (1995), *Reading Blake's Designs*. Cambridge: Cambridge University Press.

Hilton, Nelson (1983), *Literal Imagination: Blake's Vision of Words*. Berkeley: University of California Press.

—— (1986), 'An Original Story', in Nelson Hilton and Thomas A. Vogler (eds), *Unnam'd Forms: Blake and Textuality*. Berkeley: University of California Press, pp. 69–104.

Hind, A. M. (1908), *A Short History of Engraving & Etching*. London: British Museum.

Hindmarsh, Robert (1861), *The Rise and Progress of the New Jerusalem Church in England, America and Other Parts*. Edward Madely (ed.). London: Hodson.

Hinnells, John R. (1995), *A New Dictionary of Religions*. Oxford: Blackwell.

Hirano, Shigemitsu (1986), *Seiho Takeuchi – Some Anecdotes of the Artist*. Tokyo: Kodansha.

Hiratsuka, Raicho (1971), *In the Beginning Woman Was the Sun: The Autobiography of Raicho Hiratsuka's Life*. Tokyo: Otsuki-Shoten.

Hisamori, Kazuko (1977), 'Blake Juyoshi no Ichidanmen – Bernard Leach shi ni kiku [A phase in the History of the Reception of Blake in Japan: asking Mr. Bernard Leach]', in *William Blake. Bokushin-sha*, 6, 168–79.

Hobson, Christopher Z. (2000), *Blake and Homosexuality*. New York and Basingstoke: Palgrave.

Hodges, William (1793), *Travels in India, during the Years 1780, 1781, 1782, & 1783*. London: printed for the author and sold by J. Edwards, Pall Mall.

Hoff, Ursula (1986), *The Art of Arthur Boyd*. London: André Deutsch.

Honma, Hisao (1916), 'Minshu Geijutu no Igi oyobi Kachi'. *Waseda Bungaku*, 129, 2–13.

Howard, John (1976), *Blake's Milton: A Study in Selfhood*. Cranbury, NJ and London: Associated University Presses.

Hsia, C. T. (1993), 'Jinü, shibing, qiong xiaohai – Blake ming shi shangxi' [Harlots, Soldiers, Poor Children – Appreciation and Analysis of a Famous Poem by Blake]. *Zhonghua ribao* [*China Daily News*], 15–16 February, 11 (*Literary Supplement*).

Hsü, Beatrice H. C. (1993), *William Blake Revisited: A Kabbalistic Reading*. Unpublished MA thesis. National Chung-shan University.

Hudson, Nicholas (1996), 'From "Nation" to "Race": The Origins of Racial Classification in Eighteenth-Century Thought'. *Eighteenth-Century Studies*, 29, 247–64.

Hughes, Bernard (1959), 'Blake's work for Wedgwood'. *Country Life*, 126. 3261 (3 September), 194–6.

Hume, David (1758), *Essays and Treatises on Several Subjects*. A new edn. Edinburgh: printed for A. Millar, A. Kincaid and A. Donaldson.

Hunt, Leigh (1814), *The Feast of the Poets, with notes, and other pieces in verse*. London: James Cawthorn.

Hwang, I-ming (1991), 'Blake de "chou'e" meixue' [Blake's Aestheticism of 'Ugliness']. National Science Council of the Executive Yüan, microfilm No. 0103-H-80A-B-233.

Imai, Nobuo (1975), '*Shirakaba* no Shuhen: Shinshu kyoiku tono koryu ni tsuite [The Outpost of *Shirakaba*: on the interchange with the educators in Shinshu]'. Nagano: Shinano Kyoiku Shuppan-bu [Shinano Education Press].

Imperial Edict (1970), *The Shin Kokinshu: The 13th century Anthology*. H. H. Honda (trans.). Tokyo: Hokuseido Press and Eirinsha Press.

*Jachin And Boaz; Or, An Authentic Key To The Door Of Free-Masonry, Both Ancient And Modern* (1797). London: Printed for E. Newbery . . . Vernor and Hood . . . Champante and Whitrow.

Jackson, Anna and Jaffer, Amin (eds) (2004), *Encounters: The Meeting of Asia and Europe 1500–1800*. London: V & A Publications.

Jackson, John Baptist (1754), *An Essay on the Engraving and Printing in Chiaro Oscuro, as Practised by Albert Dürer, Hugo di Carpi, & c. and the Application of it to the Making Paper Hangings of Taste, Direction, and Elegance, By Mr. Jackson, of Battersea, Illustrated with Prints in proper Colours*. London: Printed for A. Millar, in the Strand; S. Baker, in York-Street, Covent Garden; J. Whiston and B. White; and L. Davis, in Fleet Street.

Jackson, Mary (1977), 'Blake and Zoroastrianism'. *Blake*, Illustrated Quarterly, XI, 74–6.

James, William (1983), *The Principles of Psychology*, Cambridge, MA: Harvard University Press.

Johnson, Mary Lynn (2004), 'Blake's Engravings for Lavater's Physiognomy: Overdue Credit to Chodowiecki, Schellenberg, and Lips'. *Blake: An Illustrated Quarterly*, 38.2, 52–74.

Jomard, E. F. (1809–28), *Description de l'Egypte*. Paris: Impr. Impériale.

Jones, David (1972), *The Anathemata: Fragments of an attempted writing*. London: Faber and Faber.

Joppien, Rüdiger and Smith, Bernard (1985), *The Art of Captain Cook's Voyages, Vol. 2: The Voyage of the Resolution and Adventure 1772–1775*. New Haven and London: Yale University Press.

Jugaku, Bunsho (ed.) (1929), *Iriamu bureiku shoshi* [William Blake: A Bibliography]. Special Binding Edition. Kobe: Guroria Sosaete.

Jugaku, Bunsho (1931), 'Blake in His Early Poems'. *Blake and Whitman*, 1:6, 262–7.

—— (1932a), 'Postscript'. *Blake and Whitman*, 2:4, 190–1.

—— (1934), *Bureiku* [*William Blake*]. Tokyo: Kenkyu-Sha.

Jugaku, Shizu (1932b), 'Postscript'. *Blake and Whitman*, 2:12, 567–8.

Kaempfer, Engelbert ([1727]1728), 'Appendix [selections from the Amoenitates exoticae]', in J. G. Scheuchzer (trans. & ed.), *The History of Japan*. London: Woodward.

Kalish, Richard A. (1973), *The Psychology of Human Behavior*. 3rd edn Monterey, CA: Brooks/Cole Publishing Company.

Kant, Immanuel (1800; 1974), *Logic*. Robert Hartman and Wolfgang Schwarz (trans.). New York: Dover.

—— (1960), *Observations on the Feeling of the Beautiful and the Sublime*, trans. John T. Goldthwait. Berkeley: University of California Press.

Kao, Tien-en (1990), 'Yingguo langmanzhuyi shiren ji qi zhongji guanhuai – Blake de lingxiang yuzhou' [English Romantic Poets and Their Ultimate Concerns – William Blake's Visionary Universe]. *Lianhe wenxue* [Unitas: A Literary Monthly], 6.3, 148–54.

—— (1999), 'Blake yu Wordsworth' [Blake and Wordsworth], in Ching-hsi Perng (ed.), *Xiyang wenxue da jiaoshi – jingdu jingdian* [Reading the Canon: Essays on Western Literature]. Taipei: Jiuke chuban she, pp. 303–27.

Kauffmann, C. M. (1984), *John Varley, 1778–1842*. London: Batsford.

Kelley, Theresa M. (2003), 'A Note About the Cover' and 'Romantic Exemplarity: Botany and "Material" Culture', in Noah Herrington (ed.), *Romantic Science: The Literary Forms of Natural History*. Albany: State University of New York Press, pp. xi–xii, 223–54.

Kennedy, Liam and Balshaw, Maria (eds) (1998), 'Singapore Soil: A Completely Different Organization of Space', in *Urban Space and Representation*. London: Pluto Press, pp. 175–95.

Kerr, Rose (2004a), 'Chinese Porcelain in Early European Collections', in Jackson and Jaffer, pp. 44–51.

—— (2004b), 'Asia in Europe: Porcelain and Enamel for the West', in Anna Jackson and Jaffer (eds), pp. 222–31.

Keynes, Geoffrey (1921), *A Bibliography of William Blake*. New York: Grolier Club.

—— (1949; 1971), *Blake Studies*. London: Rupert Hart-Davis. 2nd edn Oxford: Clarendon Press.

Kidson, Alex (2002), *George Romney, 1734–1802*. Princeton: Princeton University Press.

Kinpara, Samon (1967), *Taishō Democracy no Shakaiteki Keisei*. Tokyo: Aoki Shoten.

Kishida, Ryusei (1919; 1969–72), 'Omoide Oyobi Kondo no Tenrankai ni Saishite' [Recollections and on the Occasion of this Exhibition]. *Shirakaba*, 10.4, 361–75. Tokyo: Rakuyo Do. Rpt. by Kyoto: Rinsen Shoten.

Kitson, Peter J. (ed.) (1999), *Slavery, Abolition and Emancipation: Writings in the British Romantic Period*. Vol. 8, *Theories of Race*. London: Pickering & Chatto.

Kitson, Peter J. (2001), 'Coleridge and "the Orang-utan Hypothesis": Romantic Theories of Race', in Nicolas Roe (ed.), *Samuel Taylor Coleridge and the Sciences of Life*. Oxford: Oxford University Press, pp. 91–116.

Klein, Melanie (1988), *Love, Guilt and Reparation and other works 1921–1945*. London: Virago.

Knowles, John (ed.) (1831), *The Life and Writings of Henry Fuseli*. (2 vols) London: Henry Colburn and Richard Bentley.

Koizumi, Magane (1915), 'Henshu shitsu nite' [At the Editorial Office]. *Shirakaba*, 6.4, 367–8.

*Koizumi Yakumo Zenshu* [The Complete Works of Yakumo Koizumi] Daiichi–Shobo(1927), Tokyo: publisher.

Kornicki, P. F. (1993), 'The Japanese collection in the Bibliotheca Lindesiana'. *Bulletin of the John Rylands University Library of Manchester*. 7 75: 2, 209–300.

Kostelanetz, Annet (1960). 'Blake's 1795 Color Prints: An Interpretation', in Rosenfeld (ed.), *Essays for S. Foster Damon*. Providence: Brown University Press, pp. 117–30.

Kuroda, Jutaro (1947), *Kyoto Yoga no Reimei ki* [The Dawn of Western-style Paintings in Kyoto]. Kyoto: Koto Shoin.

Kusamitsu, Toshio (1995), 'Yanagi Sōetsu to Eikoku Chuseishugi', in Shirō Sugihara (ed.), *Kindai Nippon to Igirisu Shisō*. Tokyo: Nihon Keizai Hyoronsha.

La Belle, Jenijoy (1980), 'Michelangelo's Sistine Frescoes and Blake's 1795 Color-printed Drawings: A Study in Structural Relationships'. *Blake: An Illuminated Quarterly*, 14, 66–84

Lacan, Jacques (1977), *Ecrits: A Selection*, trans. Alan Sheridan. London: Tavistock.

—— (1979), *The Four Fundamental Concepts of Psychoanalysis*. Alan Sheridan (trans.). Harmondsworth: Penguin.

Lan, Ting (2000), 'Yingguo langmanzhuyi shidai de shiren' [British Poets during the Romantic Era]. *Yiyin yuekan* [*First Bank Monthly*] (I) 35.8 (August 2000): 86–97; (II) 35.9 (September 2000): 96–106.

Larrissy, Edward (1985), *Blake*. London: Routledge.

Lavater, Johann Caspar (1789), *Essays on Physiognomy*. Thomas Holcroft (trans.). (3 vols) London: G. G. J. & J. Robinson.

Lavater, Johann Caspar (1789–98), *Essays on Physiognomy*. Henry Hunter (trans.). (3 vols) London: for John Murray et al.

Leary, Emmeline and Walton, Peter (1976–7), *Transfer-printed Worcester Porcelain at Manchester City Art Gallery*. Catalogue. City of Manchester Cultural Services.

Leask, Nigel (2002), *Curiosity and the Aesthetics of Travel Writing 1770–1840*. Oxford: Oxford University Press.

Le Blon, Jacques Christophe (1725), *Coloritto; or the Harmony of Colouring in Painting: Reduced to Mechanical Practice, under Easy Precepts, and infallible Rules; Together with Some Coloured Figures, in order to Render the Said Precepts and Rules Intelligible, not only to Painters, but even to All lovers of Paintings*. London: n.p.

Le Brun, Charles (1701), *The Conference of the Monsieur Le Brun*. Translated from the French. London: David Mortier.

Lee, Debbie (ed.) (2001), *Travels, Explorations and Empires: Writings from the Era of Imperial Expansion 1770–1835*. London: Pickering and Chatto.

Lee, Debbie (2002), *Slavery and the Romantic Imagination*. Philadelphia: University of Pennsylvania Press.

Leonard, John (2000), 'Milton, Lucretius and "the Void Profound of Unessential Night" ', in Kristin A. Pruitt and Charles W. Durham (eds), *Living Texts: Interpreting Milton*. Selinsgrove: Susquehanna University Press, pp. 198–217.

Leu, Yün-shan (1992), 'Goodness and Evil: Human Nature in Blake's and Wordsworth's Poetry through the Relationship of Innocence and Experience'. Unpublished MA thesis. National Chung-shan University.

Levin, Thomas Y. (trans.), 'Unitary Urbanism at the End of the 1950s', in Elisabeth Sussman (ed.), *On the Passage of a few people through a rather brief moment in time: The Situationist International 1957–1972*. Cambridge, MA: MIT Press, pp. 143–7.

Levinas, Emanuel (1978), *Existence and Existents*. Alphonso Lingis (trans.). The Hague: Martinus Nijhoff.

Le Vaillant, François ([1801–] 1806), *Histoire naturelle des Oiseaux de paradis et des rolliers, suivie de celle des toucans et des barbus*. (3 vols) Paris: Denne, Perlet.

Levitine, George (1958), 'Addenda to Robert Rosenblum's "The Origin of Painting: A Problem in the Iconography of Romantic Classicism" '. *Art Bulletin*, XL, 329–31.

Lewis, Michael (1990), *Rioters and Citizens: Mass Protest in Imperial Japan*. Berkeley: University of California Press.

Li, Ch'ing-hsüan (1973), 'Innocence and Experience in Blake's Poetry'. Unpublished MA thesis. Chinese Culture University.

Liang, Shih-ch'iu (1985), 'William Blake', *Yingguo wenxue xuan* [Selections from English Literature]. Taipei: Xiezhi gongyie congshu chuban gongsi, Vol. II, pp. 1104–25.

Liao, Ping-hui (1988), 'Shi yu hua zhi bianzheng: Shi yi Wang Meng yu William Blake wei li' [The Dialectics of Poetry and Painting: Using Wang Meng and William Blake as Examples]. *Chung-wai Literary Monthly*, 16.12, 68–86.

Lichtenberg, Georg Christoph (1967–72), *Schriften und Briefe*. Wolfgang Promies (ed.). (4 vols) Munich: Carl Hanser Verlag.

Lilien, Otto M. (1985), *Jacob Christoph Le Blon, 1667–1741: Inventor of Three- and Four-Colour Printing*. Stuttgart: A. Hiersemann.

Lindsay, David W. (1989), 'The Order of Blake's Large Color Prints'. *Huntington Library Quarterly*, 52.1, 19–41.

Liu, Hwang-cheng (1993), 'Blake: Divine Vision'. *Journal of Chinese Military Academy*, 26, 177–214.

Locke, John (1975), *An Essay Concerning Human Understanding*. Peter H. Nidditch (ed.). Oxford: Clarendon Press.

Lowndes, W. T. (1864), *Bibliographer's Manual of English Literature*. Rev. edn London: H. G. Bohn.

Lowry, Malcolm (1962), *The Forest Path to the Spring. Hear Us O Lord From Heaven Thy Dwelling Place*. London: Cape, pp. 215–83.

—— (1995), *Sursum Corda! The Collected Letters of Malcolm Lowry*. Vol 1. 1926–46. Sherrill E. Grace (ed.). London: Cape.

Lu, Yujia (2002), 'Gei tianzhen yu shigu lüke de shi *Lai dao William Blake lüguan*'[A Poem to the Innocent and Experienced Traveller *A Visit to William Blake's Inn*]. *Lianhe bao* (*United Daily News*), 24 March 2002: 22 (*Dushuren* [*The Reader*]).

Lussier, Mark, 'Resisting Critical Erasure, or Blake Beyond Postmodernity'. Talk given in 2000 at Arizona State University. Online. http://english.asu.edu/ ramgen/english/lussier.rm; see also http://www.public.asu.edu/~idmsl/ postmodblake_.htm.

Macaulay, Thomas Babington (1972), *Selected Writings*. John Clive and Thomas Pinney (eds). Chicago: University of Chicago Press.

McCalman, Iain (1994), 'The Infidel as Prophet: William Reid and Blakean Radicalism', in Steve Clark and David Worrall (eds), *Historicizing Blake*. New York: St Martin's Press, pp. 24–42.

McKellar, Elizabeth (1999), 'Peripheral Visions: alternative aspects and rural presences in mid-eighteenth-century London', in Dana Arnold (ed.), *The Metropolis and its Image: Constructing Identities for London, c. 150–1950*. Oxford: Blackwell.

McKusick, James C. (1998), ' "Wisely forgetful": Coleridge and the Politics of Pantisocracy', in Tim Fulford and Peter J. Kitson (eds), *Romanticism and Colonialism: Writing and Empire, 1780–1830*. Cambridge: Cambridge University Press.

Maclagan, E. R. D. and Russell, A. G. B. (1904), *The Prophetic Books of William Blake, Jerusalem*. London: A. H. Bullen.

Madan, Martin (1780), *Thelypthora; or a treatise on Female Ruin, in its causes, effects, consequences, prevention, and remedy; considered on the basis of divine law: under the following heads, viz, marriage, whoredom, and fornication, adultery, polygamy, divorce; with many other incidental matters; particularly including an examination of the principles and tendency of Stat. 26 GEO II c.33. commonly called the Marriage act.* (2 vols) London: for J. Dodsley.

*Magna Carta Regis Johannis, xv die Juni, mccxv, anno regni xvii* (1816). London: John Whittaker.

Magno, Cettina Tramontano, and Erdman, David V. (1987), 'Introduction', in *The Four Zoas by William Blake: A Photographic Facsimile of the Manuscript with Commentary on the Illuminations*. Lewisburg: Bucknell University Press, pp. 13–21.

Maier, Michael (1617; 1989), *Atalanta fugiens*. [London]; Grand Rapids, MI: Phanes Press.

Makdisi, Saree (1998), *Romantic Imperialism: Universal Empire and the Culture of Modernity*. Cambridge: Cambridge University Press.

—— (2003a), *William Blake and the Impossible History of the 1790s*. Chicago: University of Chicago Press.

—— (2003b), 'The Political Aesthetic of Blake's Images', in Morris Eaves (ed.), *The Cambridge Companion to William Blake*. Cambridge: Cambridge University Press, pp. 110–31.

Malkin, Benjamin Health (1795), *Essays on Subjects concerned with Civilization*. London: C. Dilly.

—— (1806), *A Father's Memoirs of his Child*. London: printed for Longman, Hurst, Rees and Orme by T. Bensley.

*Man I Killed, The* (aka *Broken Lullaby*) (1932). Audio-Visual. Paramount, USA, 77 minutes, Black and White. Directed by Ernst Lubitsch. Writing Credits: Maurice Rostand, Reginald Berkeley, Samson Raphaelson. Cinematography: Victor Milner. Cast: Nancy Carroll (Elsa), Phillips Holmes (Paul), Lionel Barrymore (Dr Holderlin), Louise Carter (Frau Holderlin).

Marcus, Greil (2002), 'The Long Walk of the Situationist International', in Tom McDonough (ed.), *Guy Debord and the Situationist International: Text and Documents*. Cambridge, MA: MIT Press, pp. 1–20.

Marshall, P. J. (1965), *The Impeachment of Warren Hastings*. Oxford: Oxford University Press.

—— (1970), *The British Discovery of Hinduism in the Eighteenth Century*. Cambridge: Cambridge University Press.

Marvell, Andrew (1956), 'Bermudas'. *The Poems of Andrew Marvell*. Hugh Macdonald (ed.). London: Routledge and Kegan Paul.

Matsuhashi, Keiko (1999), *An Eternal Alto Singer: The Biography of Kaneko Yanagi*. Tokyo: Suiyo-Sha.

Matsushima, Shoichi (1986), 'Romanticism to sono Kenkyu: Blake no Juyo wo Toshite'. *Igirisu Romanha Kenkyu*, Igirisu Romanha Gakkai, 9&10, 21–7.

—— (2003), *Blake no Shiso to Kindai Nippon – Blake o yomu* [Blake's Thoughts and Modern Japan: A Reading of Blake]. Tokyo: Hokuseido.

Matthews, John (1788), *A Voyage to the River Sierra-Leone, On the Coast of Africa; Containing an Account of the Trade and Productions of the Country, and of the Civil and Religious Customs and Manners of the People in a Series of Letters . . . During his Residence With an Additional Letter on the Subject of the African Slave Trade*. [London].

Matthews, Susan (1998), 'Jerusalem and Nationalism', in John Lucas (ed.), *William Blake*. London: Longman, pp. 80–100.

Maxted, Ian (2001), *The London book trades 1775–1800 a checklist of members (Exeter Working Papers in British Book Trade History 0[sic])*. Exeter: Devon Library Services.

Mee, Jon (1992), *Dangerous Enthusiasm: William Blake and the Culture of Radicalism in the 1790s*. Oxford: Clarendon Press.

—— (1998), ' "The Doom of Tyrants": William Blake, Richard "Citizen" Lee, and the Millenarian Public Sphere', in Jackie DiSalvo, G. A. Rosso and Christopher Z. Hobson (eds), *Blake, Politics and History*. New York: Garland Publishing, pp. 97–114.

—— (2002), ' "As portentous as the written wall": Blake's Illustrations to *Night Thoughts*', in Alexander S. Gourlay (ed.), *Prophetic Character: Essays on William Blake in Honor of John E. Grant*. West Cornwall, CT: Locust Hill Press, pp. 171–203.

—— (2003), *Romanticism, Enthusiasm and Regulation: Poetics and the Policing of Culture in the Romantic Period*. Oxford: Oxford University Press.

Mellor, Anne (1974), *Blake's Human Form Divine*. Berkeley: University of California Press.

—— (1994), 'Sex, Violence, and Slavery: Blake and Wollstonecraft', in *William Blake: Images and Texts, Essays presented at a symposium held on October 29, 1994 in honor of the Huntington Library's Seventy-fifth Anniversary*. San Marino, CA: Huntington Library, pp. 69–94.

Melville, Herman (1992), *Moby Dick*. Hertfordshire: Wordsworth Classics.

Merian, Maria Sibilla (1726), *Dissertatio de generatione et metamorphosibus insectorum Surinamensium* . . . Dissertation sur la generation et les transformations des insectes de Surinam . . . [The Hague]: Pieter Gosse.

Mitani, Taichiro (1995), *The Age of Taisho Democracy: Japan's Response to American Influence in the Post-World War I Period*. Tokyo: University of Tokyo Press.

Mitchell, W. J. T. (1973), 'Blake's Radical Comedy', in Stuart Curran and Joseph Anthony Wittreich, Jr. (eds), *Blake's Sublime Allegory*. Wisconsin: University of Wisconsin Press, pp. 281–307.

—— (1978), *Blake's Composite Art*. Princeton: Princeton University Press.

Michael, Jennifer Davis (2002), 'Blake's Feet: Towards a Poetics of Incarnation', in Alexander S. Gourlay (ed.), *Prophetic Character: Essays on William Blake in Honor of John E. Grant*. West Cornwall, CT: Locust Hill Press, pp. 205–24.

Mill, James (1817–36: 1975), *The History of British India*. William Thomas (ed.). Chicago: University of Chicago Press.

Milton, John (1998), *Paradise Lost*. Alastair Fowler (ed.). 2nd edn London: Longman.

Miner, Paul (2002), 'Blake's London: Times & Spaces'. *Studies in Romanticism*, 41.2, 279–316.

Miyakawa, Toru and Hijikata, Kazuo (1977), *Jiyu Minken Shisō to Nihon no Roman Shugi*. Vol. 2. *Gendai Nihon Shisōshi*. Tokyo: Aoki Shoten.

Mizuo, Hiroshi (1992), *The Life and Work of Soetsu Yanagi*. Tokyo: Chikuma Shobo.

Moor, Edward (1810), *The Hindu Pantheon*. London: printed for Joseph Johnson.

Moore, Lisa (1992), ' "Something More Tender Still Than Friendship": Romantic Friendship in Early Nineteenth Century England'. *Feminist Studies*, 18.3, 499–520.

More, Hannah (1809), *Coelebs in search of a wife, comprehending Observations on Domestic Habits and Manners, Religion and Morals*. 4th edn (2 vols) London: Cadell and Davies.

More, Martha (1859), *Mendip annals: or, A narrative of the charitable labours of Hannah and Martha More. Edited, with additional matter, by Arthur Roberts . . . Third edition*. London: James Nisbet.

Munby, A. N. L. (1971), *Sale Catalogues of Libraries of Eminent Persons*. Vol. 2. *Poets and Men of Letters*. London: Mansell and Sotheby.

—— (1972), *Connoisseurs and Medieval Miniatures, 1750–1850*. Oxford: Clarendon Press.

Murakami, Shigeyoshi (1968), *Japanese Religion in the Modern Century*. H. Byron Earhart (trans.). Tokyo: University of Tokyo Press.

Mushanokoji, Saneatsu (1910), 'Rodan to Jinsei' [Rodin and Life]. *Shirakaba*, 1.8, 72–9.

—— (1913), ' "Aru E nitsuite" Oyobi Sono Ta Kanso' ['On a Painting' and Other Impressions]. *Shirakaba*, 4.7, 132–66.

—— (1917), 'Nikki no Kawari' [Instead of a Diary]. *Shirakaba*, 8.10, 27–53.

—— (1927), 'Bureku nitsuite' [About Blake]. *Taiyoka* [Sunflower], 10, 4–5.

Musselwhite, David (1986), 'The Trial of Warren Hastings', in Francis Barker et al. (eds), *Literature, Politics and Theory: Papers from the Essex Conference 1976–84*. London: Methuen, pp. 77–103.

Myers, Robin and Harris, Michael (eds) (1991), *Property of a Gentleman*. Winchester: St Paul's Bibliographies.

Myers, Robin, Harris, Michael and Mandelbrote, Giles (eds) (2000), *Libraries and the Book Trade*. New Castle: Oak Knoll Press.

Myrone, Martin (2001), *Henry Fuseli*. London: Tate Gallery.

Nagayo, Yoshiro (1918), 'Bijutsuka nitsuite' [About Artists]. *Geijutsu* [Art], 1.2, 1–12.

—— (1960), *Waga Kokoro no Henreki* [Journey of My Soul]. Tokyo: Chikuma Shobo.

Nakajima, Kunihiko (1991), 'Jikkan, bikan, kankyo – kindai bunkaku ni egakareta kanjusei (23): Blake inyu no imisuru mono – Yanagi Muneyoshi no kanjusei'[Actual feeling, aesthetic sense, sensation: sensibility in Japanese modern literature 23: what the reception of Blake in Japan means: sensibility in Muneyoshi Yanagi]. *Waseda Bungaku*, 176, 90–104.

Nakami, Mari (2003), *Yanagi Muneyoshi: Jidai to Shiso* [The Times and Thought of Yanagi Sōetsu]. Tokyo: University of Tokyo Press.

Nakamura, Seiko (1917), 'Minshu Geijutsu toshiteno Shousetsu'. *Waseda Bungaku*, 135, 53–5.

Nanavutty, Piloo (1957), 'William Blake and Hindu Creation Myths', in Vivian de Sola Pinto (ed.), *The Divine Vision: Studies in the Poetry and Art of William Blake*. London: Gollancz, pp. 163–82.

Newby, Herbert W. (1949), *Old Southgate*. London : T. Grove.

Newton, Isaac (1730; 1952), *Opticks or A Treatise of the Reflections, Refractions, Inflections & Colours of Light*. 4th edn London and New York: Dover.

Nordenskjöld, Augustus (1790), *Församlings Formen uti det Nya Jersualem*. Copenhagen.

Nudelman, Bryan C. (2003), 'Spaces of Transformation: Liminality and William Blake's America: A Prophecy'. *Lamar Journal of the Humanities*, 28.1, 33–46.

Nussbaum, Felicity A. (1995), *Torrid Zones: Maternity, Sexuality and Empire in Eighteenth-Century English Narratives*. Baltimore: Johns Hopkins University.

O'Connell, Sheila (2003), *London 1753*. London: British Museum Press.

Ōe, Kenzaburo (1964; 1969), *A Personal Matter* [Kojinteki na taiken. Tokyo: Shinchoshahan]. John Nathan (trans.). New York: Grove.

—— (1977), *The Day He Himself Shall Wipe My Tears Away. Teach Us to Outgrow Our Madness*. John Nathan (trans.). New York: Grove.

—— (1983; 2002), *Rouse Up O Young Men of the New Age!* [*Atarashii hito yo mezameyo*]. Tokyo: Kodansha. John Nathan (trans.). London: Atlantic.

—— (1989;1996), *An Echo of Heaven*. Margaret Mitsutani (trans.). Tokyo: Kodansha.

—— (1992), *Oe Kenzaburo. Nihon no Sakka* [Japanese Writers]. Vol. 23. Tokyo: Shogakaukan.

—— (1995a), *Japan, The Ambiguous, and Myself: The Nobel Prize Speech and Other Lectures*. Tokyo: Kodansha.

—— (1995b), *Ōi naru hi ni* [On the Great Day]. Tokyo: Shinchosha.

Ogude, S.E. (1976), 'Swedenborg and Blake's "Little Black Boy" '. *Asemka (Ghana)*, 4, 85–96.

Ohashi, Kenzaburo (1986), 'Doi Kochi no bungaku hihyou'[Kochi Doi on Literary Criticism]. *Eigoseinen* [The Rising Generation], cxxxii.8, 18–19.

Okada, Kazuya (2000), 'Orc under a Veil Revealed: Family Relationships and their Symbols in *Europe* and *The Book of Urizen*'. *Blake: An Illustrated Quarterly*, 34, 38–45.

Okumura, Kichiemon (1991), *Yanagi Soetsu to Shoki Mingei Undoō*. Tokyo: Tamagawa University Press.

Orsi, Maria Teresa (1998), 'The Colors of Shadow', in Adriana Boscaro and Anthony Hood Chambers (eds), *A Tanizaki Feast: The International Symposium in Venice*. Ann Arbor: Center for Japanese Studies, University of Michigan, pp. 1–13.

Ostriker, Alicia S. (1965), *Vision and Verse in William Blake*. Madison: University of Wisconsin Press.

Osugi, Sakae (1917), 'Atarashiki Sekai notameno Atarashiki Geijutsu'. *Waseda Bungaku*, 143, 232–51.

Otto, Peter (1991), *Constructive Vision and Visionary Deconstruction*. Oxford: Clarendon Press.

—— (2000), *Blake's Critique of Transcendence: Love, Jealousy, and the Sublime in 'The Four Zoas'*. Oxford: Oxford University Press.

—— (2001), ' "A Pompous High Priest": Urizen's ancient phallic religion in *The Four Zoas*'. *Blake: An Illustrated Quarterly*, 35, 4–22.

Owen, Robert (1920), *The Life of Robert Owen by himself*, with an Introduction by M. Beer. London: G. Bell.

Paley, Morton D. (1978), ' "Wonderful Originals": Blake and Ancient Sculpture', in Robert Essick and Donald Pearce (eds), *Blake in His Time*. Bloomington and London: Indiana University Press, pp. 170–97.

—— (1979), ' "A New Heaven is Begun": William Blake and Swedenborgianism'. *Blake: An Illustrated Quarterly*, 13, 64–90.

—— (1983), 'The Fourth of Man: Blake and Architecture', in Richard Wendorf (ed.), *Articulate Images: The Sister Arts from Hogarth to Tennyson*. Minneapolis: University of Minnesota Press, pp. 184–215.

—— (1985), ' "A New Heaven is begun": Blake and Swedenborgianism', in Harvey F. Bellin and Darrell Ruhl (eds), *Blake and Swedenborg: Opposition is true Friendship*. New York: Swedenborg Foundation, pp. 15–34.

—— (2004), *The Traveller in the Evening: The Last Works of William Blake*. Oxford: Oxford University Press.

Palmer, Samuel (1974), *The Letters of Samuel Palmer*. (2 vols) Raymond Lister (ed.). Oxford: Clarendon Press.

Parissien, Steven (2004), 'European Fantasies of Asia', in Jackson and Jaffer (eds), pp. 348–59.

Pasquin, Anthony (1786), *The Royal Academicians. A Farce*. London.

Peacock, Thomas Love (1934), 'An Essay on Fashionable Literature', Vol. 8 of H. F. B. Brett-Smith and C. E. Jones (eds), *The Works of Thomas Love Peacock, Essays, Memoirs, Letters & Unfinished Novels*. London: Constable and Gabriel Wells, pp. 261–91.

Pearce, Barry (1993), *Arthur Boyd: Retrospective*. Roseville, NSW: Beagle Press.

Pestalozzi, Karl (1975), 'Lavaters Utopie', in Helmut Arntzen et al. (eds), *Literatur-wissenschaft und Geschichtsphilosophie: Festschrift fur Wilhelm Emrich*. Berlin and New York: de Gruyter, pp. 283–301.

Peterfreund, Stuart (1998), *William Blake in a Newtonian World: Essays on Literature as Art and Science*. Norman: University of Oklahoma Press.

Phillips, John (1998), 'Singapore Soil: A Completely Different Organization of Space', in Liam Kennedy and Maria Balshaw (eds), *Urban Space and Representation*. London: Pluto Press, pp. 175–95.

Phillips, Michael (2000), *William Blake, the Creation of the Songs; from Manuscript to Illuminated Printing*. London: British Library.

Podmore, Colin (1998), *The Moravian Church in England, 1728–1760*. Oxford: Clarendon Press.

Pollack, David (1992), *Reading against Culture: Ideology and Narrative in the Japanese Novel*. Ithaca: Cornell University Press.

Pope, Alexander (1966), 'Essay on Man', in Herbert Davis (ed.), *Poetical Works*. Oxford: Oxford University Press, pp. 239–82.

Potts, Alex (2000), *Flesh and the Ideal: Winckelmann and the Origins of Art History*. New Haven: Yale University Press.

Powell, Nicholas (1973), *Fuseli: The Nightmare*. Harmondsworth: Penguin.

Pratt, Mary Louis (1992), *Imperial Eyes: Studies in Travel Writing and Trans-culturation*. New York: Routledge.

Pressly, William (1981), *The Life and Art of James Barry*. New Haven: Yale University Press.

—— (1983), *James Barry: The Artist as Hero*. London: Tate Gallery.

Price, E. Stanley (1984), *John Sadler, A Liverpool Pottery Printer*. West Kirby: Stanley Price.

Priestman, Martin (1999), *Romantic Atheism: Poetry and Freethoughts, 1780–1830*. Cambridge: Cambridge University Press.

Raine, Kathleen (1968), *Blake and Tradition*. (2 vols) Bollingen Series XXXV:11. Princeton: Princeton University Press.

—— (1969; 2002), *Blake and Tradition*. The A. W. Mellon Lectures in the Fine Arts 1962. The National Gallery of Art, Washington, DC. (2 vols) London: Routledge.

—— (1979), *Blake and the New Age*. London: Allen and Unwin.

—— (1991), 'Blake and Maya', in *Golgonooza: City of Imagination. Last Studies in William Blake*. New York: Lindisfarne.

Ramsay, James (1784), *An Essay on the Treatment and Conversion of African Slaves in the British Sugar Colonies*. [London].

Read, Dennis M. (1988), 'The Rival Canterbury Pilgrims of Blake and Cromek: Herculean Figures in the Carpet'. *Modern Philology*, LXXXVI, 171–90.

Reisner, M. E. (1979), 'Effigies of Power: Pitt and Fox as Canterbury Pilgrims'. *Eighteenth-Century Studies*, 12, 481–503.

*Retrospective Exhibition of Wada Eisaku* (1998), Exhibition catalogue.

Richards, Robert J. (2002), *The Romantic Conception of Life: Science and Philosophy in the Age of Goethe*. Chicago: University of Chicago Press.

Richardson, Alan (1990), 'Colonialism, Race, and Lyric Irony in Blake's "The Little Black Boy" '. *Papers in Language and Literature*, 26, 233–48.

—— (1994), *Literature, Education and Romanticism: Reading as Social Practice 1780–1832*. Cambridge: Cambridge University Press.

Rimer, J. Thomas (1993), 'Introduction' in Sato Haruo, *The Sick Rose: A Pastoral Elegy*. Francis B. Tenny (trans.). Honolulu: University of Hawaii Press, pp. 1–14.

Rivers, Isabel (ed.) (1982), *Books and their Readers in Eighteenth-Century England*. Leicester: University of Leicester Press.

—— (2001), *Books and their Readers in Eighteenth-Century England: New Essays*. Leicester: University of Leicester Press.

Rix, Robert W. (2001), ' "Bibles of Hell": William Blake and the Discourse of Radicalism'. Unpublished PhD thesis. University of Copenhagen.

—— (2003), 'William Blake and Radical Swedenborgianism'. *Esoterica*, 5, 73–94.

Roberts, Gaye Blake (ed.) (1998), *True Blue: Transfer Printed Earthenware*. The catalogue of an exhibition of British Blue Transfer Printed Earthenware, held at The Wedgwood Museum, Barlaston, Stoke-on-Trent, Staffordshire, 21 March to 12 July, 1998. East Hagbourne: Friends of Blue.

Robinson, B. W. (1980), *Persian Paintings in the John Rylands Library: a Descriptive Catalogue*. London: Philip Wilson Publishers Ltd for Sotheby Parke Bernet Publications.

Rocher, Rozanne (1983), *Orientalism, Poetry and the Millennium: The Checkered Life of Nathaniel Brassey Halhed 1751–1839*. Delhi: Motilal Banarsidass.

Roe, Albert S. (1969), 'The Thunder of Egypt', in Alvin Rosenfeldk (ed.), *William Blake: Essays for S. Foster Damon*. Providence: Brown University Press, pp.158–95.

Rosenblum, Robert (1957), 'The Origin of Painting: A Problem in the Iconography of Romantic Classicism'. *Art Bulletin*, XXXIX, 279–90.

—— (1967), *The Transformations in Late Eighteenth Century Art*. Princeton: Princeton University Press.

Rosenthal, Michael and Myrone, Martin (eds) (2002), *Gainsborough*. London: Tate Gallery.

Rossetti, D. G. (1863), 'Supplementary', in Alexander Gilchrist, *The Life of William Blake*, Vol. 1, p. 376.

Rossetti, William Michael (1885), *The Poetical Works of William Blake, Lyrical and Miscellaneous*. London: George Bell and Sons.

Rousseau, G. S. (1982), 'Science Books and Their Readership in the High Enlightenment', in Isabel Rivers (ed.), *Books and Their Readers*, pp. 197–255.

Rousseau, Jean-Jacques (1987), *The Basic Political Writings*. Donald A. Cress (trans.). Indianapolis: Hackett.

Rubinstein, Anne and Townsend, Camilla (1998), 'Revolted Negroes and the Devilish Principle: William Blake and Conflicting Visions of Boni's Wars in Surinam, 1772–1796', in Jackie DiSalvo, G. A. Rosso and Christopher Hobson (eds), *Blake, Politics, and History*. New York: Garland, pp. 273–98.

Sack, Ronald H. (1991), *Images of Nebuchadnezzar: The Emergence of a Legend*. Selinsgrove: Susquehanna University Press.

*Sacred Books of the East: The Upanishads, The* (1879). F. Max Müller (ed.). Vols 1, 15. Oxford: Oxford University Press.

Sadler, Simon (1998), *The Situationist City*. Cambridge, MA: MIT Press.

Said, Edward (1979), *Orientalism*. New York: Random House.

Saito, Takeshi (1915), 'Yanagi Muneyoshi no Toaicho "William Blake" oyobi Sonogo no Blake Kenkyu ni Tsuite'. *Geppo* [Monthly Report], 8, supplement to Vol. 4 of *Yanagi Muneyoshi Zenshu*.

Sakimura, Hisao (1965), 'Seiyo Bunka no Juyo Katei'. *Taishō Bunka*. Hiroshi Minami (ed.). Tokyo: Keisō Shobō.

Salman, Malcolm C. (1920), *The Modern Colour-Print of Original Design*. London: Bromhead.

Sato, Haruo (1993), *The Sick Rose: A Pastoral Elegy*. Francis B. Tenny (trans.). Honolulu: University of Hawaii Press.

Schorer, Mark (1946), *William Blake: The Politics of Vision*. New York: Henry Holt and Company.

Schuchard, Marsha Keith (1992), 'The Secret Masonic History of Blake's Swedenborg Society'. *Blake*, 26, 40–51.

—— (1999), 'Blake and the Grand Masters', in Steve Clark and David Worrall (eds), *Blake in the Nineties*. London: Macmillan Press, pp. 173–93.

—— (2000), 'Why Mrs Blake Cried: Blake, Swedenborg, and the Sexual Basis of Spiritual Vision'. *Esoterica*, 2, 45–93.

Schwab, Raymond (1975), *The Oriental Renaissance: Europe's Rediscovery of India and the East, 1680–1880*. Gene Patterson-Black and Victor Reinking (trans.). New York: Columbia University Press.

Seidensticker, Edward (1966), 'Tanizaki Ju-ichiro, 1886–1965'. *Monumenta Nipponica*, 21, 258.

Senge, Motomaro (1927), 'Bureku nitsuite' [Concerning Blake]. *Taiyoka*, 10, 5.

Shabetai, Karen (1996), 'The Question of Blake's Hostility Toward The Jews'. *ELH*, 63.1, 139–52.

Shaffer, Elinor (1975), *Kubla Khan and the Fall of Jerusalem*. Cambridge: Cambridge University Press.

Shakespeare, William (1960), *Lucrece. The Poems*. F. T. Prince (ed.). Walton-on-Thames: Arden.

—— (1985), *King Lear*. Kenneth Muir (ed.). London: Methuen.

—— (1997), *The Norton Shakespeare*. Stephen Greenblatt (ed.). New York: Norton.

Sharp, Granville (1786), *Short Sketch of Temporary Regulations*, London.

Shikibu, Muraski (1981), *The Tale of Genji*. Edward Seidensticker (trans.). Harmondsworth: Penguin Classics.

Shimamura, Hogetsu (1917), 'Minshu Geijutsu toshiteno Engeki'. *Waseda Bungaku*, 135, 42–9.

*Shin Kokinshu, The* (1970): *The 13th Century Anthology Edited by Imperial Edict*. H. H. Honda (trans.). Tokyo: The Hokuseido Press and The Eirinsha Press.

Shioe, Kozo (1995), 'Blake and Japan – his Short-Lived Influence on the Kyoto School'. Japan and Europe in Art History, C.I.H.A. Tokyo Colloquium 1991, pp. 139–50.

Shirakaba Dojin [members] (1914), 'Henshu shitsu nite' [At the Editorial Office]. *Shirakaba*, 5.11, 272–4.

—— (1917), (written by Saneatsu Mushanokoji) 'Bijutsukan wo Tsukuru Keikaku nitsuite (Narabi ni Doshi no Hito no Kifu wo Tsunoru)' [About the plan to build a museum (and a request for contributions from like-minded people)]. *Shirakaba*, 8.10, 146–8.

Sinclair, Iain (1991), *Downriver: (Or, The Vessels of Wrath): A Narrative in Twelve Tales*. London: Vintage.

—— (1997), *Lights out for the Territory*. London: Granta Books.

—— (1998), *Lud Heat and Suicide Bridge*. London: Granta Books.

—— (2002), *London Orbital: A Walk Around the M25*. London and New York: Granta Books.

Singh, Charu Sheel (1981), *The Chariot of Fire: A Study of William Blake in the Light of Hindu Thought*. Salzburg Studies in English Literature: Romantic Reassessment. Salzburg: Institut fur Anglistik und Amerikanistik.

—— (1988), 'Bhagavadgita, Typology and William Blake', in T. R. Sharma (ed.), *Influence of Bhagavadgita on Literature Written in English*. Meerut: Shalabh Prakashan, pp. 23–36.

Sitwell, Sacheverell, Buchanan, Handasyde and Fisher, James (eds) (1953), *Fine bird books, 1700–1900*. London: Collins, Van Nostrand.

Smeathman, Henry (1786), *Plan of a Settlement To Be Made Near Sierra Leona, on the Grain Coast of Africa*. London.

Smith, Bernard (1960; 1985), *European Vision and the South Pacific*. 2$^{nd}$ edn New Haven: Yale University Press, pp. 80, 81–5.

Smith, Samuel Stanhope (1787), *An Essay on the Causes of the Variety of Complexion and Figure in the Human Species*. Philadelphia.

Snodin, Michael (ed.) (1984), *Rococo: Art and Design in Hogarth's England*. Exhibition Catalogue, 16 May – 30 September 1984. London: V & A, Trefoil Books.

Solvyns, F. Balthazard (1808), *Les hindoûs*. (2 vols) Paris: chez l'auteur, place Saint-Andre-des-Arcs, no. 11, et chez H. Nicolle, rue de Seine, no. 12, à la librairie stéréotype, de l'imprimerie de Mame frères.

' "The Sorrows of Yamba", by Eaglesfield Smith and Hannah More: Authorship, Ideology and The Fractures of Antislavery Discourse' (2002). *Romanticism on the Net*, no. 28.

Spenser, Edmund (2001), *The Faerie Quene*. A. C. Hamilton, Hiroshi Yamashita and Toshiyuki Suzuki (eds). London: Longman.

Stafford, Barbara (1991), *Body Criticism: Imaging the Unseen in Enlightenment Art and Medicine*. Cambridge, MA: MIT Press.

Staley, Allen (1989), *Benjamin West: American Painter at the English Court*. Baltimore: Baltimore Museum of Art.

Stanley, Thomas A. (1982), *Ōsugi Sakae, Anarchist in Taishō Japan: The Creativity of Ego*. Cambridge, MA: Harvard University Press.

Stedman, John (1796), *Narrative of a five years' expedition against the Revolted Negroes of Surinam, in Guiana, on the Wild Coast of South America; from the year 1772, to 1777*. (2 vols) London: J. Johnson.

Stemmler, Joan, K. (1993), 'The Physiognomical Portraits of Johann Caspar Lavater'. *The Art Bulletin*, 75.1, 151–68.

Suleri, Sara (1995), *The Rhetoric of English India*. Chicago: University of Chicago Press.

Sung, Mei-Ying (2005), *Technical and Material Studies of William Blake's Engraved Illustrations of the Book of Job* (1826). Diss: Nottingham Trent University.

Sussman, Elisabeth (1989), *On the Passage of a few people through a rather brief moment in time: The Situationist International 1957–1972*. Cambridge, MA: MIT Press.

Sutherland, John (1970), 'Blake and Urizen', in David V. Erdman and John E. Grant (eds), *Blake's Visionary Forms Dramatic*. Princeton: Princeton University Press, pp. 244–62.

Suzuki, Teitaro Daisetz (1926), *Zen Buddhism*. New Delhi: Aryan Books International.

—— (1950; 1972), *Living by Zen: A Synthesis of the Historical and Practical Aspects of Zen Buddhism*. York Beach: Samuel Weiser.

—— (1957), *Mysticism: Christian and Buddhist*. New York: Harper.

Suzuki, Masashi (2001), ' "Signal of Solemn Mourning": Los/Blake's Sandals and Ancient Israelite Custom'. *Journal of English and Germanic Philology*, 100, 40–56.

Suzuki, Masashi and Clark, Steve (eds) (2003), *The International Blake Conference: 'Blake in the Orient' with a Concurrent Exhibition 'The Glad Days in the Reception of Blake in Japan': Exhibition Catalogue*. Kozo Shioe and Yumiko Goto (entries). Kyoto: Nakanishi-shuppan.

Suzuki, Masashi and Clark, Steve (eds) (2003), *The International Blake Conference 'Blake in the Orient': Programme*. Kyoto: Nakanishi-shuppan.

Suzuki, Zenzo (1999), 'Doi Kochi to Northrop Frye' [Kochi Doi and Northrop Frye]. *Eigoseinen* [The Rising Generation], cvliv.10, 14–16.

Swedenborg, Emanuel (1781), *The True Christian Religion; containing the universal theology of the New Church*. (2 vols) London: J. Phillips; J. Denis & Son.

—— (1781: 1975), *The True Christian Religion*. Wm. C. Dick (trans.). London: Swedenborg Society.

—— (1788), *The Wisdom of Angels, concerning Divine Love and Divine Wisdom*. Tr. from the original Latin. London: printed and sold by W. Chalken.

—— (1789), *A Sketch of the Chaste Delights of Conjugal Love, and the Impure Pleasures of Adulterous Love. Translated from the Apocalypsis Explicata, a manuscript of the posthumous works of the Hon. Emanuel Swedenborg*. London: J. Denew.

—— (1790), *The Delights of Wisdom Respecting Conjugal Love. After which follow the Pleasures of Insanity Respecting Scortatory Love*. London: for the Society.

Swinburne, Algernon Charles (1868; 1906), *William Blake: a Critical Essay*. A new edn London: Chatto & Windus.

Symons, Arthur (1907), *William Blake*. London: Archibald Constable.

Tambling, Jeremy (1998), 'Dante and Blake: Allegorizing the Event', in Nick Havely (ed.), *Dante's Modern Afterlife*, London: Macmillan, pp. 33–48.

—— (2004a), *Blake's Night Thought*. London: Palgrave.

—— (2004b), 'Levinas and Macbeth's "Strange Images of Death" '. *Essays in Criticism*, 54, 351–72.

*Tame 'Shirakaba Bijutsukan' Setsuritsu: Uiriamu Bureku Fukusei Hanga Tenrankai Mokuroku* [Catalogue of the Exhibition of Reproductions from the Works of William Blake: For the Establishment of the Shirakaba Art Museum] (1919).

Tanizaki, Jun'ichiro (1933; 1984), *In Praise of Shadows*. Thomas J. Harper and Edward G. Seidensticker (trans.). Rutland, VT and Tokyo: Charles E. Tuttle.

Tannenbaum, Leslie (1982), *Biblical Tradition in Blake's Early Prophecies: The Great Code of Art*. Princeton: Princeton University Press.

Tayler, Irene (1971), *Blake's Illustrations to the Poems Of Gray*. Princeton: Princeton University Press.

Taylor, Dena Bain (2004), Rev. of *'Wonders Divine': The Development of Blake's*

*Kabbalistic Myth*, by Sheila A. Spector. *Blake: An Illustrated Quarterly*, 38.2, 79–85.

Teltscher, Kate (1995), *India Inscribed: European and British Writing on India 1600– 1800*. Oxford: Oxford University Press.

Thomas, Nicholas (2004), 'Hodges as anthropologist and historian', in Geoff Quilley and John Bonehill (eds), *William Hodges 1744–1797: The Art of Exploration*. New Haven: Yale University Press, pp. 27–34.

Thompson, E. P. (1963), *The Making of the English Working Class*. Harmondsworth: Penguin.

—— (1993), *Witness against the Beast: William Blake and the Moral Law*. Cambridge: Cambridge University Press.

Thornton, Robert John (1799–), *Temple of Flora, or The New Illustration of the Sexual System of Carolus von Linnaeus*. London.

Thorpe, Robert (1815), *A Letter to William Wilberforce . . . Vice President of the African Institution . . . Containing Remarks on the Reports of the Sierra Leone Company, and African Institution*. London.

'Tippoo's Tiger' (1835). *The Penny Magazine*, 216 (Aug. 15). 13 August 2002. University of Rochester, 1995 [http://www.history.rochester.edu/ pennymag/216/tt.htm].

Todd, Ruthven (1972), 'Two Blake Prints and Two Fuseli Drawings'. *Blake Newsletter*, V, 176–7.

Tomita, Saika (1917), 'Minshu Geijutsu toshiteno Shiika'. *Waseda Bungaku*, 135, 49–53.

Tomory, Peter (1972), *The Life and Art of Henry Fuseli*. London: Thames and Hudson.

—— (1975), 'A Blake Sketch for Hayley's Ballad "The Lion" and a Connection with Fuseli'. *Burlington Magazine*, 117, 377–8.

Tong, Yuanfang (1988), ' "Tiedani hao" shang de zhen gushi: Weidener tushu-guan yu Harvard daxue (zhong)' [A True Story on the *Titanic*: Widener Library and Harvard University [II]]. *Lianhe bao* [*United Daily News*], 1 May 1998, 37 (*Literary Supplement*).

Trawick, Leonard M. (1967), *Backgrounds of Romanticism: English Philosophical Prose of the Eighteenth Century*. Bloomington: Indiana University Press.

Ts'ai, Yüan-hwang (1986), 'Langmanzhuyi' [Romanticism]. *Youth wenyi* [*Youth Literary Arts*], 64.5, 52–9.

Tsurumi, Shunsuke (1994), *Yanagi Muneyoshi*. Tokyo: Heibonsha.

Tung, Ch'ung-hsüan (1997), 'Blake's Dialectical Vision'. *Wenshi xuebao* [Journal of the College of Liberal Arts], National Chung-hsing University), 27, 193–211.

Uchida, Yoshihiko and Shioda, Shobē (1959), 'Chishiki Seinen no Shoruikei', in Shuichi Kato and Osamu Hisano (eds), *Chishikijin no Seisei to Yakuwari*. Tokyo: Chikuma Shobo.

Umetsu, Narumi (trans.) (1989), *Bureiku Zen Chosaku* [The Complete Translation of Blake's Works]. (2 vols) Nagoya: Nagoya University Press.

*Umi no Sachi (1762)*, compiled by Sekijuken Shūkoku and illustrated by Katsuma Ryūsui. Tokyo.

*Valuable books and manuscripts* (1842), *A catalogue of the very select and elegant library, printed & manuscript, of a private gentleman, together with another collection, including the most beautiful and valuable collection of missals, and other richly illuminated manuscripts, which have been offered for sale during many years; some of the delicately and highly finished paintings in which, have been engraved in Dr. Dibdin's decameron. Also some splendidly illuminated manuscripts in the Hebrew, Chinese, Arabic, Persian, Burmese, Hindostan, Sanscrit, Singalese, Japonese, Russian, Italian, French, and English languages, with curious specimens of ancient music . . . (Which will be sold by auction, by Mr. Fletcher . . . on Thursday, April 21st, 1842, and 3 following days).* [London].

Vaneigem, Raoul (1967), *The Revolution of Everyday Life.* Trans. Donald Nicholson-Smith. London: Left Bank Books.

Varenius, Bernhardus (Bernhard Varen) (1649; 1974), *Descriptio Regni Iaponiae* [Beschreibung des Japanischen Reiches]. Amsterdam; Ernst Christian Volkmann (trans.). Darmstadt: Wissenschaftliche Buchgesellschaft.

Vaughan, Henry (1976), 'The Night'. *Henry Vaughan: The Complete Poems.* Alan Rudrum (ed.). Harmondsworth: Penguin.

Vincent-Kemp, Ruth (1986), *George Stubbs and the Wedgwood Connection.* Stoke-on-Trent: R. Vincent-Kemp.

Vine, Stephen (1993), *Blake's Poetry.* New York: St Martin's Press.

Viscomi, Joseph (1993), *Blake and the Idea of the Book.* Princeton: Princeton University Press.

—— (1997), 'The Evolution of *The Marriage of Heaven and Hell'. Huntington Library Quarterly,* 58, 281–344

—— (1998), 'The Lessons of Swedenborg; or, The Origin of William Blake's *The Marriage of Heaven and Hell'*, in Thomas Pfau and Robert F. Gleckner (eds), *Lessons of Romanticism.* Durham, NC and London: Duke University Press, pp. 173–212.

—— (1999), 'In the Caves of Heaven and Hell: Swedenborg and Printmaking in Blake's *The Marriage'*, in Steve Clark and David Worrall (eds), *Blake in the Nineties.* Basingstoke: Macmillan, pp. 27–60.

Visser, Robert Paul Willem (1985), *The Zoological Work of Petrus Camper (1722–1789).* Amsterdam: Rodopi.

Volney, Constantin F. (1805), *Travels Through Syria and Egypt in the years of 1783, 1784, and 1785: containing the present natural political state of those countries.* London: Joseph Johnson.

Wada, Ayako (2004), 'Yanagi Muneyoshi, William Blake (1914) no sono zenshu-ban (1981) tono chigai kara ukibori ni naru sono tokusei' [The 'academic exactitude' of Muneyoshi Yanagi's 1914 William Blake as exhibited by comparison to the inadequate 1981 reprinted edition]. *Tottori Daigaku Eigo Kenkyu,* 4, 17–36.

Wadström, Carl Bernhard (1789a), *A Plan For A Free Community Upon The Coast Of Africa, Under The Protection Of Great Britain; But Intirely [sic] Independent Of All European Laws And Governments. With An Invitation, under certain Conditions, to all Persons desirous of partaking the Benefits thereof.* London: R. Hindmarsh.

—— (1789b), *Observations on the Slave Trade, and a Description of some part of the Coast of Guinea, During a Voyage Made in 1787, and 1788.* London: John Phillips.

—— (1794; 1968), *An essay on Colonization, particularly applied to the Western coast of Africa, with some free thoughts on Cultivation and Commerce.* Newton Abbot: David and Charles.

Wang, Chung-lin (1985), 'A Special Frame of Mind to Approach William Blake'. *Studies in English Literature & Linguistics*, 11, 1–5.

Ward, Aileen (1988–89), 'Canterbury Revisited: The Blake–Cromek Controversy'. *Blake: an Illustrated Quarterly*, XXII, 80–92.

Wakeman, Geoffrey (1976), *The Production of Nineteenth Century Colour Illustration*. Loughborough, Leicestershire: Plough Press.

Wang, Xiaoying (2000), 'Hong Kong, China and the Question of Postcoloniality', in Arif Dirlik and Xudong Zhang (eds), *Postmodernism and China*. Durham: Duke University Press, pp. 89–119.

Wardi, Eynel (2003), 'Space, the Body, and the Text in *The Marriage of Heaven and Hell*'. *Orbis Litterarum*, 58, 253–70.

Wardle, Judith (1974), 'Satan not having the Science of Wrath, but only of Pity'. *Studies in Romanticism*, 13, 147–54.

Warner, Janet (1984), *Blake and the Language of Art*. Kingston, Ontario: McGill-Queen's University Press.

Watney, Bernard (1966), 'Engravings as the Origin of Designs and Decorations for English Eighteenth-century Ceramics'. *Burlington Magazine*, 108, 761, August 1966: 406–10.

Webster, Brenda S. (1983), *Blake's Prophetic Psychology*. London: Macmillan.

Wechsler, Judith (1993), 'Lavater, Stereotype, and Prejudice', in Ellis Shookman (ed.), *Faces of Physiognomy: Interdisciplinary Approaches to Johann Caspar Lavater*. Columbia, SC: Camden House, pp. 104–25.

Wedgwood, Barbara and Hensleigh (1980), *The Wedgwood Circle 1730–1897*. London: Studio Vista.

Weinglass, David (1994), *Prints and Engraved Illustrations by and after Henry Fuseli: A Catalogue Raissonné*, Aldershot, England: Scolar Press.

Weir, David (2003), *Brahma in the West: William Blake and the Oriental Renaissance*. New York: State University of New York Press.

Weng, Jerry Chia-je (2003), 'Re-visioning Milton: William Blake and the Poetics of Appropriation'. Unpublished MA thesis. National Taiwan University.

Weng, T. S. (1979), 'Notes and Observations on William Blake's *Songs of Innocence and Songs of Experience*, Showing the Two Contrary States of the Human Soul'. *Guoli bianyi guan guankan* [Journal of National Institute for Compilation and Translation], 8.1, 1–95.

Werner, Bette Charlene (1986), *Blake's Vision of the Poetry of Milton*. London and Toronto: Associated University Presses.

White, Charles (1799), *An Account of the Regular Gradation in Man*. London: C. Dilly.

Whittaker, Jason (1999), *William Blake and the Myths of Britain*. Basingstoke: Macmillan Press.

Wilford, Francis (1792), 'On Egypt and Other Countries adjacent to the Ca'li' River, or Nile of Ethiopia. From the Ancient Books of the Hindus'. *Asiatick Researches*, 3, 295–468.

Williams, Nicholas M. (1998), *Ideology and Utopia in the Poetry of William Blake*. Cambridge: Cambridge University Press.

William-Wood, Cyril (1981), *English Transfer-Printed Pottery and Porcelain: A History of Over-Glaze Printing*. London and Boston: Faber and Faber.

Wilson, Mona (1927; 1971), *The Life of William Blake*. A New edn Oxford: Oxford University Press.

Wilton, Andrew (1973–4), 'A Fan Design by Blake'. *Blake Newsletter*, 27. 7: 3, 60–3.

Winckelmann, Johann Joachim (1765), *Reflections on the Painting and Sculpture of the Greeks. With Instructions for the Connoisseur, and an Essay on Grace in Works of Art*. Henry Fuseli (trans.). London: the Translator.

—— (1766), *Versuch einer Allegorie, besonders fur die Kunst* [Attempt at an Allegory, Particularly for Art]. Dresden.

Wiseman, D. J. (1985), *Nebuchadnezzar and Babylon*. Oxford: Oxford University Press.

Wittreich, Joseph Anthony, Jr (1972), 'Domes of Mental Pleasure: Blake's Epic and Hayley's Epic Theory'. *Studies in Philology*, 69, 101–29.

Wollstonecraft, Mary (1989), *A Vindication of the Rights of Woman*. Vol. 5. *The Works of Mary Wollstonecraft*. Janet Todd and Marilyn Butler (eds). (7 vols) London: Pickering and Chatto.

—— (1994), *Political Writings*. Janet Todd (ed.). Oxford: Oxford University Press.

Wood, Marcus (2000), *Blind Memory: Visual representations of slavery in England and America 1780–1865*. Manchester: Manchester University Press.

—— (2002), *Slavery, Empathy, and Pornography*. Oxford: Oxford University Press.

Woof, Robert and Hebron, Stephen, with Woof, Pamela (2000), *English Poetry 850–1850: the First Thousand Years with Some Romantic Perspectives*. Grasmere: Wordsworth Trust.

Wordsworth, William (1952–63), *The Poetical Works of William Wordsworth*. Ernest de Selincourt and Helen Darbishire (eds). 2nd edn (5 vols) Oxford: Clarendon Press.

Worrall, David (2000), 'William Bryan: Another Anti-Swedenborgian Engraver of 1789'. *Blake: An Illustrated Quarterly*, 34, 1–14.

Worrall, David and Clark, Steve (eds) (2006), *Blake, Nation and Empire*. Basingstoke: Palgrave Macmillan.

Wright, Julia M. (2004), *Blake, Nationalism, and the Politics of Alienation*. Athens: Ohio University Press.

Xie, Jin-li (1994), 'Chastity and the Feminine in William Blake's Poetry'. Unpublished MA thesis. Providence University.

Yanagi, Kaneko (1975), 'My Music and Its History'. Friends of *Music* 33:8 (rpt in Matsuhashi 1999: 153).

Yanagi, Soetsu [Muneyoshi] (1912), 'Kakumei no Gaka' [Revolutionary Painters]. *Shirakaba*, 3.1, 1–31.

—— (1913a), *Problems of the Life*. Place: publisher.

—— (1913b), 'Hyoushi Ga nitsuite' [Concerning the Cover Art]. *Shirakaba*, 4.1, 269–70.

—— (1914a), *William Blake: Kare no shogai to seisaku oyobi sono shiso* [William Blake: His Life, Works and Thought]. Tokyo: Rakuyodo.

—— (1914b), 'Uiriamu Bureku' [William Blake]. *Yanagi Soetsu Zenshu* [The Complete Works of Soetsu Yanagi]. Vol. 4. Tokyo: Chikuma Shobo, 1980–92, pp. 3–514. Rpt. *William Blake: Kare no Shogai to Seisaku Oyobi Sono Shiso* [William Blake: His Life, Works and Thought]. Tokyo: Rakuyo Do.

—— (1914c), 'Bureku Tenrankai ni Tsuite' [On Blake Exhibition]. *Shirakaba*, 5.11, 272.

—— (1914d), 'Bureku Tenrankai ni Tsuite' [On Blake Exhibition]. *Shirakaba*, 5.12, 137.

—— (1915a), 'Dai Nana Kai Bijutsu Tenrankai' [7th Art Exhibition]. *Shirakaba*, 6.2, 165.

—— (1915b;1981), 'About My Blake Study'. Vol. 5. *Yanagi Soetsu Zenshu* [The Complete Works of Soetsu Yanagi]. Place: publisher.

—— (1919), 'Bureku Tenrankai' [Blake Exhibition]. *Shirakaba*, 10.11–12, 180.

—— (1920a), 'Bureku no E wo Chumon sareta Kata ni' [To Whom Ordered Blake's Paintings]. *Shirakaba*, 11.5, 126.

—— (1920b), 'Bureku no E wo Chumon sareta Kata ni Futatabi' [Again to Whom Ordered Blake's Paintings]. *Shirakaba*, 11.7, 147.

—— (1927; 1988), *Beauty of Crafts*. Tokyo: Iwanami Shoten.

—— (1931), 'Postscript'. *Blake and Whitman*, 1.10, 475–9.

—— (1955; 1988), *Namuamidabutsu*. Tokyo: Iwanami Shoten.

—— (1972; 1989), *The Unknown Craftsman: A Japanese Insight into Beauty*. Adapted by Bernard Leach. Foreword by Shoji Hamada. Rev. Tokyo: Kodansha.

—— (1980–92), *Yanagi Muneyoshi Zenshu* [The Complete Works of Muneyoshi Yanagi]. Writings: 22 vols. Illustrated books: 5 vols. Bunsho Jugaku, Shunsuke Tsurumi, Hiroshi Minao and Sori Yanagi (eds). Tokyo: Chikuma-shobo.

—— (1984), 'Kogei no Bi [Beauty of Crafts]', in *Mingei Yonjuu-nen* [40 years of Mingei]. Tokyo: Iwanami Shoten.

Yangmu (1993), 'Wei Blake chenqing' [A Petition for Blake]. *Lianhe bao* [*United Daily News*], 21 November 1993: 37 (*Literary Supplement*).

Yano, Kazumi (1957), 'Blake inyushi oboegaki' [Notes on the history of introducing Blake to Japan]. *Eigo Seinen* [The Rising Generation], CIII, 535–6.

Yen, Aizhu and Zhang, Chunrong (eds) (1996), *Ying Mei ming shi shangxi* [Appreciations and Analyses of Famous English-American Poems]. Taipei: Wenhe chuban gongsi [Crane Publishing Company], pp. 114–21.

Young, Edward (1989). *Night Thoughts*. Stephen Cornford (ed.). Cambridge: Cambridge University Press.

Young, Hilary (ed.) (1995), *The Genius of Wedgwood*. London: Victoria & Albert Museum.

Youngquist, Paul (2003), *Monstrosities: Bodies and Romanticism*. Minneapolis: University of Minnesota Press.

Yü, Kuang-chung (trans. and anno.) (1960), *Ying shi yi zhu* [English Poems: Translations and Annotations]. Taipei: Wenxing shudian.

Yura, Kimiyoshi (1990), 'Kaisetsu: Yanagi shiso no shihatsu eki, William Blake' [The starting station of Yanagi's thought: his William Blake]. *Yanagi Muneyoshi Zenshu*. Vol. 4, pp. 679–707. Abridged and translated into English as 'The Great Encounter: Sôetsu Yanagi and William Blake'. *William Blake* (Yanagi: Blake no Deai [Great Encounter: Yanagi and Blake]). Tokyo: Nippon Mingeikan, pp. 30–1.

Zhang, Shiyin (trans.) (1980), 'Qing ke' [Love Song]. *Mingdao weni* [Mindao Literary Arts], 47.2, 24.

—— (1982), 'Xiao yang' [The Lamb]. *Mingdao weni* [Mindao Literary Arts], 73.4, 97.

Zhong, Li (trans.) (1988), 'Shangdi zao Yadang' [God Creating Adam]. *Youth wenyi* [Youth Literary Arts], 67.5, 135.

Zhongguo shibao bianjibu (Editorial Section of *China Times*) (2001), 'William Blake hua Shangdi chuangzao tiandi' [William Blake Illustrating God's Creation of the World]. *Zhongguo shibao* [*China Times*], 20 March 2001: 23 (*Literary Supplement*).

Zhou, Wenbin (trans.) (1966), *Blake shi xuan* [Selections of Blake's Poems]. Taipei: Wuzhou chuban she.

# Index

The index covers chapters, illustrations and principal notes. A page number in italics indicates an illustration; a page number followed by 'n.' and number indicates a note.

Eden
  civilization in 115
    as non-African 116
  fertility 115
  freedom 115
  identity 115
  location 116
  luxury 115–16
Edo, Ukiyo-e colour printing 85
Edwards, George 68, 70
Edwards, James 54, 55
eggs 29–30
ego 174–5, 176–7
Egypt
  accessibility 29
  as destructive power 31, 32, 33–5
  as fallen world 29
  false gods 31, 32, 33, 34
  Nile 111, *112*, 118
  Swedenborgianism on 33
  symbolism 3, 29–35, 36 n. 16, 36 n. 19, 37
    n. 31
*Ehon mushi erami* 57, 58
elephants 136, 137
engraving
  copper-plate 3, *64–5*, 73
    business acumen lacking on 74–5
    fees 71
    markets, flourishing 63
    as neglected 63, 74
    transfer-printing and 64, 65
  stipple 80–1
Enoch, Book of 111
Equiano, Olaudah 107
Erle, Sibylle 4, 87–103
escape 96
*Essay Concerning Human Understanding, An* (Locke) 174
*Essay on Man, An* (Pope) 294–5, 296, 297–8
*Essay on the Causes of the Variety of Complexion and Figure* (S. S. Smith) 97–8
*Essay on the History of Civil Society* (A. Ferguson) 113
*Essays on Physiognomy* (Lavater, trans. Holcroft) 95, 101 n. 14
*Essays on Physiognomy* (Lavater, trans. Hunter) 88, 93
Essick, Robert N. 77–8, 258
'Eternity' 213
eternity 265, *266*, 266–7
Etruria 75 n. 12
Etruria Hall 71

*Europe* 200, 244, 292
Europe 301
exhibitions 5, 6, 169 nn. 5–6, 221, 222, *222*, 223, *224*, 225, *225*, 233 n. 13, 301
  catalogue *223*, *226*
exile 107
exotica 122–3
experience 174
export paintings 43
Ezekiel 166

Faderman, Lillian 40
*Faerie Queene, The* (Spenser) 241
fantasies 273
*Father's Memoirs of His Child, A* (Malkin) 45
Felpham 134–5
feminist consciousness 195, 198–9
  challenge from 203
  pioneers 203
Ferguson, Adam 113–14
fiends 268–9, *269*, 270
Fifteen Years' War 8–9, 213
film 242
  *Man I Killed, The* 205, 206, *206*, 207, *207*, 208, *209*
fish 56, *57*, 58
Flaxman, John 29, 70–1, 75–6 n. 15
floods 31, 32, 111
Foersch, N. P. 127
folk art 173, 181, 183, 188, 190, 191, 192, 213–14, 231–2, 247–8
*For Children* 39, 44–5
*For the Sexes* 124, *127*
  'The Traveller Hasteth in the Evening' 238
foreigners 105
*Four Zoas, The* 196–8, 199–200, 297
freedom 107–8, 115, 270
  in love 112
Freemasonry 34
French Revolution 18, 79–80
  despotism and madness in 261
friendships, romantic, women 40, 47
frigidity 113
Frye, Northrop 7, 134
Fulford, Tim 121–2
Fuller Maitland, William 45–6
Fuseli, Henry 88, 89, *90*, 91, 92, 105
future 288–9
  unknowable 297–8

Gandy, Henry 21
Garuda 49, *49*

Printed in the United States
152360LV00002B/32/P

9 780826 438058